8

Hina matsuri

Masao Ohtake

HINA MATSURI Vol.8

CONTENTS

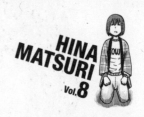

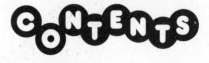

CHAPTER 39

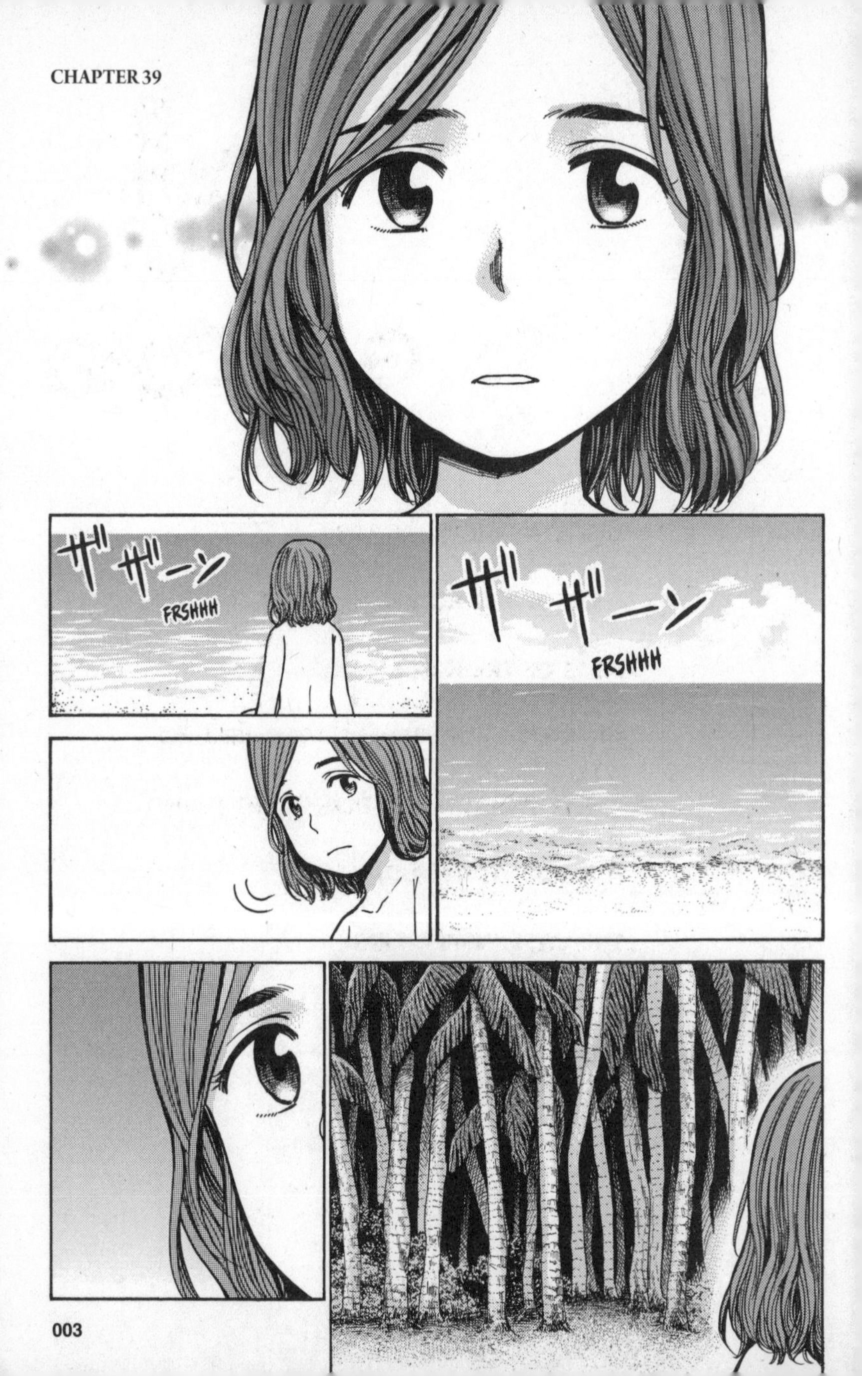
ザザーン
FRSHHH
ザザーン
FRSHHH

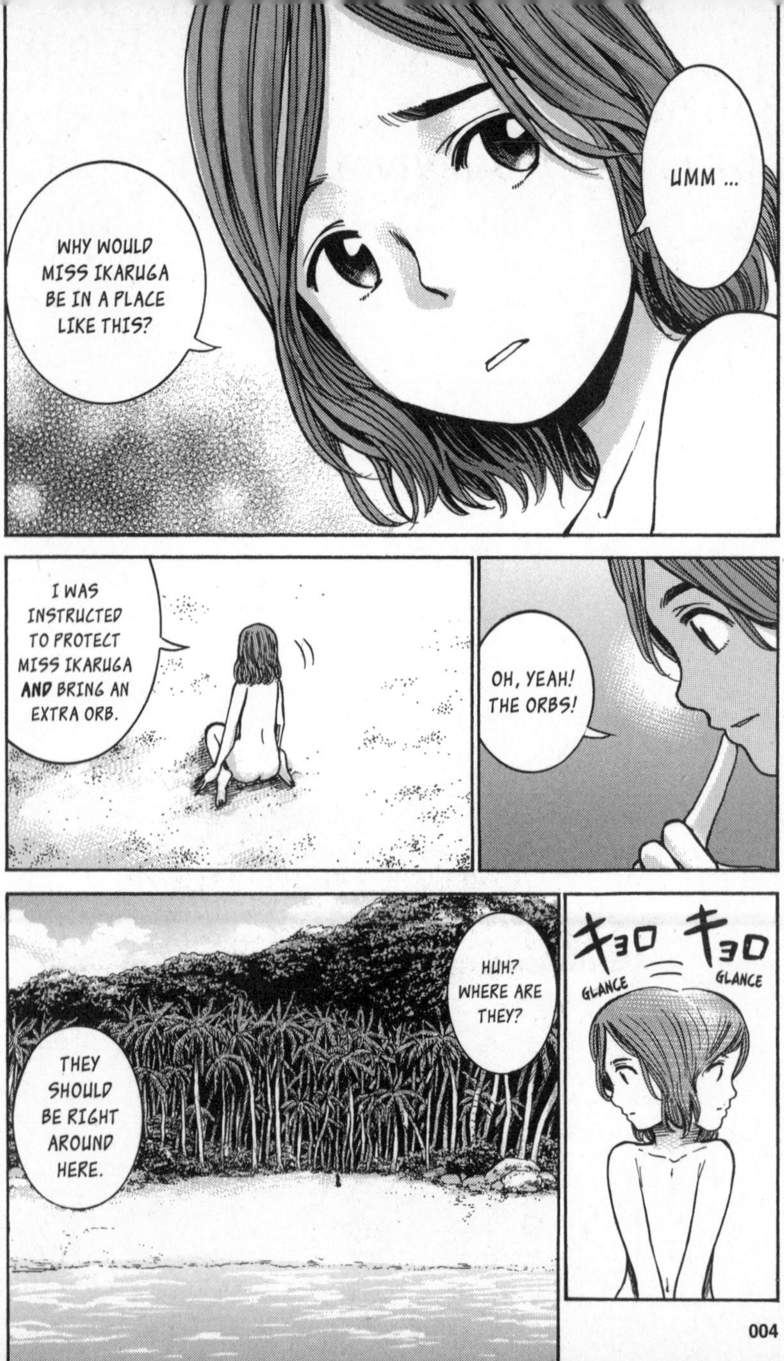
UMM ...
WHY WOULD MISS IKARUGA BE IN A PLACE LIKE THIS?
OH, YEAH! THE ORBS!
I WAS INSTRUCTED TO PROTECT MISS IKARUGA **AND** BRING AN EXTRA ORB.
キョロ
GLANCE
キョロ
GLANCE
HUH? WHERE ARE THEY?
THEY SHOULD BE RIGHT AROUND HERE.

CHAPTER 39
LIFE IS ABOUT SURVIVAL

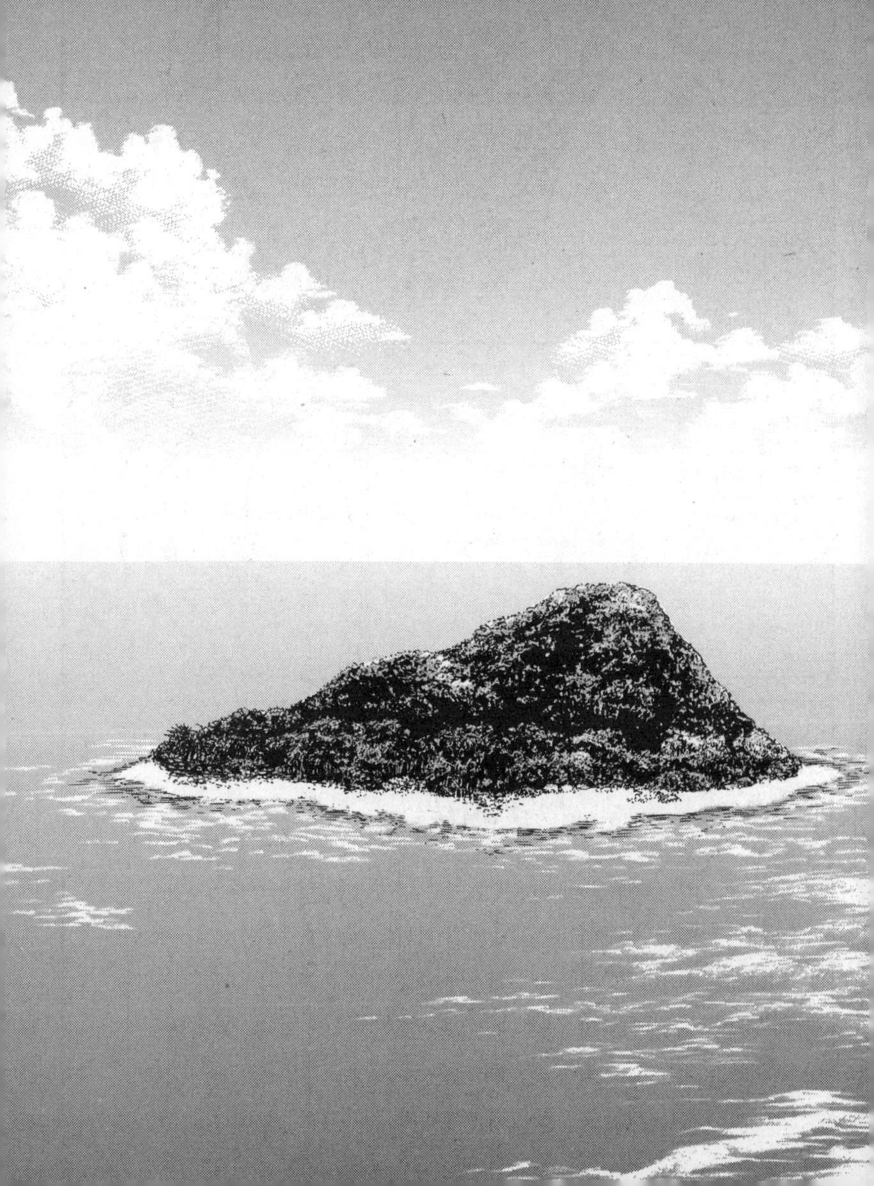

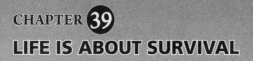

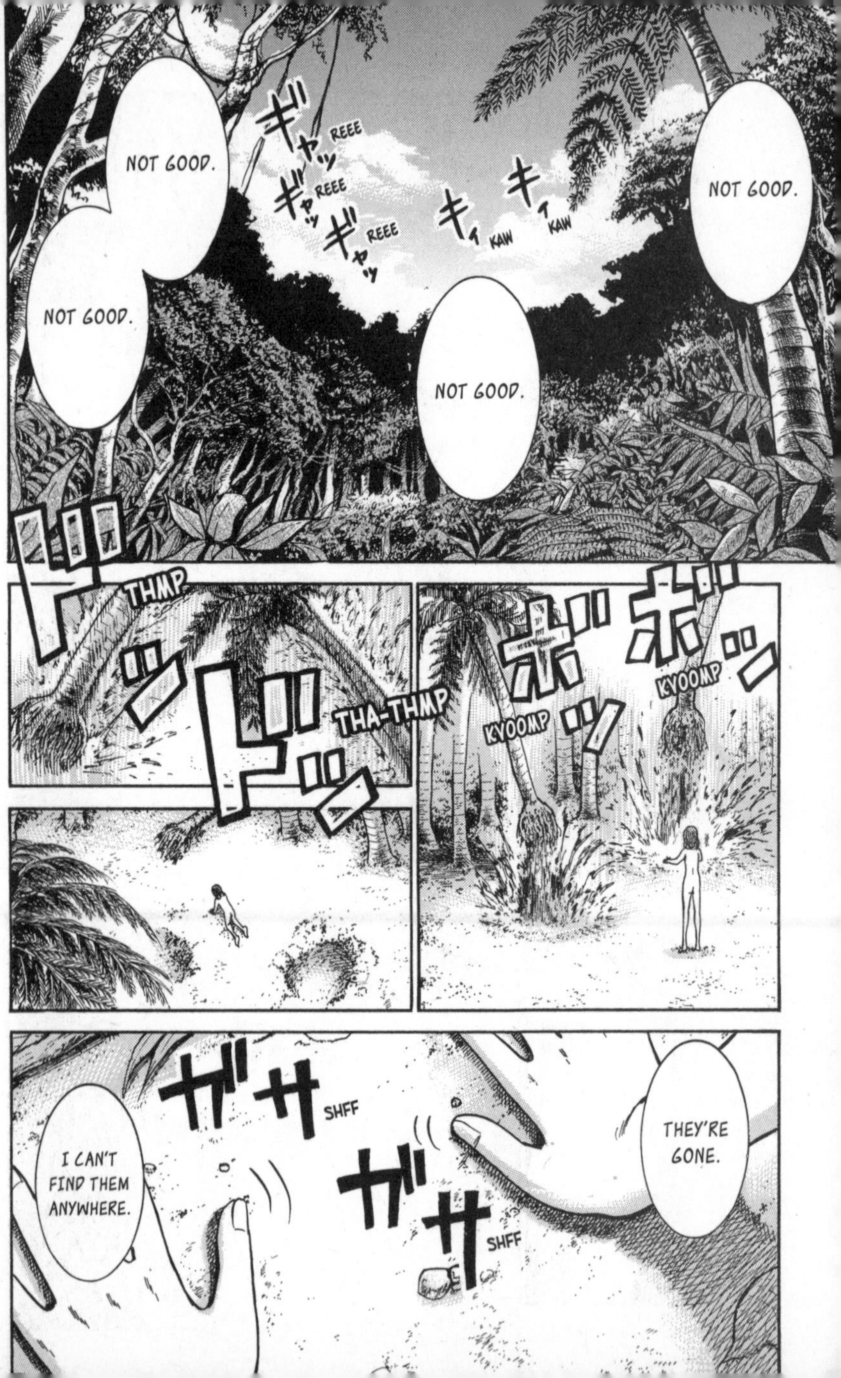
NOT GOOD.
キィ KAW
キィ KAW
ギャッ REEE
ギャッ REEE
ギャッ REEE
NOT GOOD.
NOT GOOD.
NOT GOOD.
ボッ KYOOMP
ボッ KYOOMP
ドッ THMP
ドッ THA-THMP
THEY'RE GONE.
ガサ SHFF
ガサ SHFF
I CAN'T FIND THEM ANYWHERE.

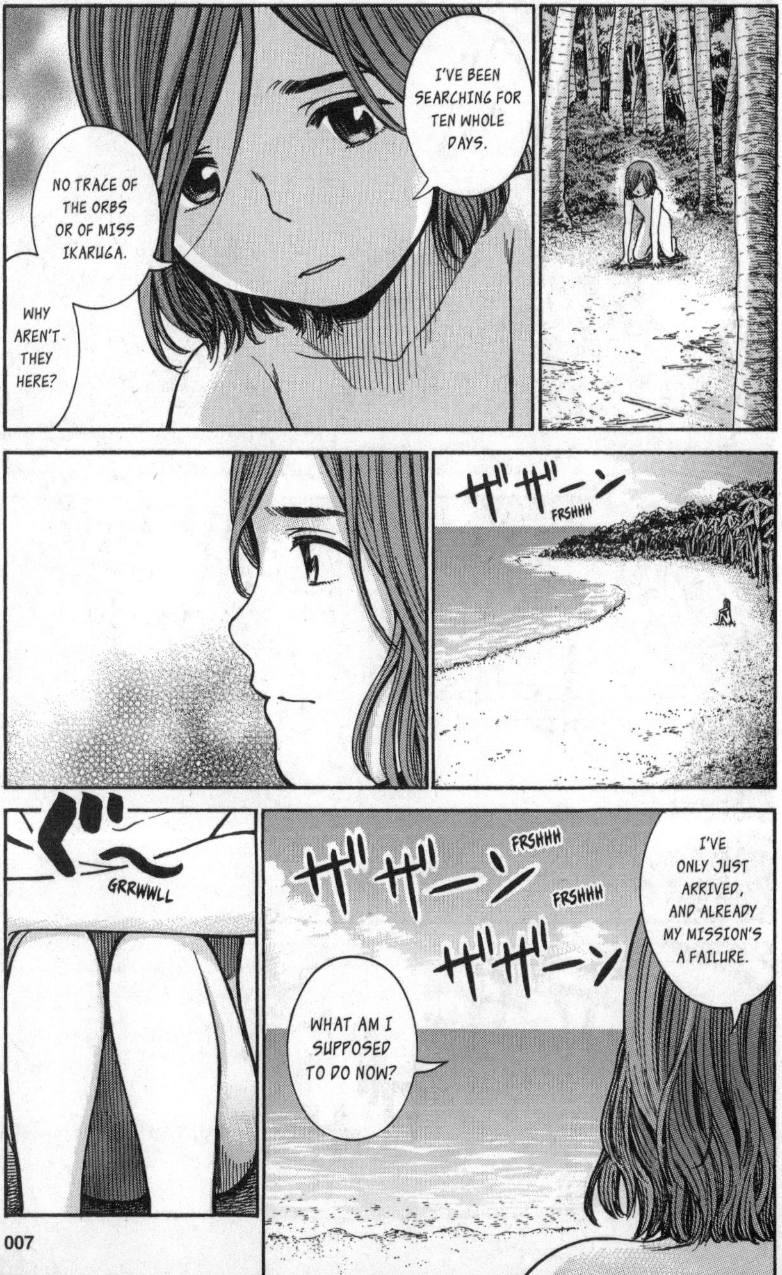
I'VE BEEN SEARCHING FOR TEN WHOLE DAYS.
NO TRACE OF THE ORBS OR OF MISS IKARUGA.
WHY AREN'T THEY HERE?
ザザーン
FRSHHH
ザザーン
FRSHHH
ザザーン
FRSHHH
I'VE ONLY JUST ARRIVED, AND ALREADY MY MISSION'S A FAILURE.
WHAT AM I SUPPOSED TO DO NOW?
ぐ～
GRRWWLL

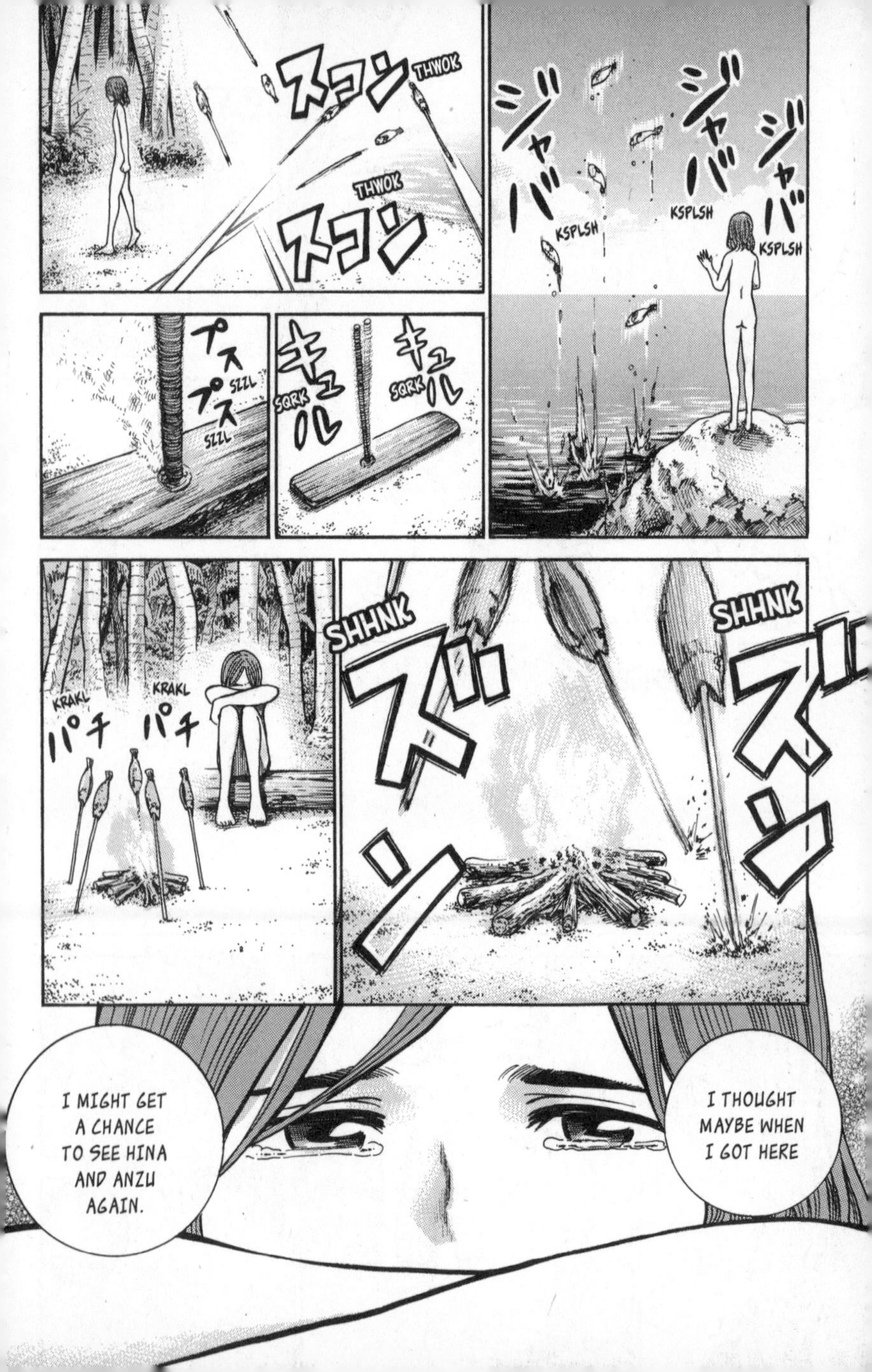
ジャバ
KSPLSH
ジャバ
KSPLSH
ジャバ
KSPLSH
スコン
THWOK
スコン
THWOK
キュル
SQRK
キュル
SQRK
プス
SZZL
プス
SZZL
ズン
SHHNK
ズン
SHHNK
パチ
KRAKL
パチ
KRAKL
I THOUGHT MAYBE WHEN I GOT HERE
I MIGHT GET A CHANCE TO SEE HINA AND ANZU AGAIN.

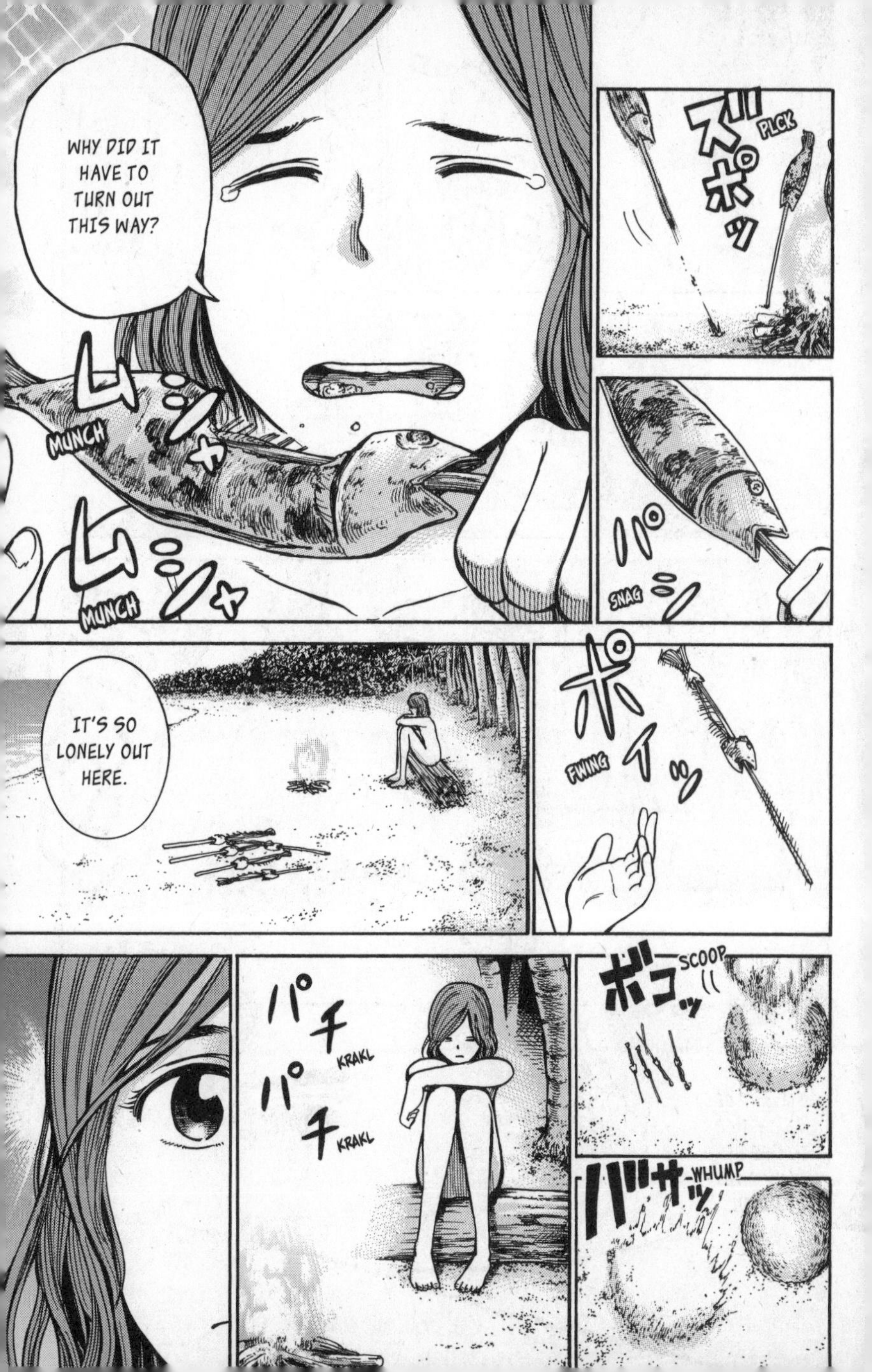
PLCK
SNAG
WHY DID IT HAVE TO TURN OUT THIS WAY?
MUNCH
MUNCH
FWING
IT'S SO LONELY OUT HERE.
SCOOP
WHUMP
KRAKL
KRAKL

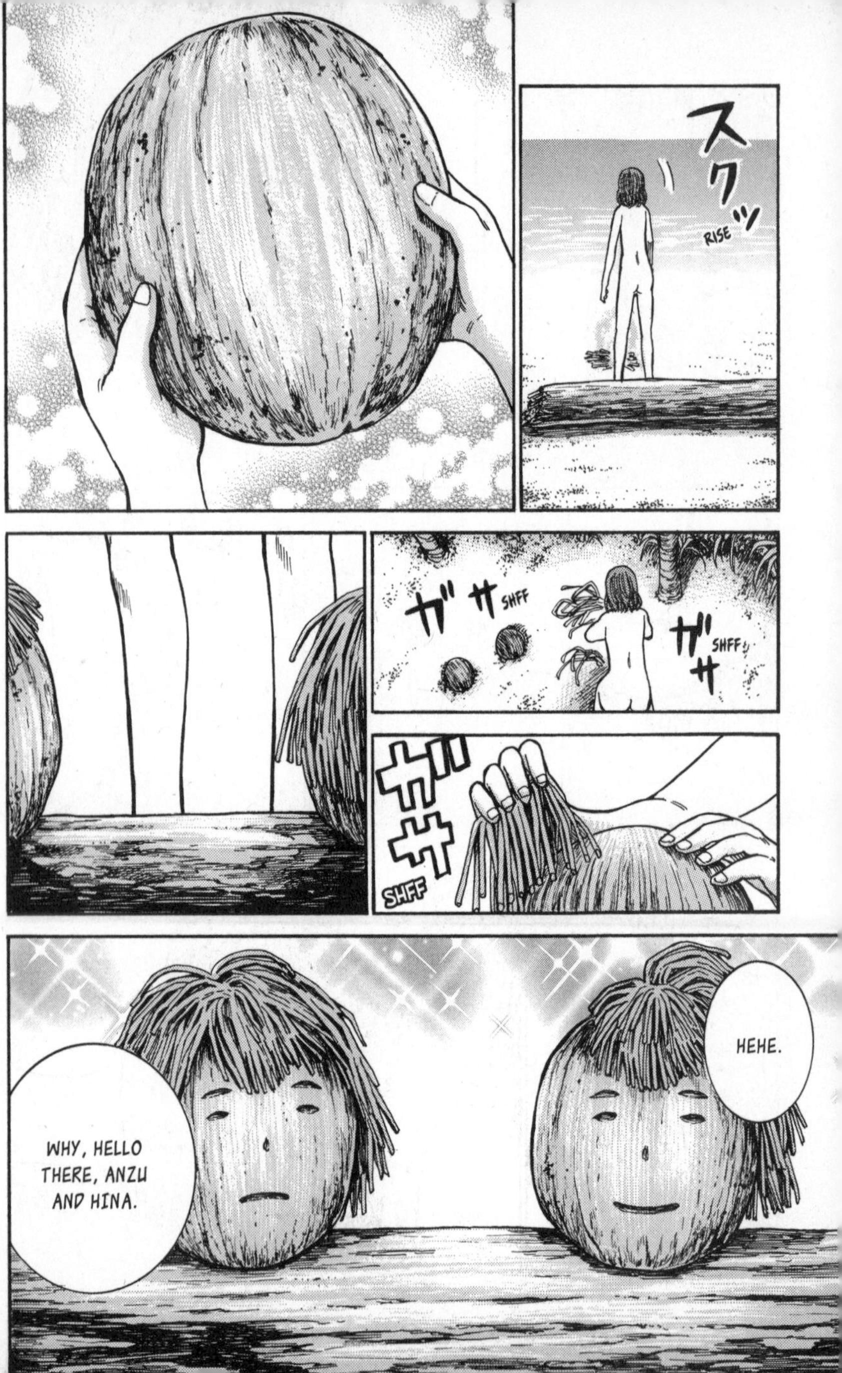

スクッ
RISE
ガサ
SHFF
ガサ
SHFF
ガサ
SHFF
HEHE.
WHY, HELLO THERE, ANZU AND HINA.

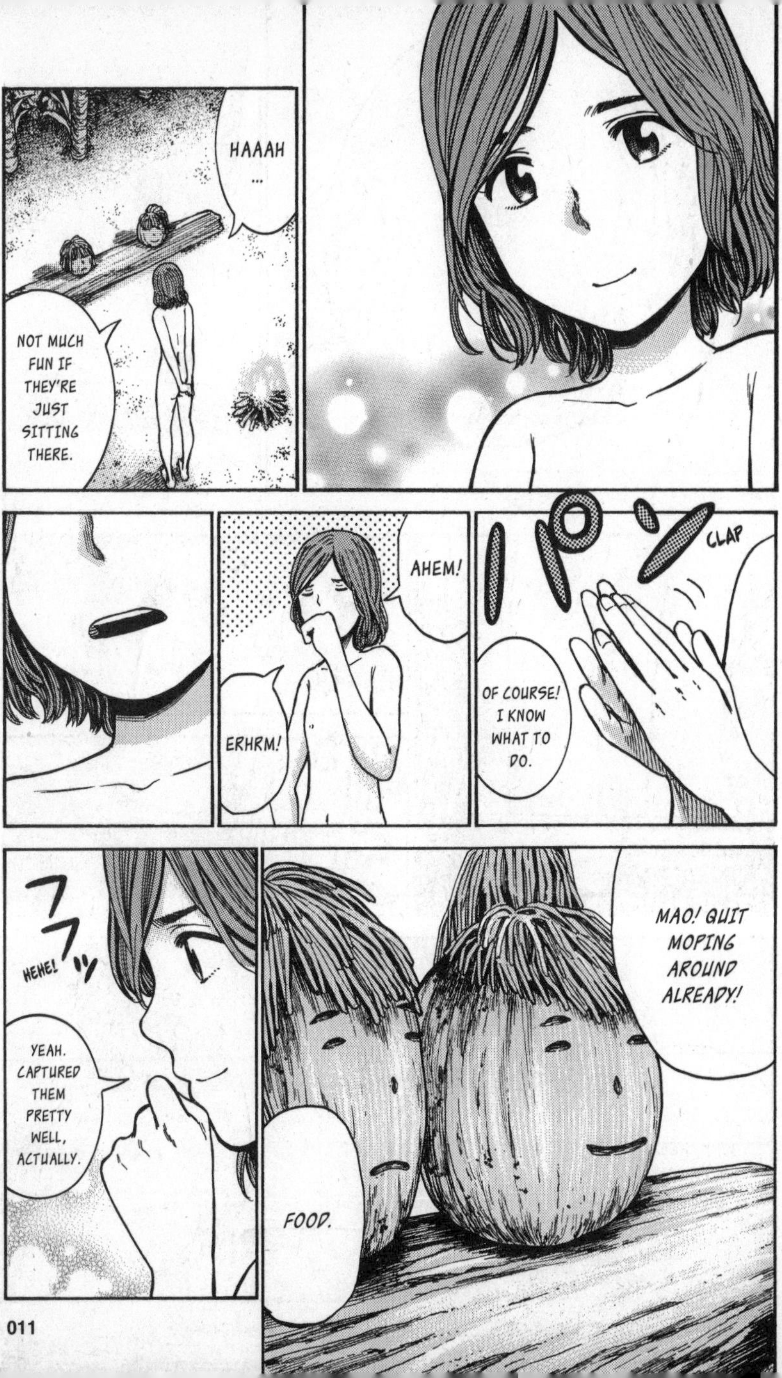
HAAAH ...
NOT MUCH FUN IF THEY'RE JUST SITTING THERE.
CLAP
OF COURSE! I KNOW WHAT TO DO.
AHEM!
ERHRM!
MAO! QUIT MOPING AROUND ALREADY!
FOOD.
HEHE!
YEAH. CAPTURED THEM PRETTY WELL, ACTUALLY.

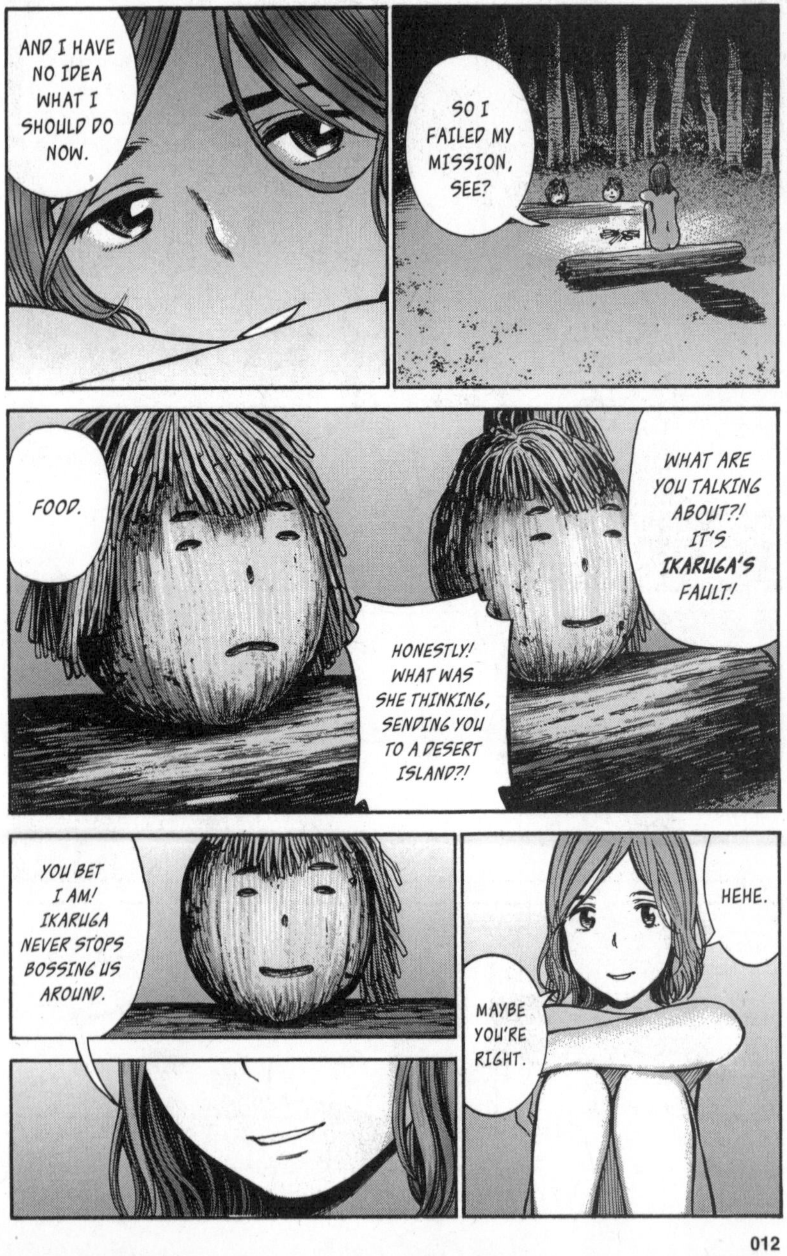
SO I FAILED MY MISSION, SEE?
AND I HAVE NO IDEA WHAT I SHOULD DO NOW.
WHAT ARE YOU TALKING ABOUT?! IT'S IKARUGA'S FAULT!
HONESTLY! WHAT WAS SHE THINKING, SENDING YOU TO A DESERT ISLAND?!
FOOD.
HEHE.
MAYBE YOU'RE RIGHT.
YOU BET I AM! IKARUGA NEVER STOPS BOSSING US AROUND.

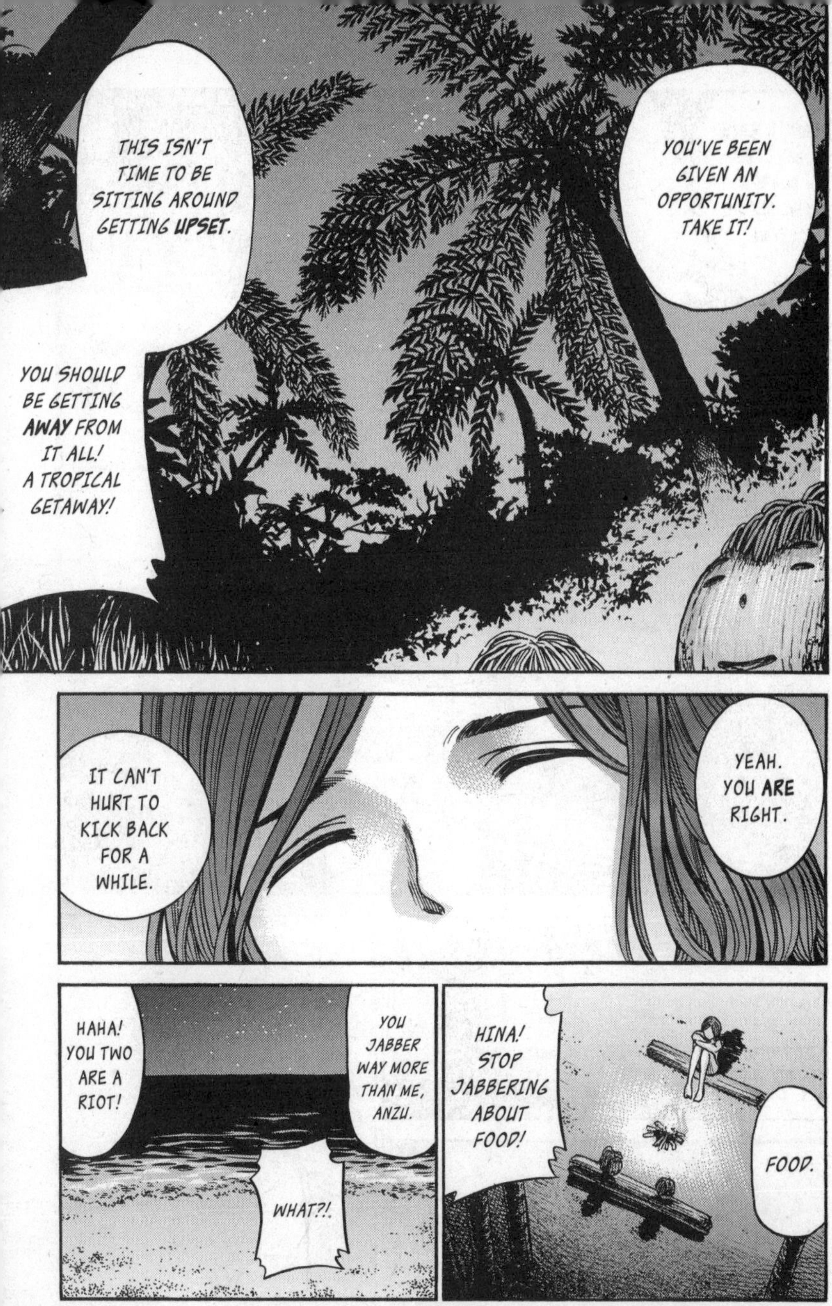
YOU'VE BEEN GIVEN AN OPPORTUNITY. TAKE IT!
THIS ISN'T TIME TO BE SITTING AROUND GETTING **UPSET**.
YOU SHOULD BE GETTING **AWAY** FROM IT ALL! A TROPICAL GETAWAY!
YEAH. YOU **ARE** RIGHT.
IT CAN'T HURT TO KICK BACK FOR A WHILE.
FOOD.
HINA! STOP JABBERING ABOUT FOOD!
YOU JABBER WAY MORE THAN ME, ANZU.
WHAT?!.
HAHA! YOU TWO ARE A RIOT!

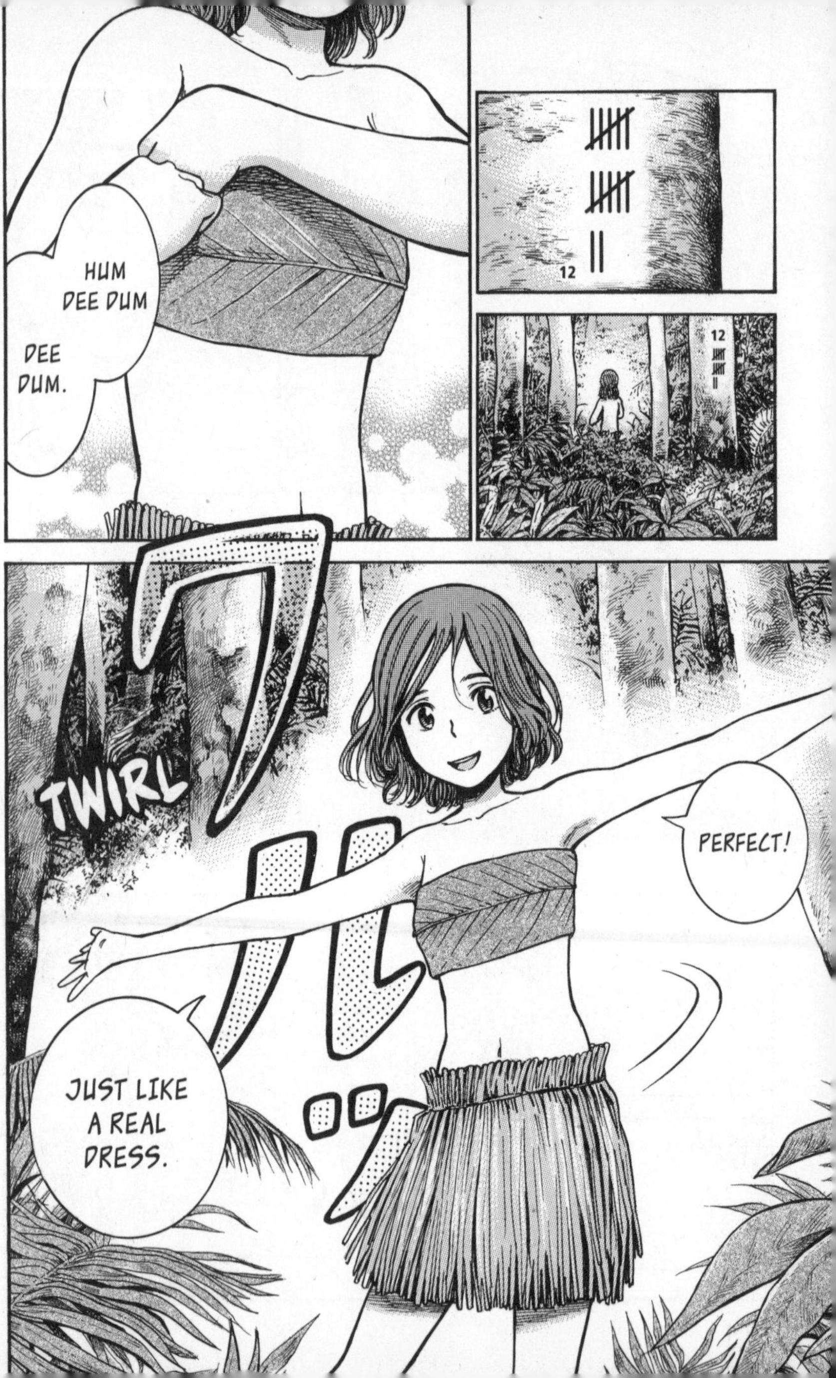
12
12
HUM DEE DUM
DEE DUM.
PERFECT!
TWIRL
JUST LIKE A REAL DRESS.

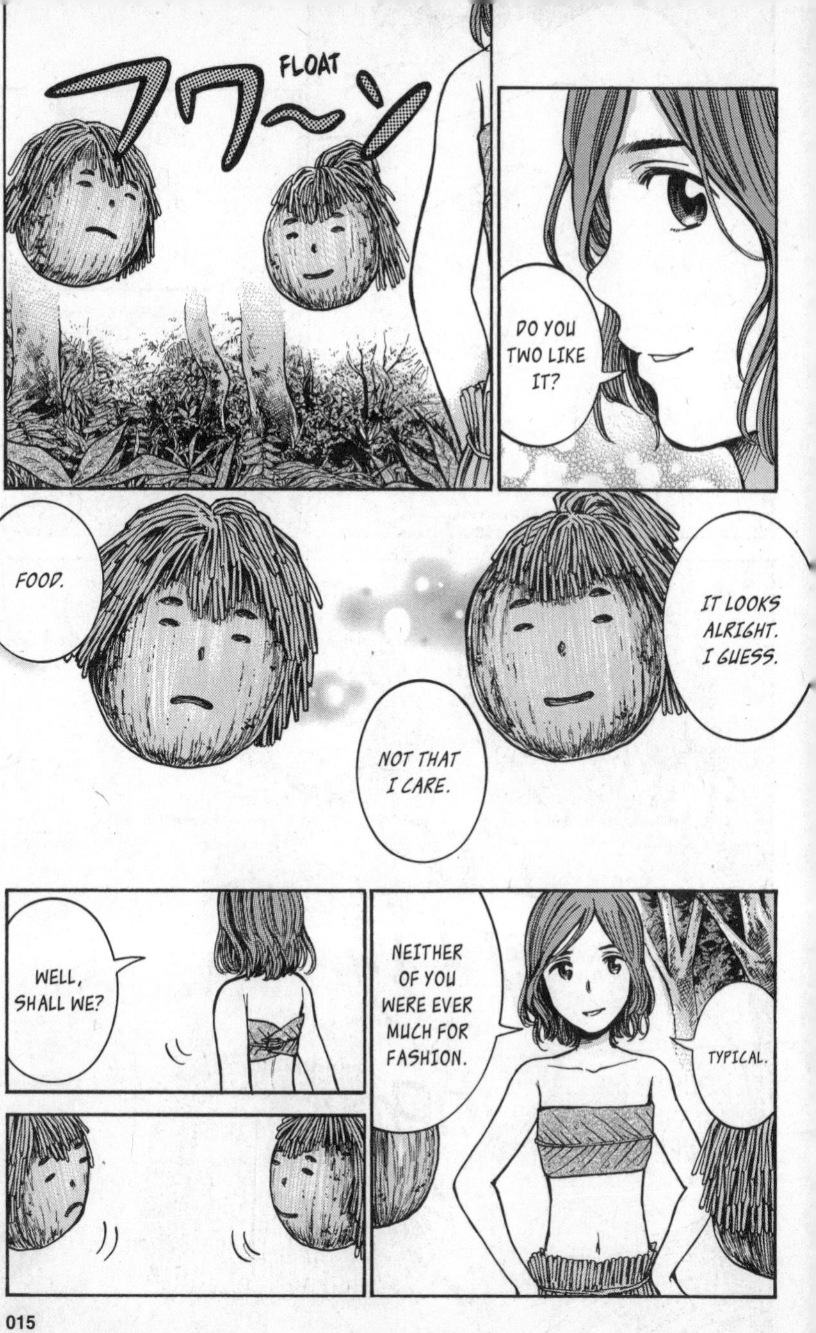
DO YOU TWO LIKE IT?
フワ〜ン
FLOAT
IT LOOKS ALRIGHT. I GUESS.
NOT THAT I CARE.
FOOD.
NEITHER OF YOU WERE EVER MUCH FOR FASHION.
TYPICAL.
WELL, SHALL WE?

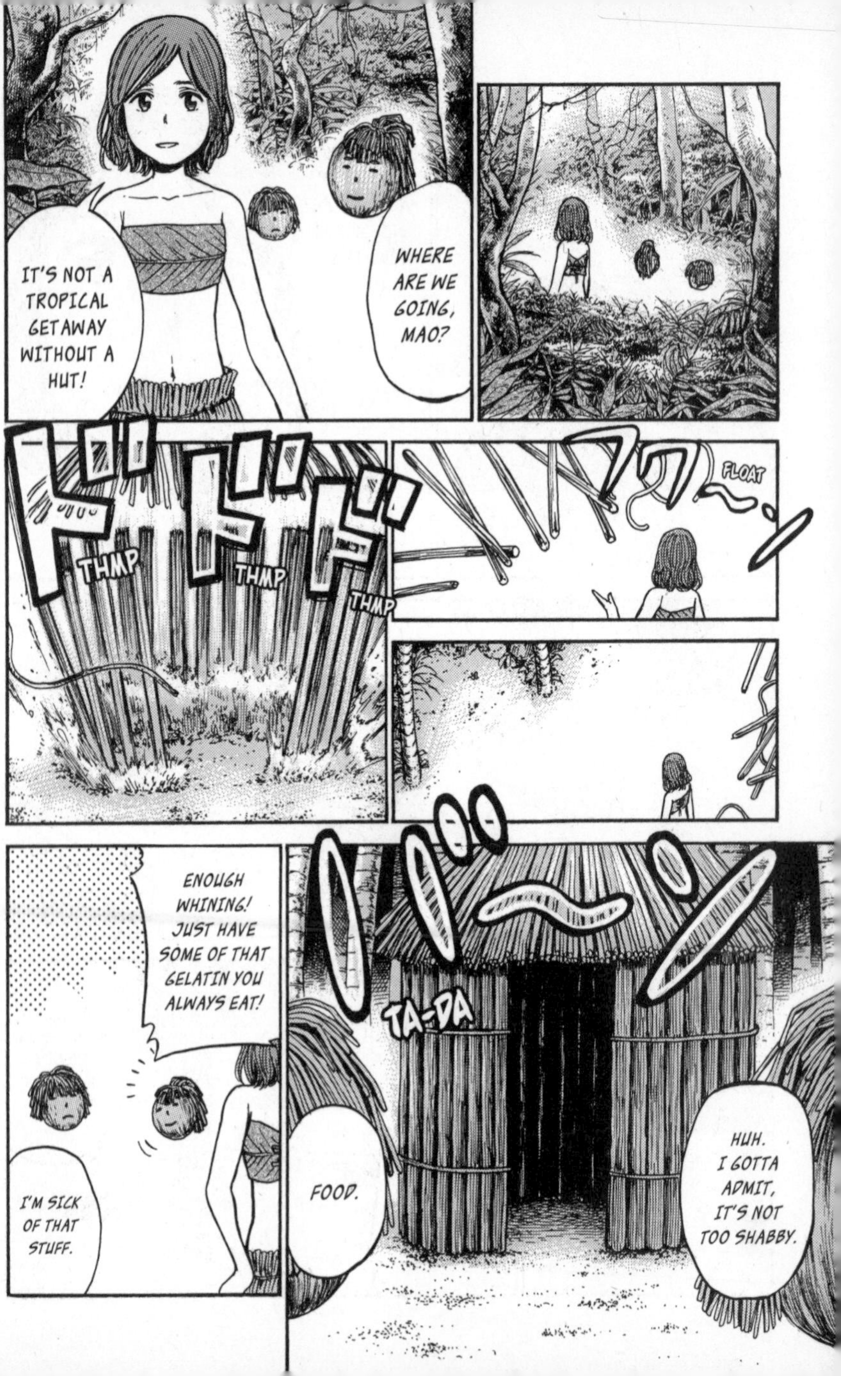
WHERE ARE WE GOING, MAO?
IT'S NOT A TROPICAL GETAWAY WITHOUT A HUT!
FLOAT
THMP
THMP
THMP
TA-DA
HUH. I GOTTA ADMIT, IT'S NOT TOO SHABBY.
FOOD.
ENOUGH WHINING! JUST HAVE SOME OF THAT GELATIN YOU ALWAYS EAT!
I'M SICK OF THAT STUFF.

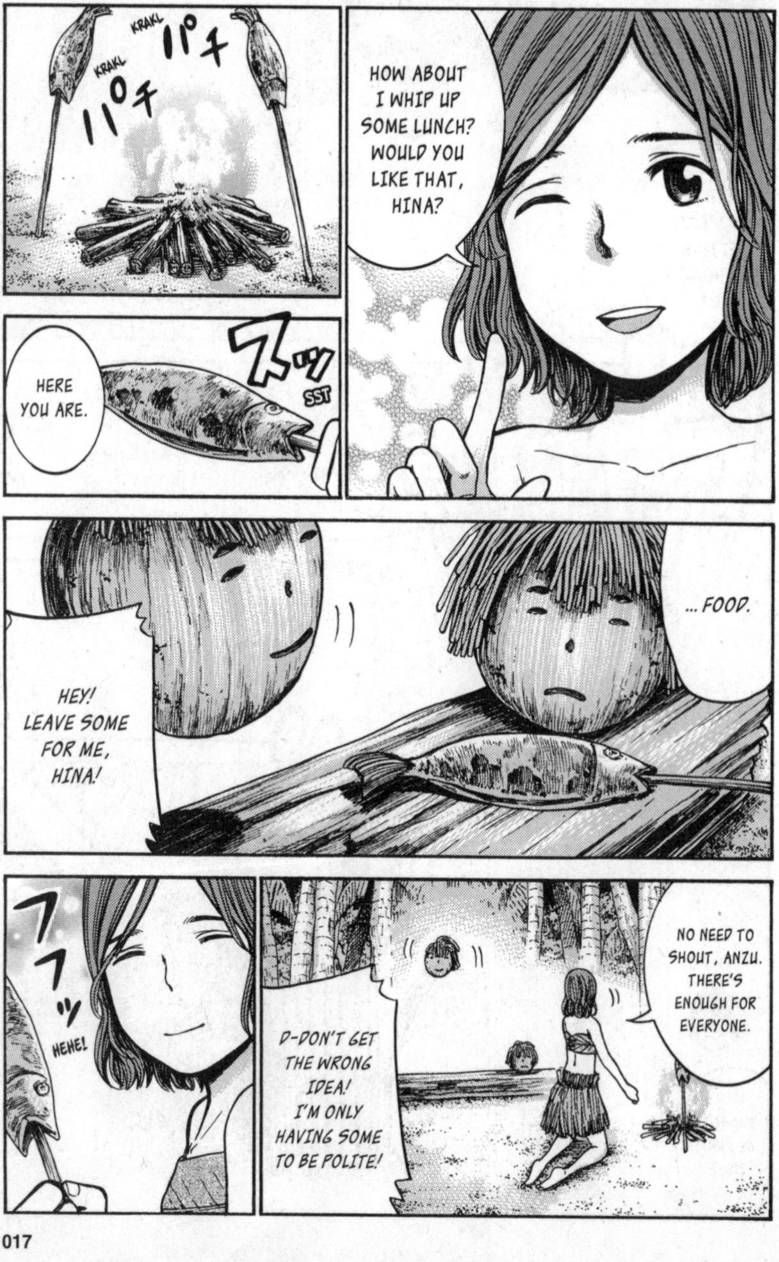
HOW ABOUT I WHIP UP SOME LUNCH? WOULD YOU LIKE THAT, HINA?
KRAKL
パチ
KRAKL
パチ
HERE YOU ARE.
スッ
SST
... FOOD.
HEY! LEAVE SOME FOR ME, HINA!
NO NEED TO SHOUT, ANZU. THERE'S ENOUGH FOR EVERYONE.
D-DON'T GET THE WRONG IDEA! I'M ONLY HAVING SOME TO BE POLITE!
フフッ
HEHE!

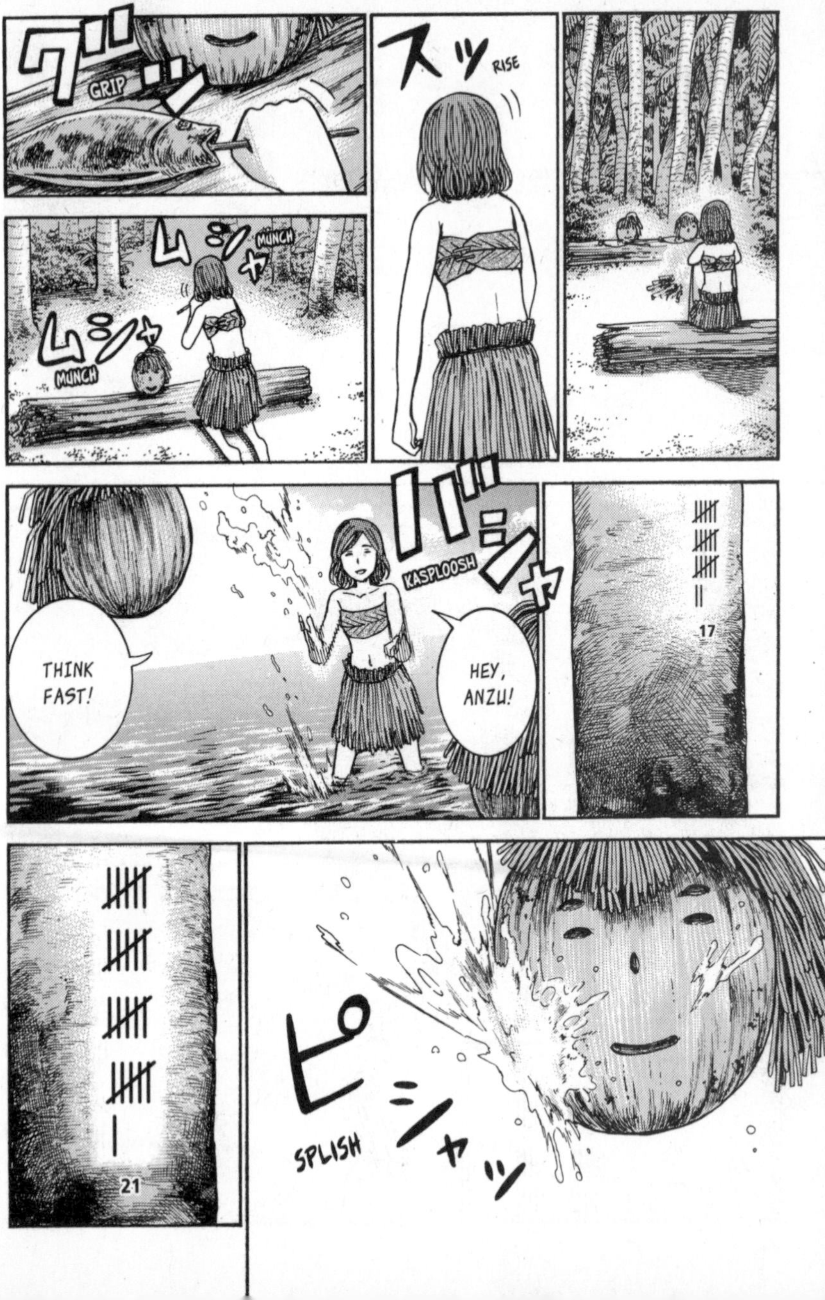
スッ
RISE
グッ
GRIP
ムシャ
MUNCH
ムシャ
MUNCH
17
バシャ
KASPLOOSH
HEY, ANZU!
THINK FAST!
ピシャッ
SPLISH
21

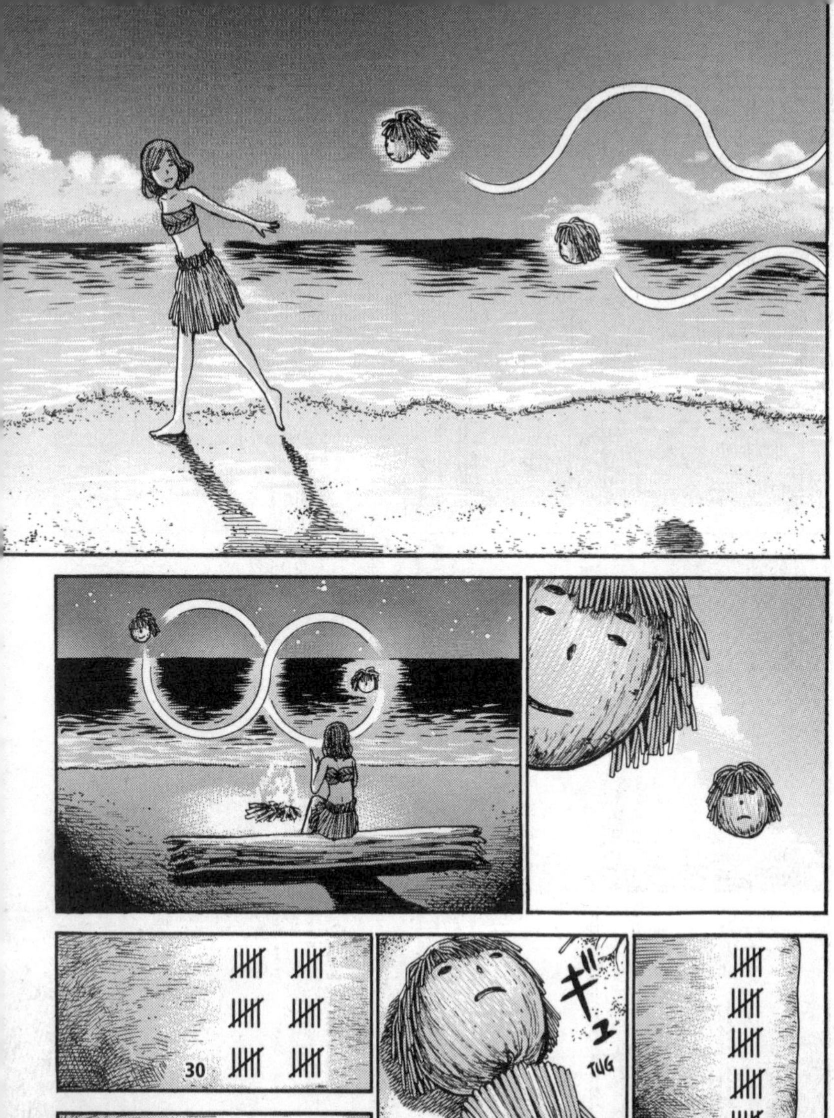
33
ギュ
TUG
30
48

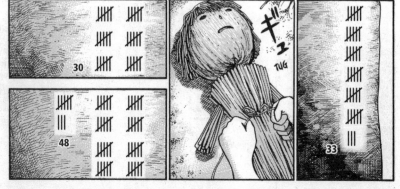

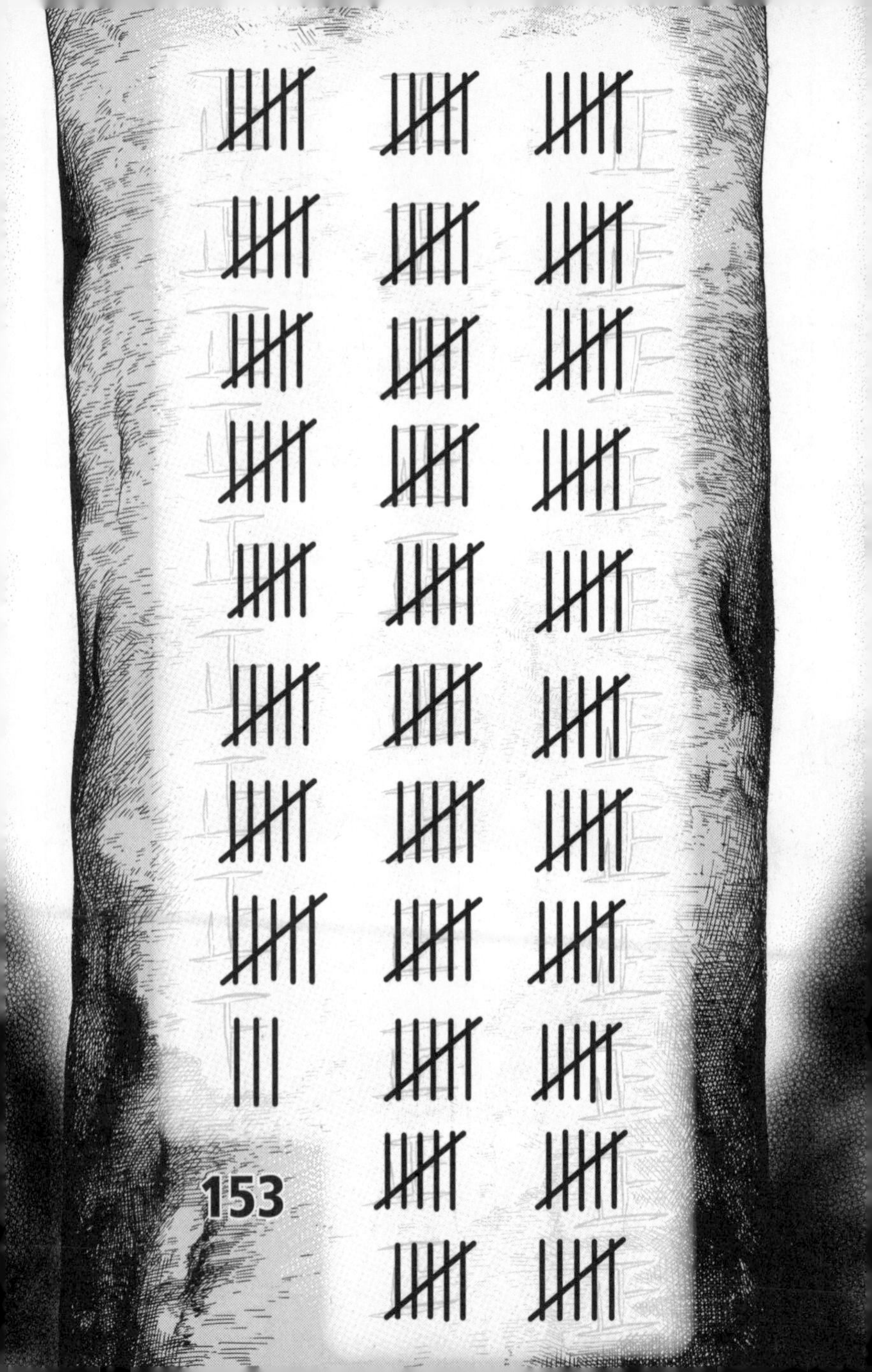
153

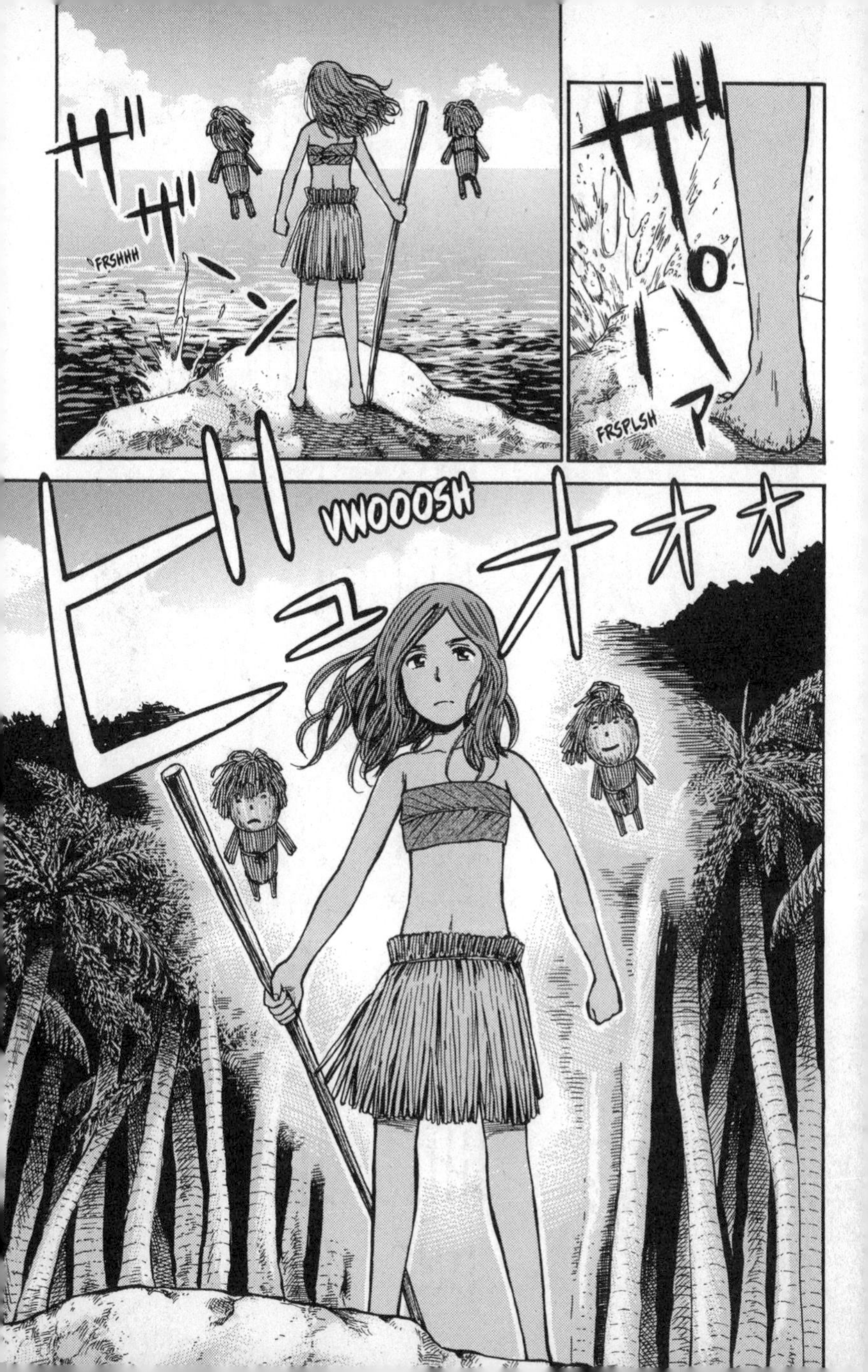
FRSPLSH
FRSHHH
VWOOOSH

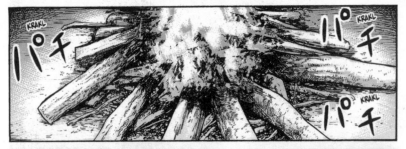

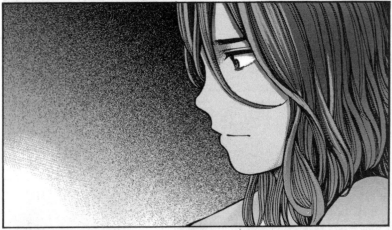

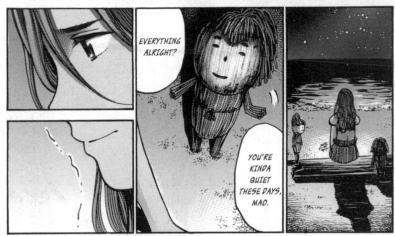

パチ
KRAKL
KRAKL
パチ
パチ
KRAKL
EVERYTHING ALRIGHT?
YOU'RE KINDA QUIET THESE DAYS, MAO.

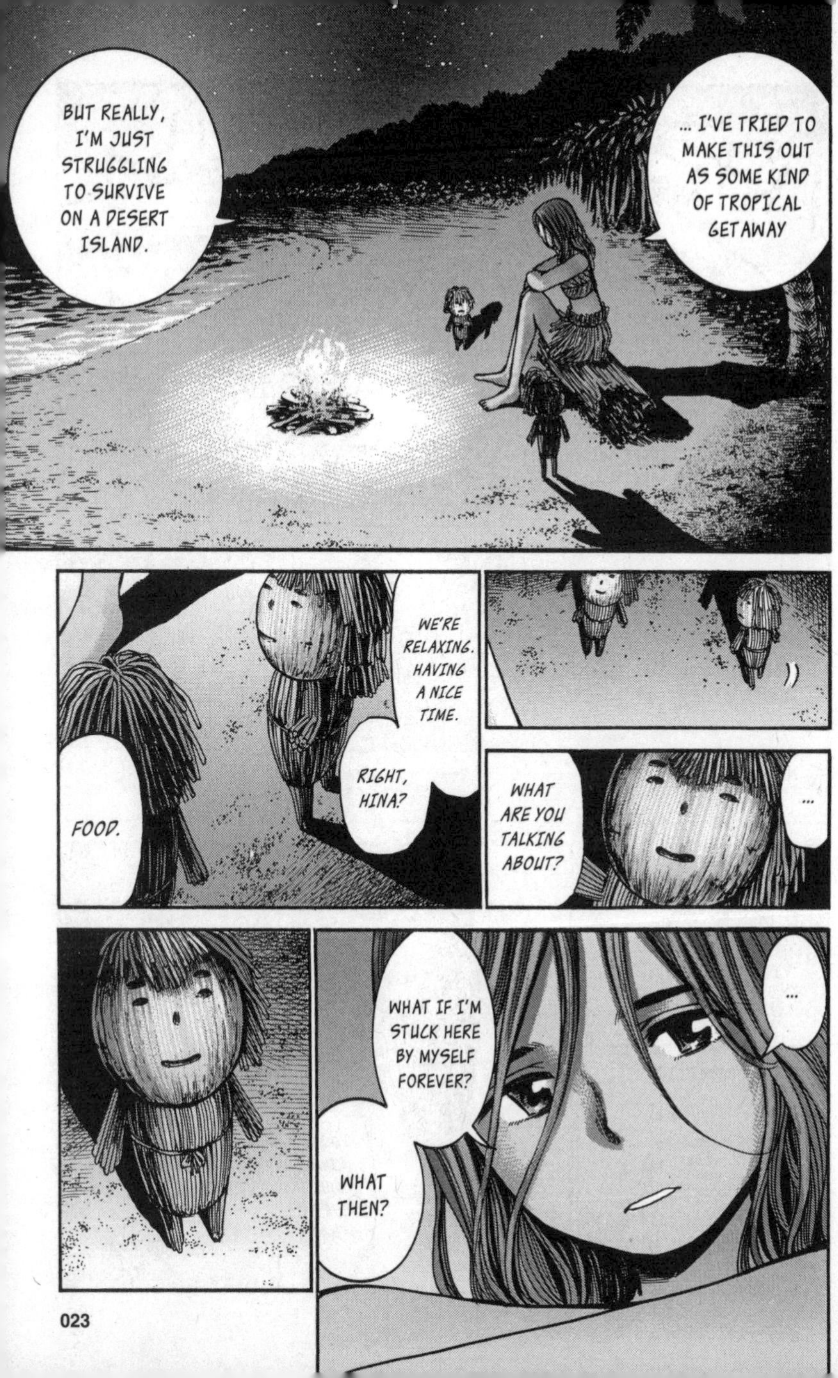
... I'VE TRIED TO MAKE THIS OUT AS SOME KIND OF TROPICAL GETAWAY
BUT REALLY, I'M JUST STRUGGLING TO SURVIVE ON A DESERT ISLAND.
...
WHAT ARE YOU TALKING ABOUT?
WE'RE RELAXING. HAVING A NICE TIME.
RIGHT, HINA?
FOOD.
...
WHAT IF I'M STUCK HERE BY MYSELF FOREVER?
WHAT THEN?

YOU'VE GOT US!

WH-WHAT DO YOU MEAN?

YOU'RE NOT ALONE, MAO!

Y ...

ガシ

GRAB

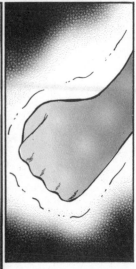

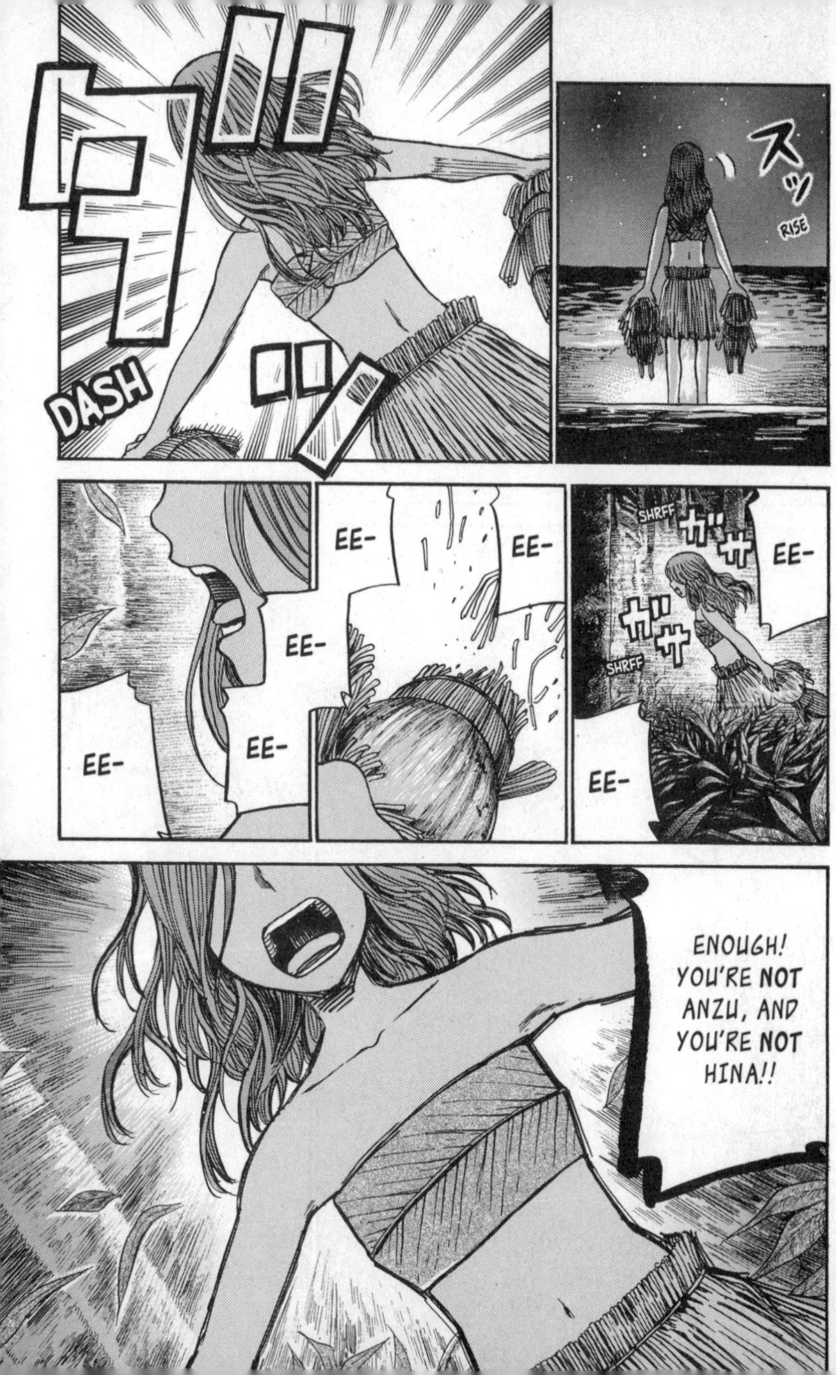

スッ
RISE
DASH
SHRFF
ガサ
EE-
ガサ
SHRFF
EE-
EE-
EE-
EE-
EE-
EE-
EE-
ENOUGH! YOU'RE NOT ANZU, AND YOU'RE NOT HINA!!

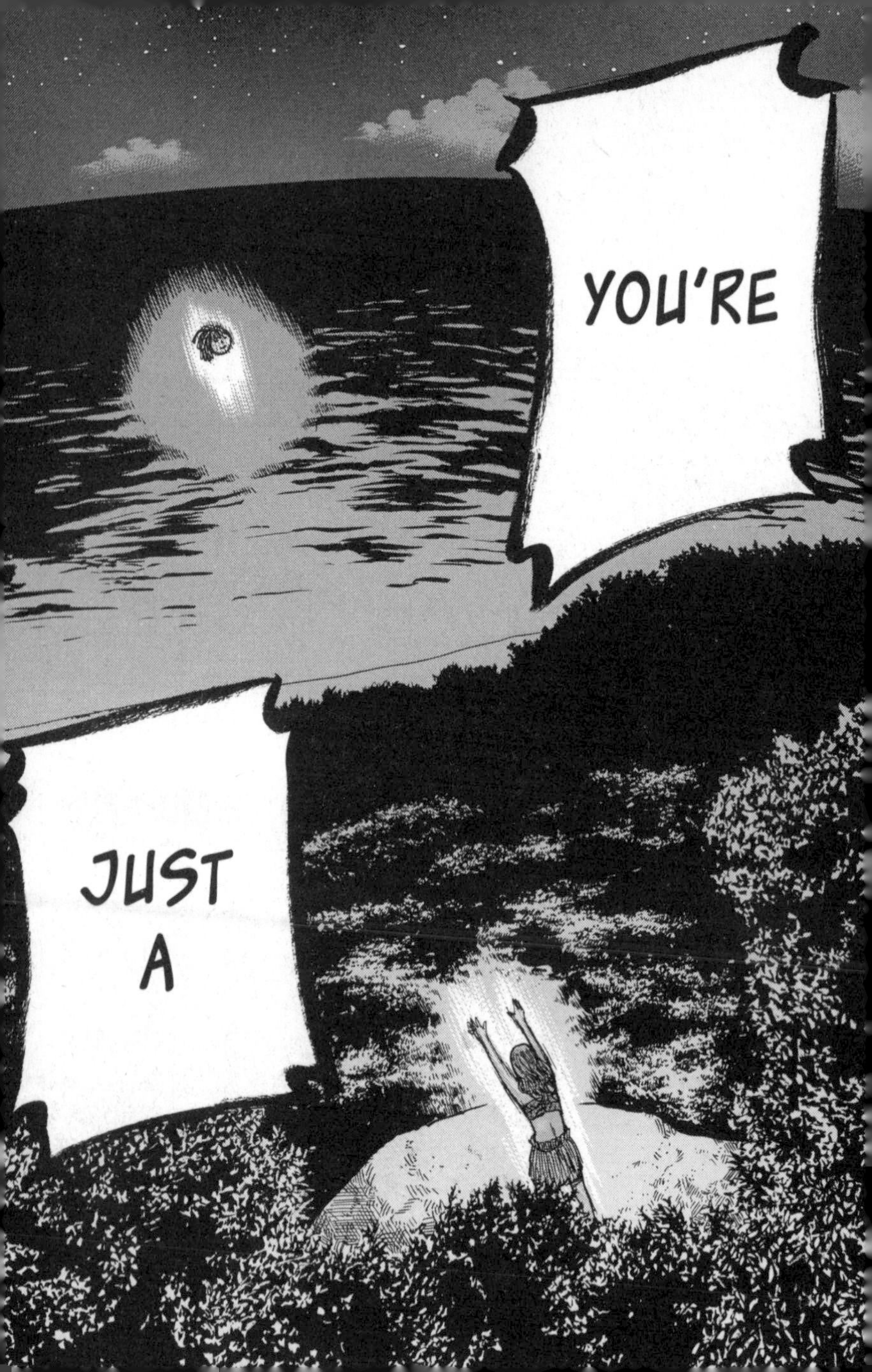
YOU'RE
JUST A

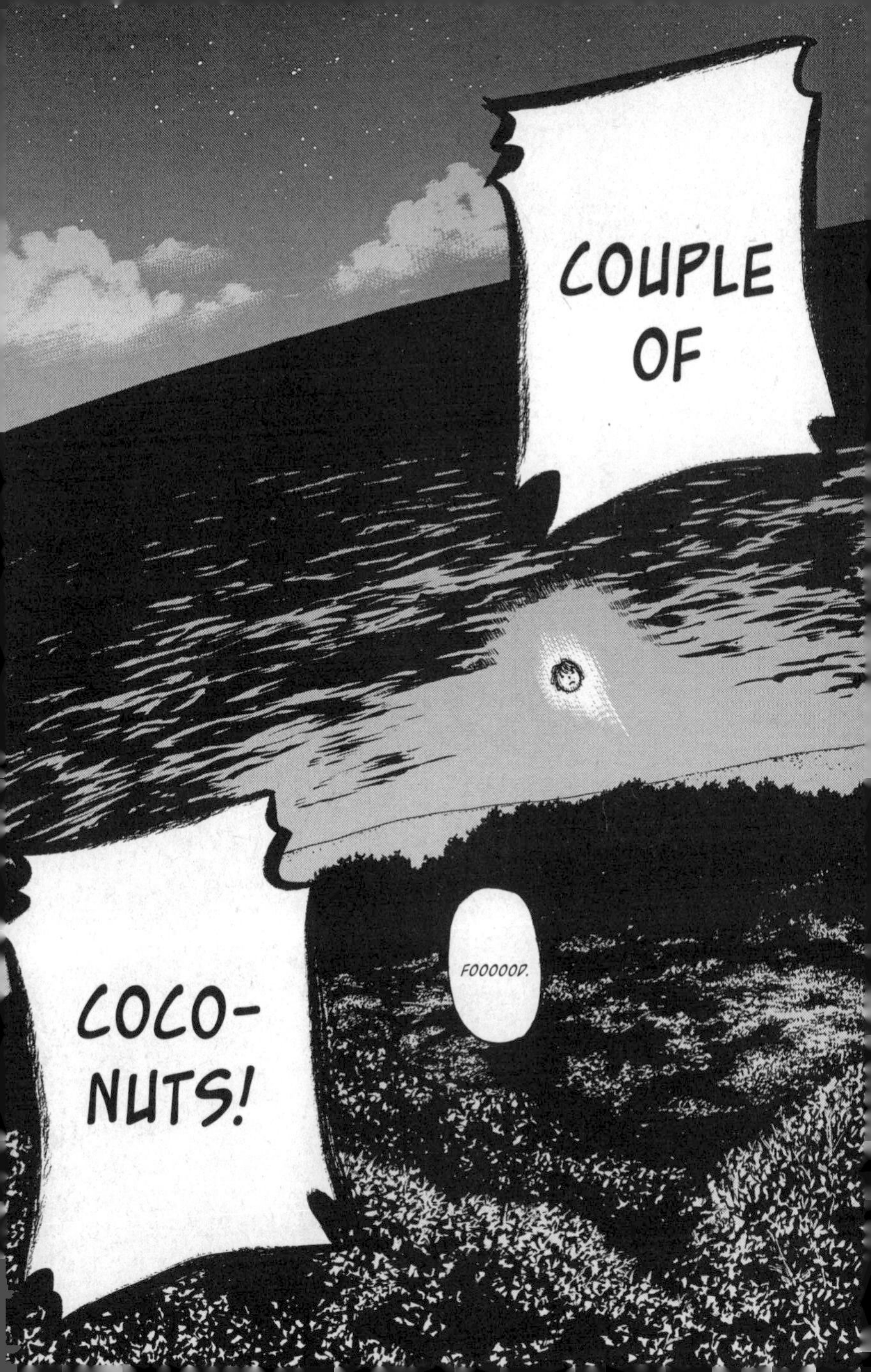
COUPLE OF
FOOOOOD.
COCO-NUTS!

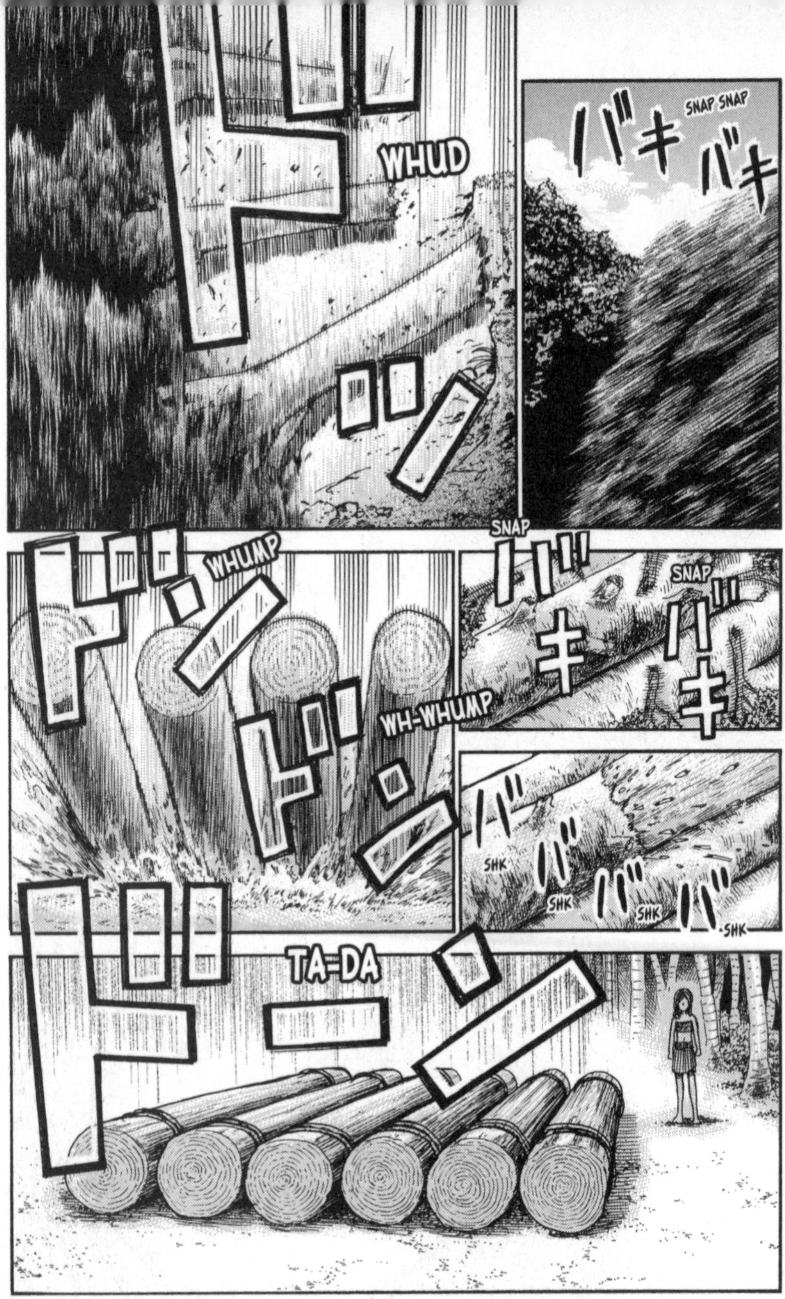
バキバキ
SNAP SNAP
WHUD
SNAP
SNAP
SHK
SHK
SHK
SHK
WHUMP
WH-WHUMP
TA-DA

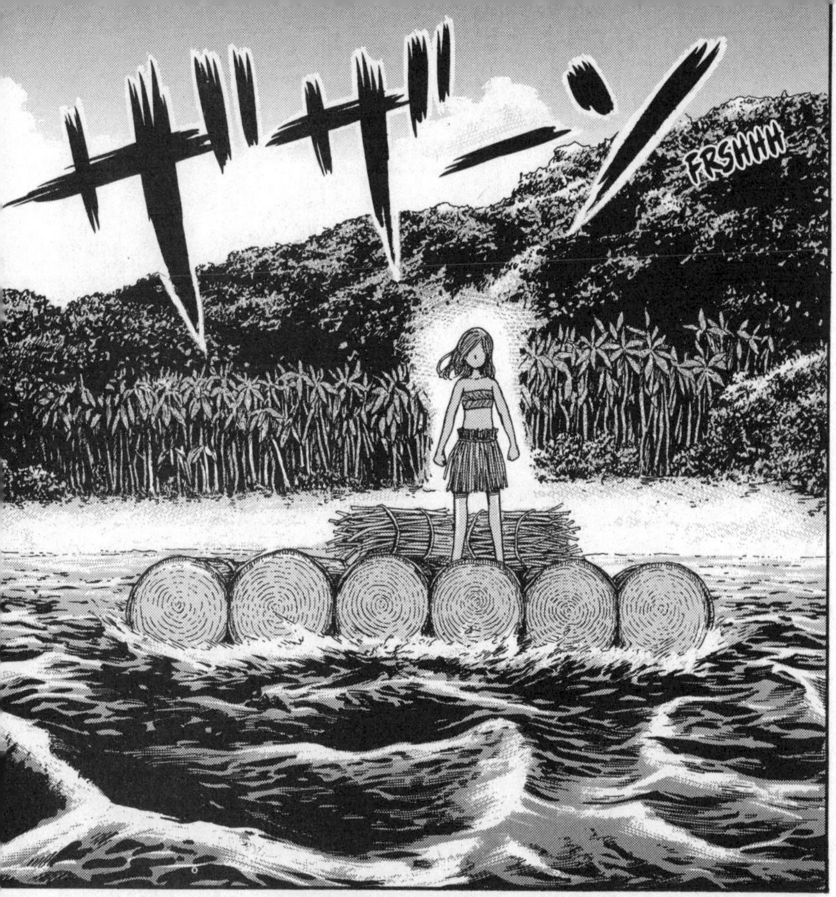
ザザーン
FRSHHH
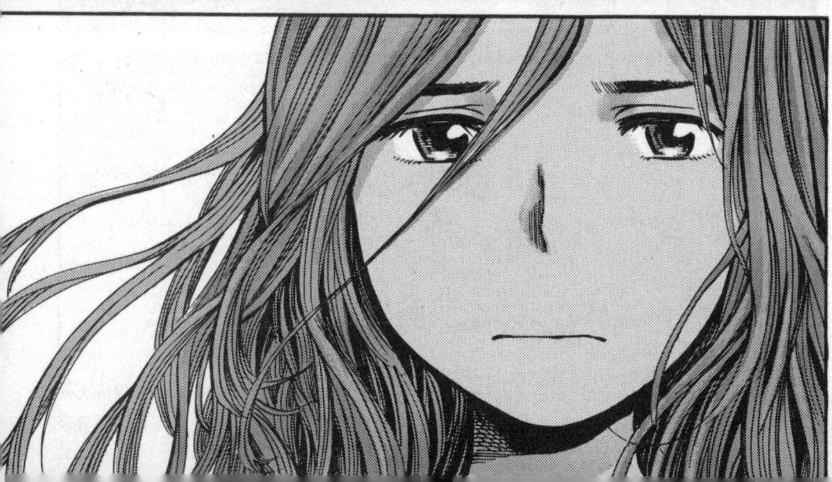

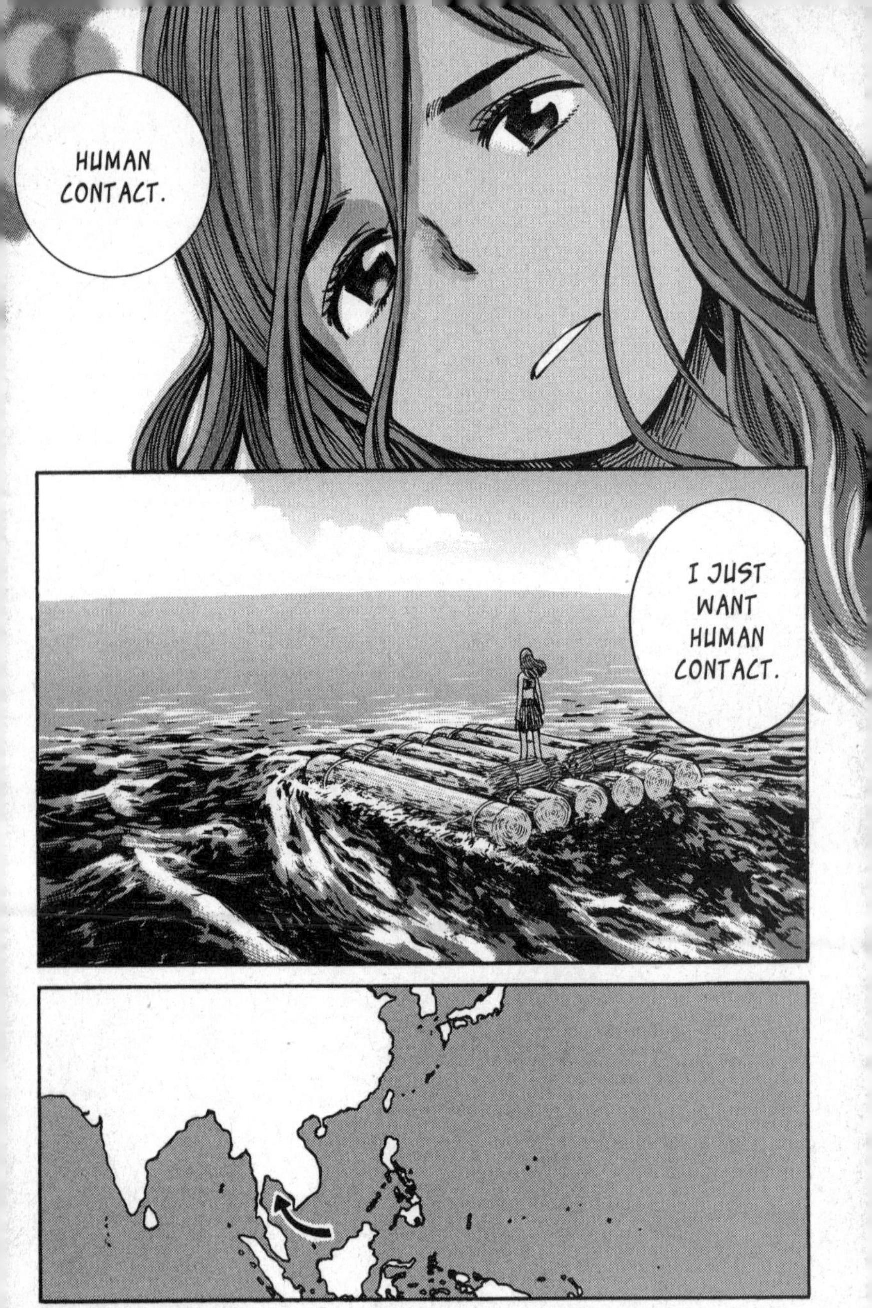
HUMAN CONTACT.
I JUST WANT HUMAN CONTACT.

CHAPTER 39 END

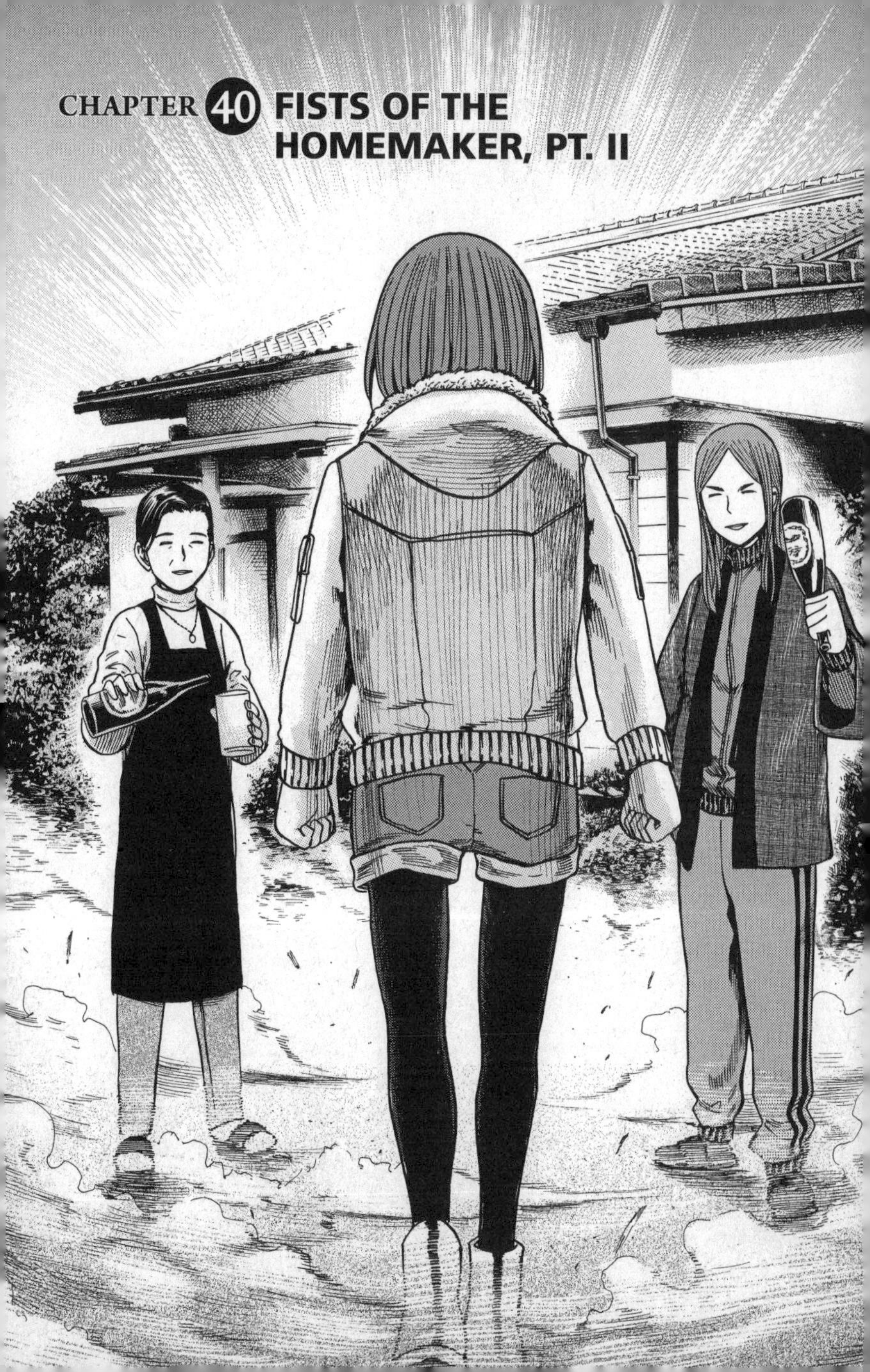
CHAPTER 40 FISTS OF THE HOMEMAKER, PT. II

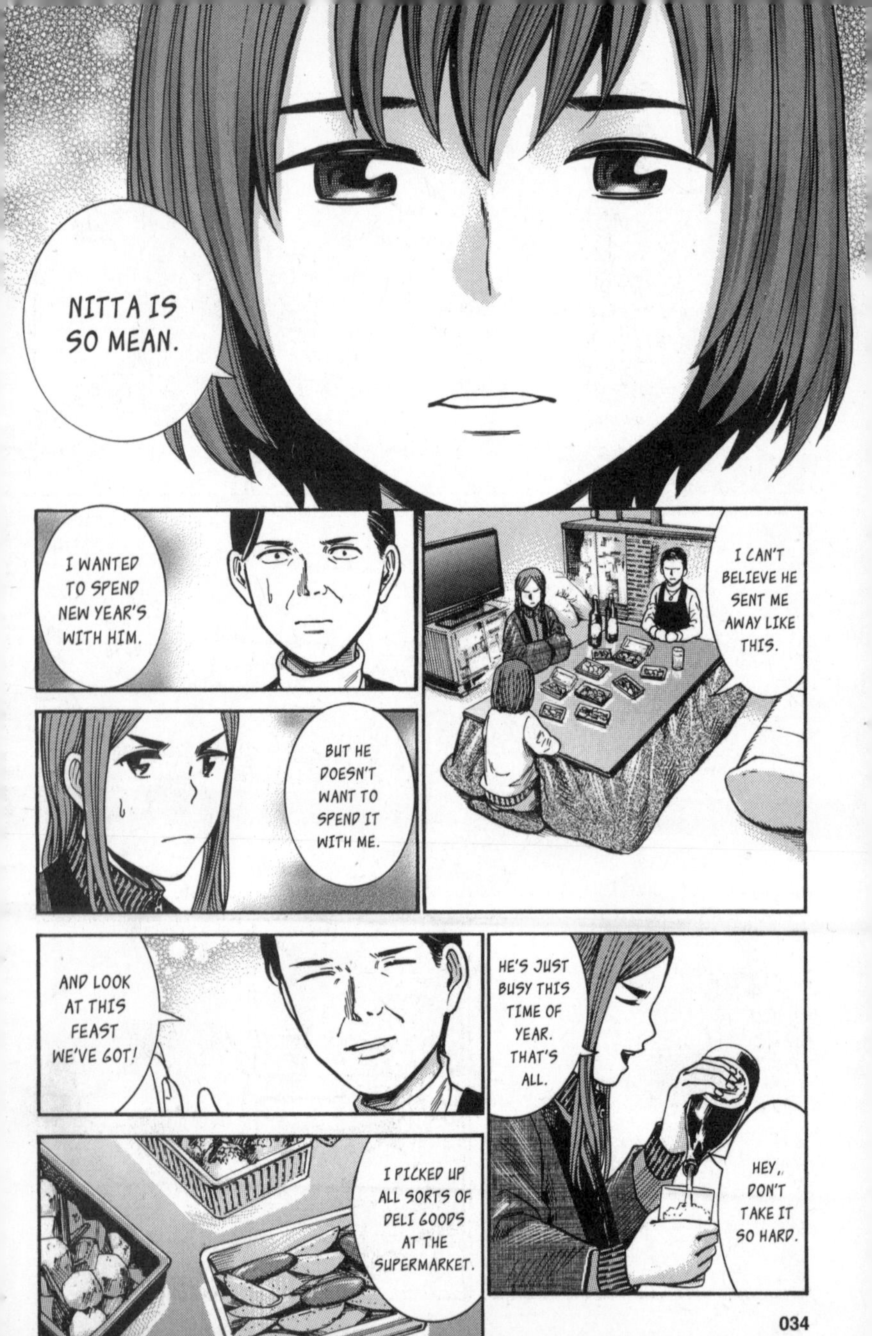
NITTA IS SO MEAN.
I CAN'T BELIEVE HE SENT ME AWAY LIKE THIS.
I WANTED TO SPEND NEW YEAR'S WITH HIM.
BUT HE DOESN'T WANT TO SPEND IT WITH ME.
HE'S JUST BUSY THIS TIME OF YEAR. THAT'S ALL.
HEY,, DON'T TAKE IT SO HARD.
AND LOOK AT THIS FEAST WE'VE GOT!
I PICKED UP ALL SORTS OF DELI GOODS AT THE SUPERMARKET.

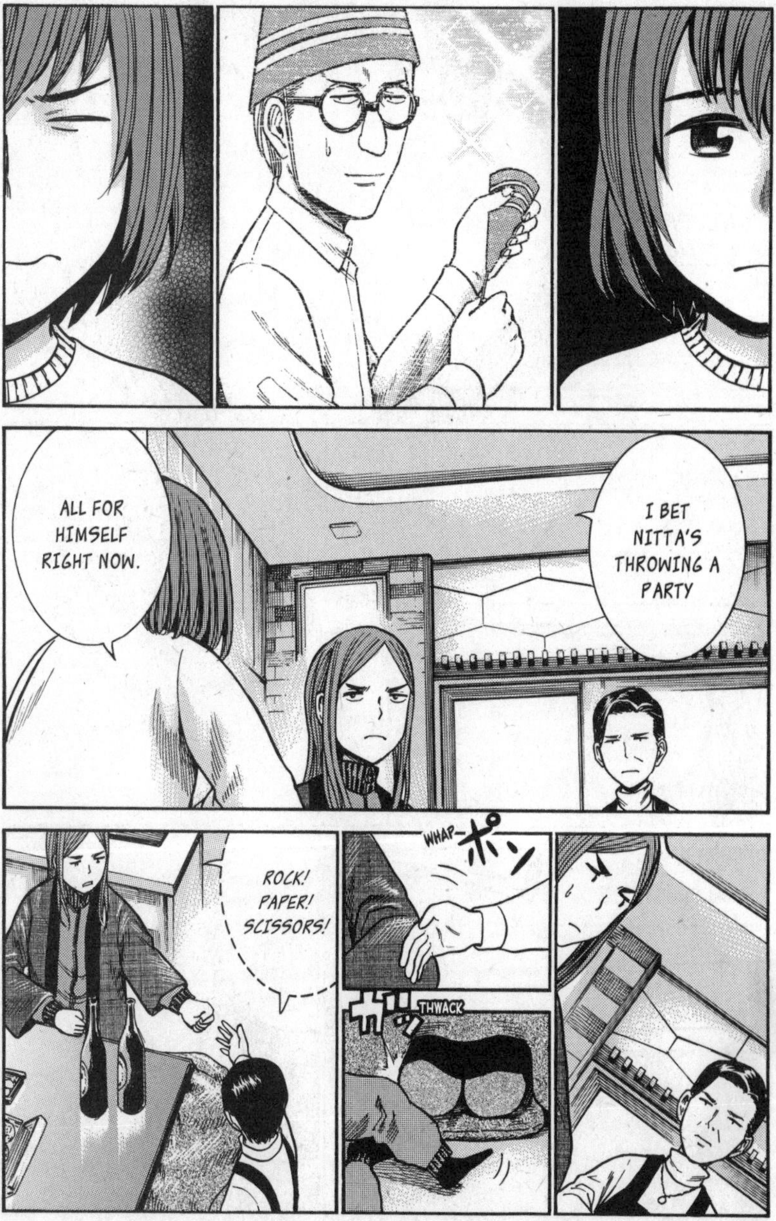
I BET NITTA'S THROWING A PARTY
ALL FOR HIMSELF RIGHT NOW.
WHAP
ポン
THWACK
ガッ
ROCK! PAPER! SCISSORS!

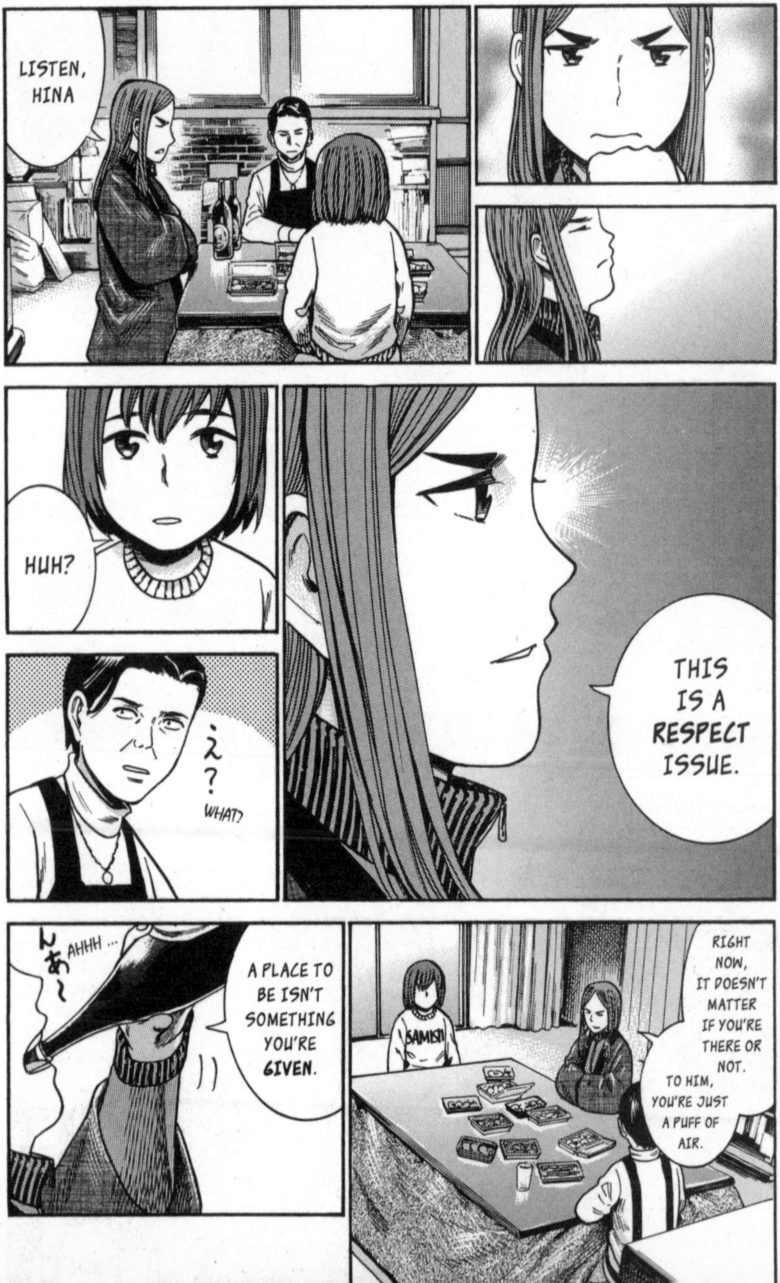
LISTEN, HINA
THIS IS A RESPECT ISSUE.
HUH?
え? WHAT?
RIGHT NOW, IT DOESN'T MATTER IF YOU'RE THERE OR NOT.
TO HIM, YOU'RE JUST A PUFF OF AIR.
A PLACE TO BE ISN'T SOMETHING YOU'RE GIVEN.
んあ~ AHHH ...

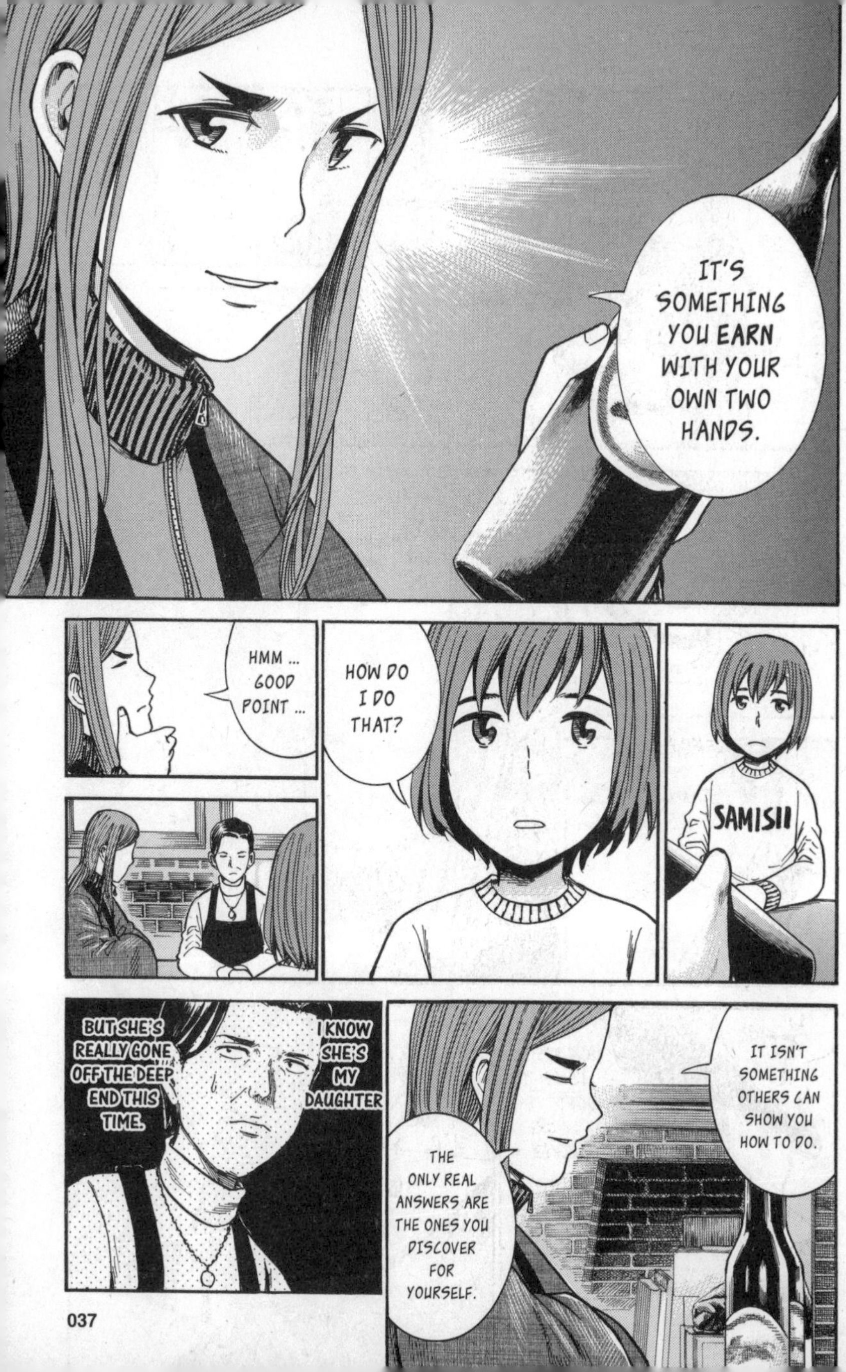
IT'S SOMETHING YOU EARN WITH YOUR OWN TWO HANDS.
SAMISII
HOW DO I DO THAT?
HMM ... GOOD POINT ...
IT ISN'T SOMETHING OTHERS CAN SHOW YOU HOW TO DO.
THE ONLY REAL ANSWERS ARE THE ONES YOU DISCOVER FOR YOURSELF.
I KNOW SHE'S MY DAUGHTER
BUT SHE'S REALLY GONE OFF THE DEEP END THIS TIME.

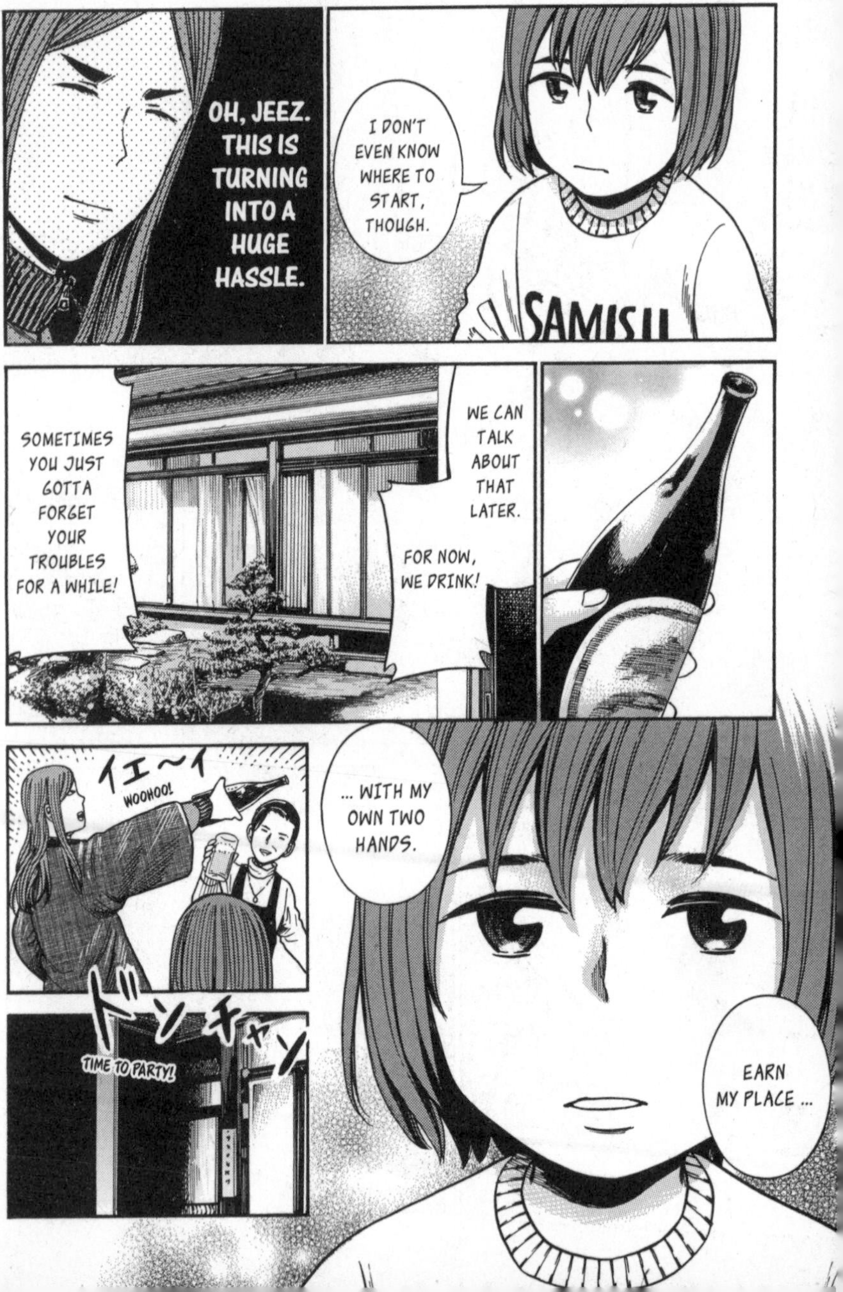
I DON'T EVEN KNOW WHERE TO START, THOUGH.
OH, JEEZ. THIS IS TURNING INTO A HUGE HASSLE.
SAMISU
WE CAN TALK ABOUT THAT LATER.
FOR NOW, WE DRINK!
SOMETIMES YOU JUST GOTTA FORGET YOUR TROUBLES FOR A WHILE!
... WITH MY OWN TWO HANDS.
EARN MY PLACE ...
イエ～イ
WOOHOO!
ドンチャン
TIME TO PARTY!

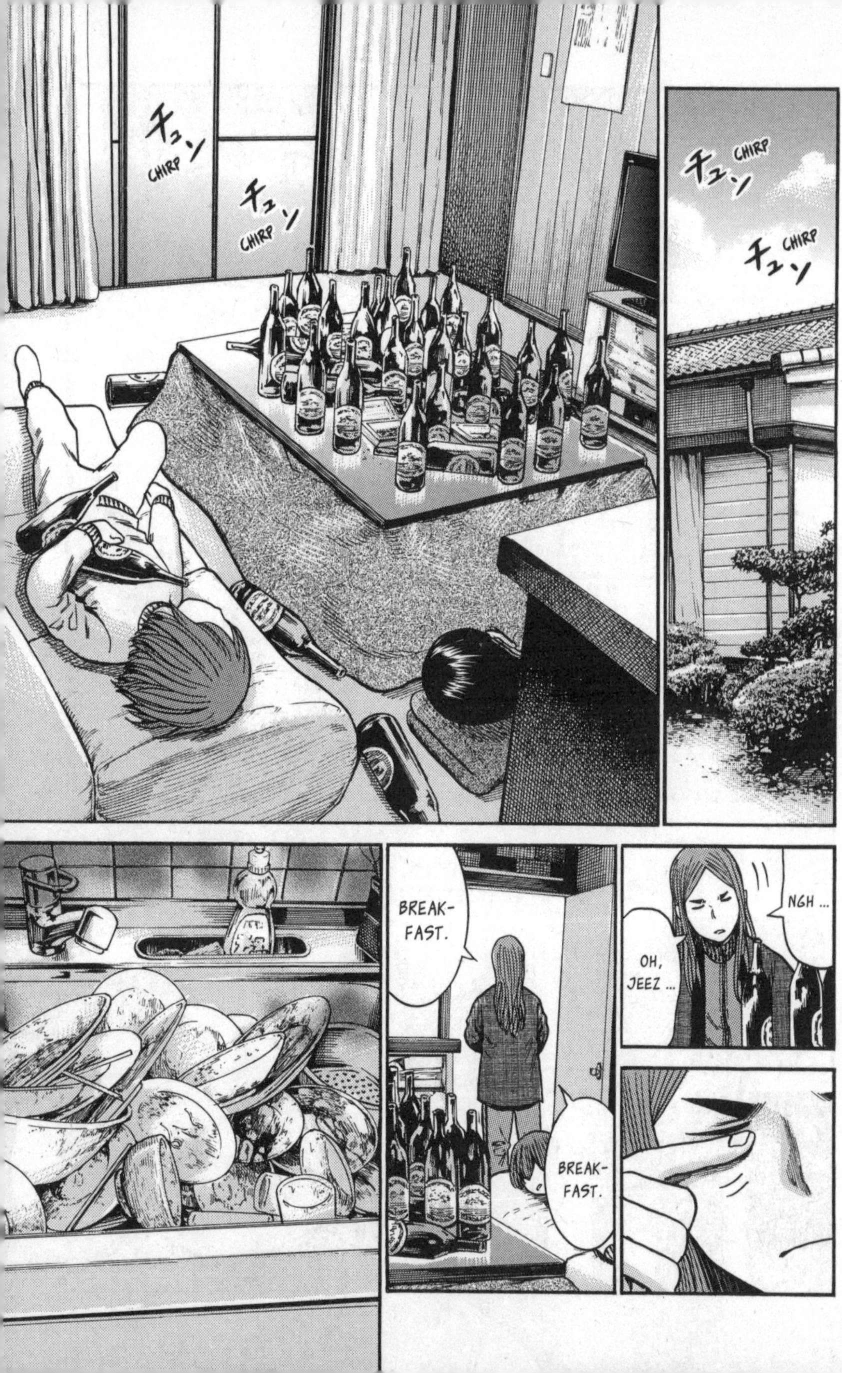
チュン CHIRP
チュン CHIRP
チュン CHIRP
チュン CHIRP
NGH ...
OH, JEEZ ...
BREAK-FAST.
BREAK-FAST.

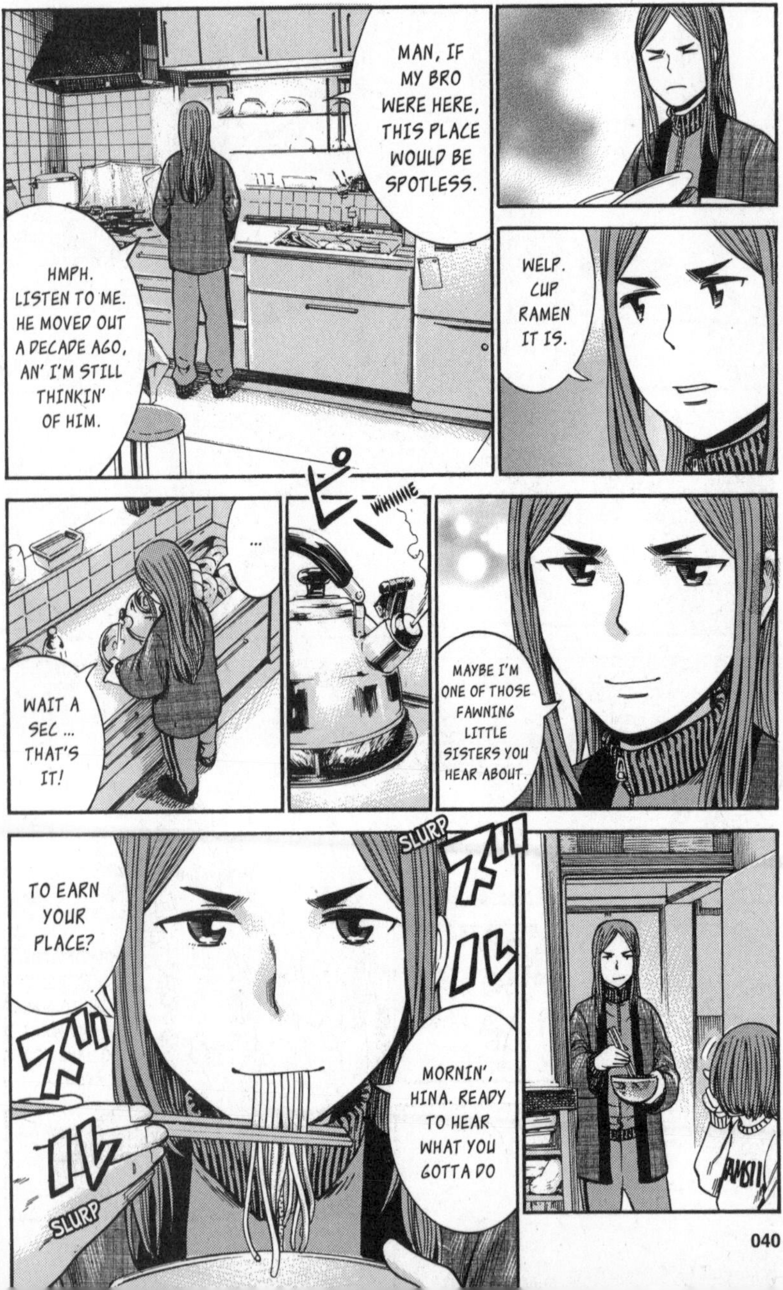
WELP. CUP RAMEN IT IS.
MAN, IF MY BRO WERE HERE, THIS PLACE WOULD BE SPOTLESS.
HMPH. LISTEN TO ME. HE MOVED OUT A DECADE AGO, AN' I'M STILL THINKIN' OF HIM.
MAYBE I'M ONE OF THOSE FAWNING LITTLE SISTERS YOU HEAR ABOUT.
ピー
WHIIIIE
...
WAIT A SEC ... THAT'S IT!
MORNIN', HINA. READY TO HEAR WHAT YOU GOTTA DO
ズル
SLURP
TO EARN YOUR PLACE?
ズル
SLURP

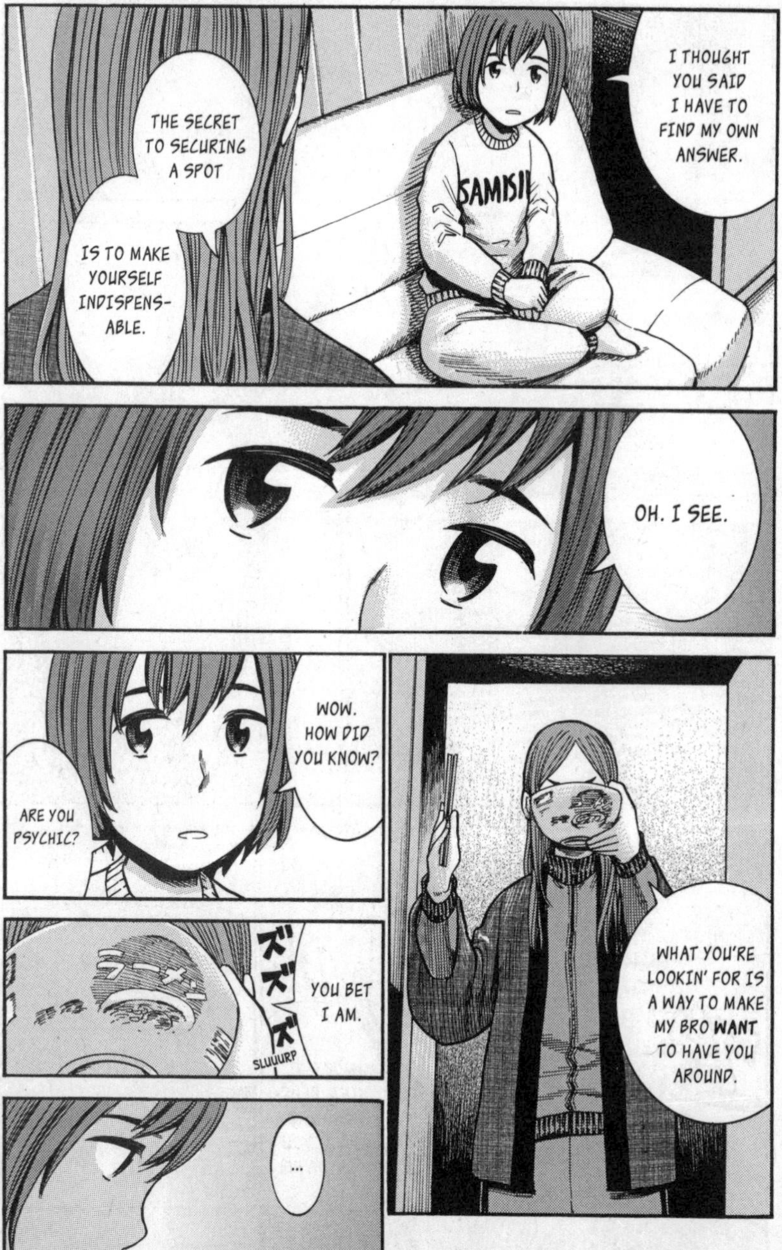
I THOUGHT YOU SAID I HAVE TO FIND MY OWN ANSWER.
THE SECRET TO SECURING A SPOT
IS TO MAKE YOURSELF INDISPENS-ABLE.
OH. I SEE.
WHAT YOU'RE LOOKIN' FOR IS A WAY TO MAKE MY BRO **WANT** TO HAVE YOU AROUND.
WOW. HOW DID YOU KNOW?
ARE YOU PSYCHIC?
ズズズ
SLUUURP
YOU BET I AM.
ラーメン
...

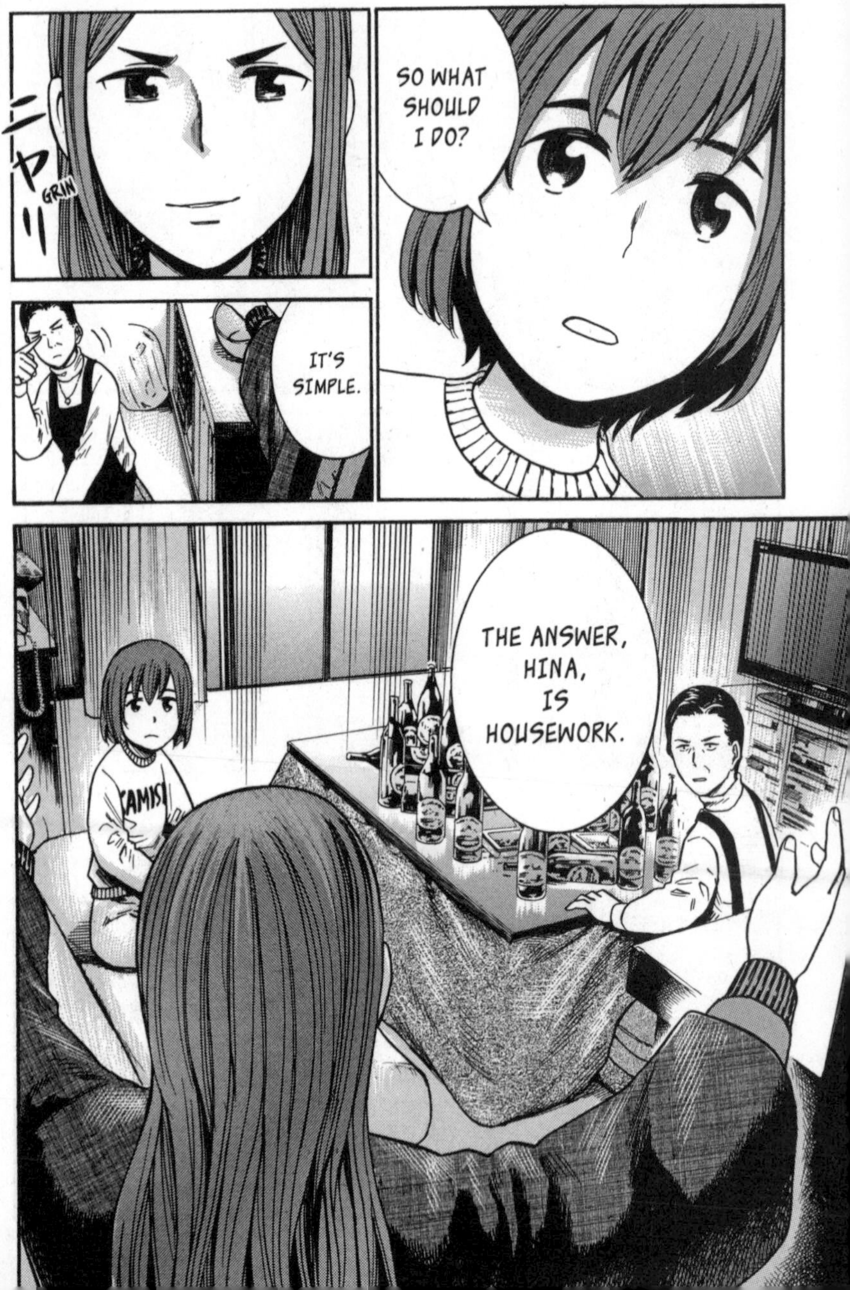
SO WHAT SHOULD I DO?
ニヤリ
GRIN
IT'S SIMPLE.
THE ANSWER, HINA, IS HOUSEWORK.

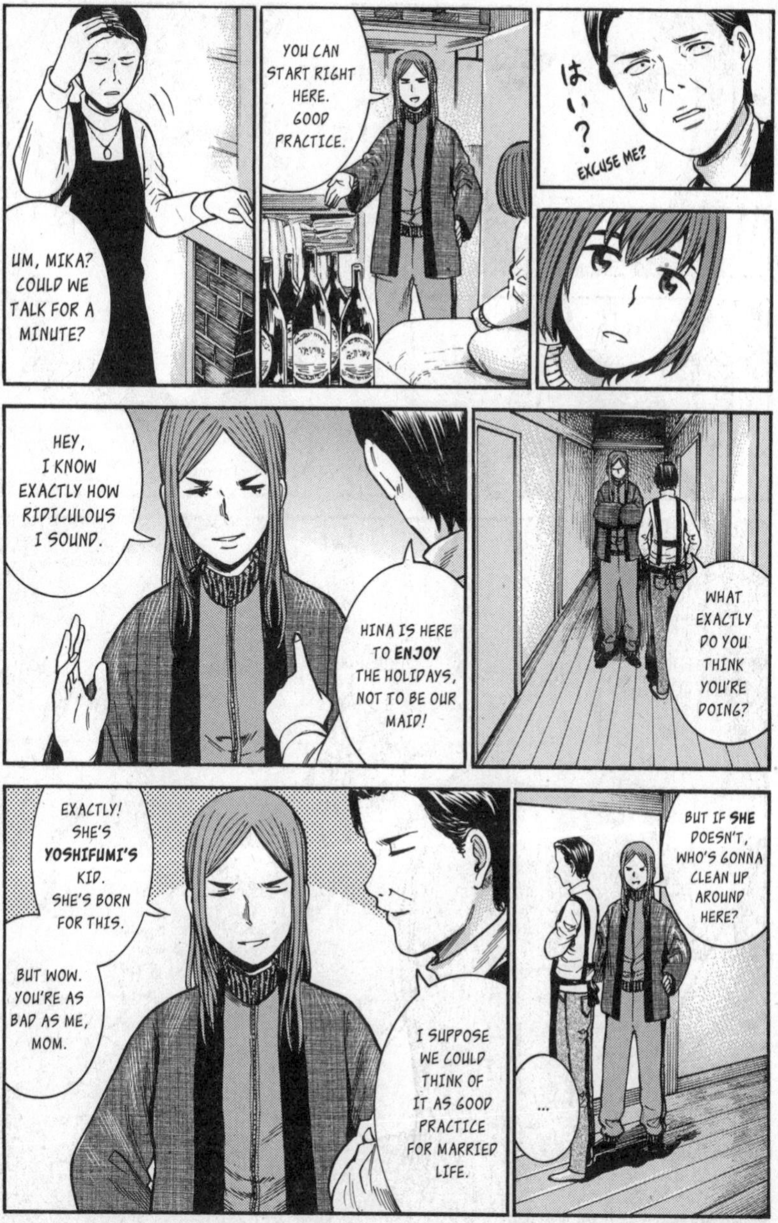
はい?
EXCUSE ME?
YOU CAN START RIGHT HERE. GOOD PRACTICE.
UM, MIKA? COULD WE TALK FOR A MINUTE?
WHAT EXACTLY DO YOU THINK YOU'RE DOING?
HINA IS HERE TO **ENJOY** THE HOLIDAYS, NOT TO BE OUR MAID!
HEY, I KNOW EXACTLY HOW RIDICULOUS I SOUND.
BUT IF **SHE** DOESN'T, WHO'S GONNA CLEAN UP AROUND HERE?
...
I SUPPOSE WE COULD THINK OF IT AS GOOD PRACTICE FOR MARRIED LIFE.
EXACTLY! SHE'S **YOSHIFUMI'S** KID. SHE'S BORN FOR THIS.
BUT WOW. YOU'RE AS BAD AS ME, MOM.

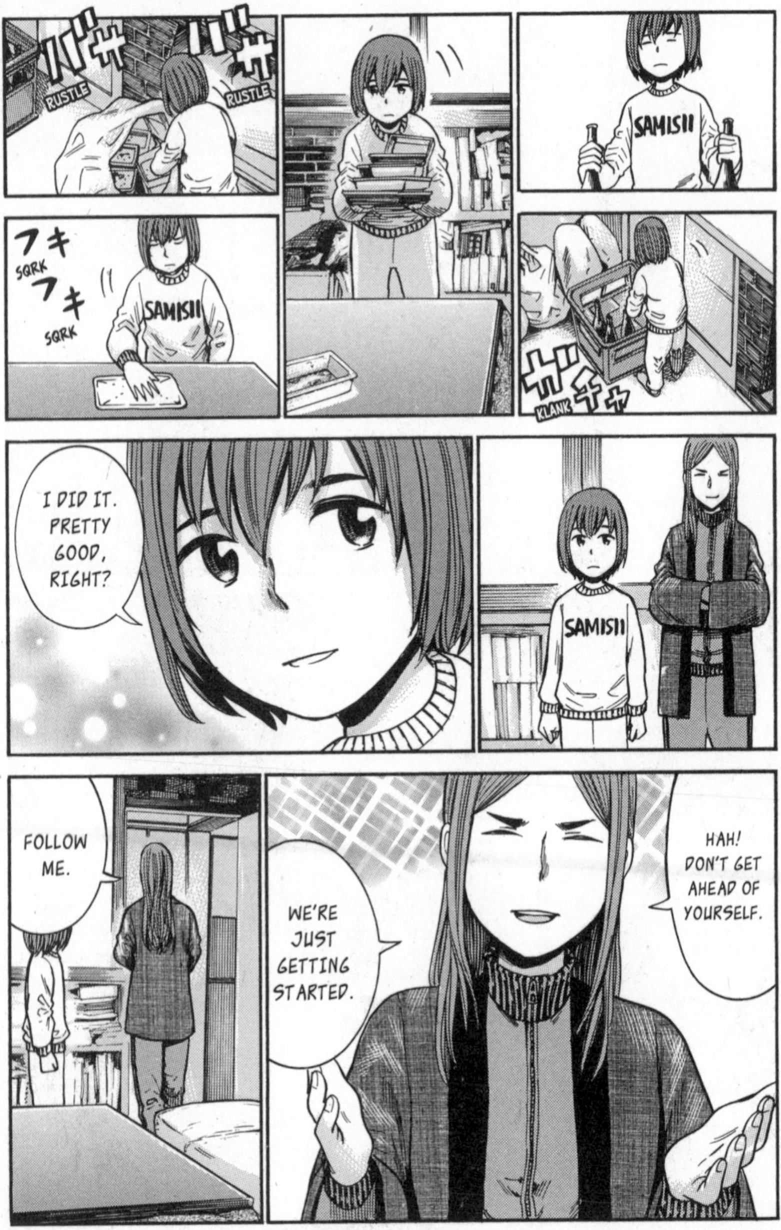
ガチャ
KLANK
バサ
RUSTLE
バサ
RUSTLE
フキ
SQRK
フキ
SQRK
I DID IT. PRETTY GOOD, RIGHT?
HAH! DON'T GET AHEAD OF YOURSELF.
WE'RE JUST GETTING STARTED.
FOLLOW ME.

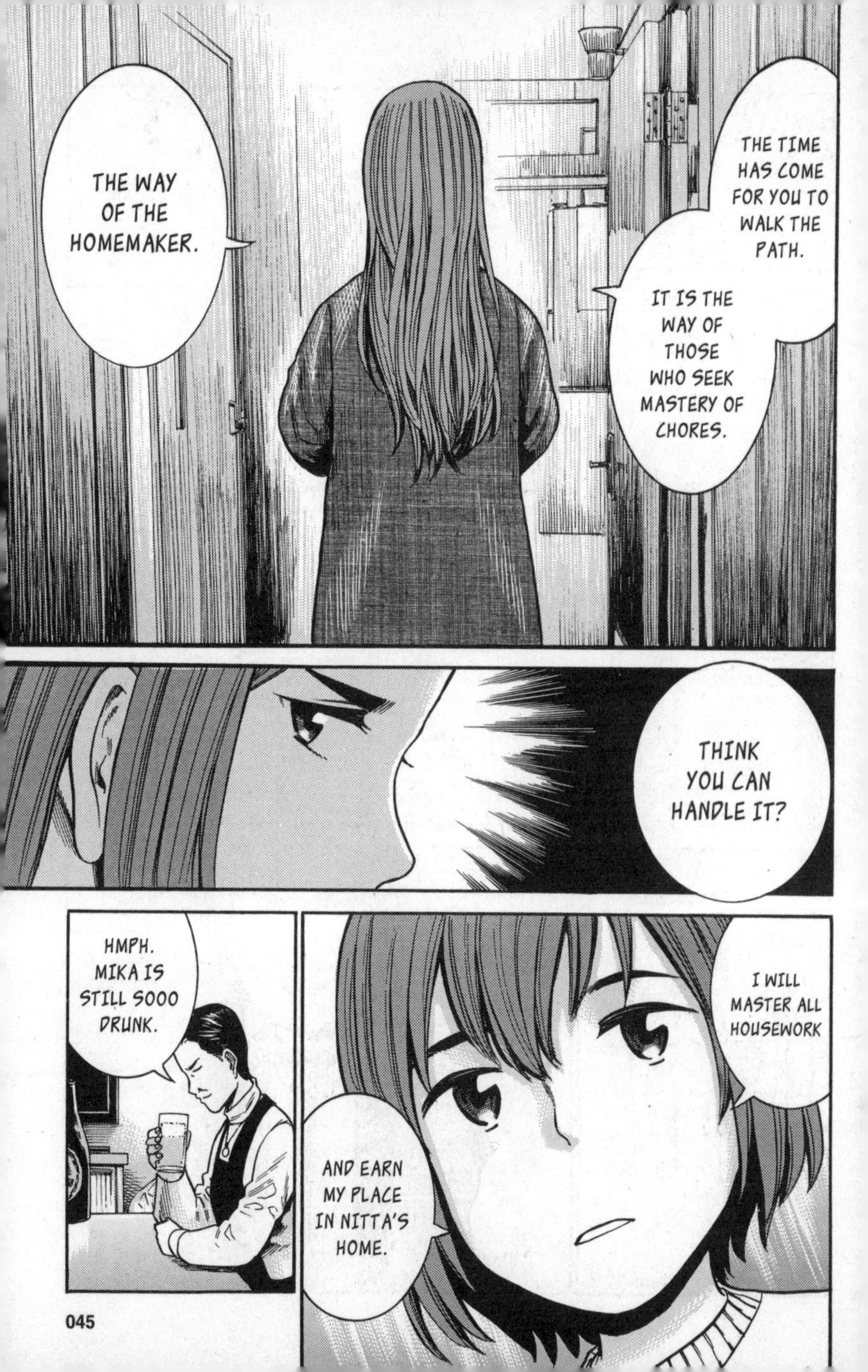
THE TIME HAS COME FOR YOU TO WALK THE PATH.
IT IS THE WAY OF THOSE WHO SEEK MASTERY OF CHORES.
THE WAY OF THE HOMEMAKER.
THINK YOU CAN HANDLE IT?
I WILL MASTER ALL HOUSEWORK
AND EARN MY PLACE IN NITTA'S HOME.
HMPH. MIKA IS STILL SOOO DRUNK.

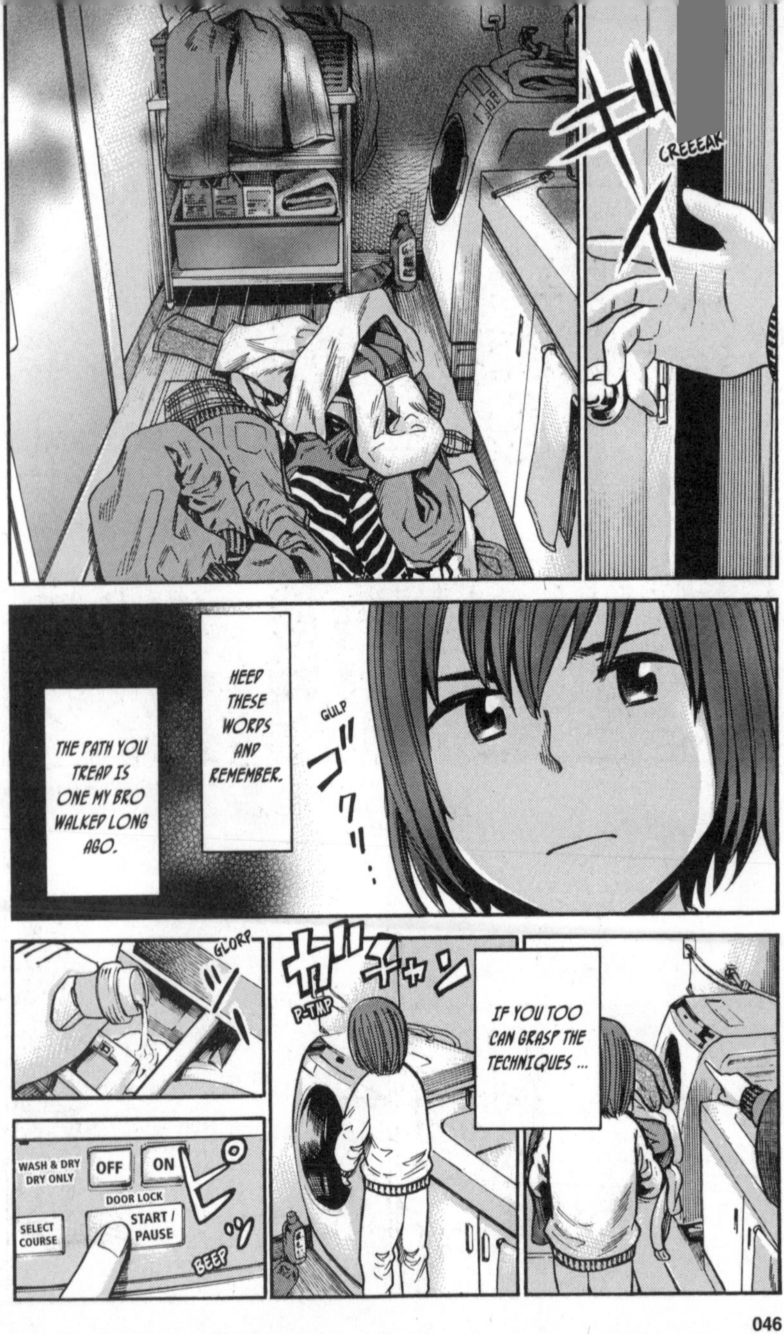
CREEEAK
GULP
HEED THESE WORDS AND REMEMBER.
THE PATH YOU TREAD IS ONE MY BRO WALKED LONG AGO.
IF YOU TOO CAN GRASP THE TECHNIQUES ...
P-TMP
GLORP
WASH & DRY
DRY ONLY
OFF
ON
DOOR LOCK
SELECT COURSE
START / PAUSE
BEEP

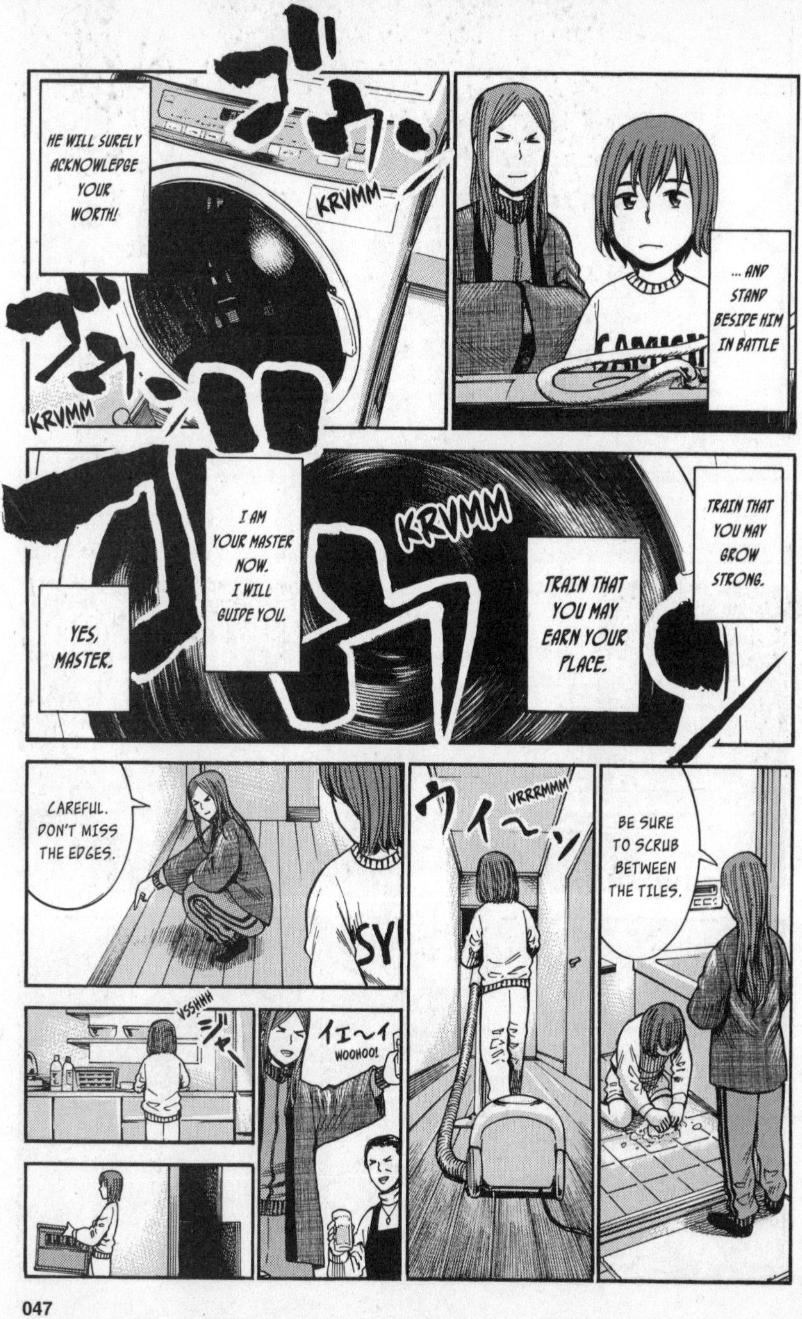
... AND STAND BESIDE HIM IN BATTLE
KRVMM
HE WILL SURELY ACKNOWLEDGE YOUR WORTH!
KRVMM
TRAIN THAT YOU MAY GROW STRONG.
KRVMM
TRAIN THAT YOU MAY EARN YOUR PLACE.
I AM YOUR MASTER NOW. I WILL GUIDE YOU.
YES, MASTER.
BE SURE TO SCRUB BETWEEN THE TILES.
ウィ〜ン
VRRRMMM
CAREFUL. DON'T MISS THE EDGES.
イエ〜イ
WOOHOO!
VSSHHH
ジャ

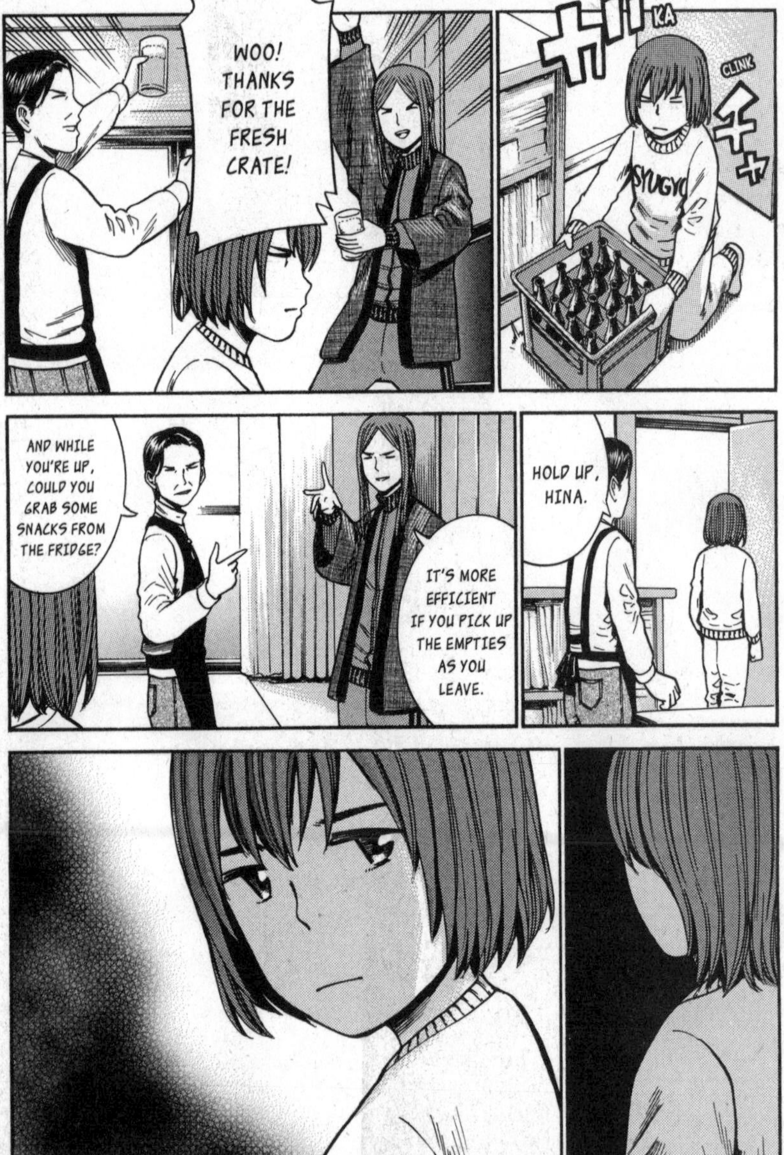
KA
CLINK
WOO! THANKS FOR THE FRESH CRATE!
HOLD UP, HINA.
AND WHILE YOU'RE UP, COULD YOU GRAB SOME SNACKS FROM THE FRIDGE?
IT'S MORE EFFICIENT IF YOU PICK UP THE EMPTIES AS YOU LEAVE.

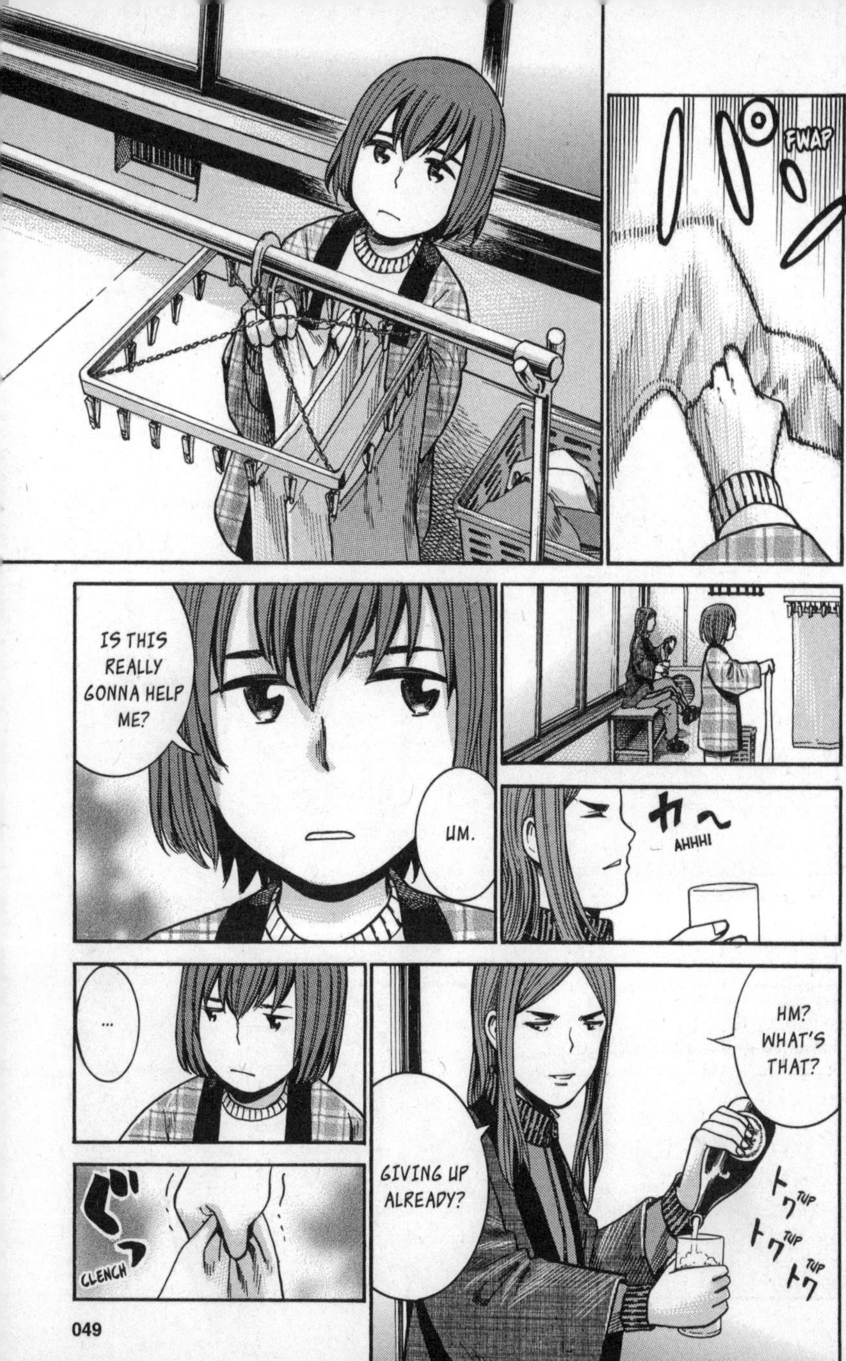
パ
FWAP
カ〜
AHHH!
UM.
IS THIS REALLY GONNA HELP ME?
HM? WHAT'S THAT?
GIVING UP ALREADY?
トクトクトク
TUP TUP TUP
...
ぐっ
CLENCH

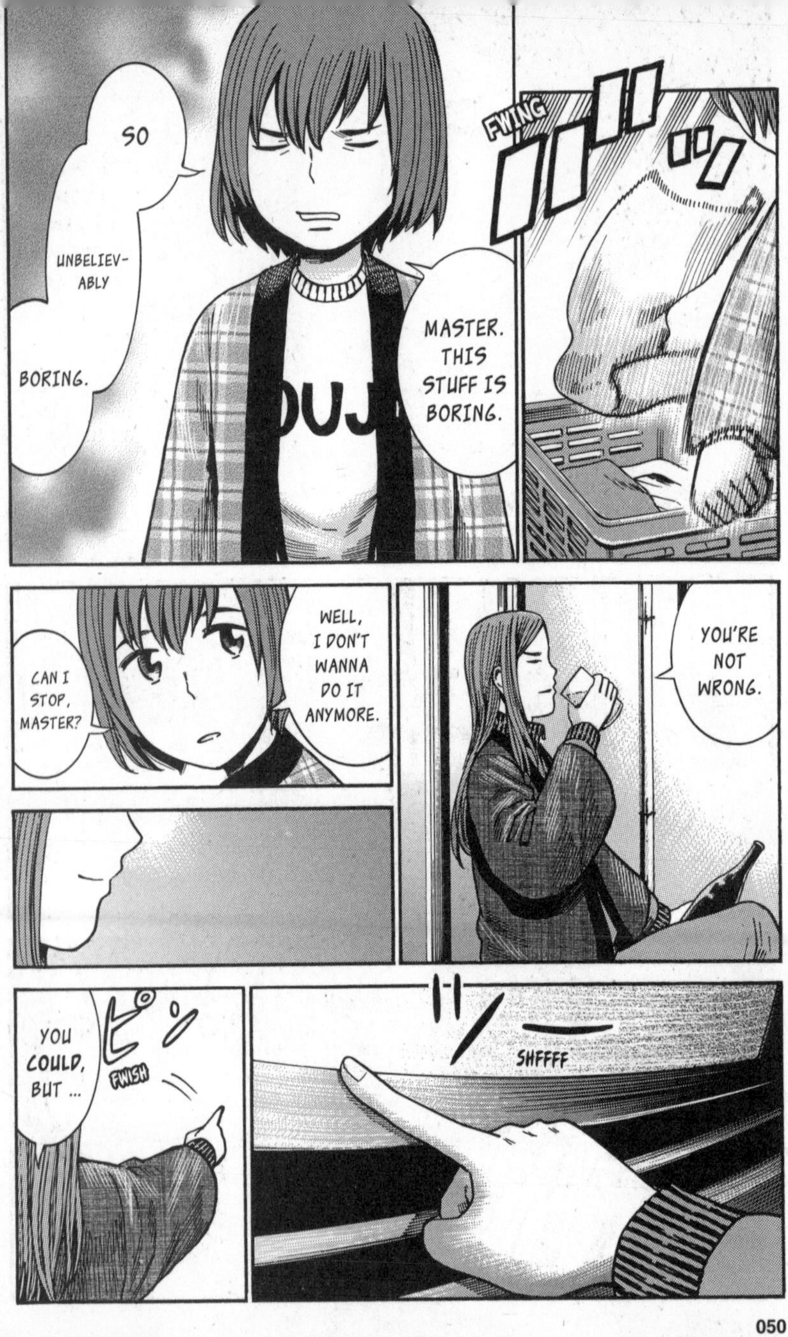

FWING
MASTER. THIS STUFF IS BORING.
SO UNBELIEVABLY BORING.
YOU'RE NOT WRONG.
WELL, I DON'T WANNA DO IT ANYMORE.
CAN I STOP, MASTER?
SHFFFF
FWISH
YOU COULD, BUT ...

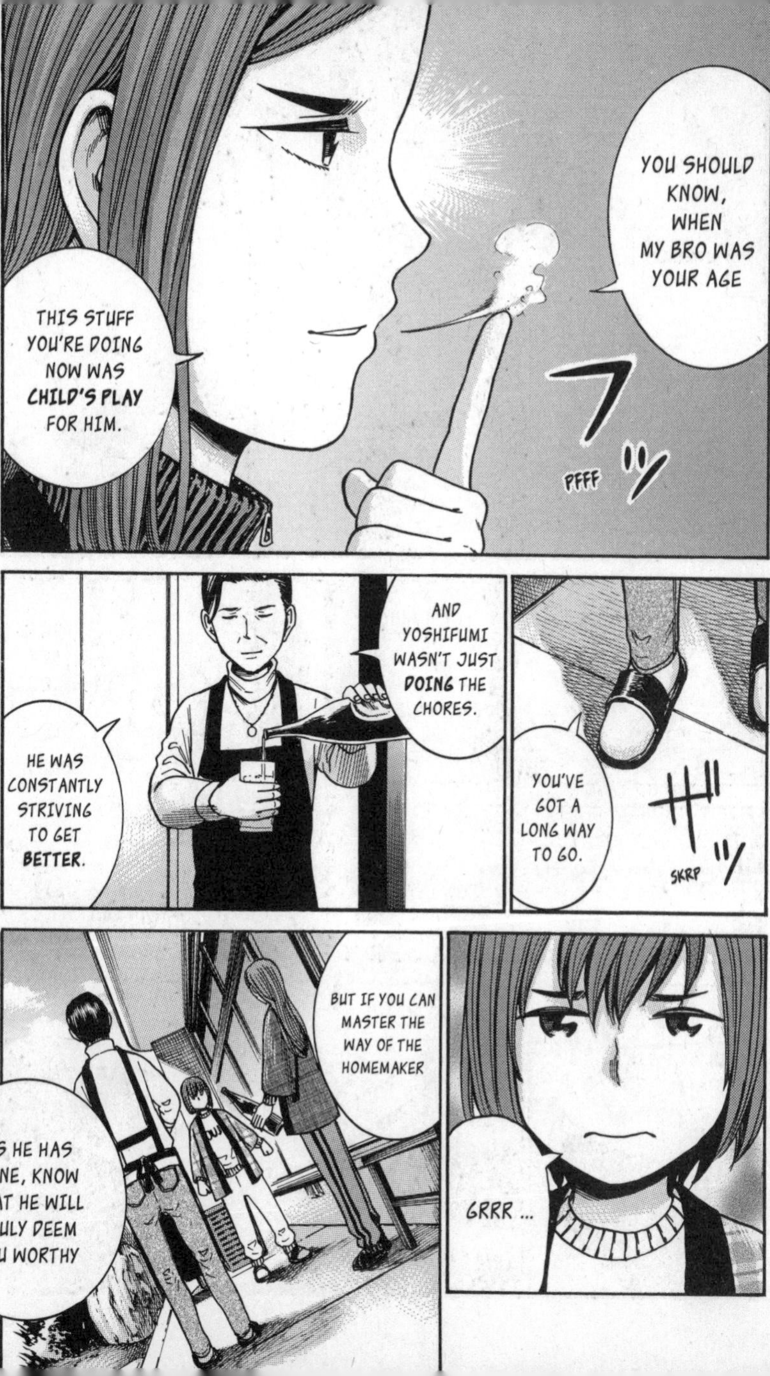
YOU SHOULD KNOW, WHEN MY BRO WAS YOUR AGE
THIS STUFF YOU'RE DOING NOW WAS **CHILD'S PLAY** FOR HIM.
PFFF
YOU'VE GOT A LONG WAY TO GO.
SKRP
AND YOSHIFUMI WASN'T JUST **DOING** THE CHORES.
HE WAS CONSTANTLY STRIVING TO GET **BETTER**.
GRRR ...
BUT IF YOU CAN MASTER THE WAY OF THE HOMEMAKER
AS HE HAS DONE, KNOW THAT HE WILL TRULY DEEM YOU WORTHY

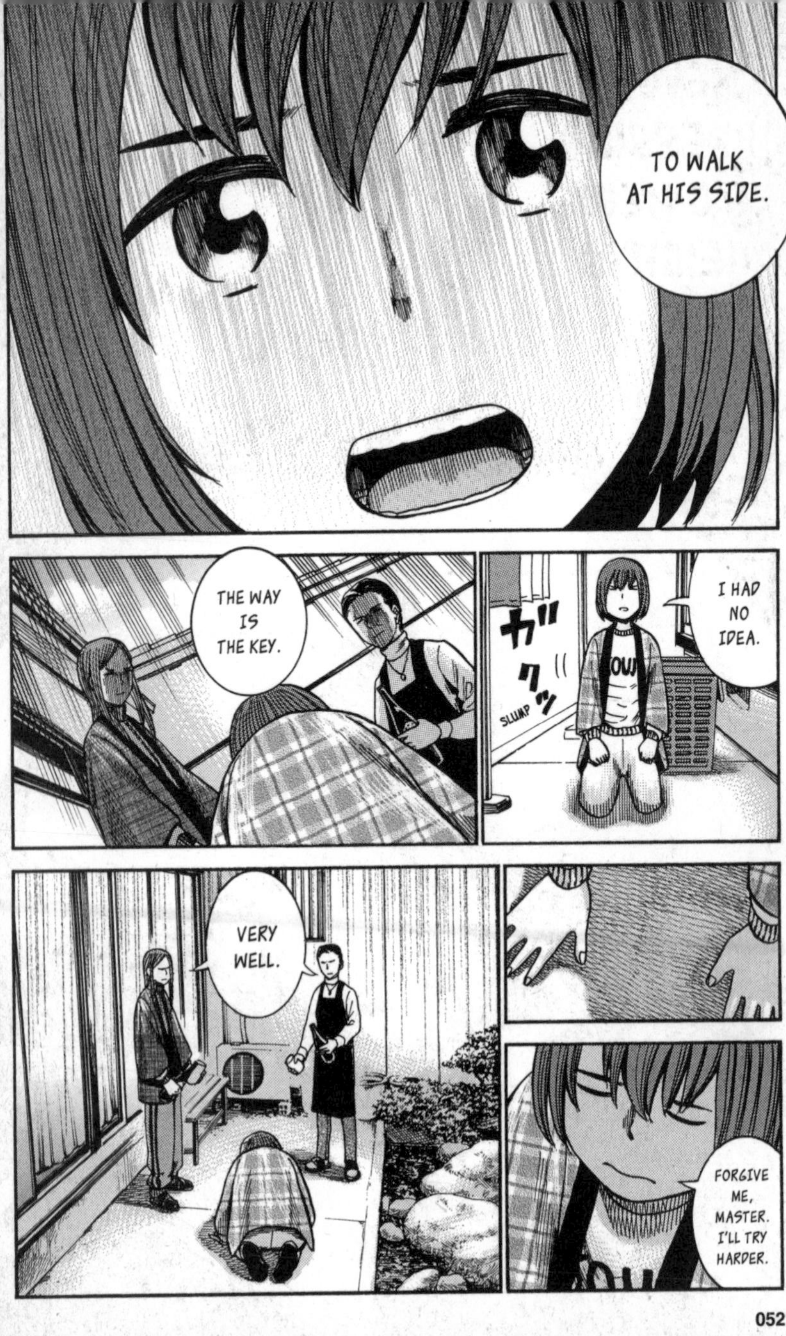
TO WALK AT HIS SIDE.
I HAD NO IDEA.
ガクッ
SLUMP
THE WAY IS THE KEY.
FORGIVE ME, MASTER. I'LL TRY HARDER.
VERY WELL.

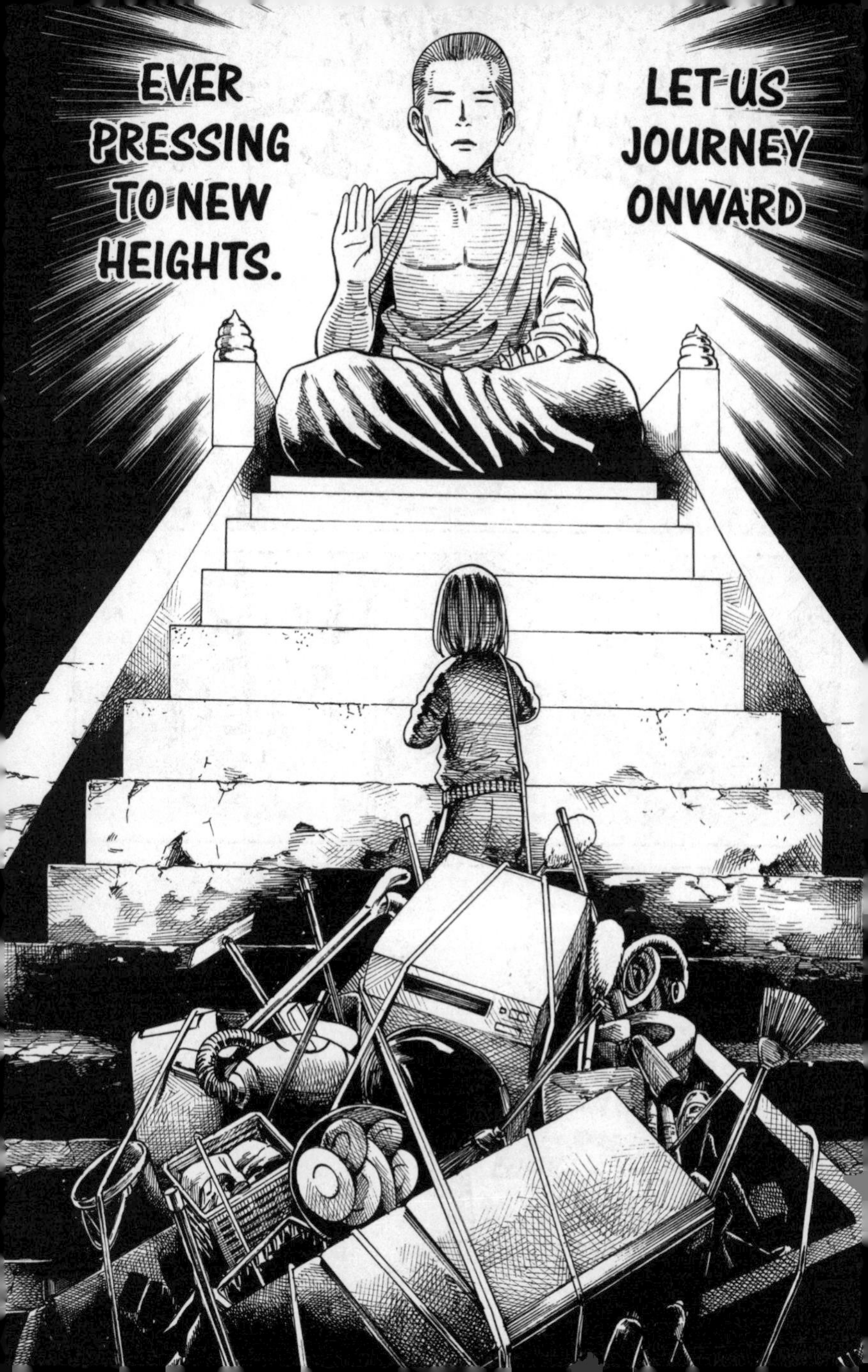
LET US JOURNEY ONWARD
EVER PRESSING TO NEW HEIGHTS.

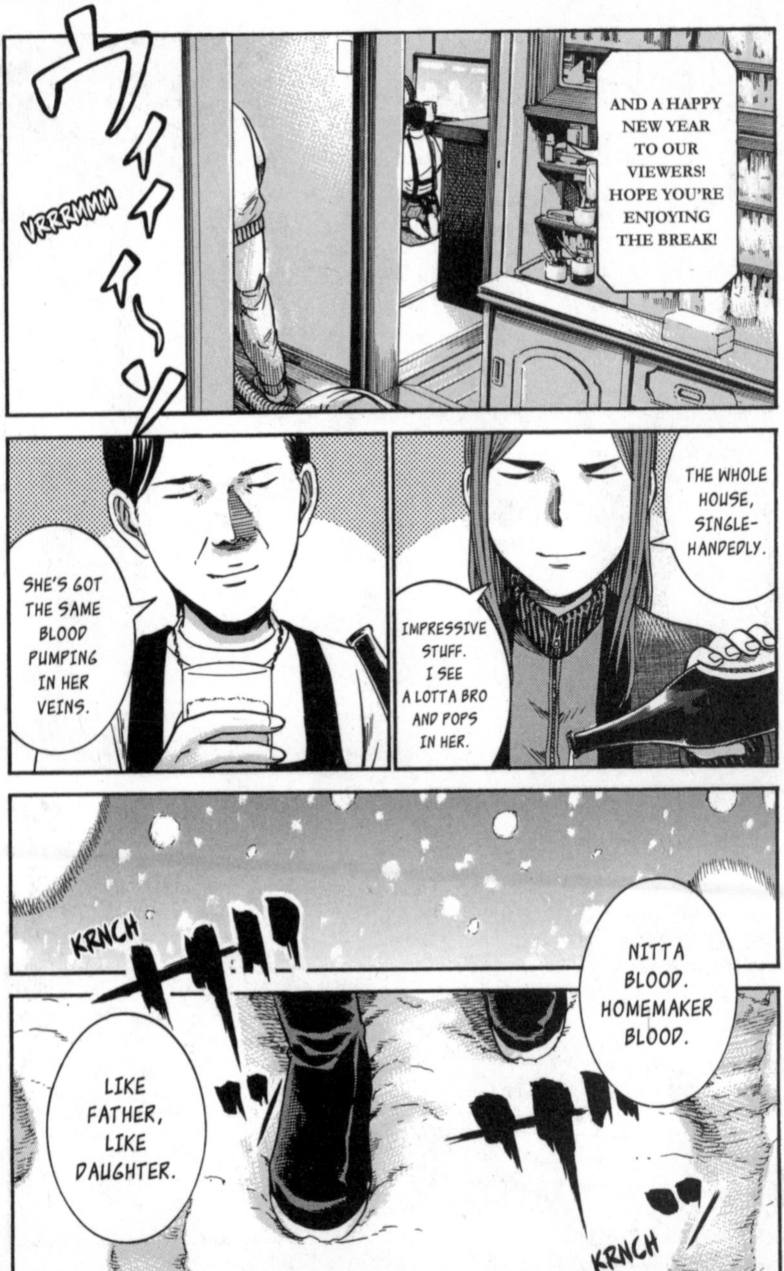
AND A HAPPY NEW YEAR TO OUR VIEWERS! HOPE YOU'RE ENJOYING THE BREAK!
ウィィ〜ン
VRRRMMM
THE WHOLE HOUSE, SINGLE-HANDEDLY.
IMPRESSIVE STUFF. I SEE A LOTTA BRO AND POPS IN HER.
SHE'S GOT THE SAME BLOOD PUMPING IN HER VEINS.
KRNCH
NITTA BLOOD. HOMEMAKER BLOOD.
LIKE FATHER, LIKE DAUGHTER.
KRNCH

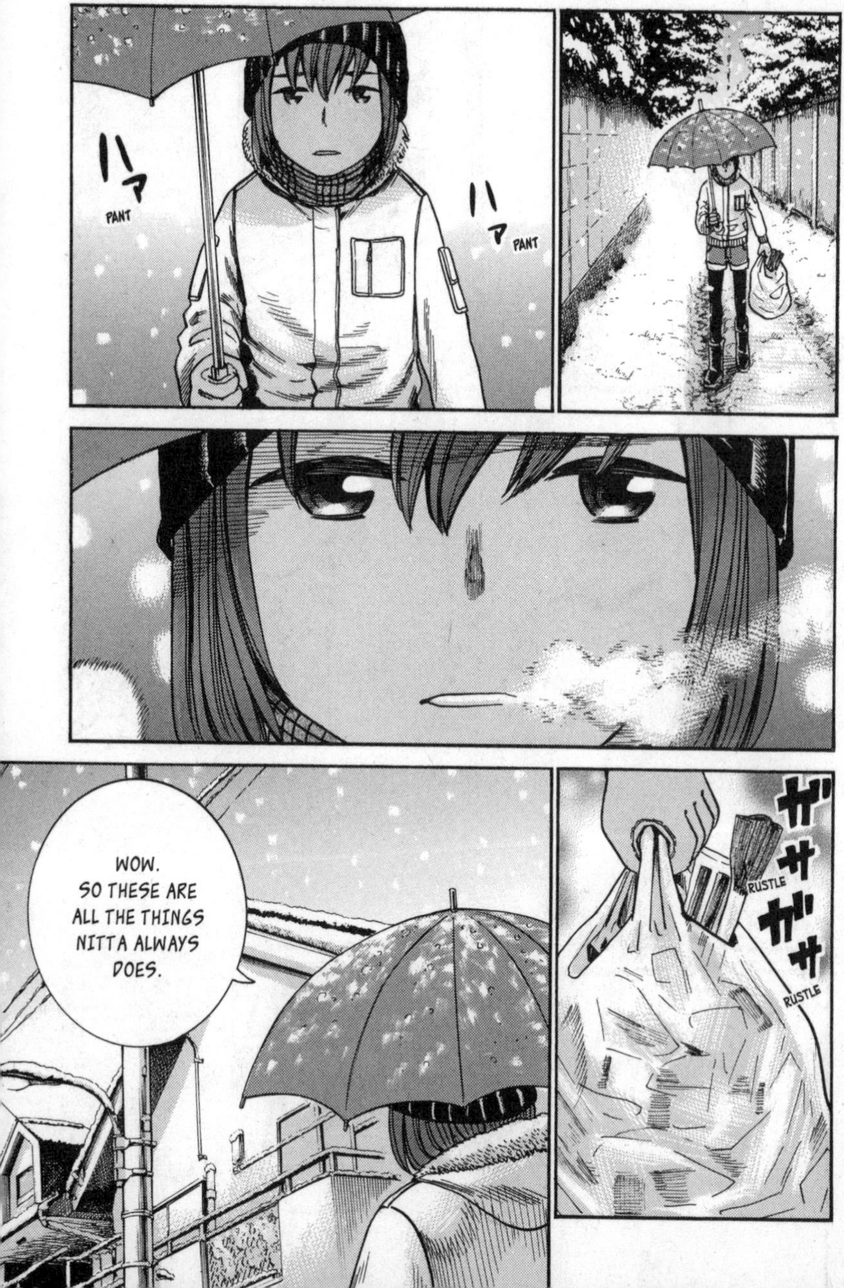
ハァ
PANT
ハァ
PANT
ガサ
RUSTLE
ガサ
RUSTLE
WOW. SO THESE ARE ALL THE THINGS NITTA ALWAYS DOES.

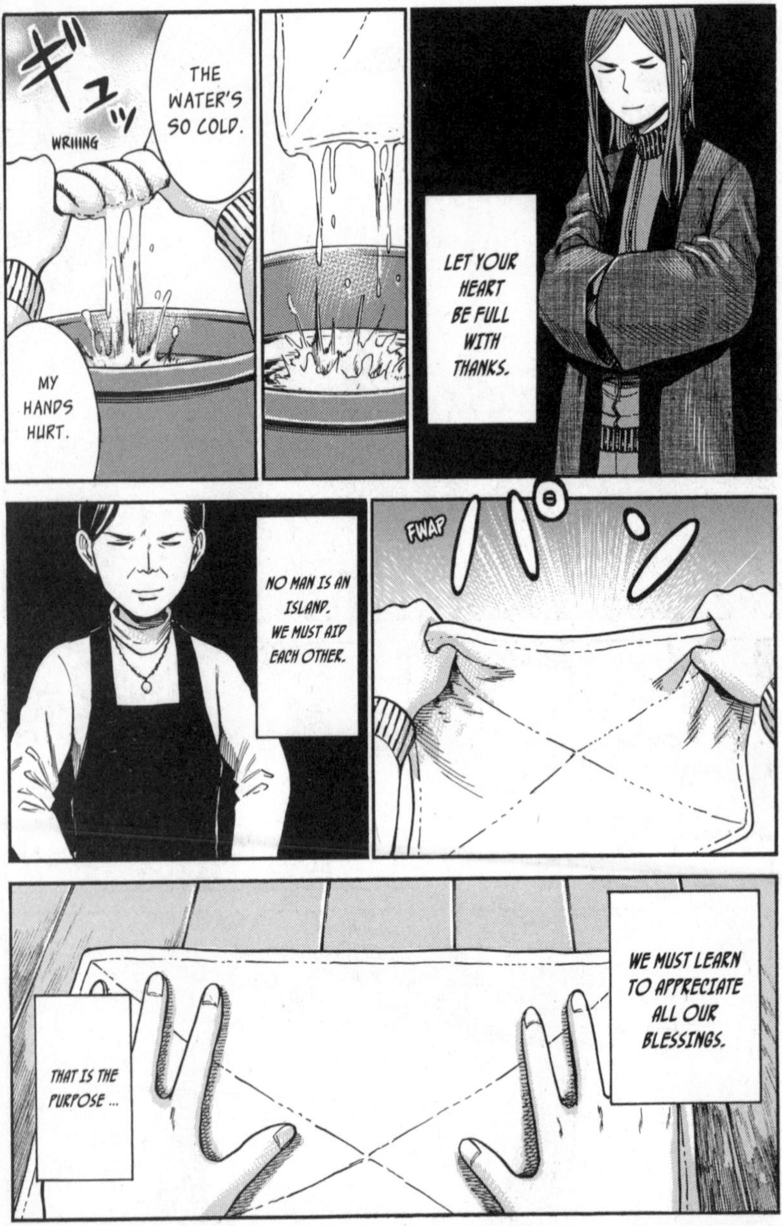
LET YOUR HEART BE FULL WITH THANKS.
ギュッ
WRIIING
THE WATER'S SO COLD.
MY HANDS HURT.
FWAP
NO MAN IS AN ISLAND. WE MUST AID EACH OTHER.
WE MUST LEARN TO APPRECIATE ALL OUR BLESSINGS.
THAT IS THE PURPOSE ...

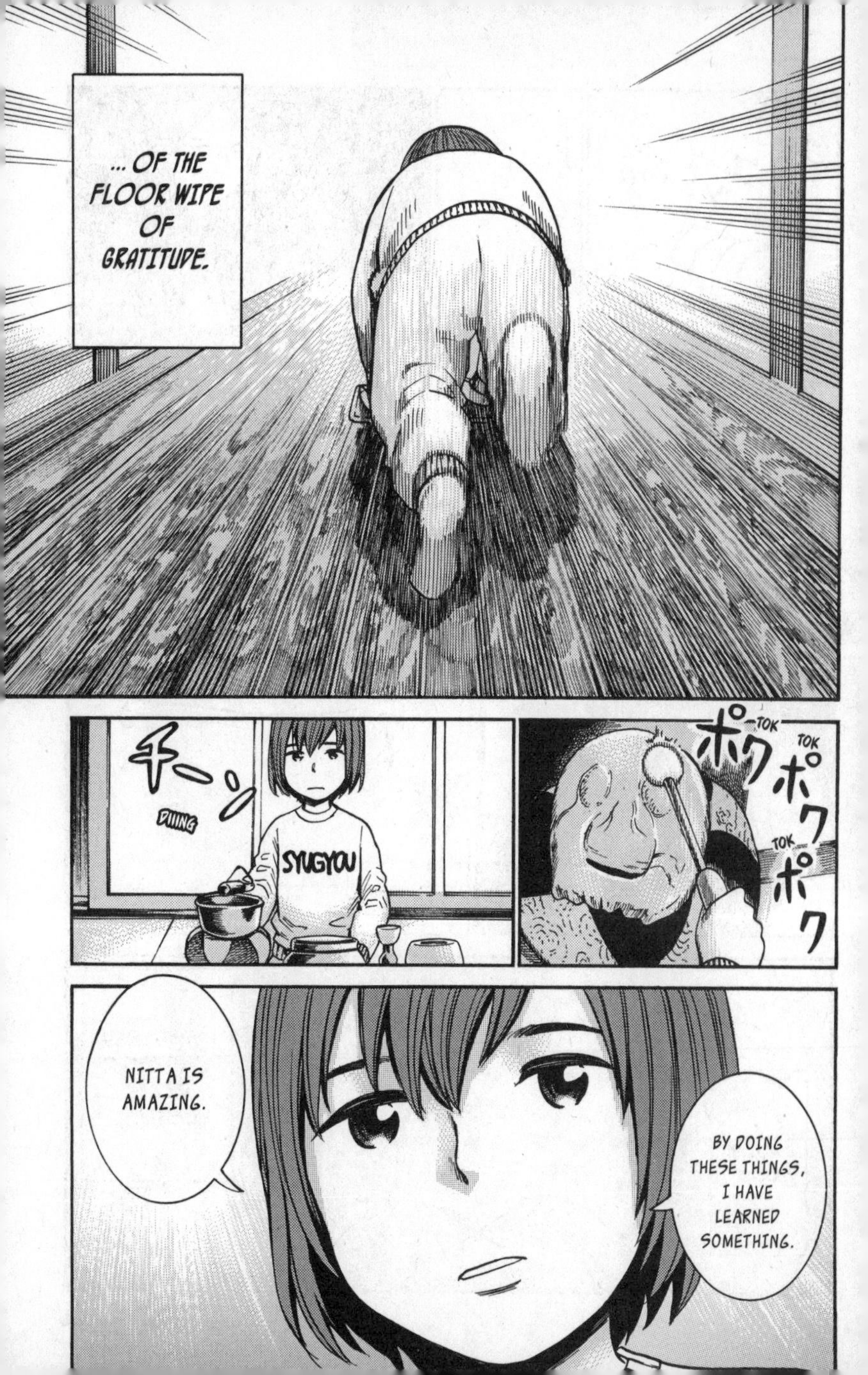
... OF THE FLOOR WIPE OF GRATITUDE.
ポクポクポク
TOK TOK TOK
チーン
DIIING
SYUGYOU
NITTA IS AMAZING.
BY DOING THESE THINGS, I HAVE LEARNED SOMETHING.

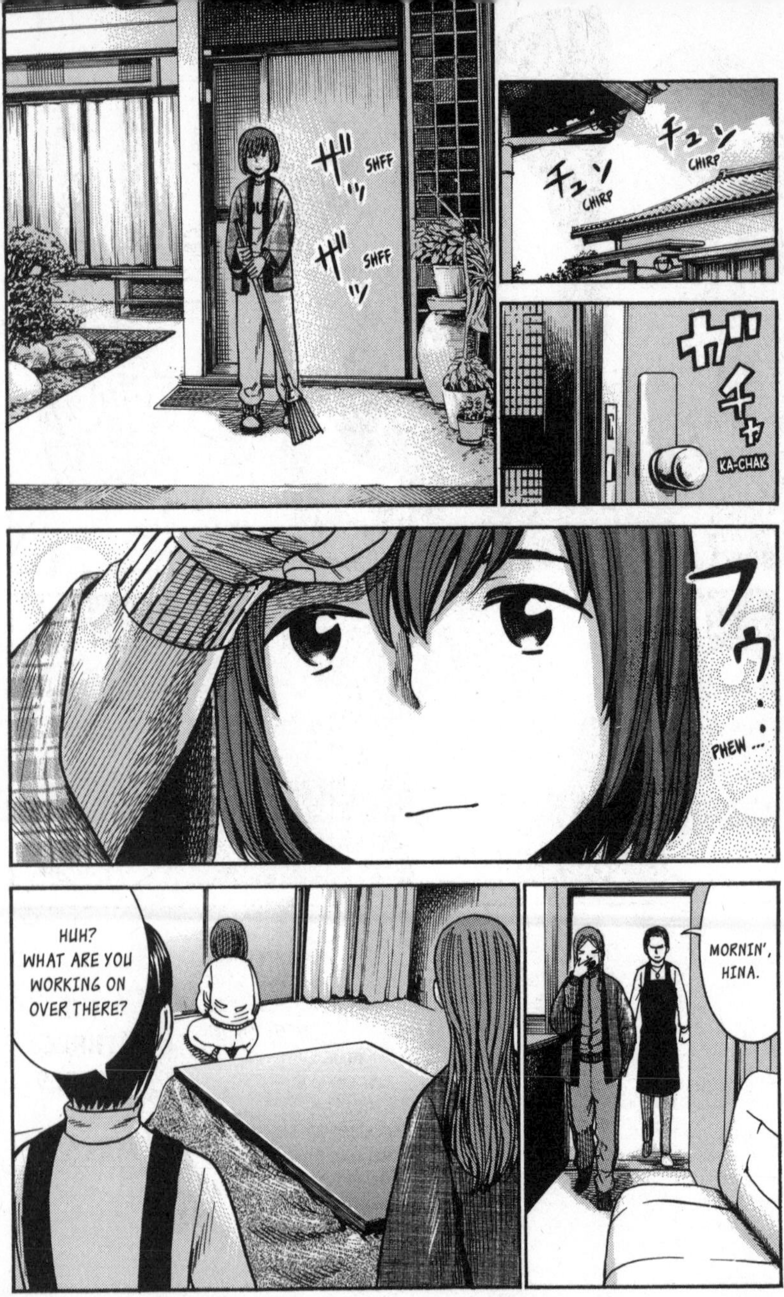
チュン
CHIRP
チュン
CHIRP
ガチャ
KA-CHAK
ザッ
SHFF
ザッ
SHFF
フウ…
PHEW...
MORNIN', HINA.
HUH? WHAT ARE YOU WORKING ON OVER THERE?

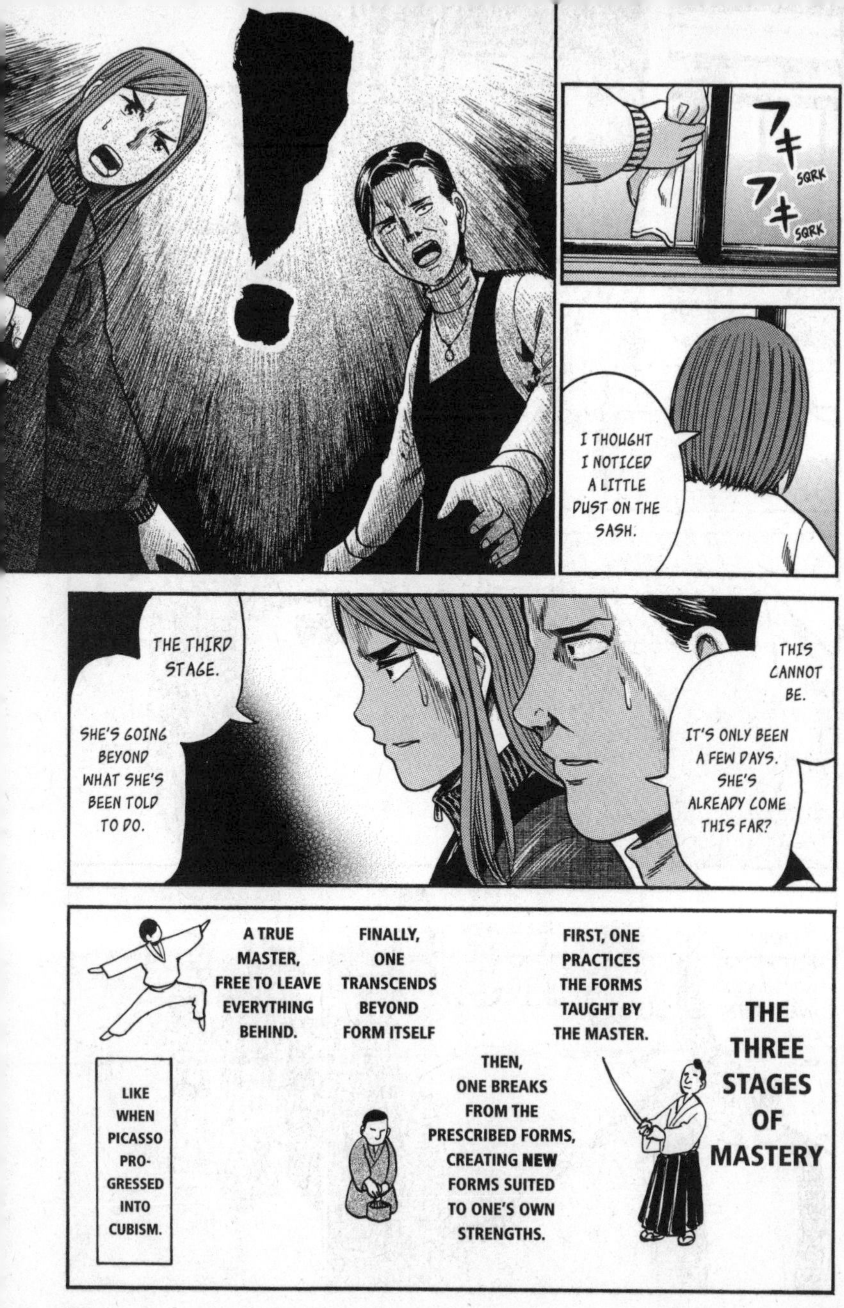
フキ SQRK
フキ SQRK
I THOUGHT I NOTICED A LITTLE DUST ON THE SASH.
THIS CANNOT BE.
IT'S ONLY BEEN A FEW DAYS. SHE'S ALREADY COME THIS FAR?
THE THIRD STAGE.
SHE'S GOING BEYOND WHAT SHE'S BEEN TOLD TO DO.
THE THREE STAGES OF MASTERY
FIRST, ONE PRACTICES THE FORMS TAUGHT BY THE MASTER.
THEN, ONE BREAKS FROM THE PRESCRIBED FORMS, CREATING NEW FORMS SUITED TO ONE'S OWN STRENGTHS.
FINALLY, ONE TRANSCENDS BEYOND FORM ITSELF
A TRUE MASTER, FREE TO LEAVE EVERYTHING BEHIND.
LIKE WHEN PICASSO PRO-GRESSED INTO CUBISM.

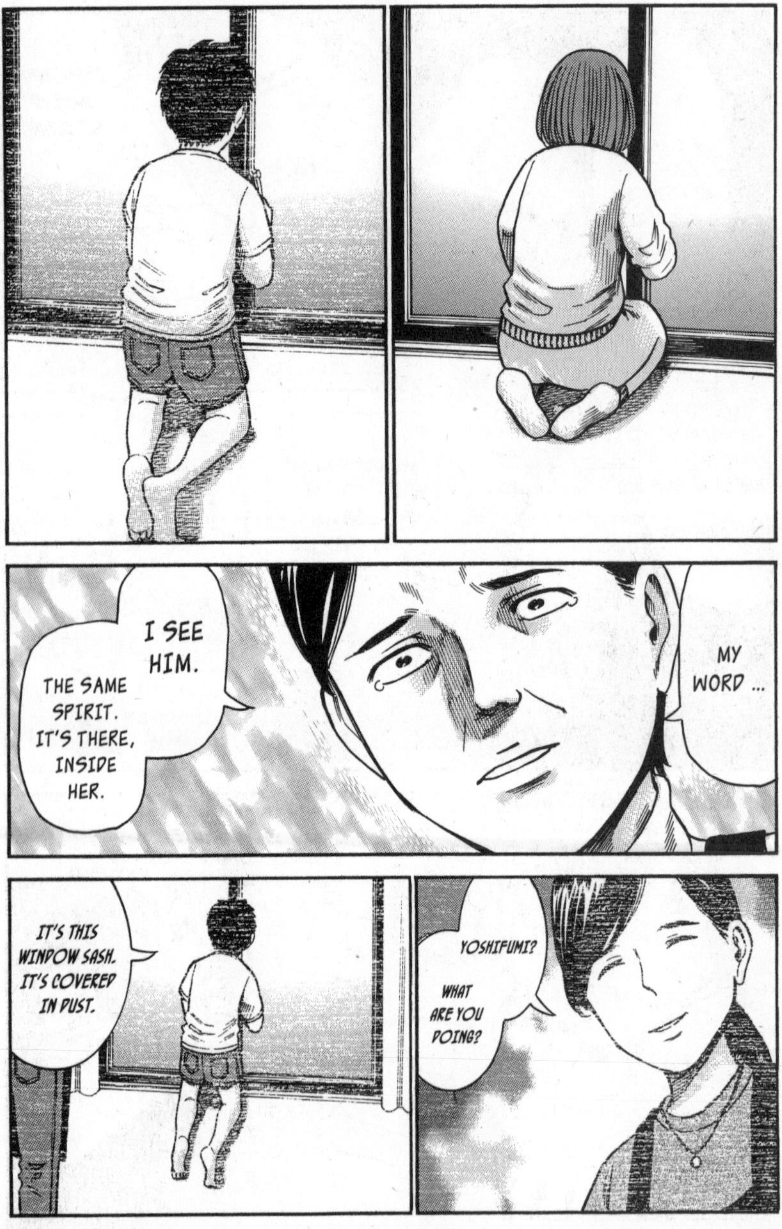
MY WORD ...
I SEE HIM.
THE SAME SPIRIT. IT'S THERE, INSIDE HER.
YOSHIFUMI?
WHAT ARE YOU DOING?
IT'S THIS WINDOW SASH. IT'S COVERED IN DUST.

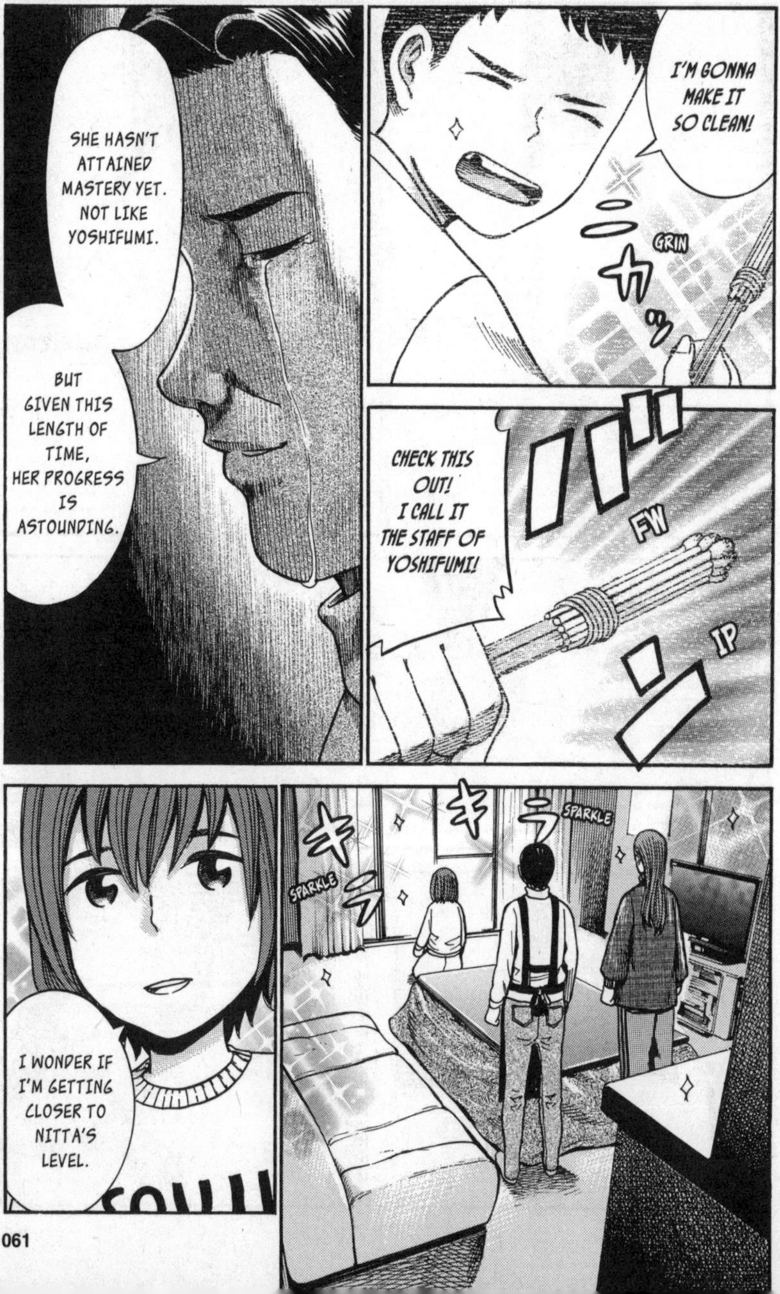
I'M GONNA MAKE IT SO CLEAN!
GRIN
CHECK THIS OUT! I CALL IT THE STAFF OF YOSHIFUMI!
FW
IP
SHE HASN'T ATTAINED MASTERY YET. NOT LIKE YOSHIFUMI.
BUT GIVEN THIS LENGTH OF TIME, HER PROGRESS IS ASTOUNDING.
SPARKLE
SPARKLE
I WONDER IF I'M GETTING CLOSER TO NITTA'S LEVEL.

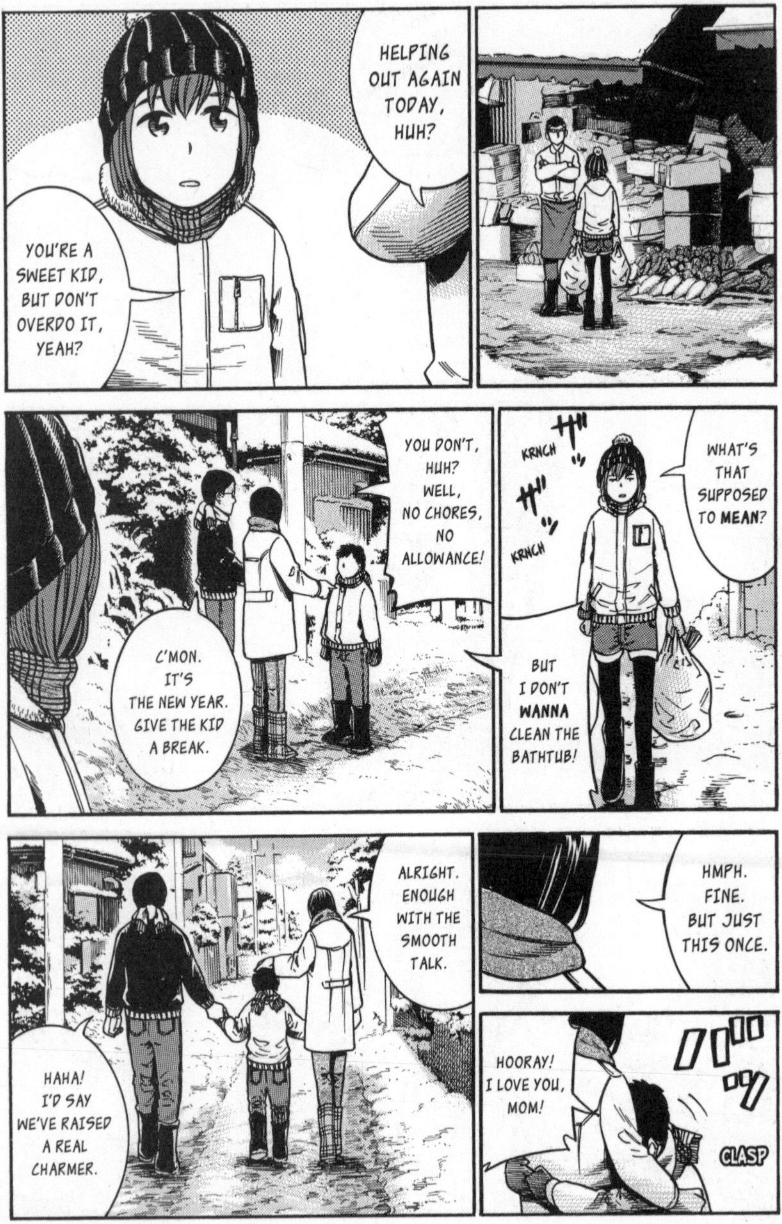
HELPING OUT AGAIN TODAY, HUH?
YOU'RE A SWEET KID, BUT DON'T OVERDO IT, YEAH?
KRNCH
KRNCH
WHAT'S THAT SUPPOSED TO MEAN?
BUT I DON'T WANNA CLEAN THE BATHTUB!
YOU DON'T, HUH? WELL, NO CHORES, NO ALLOWANCE!
C'MON. IT'S THE NEW YEAR. GIVE THE KID A BREAK.
HMPH. FINE. BUT JUST THIS ONCE.
HOORAY! I LOVE YOU, MOM!
CLASP
ALRIGHT. ENOUGH WITH THE SMOOTH TALK.
HAHA! I'D SAY WE'VE RAISED A REAL CHARMER.

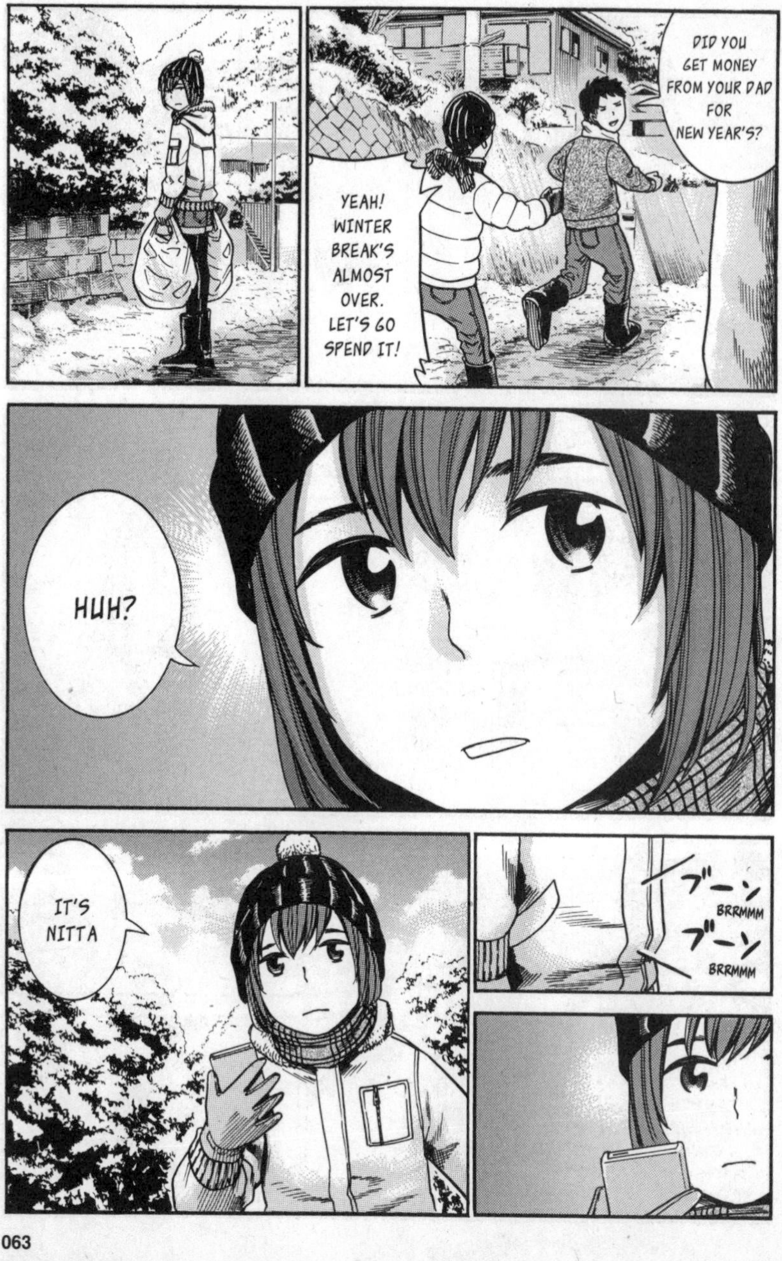
DID YOU GET MONEY FROM YOUR DAD FOR NEW YEAR'S?
YEAH! WINTER BREAK'S ALMOST OVER. LET'S GO SPEND IT!
HUH?
ブーン
BRRMMM
ブーン
BRRMMM
IT'S NITTA

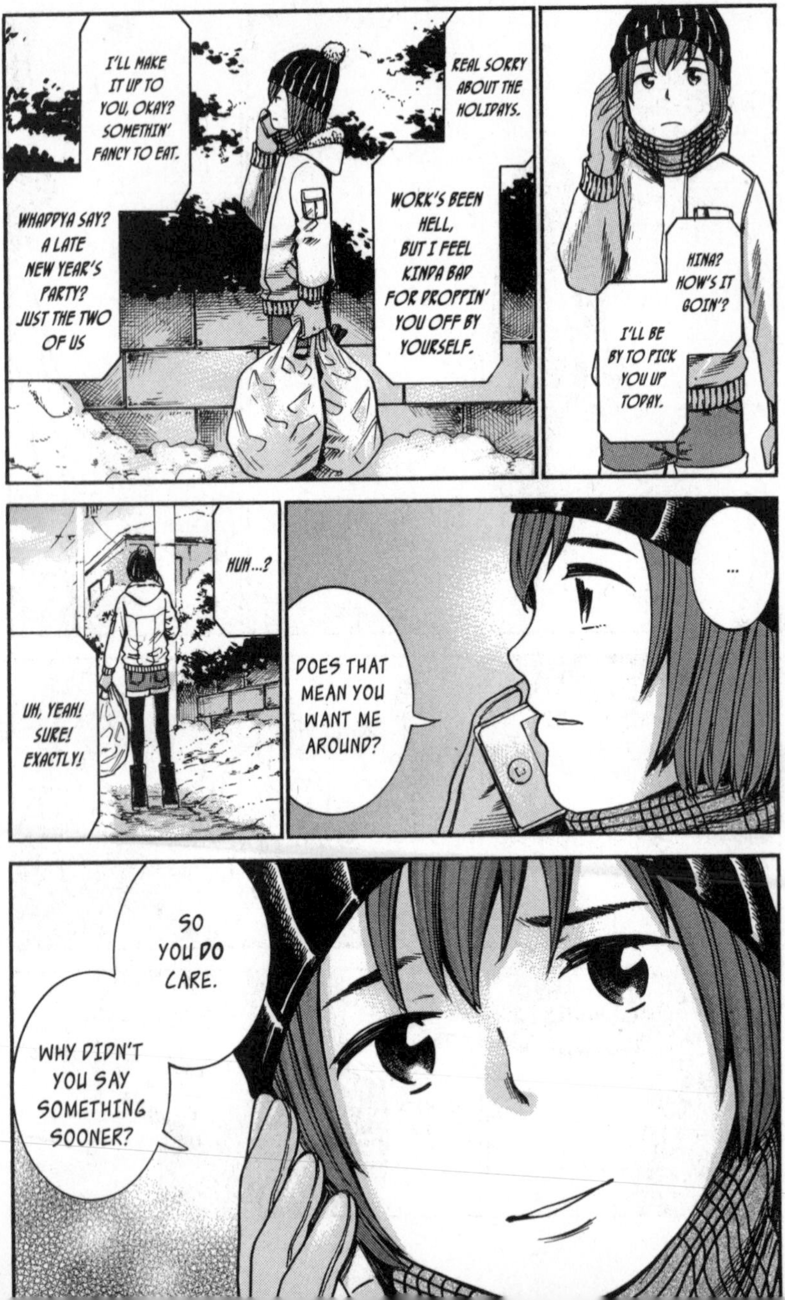
HINA? HOW'S IT GOIN'?
I'LL BE BY TO PICK YOU UP TODAY.
REAL SORRY ABOUT THE HOLIDAYS.
WORK'S BEEN HELL, BUT I FEEL KINDA BAD FOR DROPPIN' YOU OFF BY YOURSELF.
I'LL MAKE IT UP TO YOU, OKAY? SOMETHIN' FANCY TO EAT.
WHADDYA SAY? A LATE NEW YEAR'S PARTY? JUST THE TWO OF US
...
DOES THAT MEAN YOU WANT ME AROUND?
HUH...?
UH, YEAH! SURE! EXACTLY!
SO YOU DO CARE.
WHY DIDN'T YOU SAY SOMETHING SOONER?

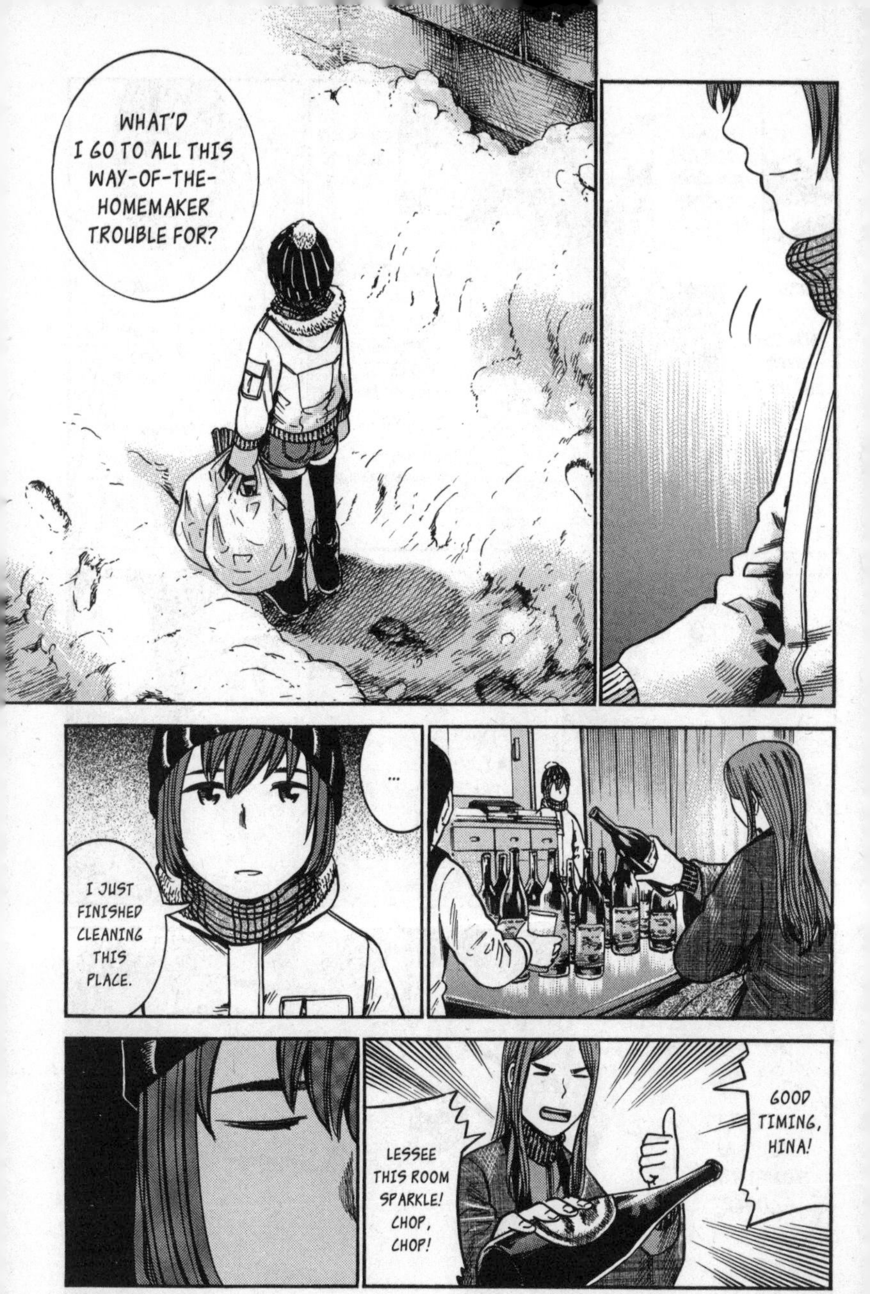
WHAT'D I GO TO ALL THIS WAY-OF-THE-HOMEMAKER TROUBLE FOR?
...
I JUST FINISHED CLEANING THIS PLACE.
GOOD TIMING, HINA!
LESSEE THIS ROOM SPARKLE! CHOP, CHOP!

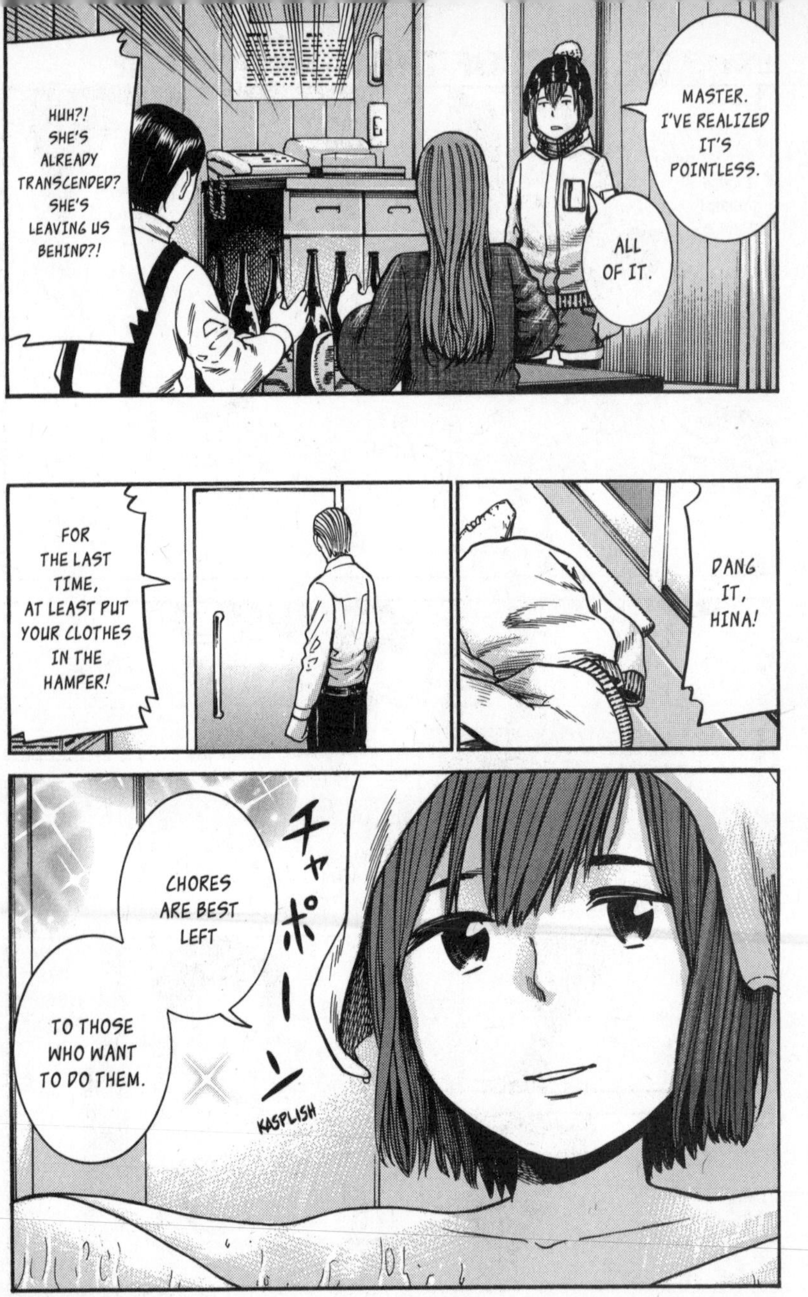
MASTER. I'VE REALIZED IT'S POINTLESS.
ALL OF IT.
HUH?! SHE'S ALREADY TRANSCENDED? SHE'S LEAVING US BEHIND?!
DANG IT, HINA!
FOR THE LAST TIME, AT LEAST PUT YOUR CLOTHES IN THE HAMPER!
チャポーン
KASPLISH
CHORES ARE BEST LEFT
TO THOSE WHO WANT TO DO THEM.

CHAPTER 40 END

EXTRA 16 FISTS OF THE HOMEMAKER

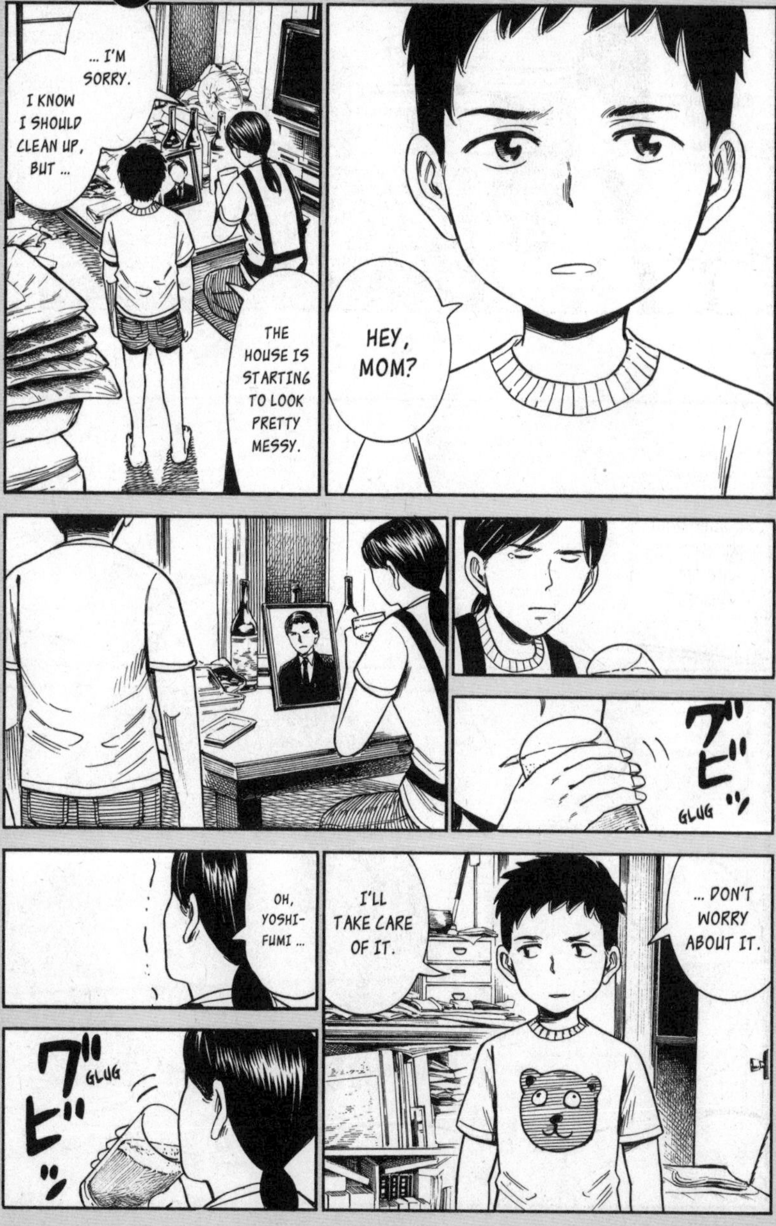
HEY, MOM?
THE HOUSE IS STARTING TO LOOK PRETTY MESSY.
... I'M SORRY.
I KNOW I SHOULD CLEAN UP, BUT ...
GLUG
... DON'T WORRY ABOUT IT.
I'LL TAKE CARE OF IT.
OH, YOSHI-FUMI ...
GLUG

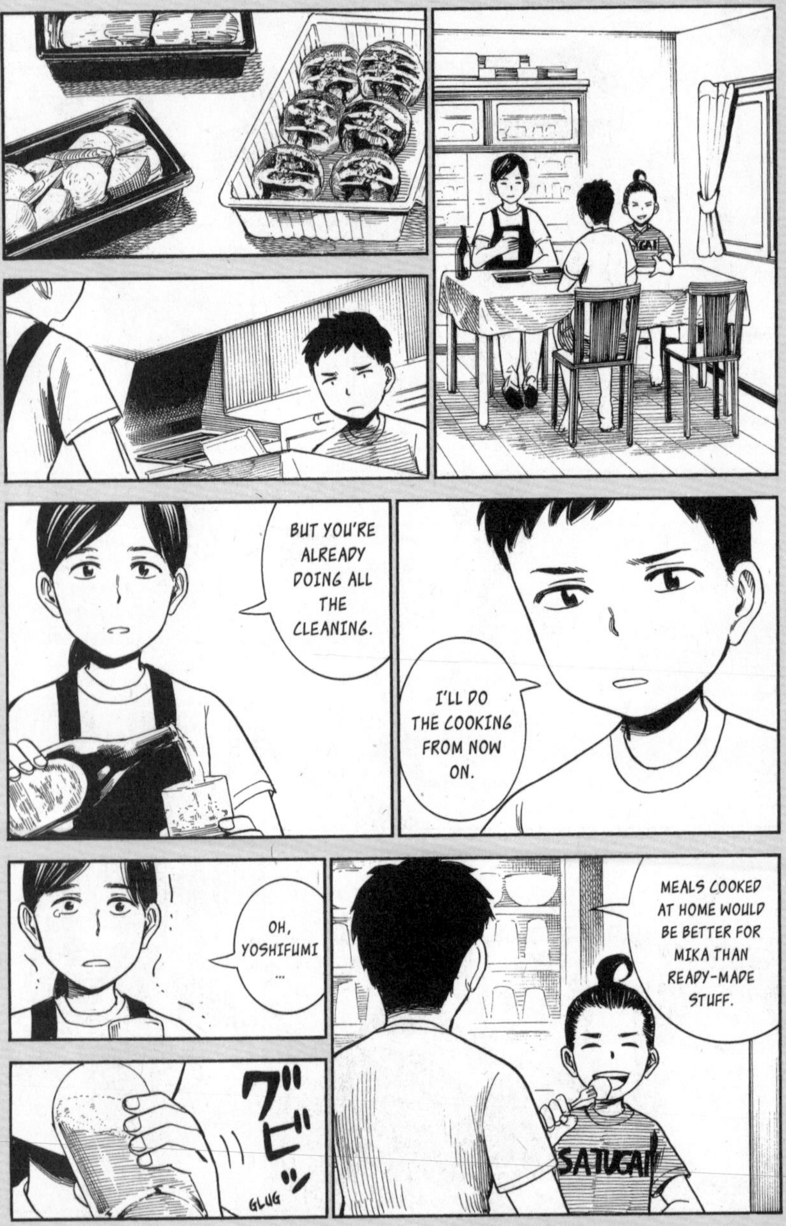
I'LL DO THE COOKING FROM NOW ON.
BUT YOU'RE ALREADY DOING ALL THE CLEANING.
MEALS COOKED AT HOME WOULD BE BETTER FOR MIKA THAN READY-MADE STUFF.
SATUGAI
OH, YOSHIFUMI ...
グビッ
GLUG

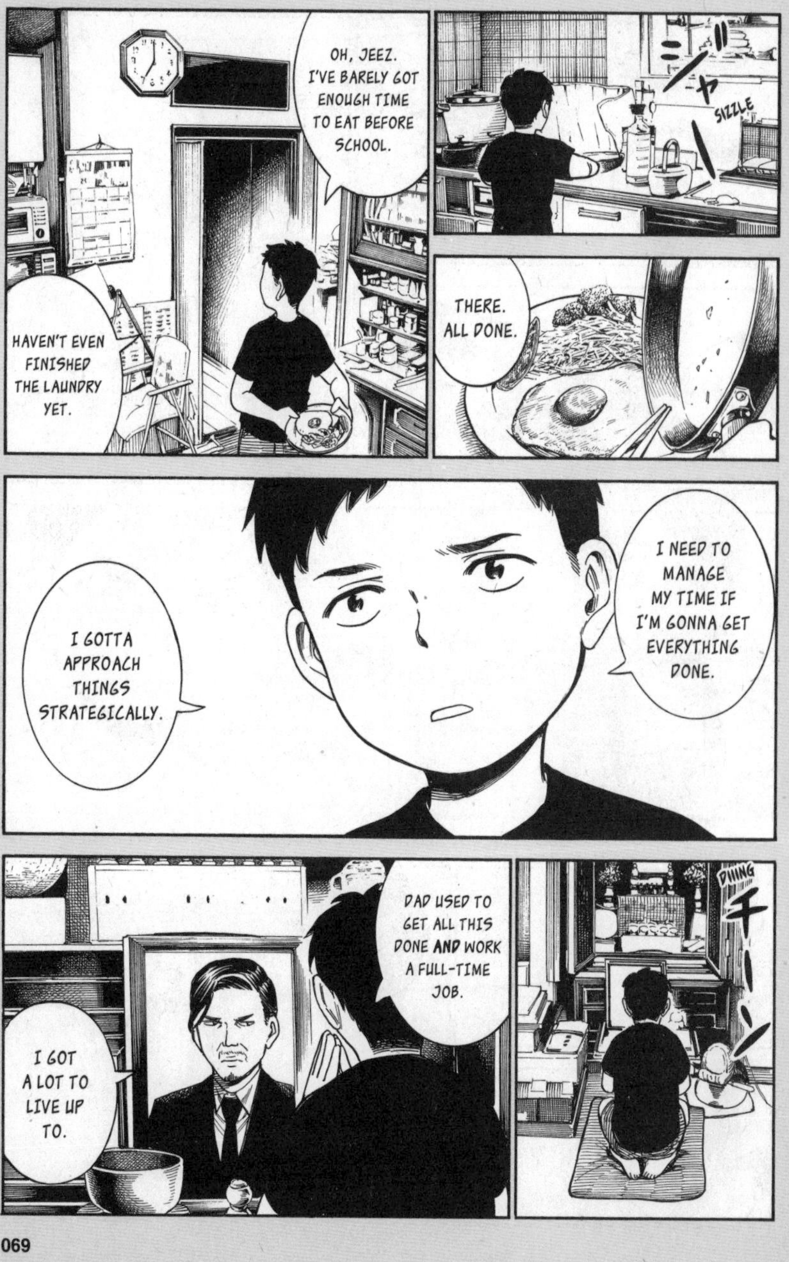
SIZZLE
THERE. ALL DONE.
OH, JEEZ. I'VE BARELY GOT ENOUGH TIME TO EAT BEFORE SCHOOL.
HAVEN'T EVEN FINISHED THE LAUNDRY YET.
I NEED TO MANAGE MY TIME IF I'M GONNA GET EVERYTHING DONE.
I GOTTA APPROACH THINGS STRATEGICALLY.
DIIING
DAD USED TO GET ALL THIS DONE **AND** WORK A FULL-TIME JOB.
I GOT A LOT TO LIVE UP TO.

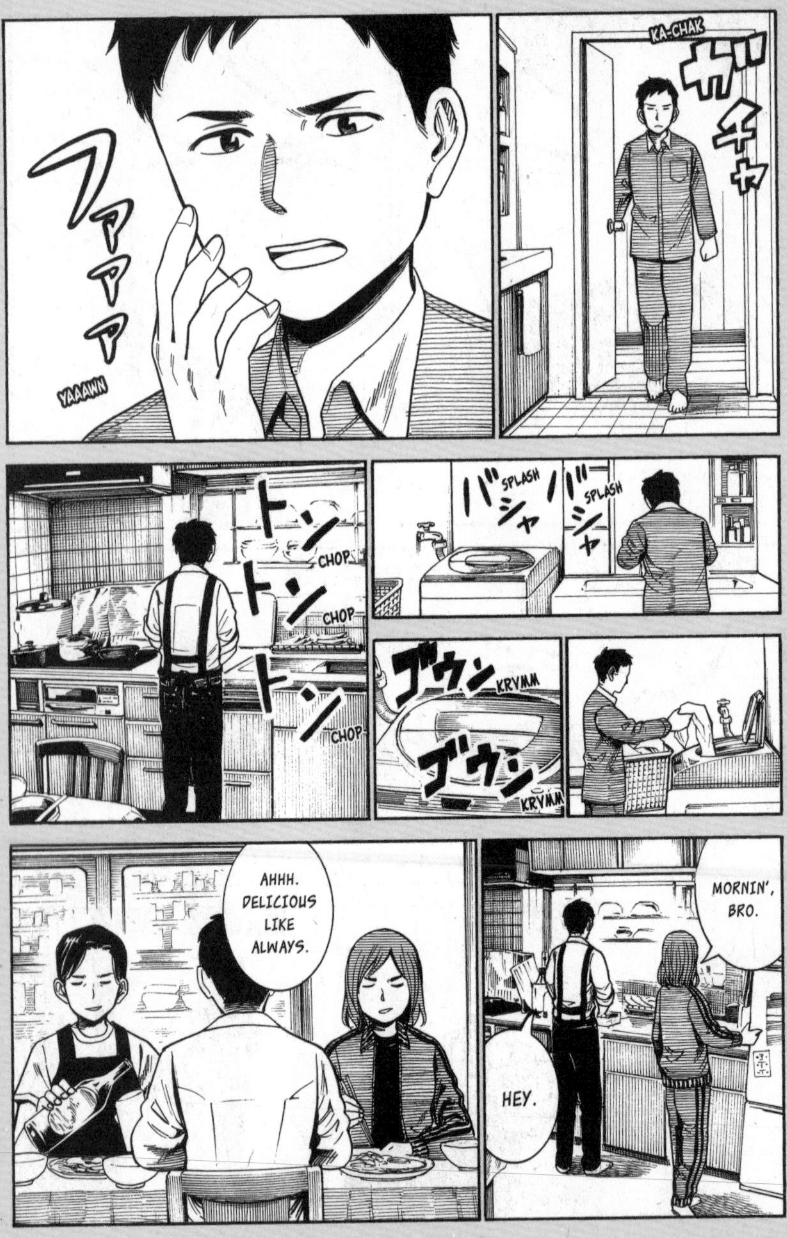
ガチャ
KA-CHAK
ファアアア
YAAAWN
バシャ
SPLASH
バシャ
SPLASH
ゴウン
KRYMM
ゴウン
KRYMM
トン
CHOP
トン
CHOP
トン
CHOP
MORNIN', BRO.
HEY.
AHHH. DELICIOUS LIKE ALWAYS.

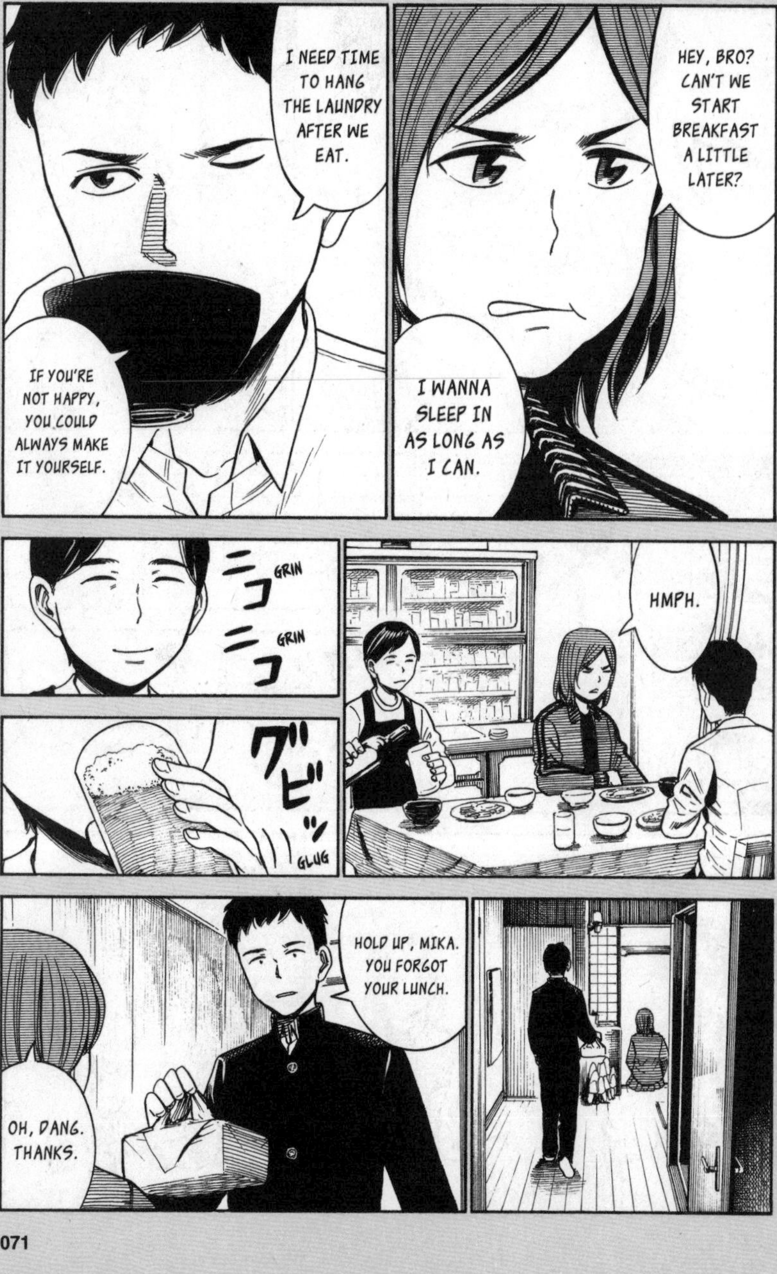
HEY, BRO? CAN'T WE START BREAKFAST A LITTLE LATER?
I WANNA SLEEP IN AS LONG AS I CAN.
I NEED TIME TO HANG THE LAUNDRY AFTER WE EAT.
IF YOU'RE NOT HAPPY, YOU COULD ALWAYS MAKE IT YOURSELF.
HMPH.
ニコ GRIN
ニコ GRIN
グビッ GLUG
HOLD UP, MIKA. YOU FORGOT YOUR LUNCH.
OH, DANG. THANKS.

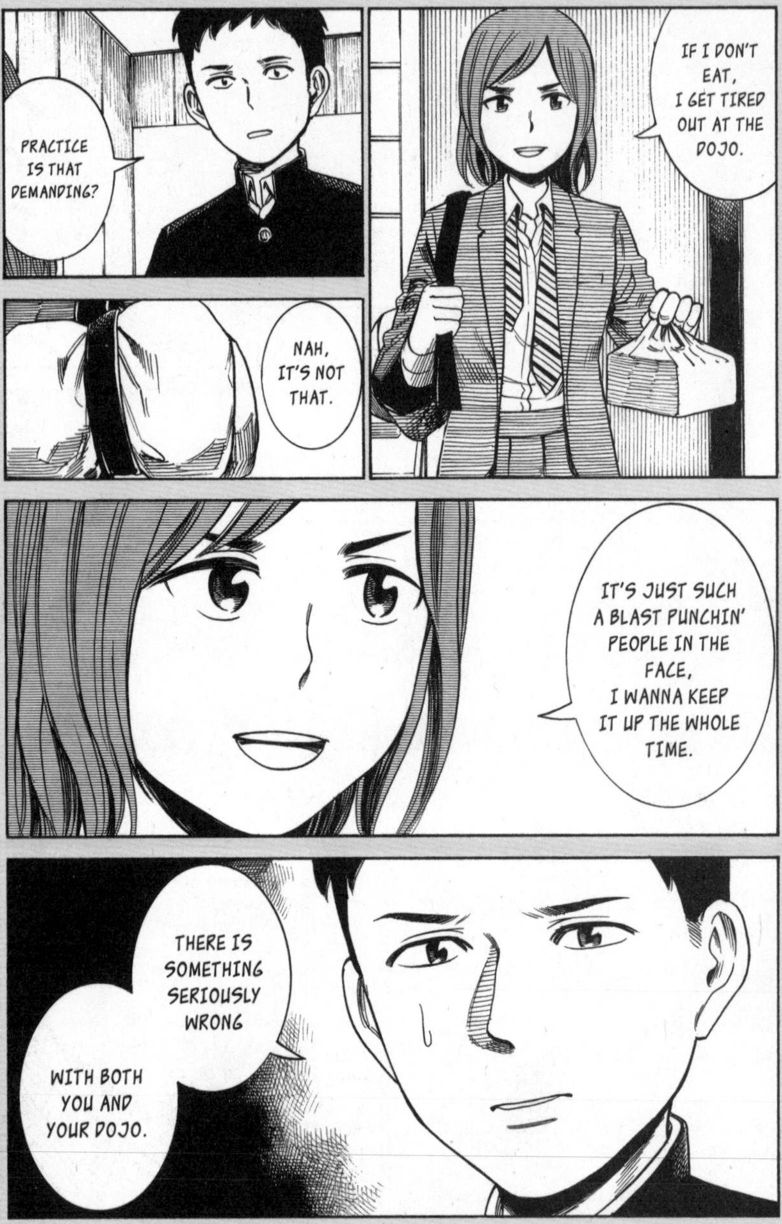
IF I DON'T EAT, I GET TIRED OUT AT THE DOJO.
PRACTICE IS THAT DEMANDING?
NAH, IT'S NOT THAT.
IT'S JUST SUCH A BLAST PUNCHIN' PEOPLE IN THE FACE, I WANNA KEEP IT UP THE WHOLE TIME.
THERE IS SOMETHING SERIOUSLY WRONG
WITH BOTH YOU AND YOUR DOJO.

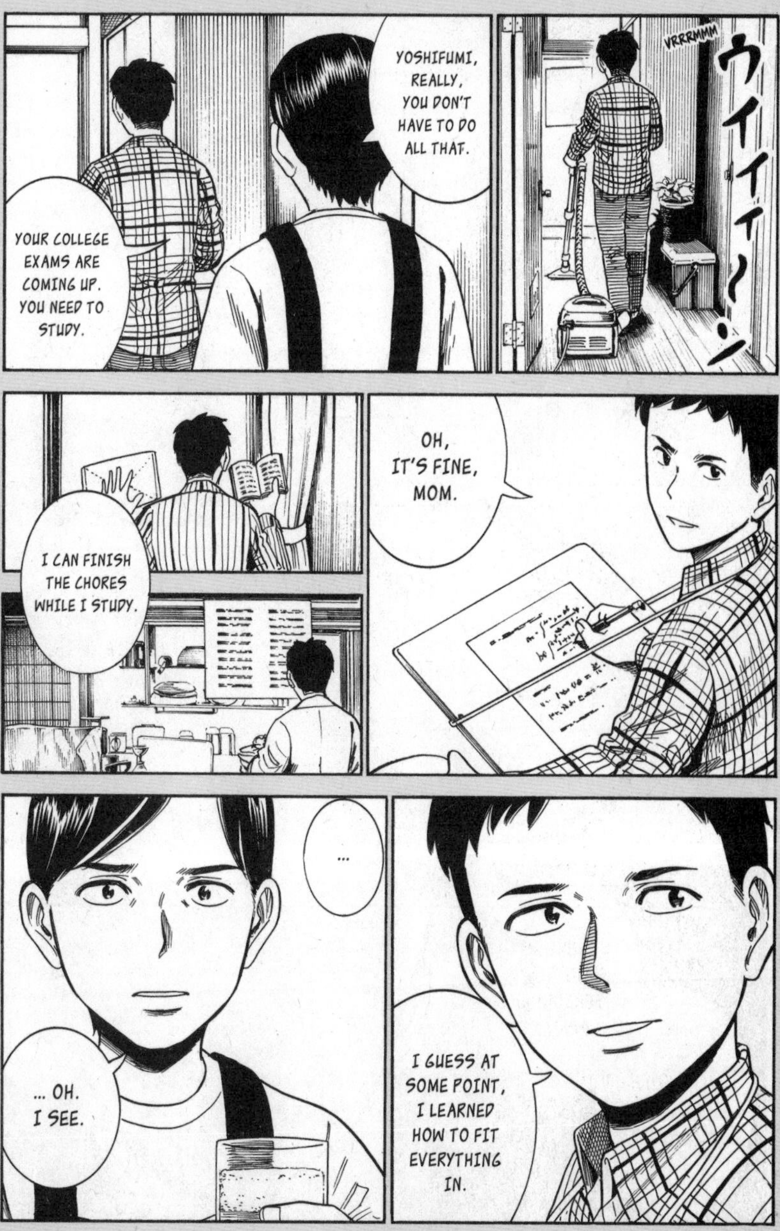
VRRRMMM
ウイイイ〜ン
YOSHIFUMI, REALLY, YOU DON'T HAVE TO DO ALL THAT.
YOUR COLLEGE EXAMS ARE COMING UP. YOU NEED TO STUDY.
OH, IT'S FINE, MOM.
I CAN FINISH THE CHORES WHILE I STUDY.
I GUESS AT SOME POINT, I LEARNED HOW TO FIT EVERYTHING IN.
...
... OH. I SEE.

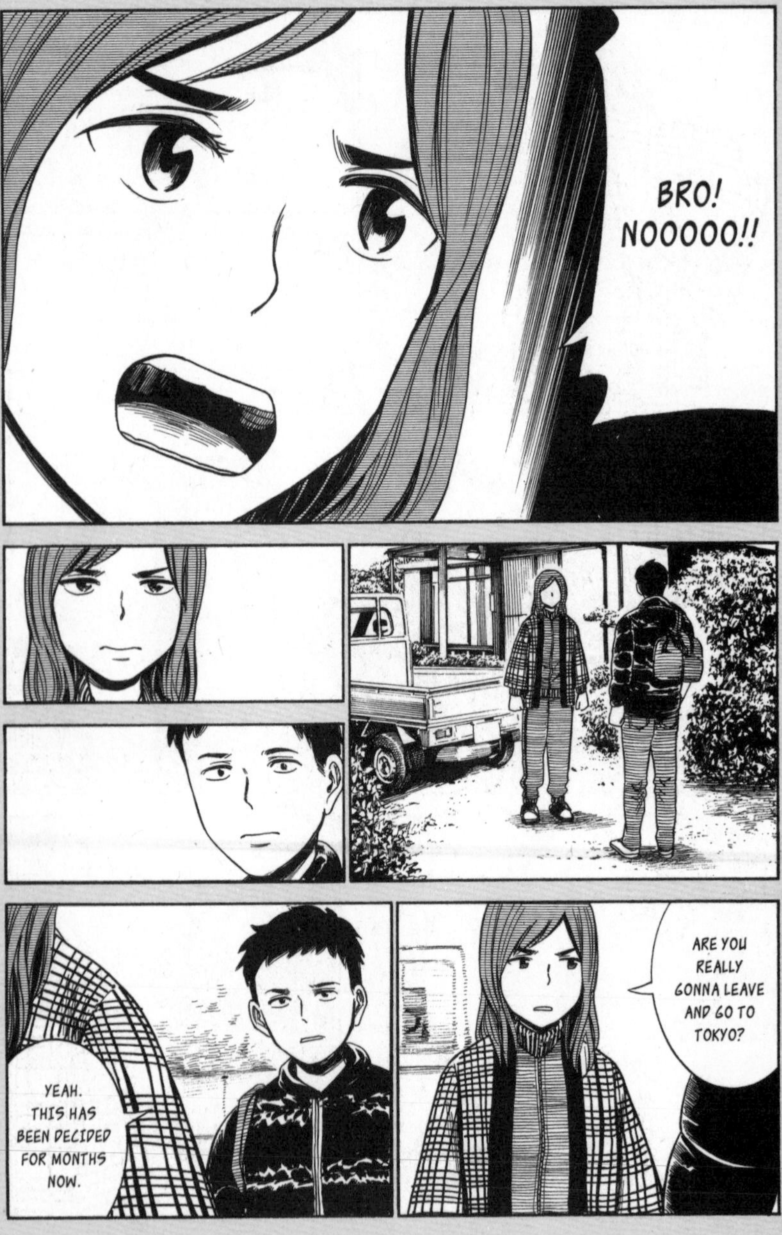
BRO! NOOOOO!!
ARE YOU REALLY GONNA LEAVE AND GO TO TOKYO?
YEAH. THIS HAS BEEN DECIDED FOR MONTHS NOW.

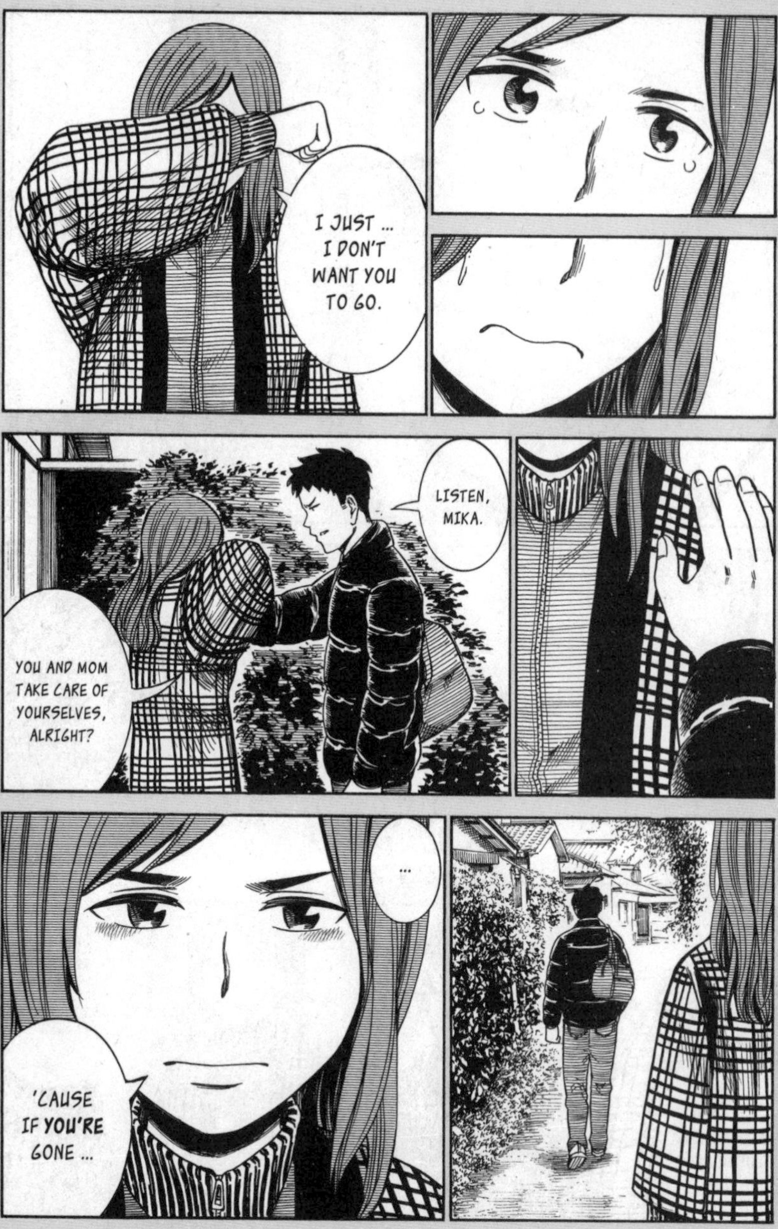
I JUST ... I DON'T WANT YOU TO GO.
LISTEN, MIKA.
YOU AND MOM TAKE CARE OF YOURSELVES, ALRIGHT?
...
'CAUSE IF YOU'RE GONE ...

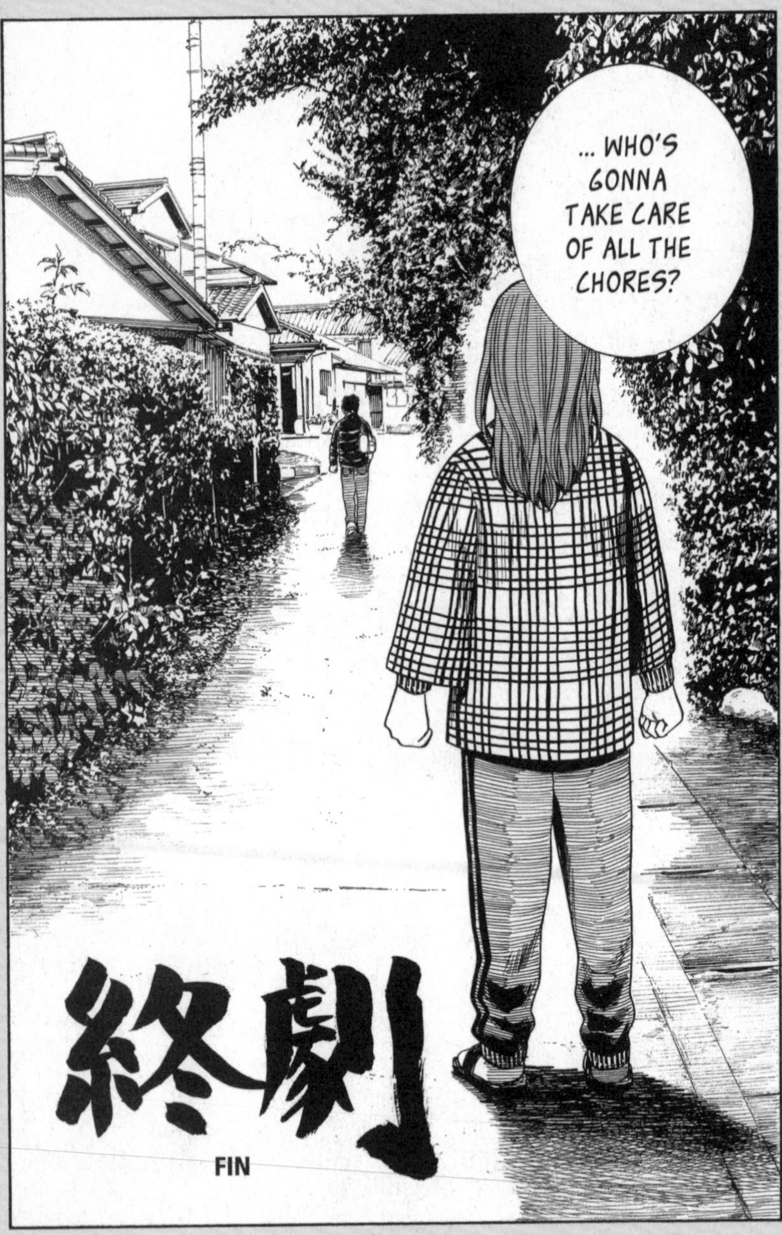
... WHO'S GONNA TAKE CARE OF ALL THE CHORES?
終劇
FIN

CHAPTER 41 HITOMI'S SHORT-TERM STUDY ABROAD

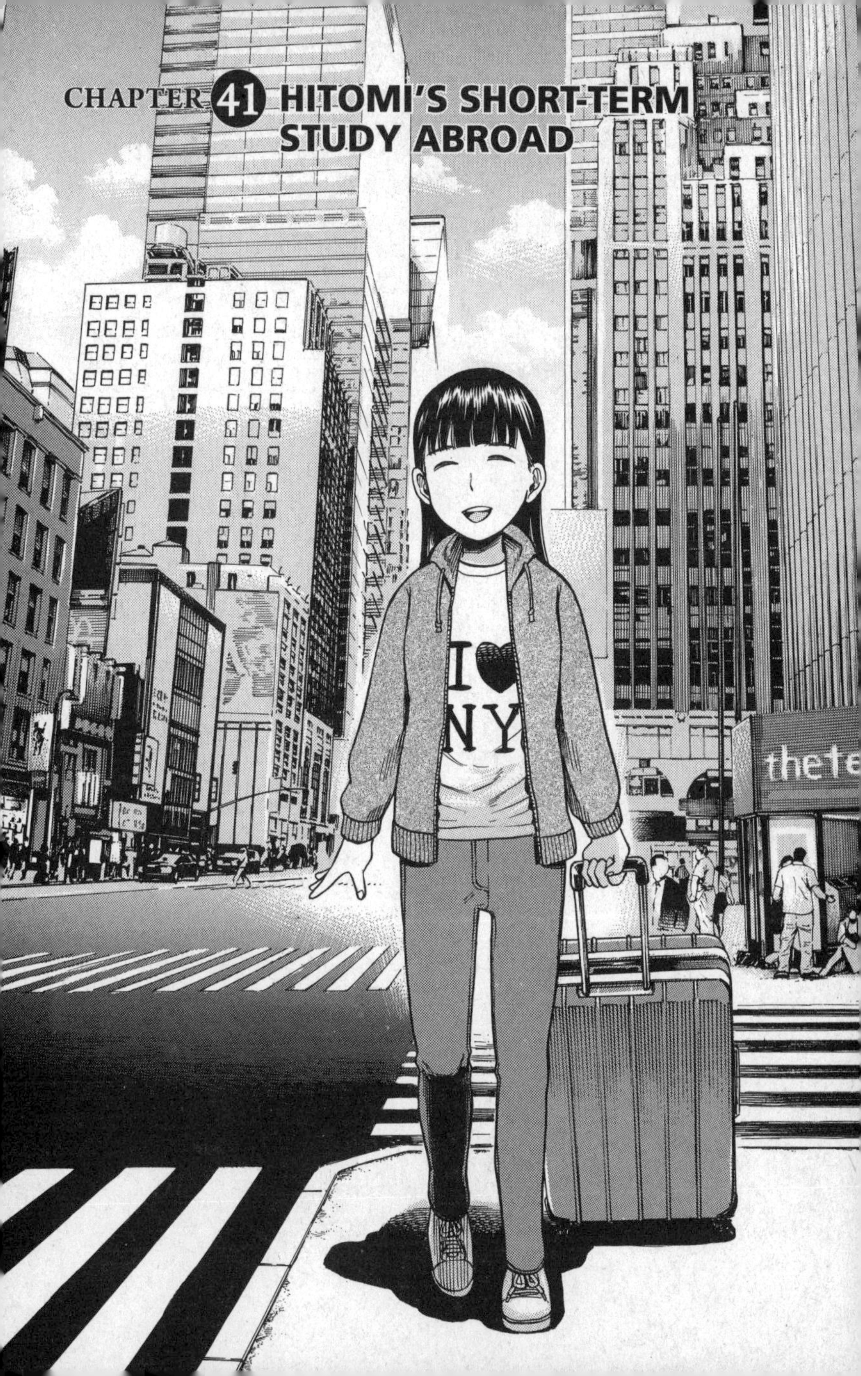
I ♥ NY
thete

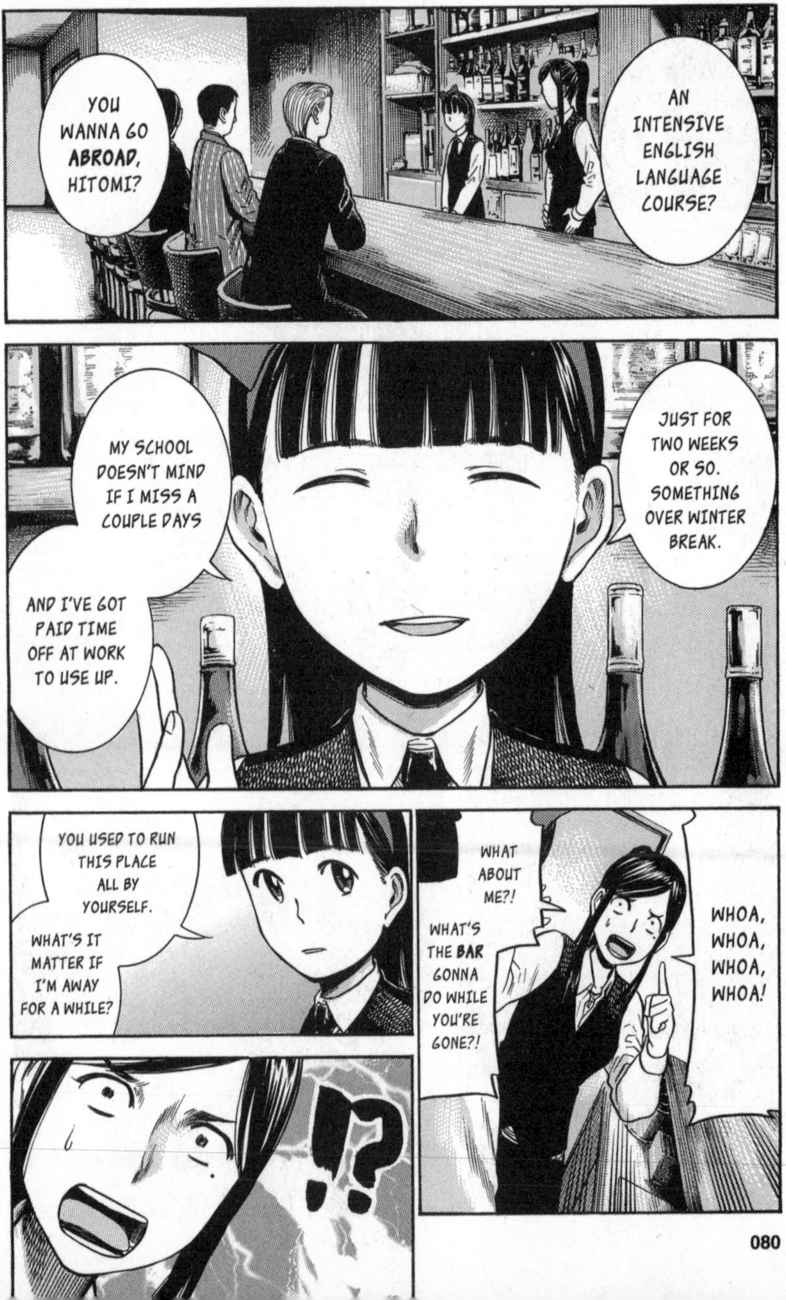

AN INTENSIVE ENGLISH LANGUAGE COURSE?
YOU WANNA GO ABROAD, HITOMI?
JUST FOR TWO WEEKS OR SO. SOMETHING OVER WINTER BREAK.
MY SCHOOL DOESN'T MIND IF I MISS A COUPLE DAYS
AND I'VE GOT PAID TIME OFF AT WORK TO USE UP.
WHOA, WHOA, WHOA, WHOA!
WHAT ABOUT ME?!
WHAT'S THE BAR GONNA DO WHILE YOU'RE GONE?!
YOU USED TO RUN THIS PLACE ALL BY YOURSELF.
WHAT'S IT MATTER IF I'M AWAY FOR A WHILE?
!?

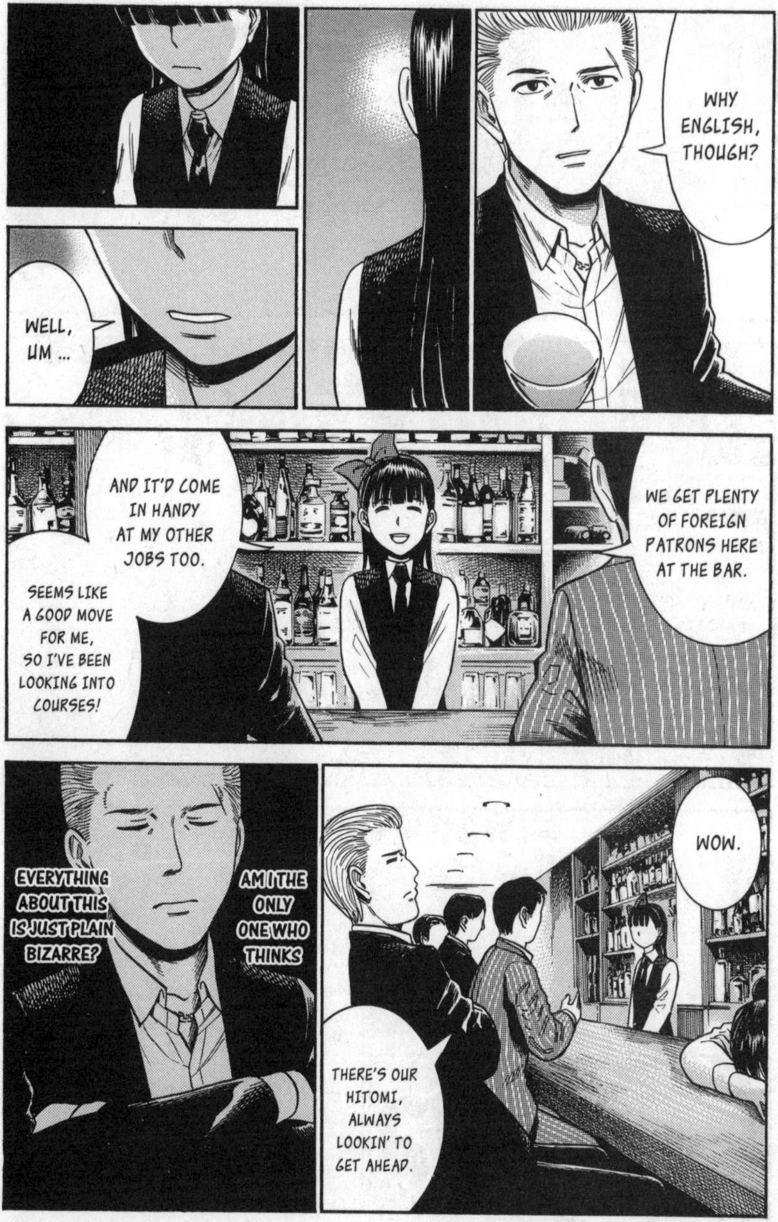
WHY ENGLISH, THOUGH?
WELL, UM ...
WE GET PLENTY OF FOREIGN PATRONS HERE AT THE BAR.
AND IT'D COME IN HANDY AT MY OTHER JOBS TOO.
SEEMS LIKE A GOOD MOVE FOR ME, SO I'VE BEEN LOOKING INTO COURSES!
WOW.
THERE'S OUR HITOMI, ALWAYS LOOKIN' TO GET AHEAD.
AM I THE ONLY ONE WHO THINKS
EVERYTHING ABOUT THIS IS JUST PLAIN BIZARRE?

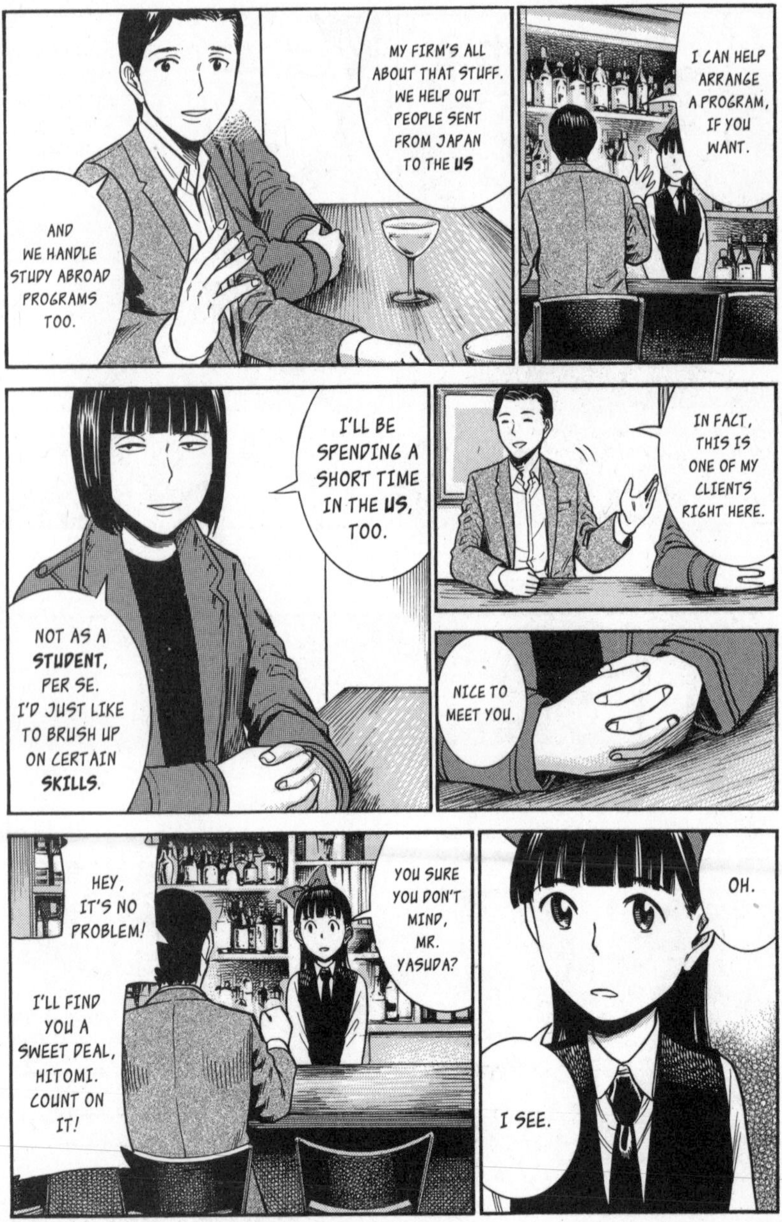
I CAN HELP ARRANGE A PROGRAM, IF YOU WANT.
MY FIRM'S ALL ABOUT THAT STUFF. WE HELP OUT PEOPLE SENT FROM JAPAN TO THE US
AND WE HANDLE STUDY ABROAD PROGRAMS TOO.
IN FACT, THIS IS ONE OF MY CLIENTS RIGHT HERE.
NICE TO MEET YOU.
I'LL BE SPENDING A SHORT TIME IN THE US, TOO.
NOT AS A STUDENT, PER SE. I'D JUST LIKE TO BRUSH UP ON CERTAIN SKILLS.
OH.
I SEE.
YOU SURE YOU DON'T MIND, MR. YASUDA?
HEY, IT'S NO PROBLEM!
I'LL FIND YOU A SWEET DEAL, HITOMI. COUNT ON IT!

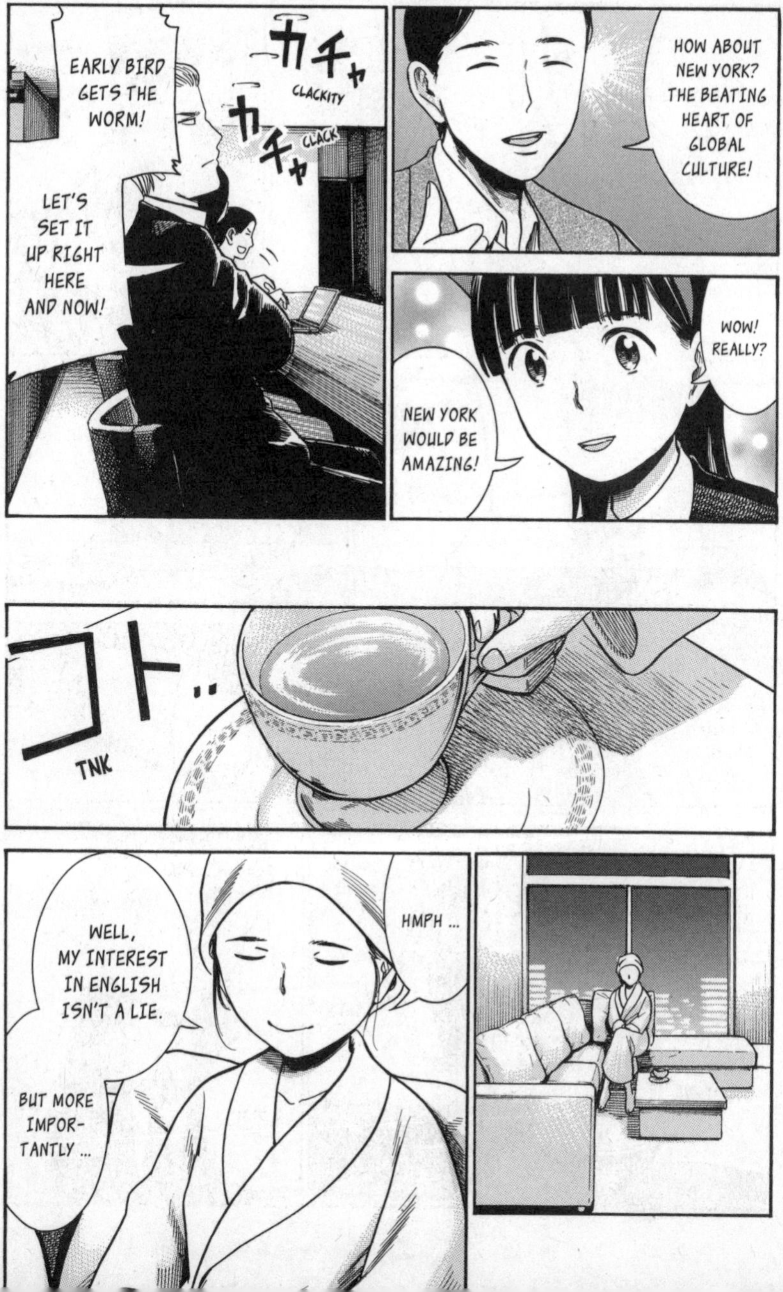
HOW ABOUT NEW YORK? THE BEATING HEART OF GLOBAL CULTURE!
WOW! REALLY?
NEW YORK WOULD BE AMAZING!
カチャ
CLACKITY
カチャ
CLACK
EARLY BIRD GETS THE WORM!
LET'S SET IT UP RIGHT HERE AND NOW!
コト..
TNK
HMPH ...
WELL, MY INTEREST IN ENGLISH ISN'T A LIE.
BUT MORE IMPOR-TANTLY ...

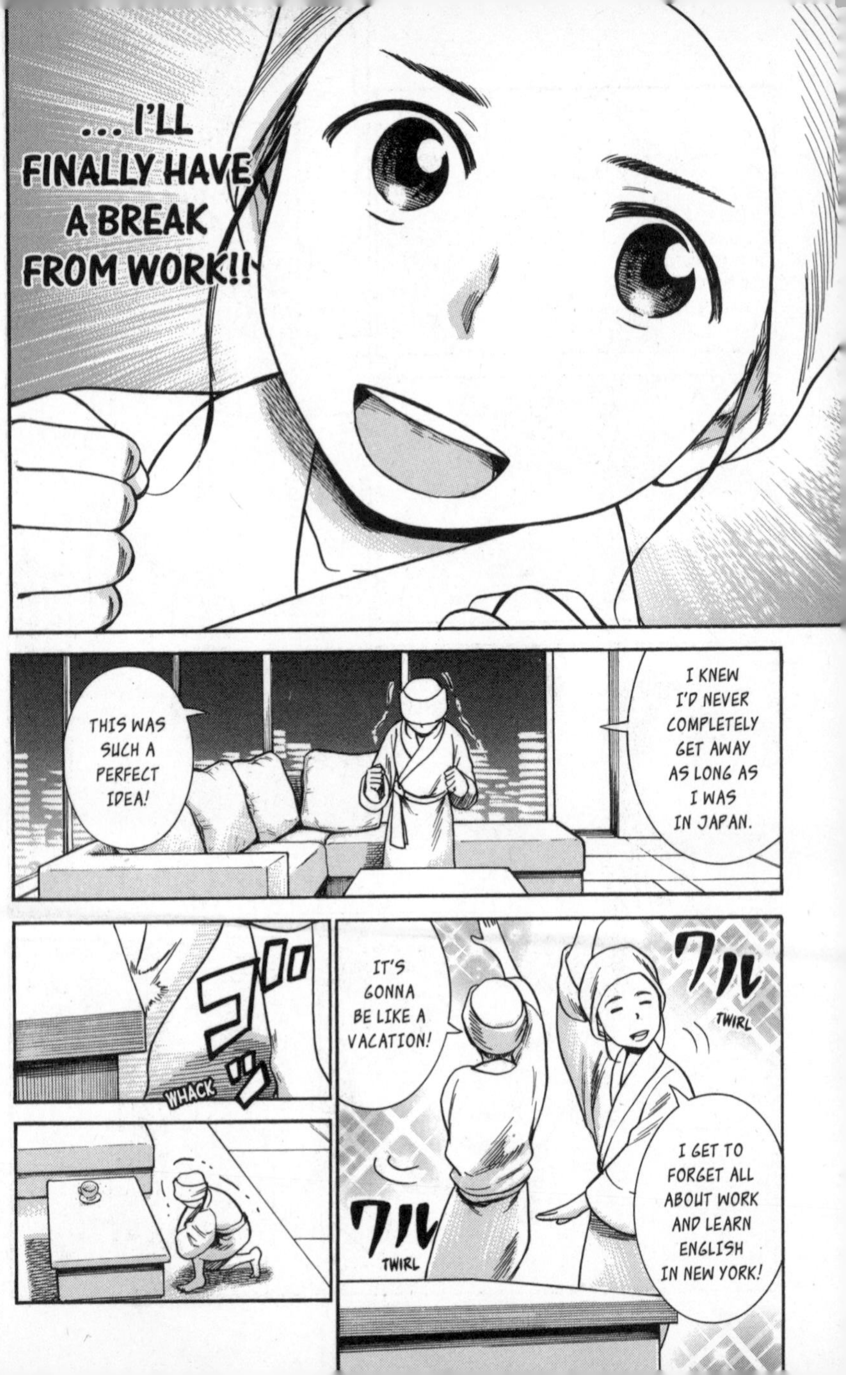

... I'LL FINALLY HAVE A BREAK FROM WORK!!
I KNEW I'D NEVER COMPLETELY GET AWAY AS LONG AS I WAS IN JAPAN.
THIS WAS SUCH A PERFECT IDEA!
ワル
TWIRL
IT'S GONNA BE LIKE A VACATION!
I GET TO FORGET ALL ABOUT WORK AND LEARN ENGLISH IN NEW YORK!
ワル
TWIRL
ゴッ
WHACK

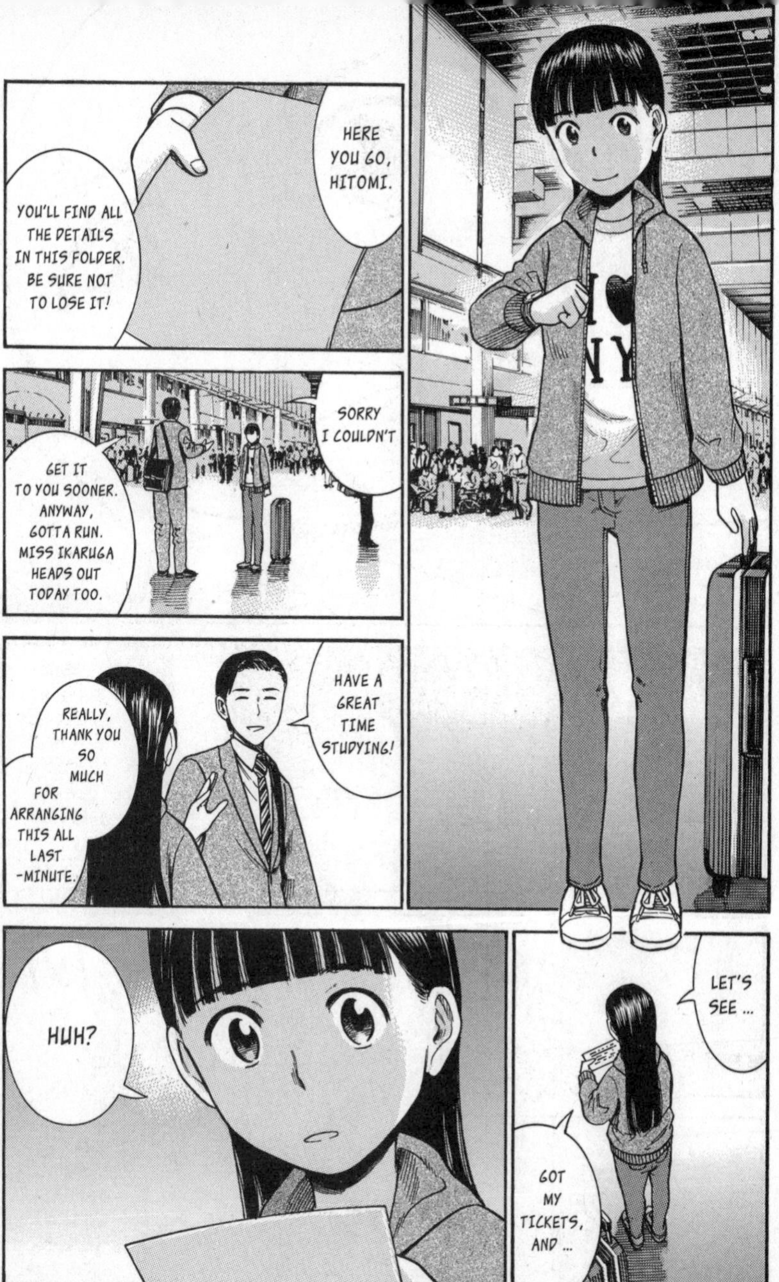
HERE YOU GO, HITOMI.
YOU'LL FIND ALL THE DETAILS IN THIS FOLDER. BE SURE NOT TO LOSE IT!
SORRY I COULDN'T
GET IT TO YOU SOONER. ANYWAY, GOTTA RUN. MISS IKARUGA HEADS OUT TODAY TOO.
HAVE A GREAT TIME STUDYING!
REALLY, THANK YOU SO MUCH FOR ARRANGING THIS ALL LAST-MINUTE.
LET'S SEE ...
GOT MY TICKETS, AND ...
HUH?

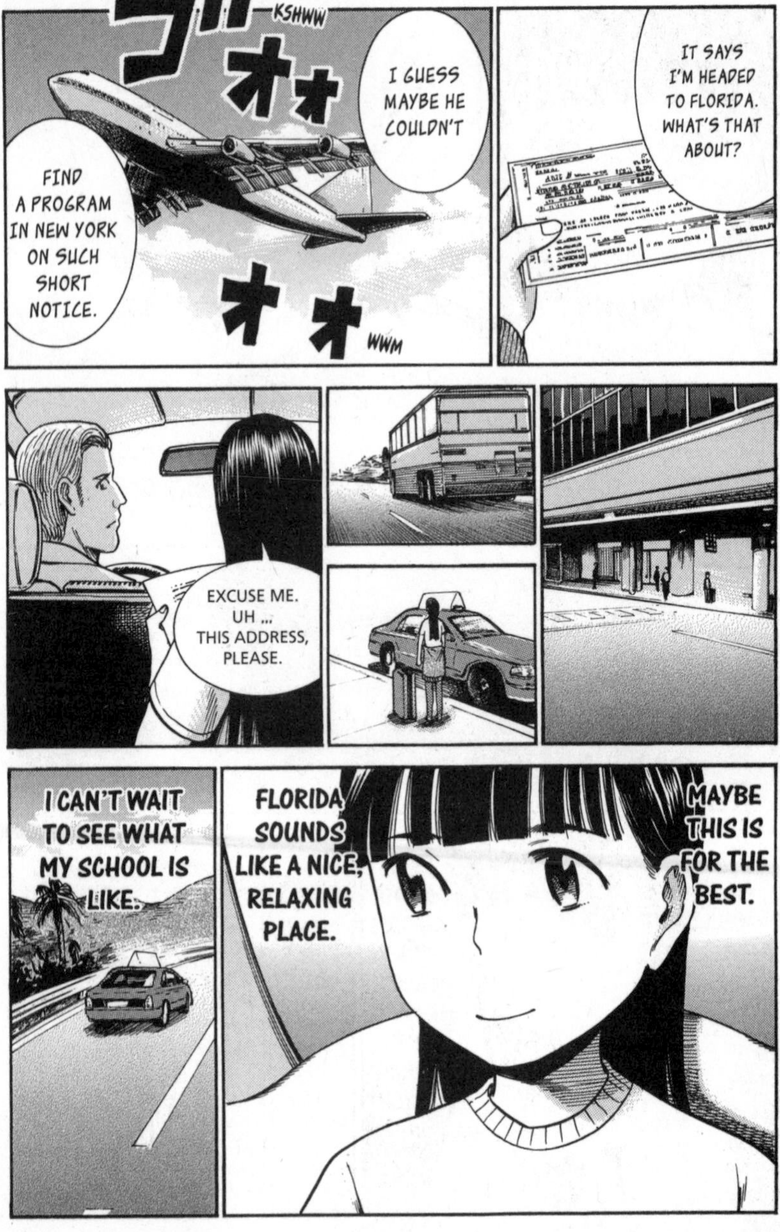
IT SAYS I'M HEADED TO FLORIDA. WHAT'S THAT ABOUT?
ゴオオ
KSHWW
I GUESS MAYBE HE COULDN'T
FIND A PROGRAM IN NEW YORK ON SUCH SHORT NOTICE.
オオ
WWM
EXCUSE ME. UH ... THIS ADDRESS, PLEASE.
MAYBE THIS IS FOR THE BEST.
FLORIDA SOUNDS LIKE A NICE, RELAXING PLACE.
I CAN'T WAIT TO SEE WHAT MY SCHOOL IS LIKE.

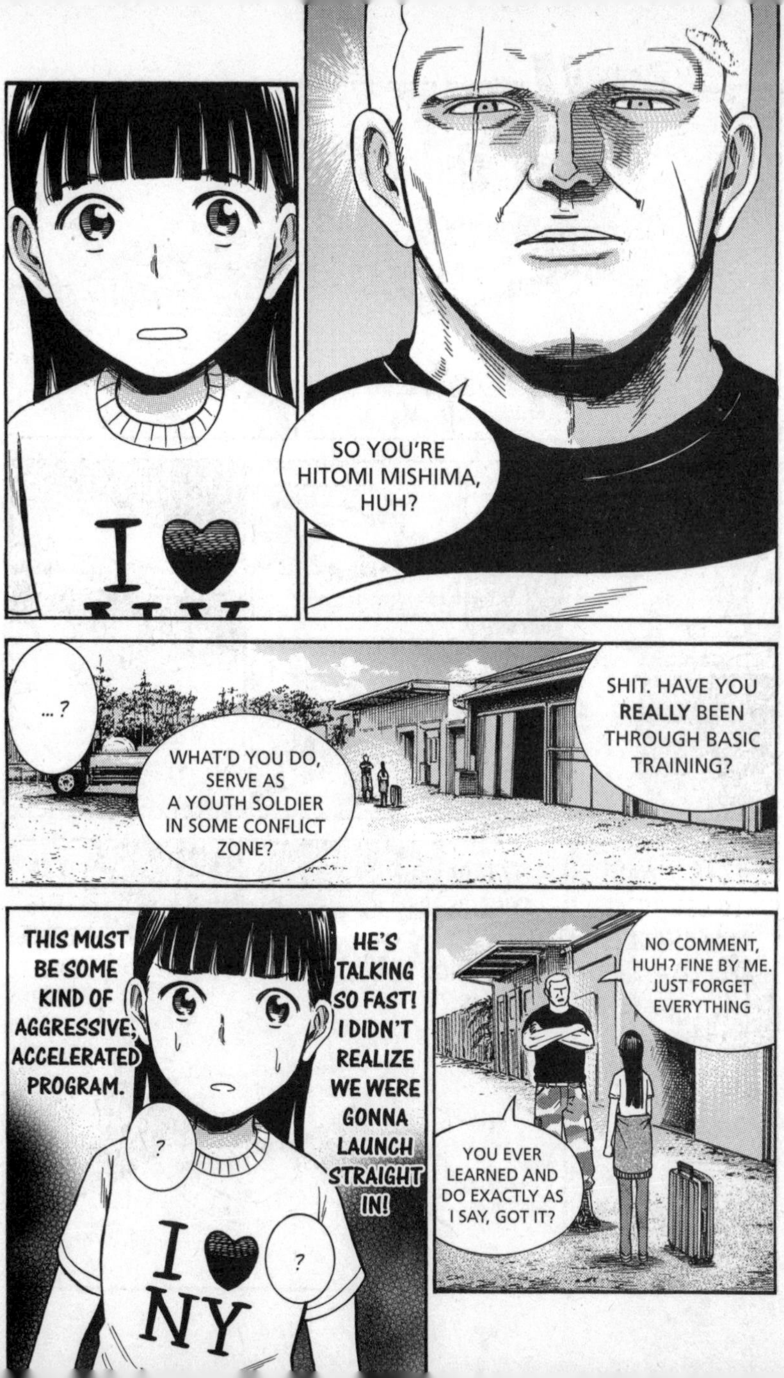
SO YOU'RE HITOMI MISHIMA, HUH?
SHIT. HAVE YOU **REALLY** BEEN THROUGH BASIC TRAINING?
WHAT'D YOU DO, SERVE AS A YOUTH SOLDIER IN SOME CONFLICT ZONE?
...?
NO COMMENT, HUH? FINE BY ME. JUST FORGET EVERYTHING
YOU EVER LEARNED AND DO EXACTLY AS I SAY, GOT IT?
HE'S TALKING SO FAST! I DIDN'T REALIZE WE WERE GONNA LAUNCH STRAIGHT IN!
THIS MUST BE SOME KIND OF AGGRESSIVE, ACCELERATED PROGRAM.
?
?

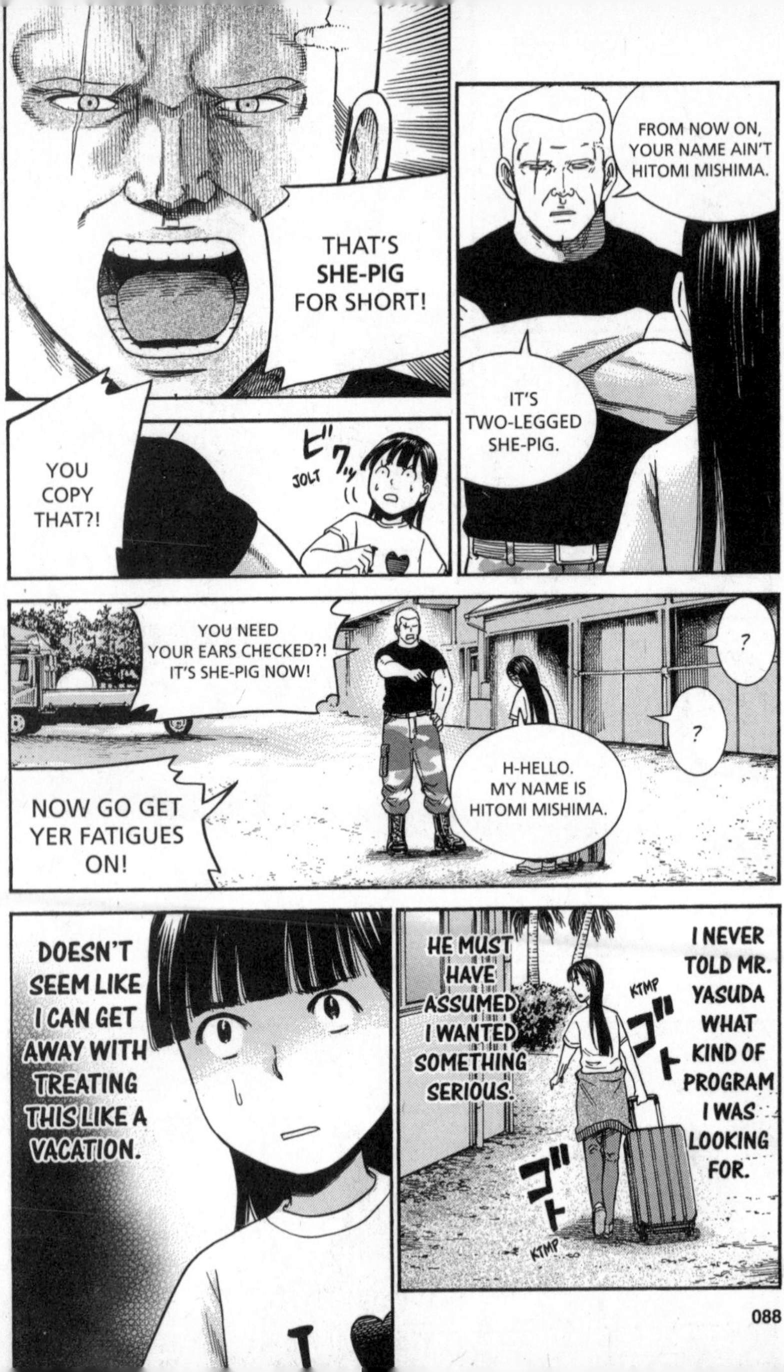
FROM NOW ON, YOUR NAME AIN'T HITOMI MISHIMA.
IT'S TWO-LEGGED SHE-PIG.
THAT'S **SHE-PIG** FOR SHORT!
JOLT
YOU COPY THAT?!
?
?
H-HELLO. MY NAME IS HITOMI MISHIMA.
YOU NEED YOUR EARS CHECKED?! IT'S SHE-PIG NOW!
NOW GO GET YER FATIGUES ON!
I NEVER TOLD MR. YASUDA WHAT KIND OF PROGRAM I WAS LOOKING FOR.
KTMP
HE MUST HAVE ASSUMED I WANTED SOMETHING SERIOUS.
KTMP
DOESN'T SEEM LIKE I CAN GET AWAY WITH TREATING THIS LIKE A VACATION.

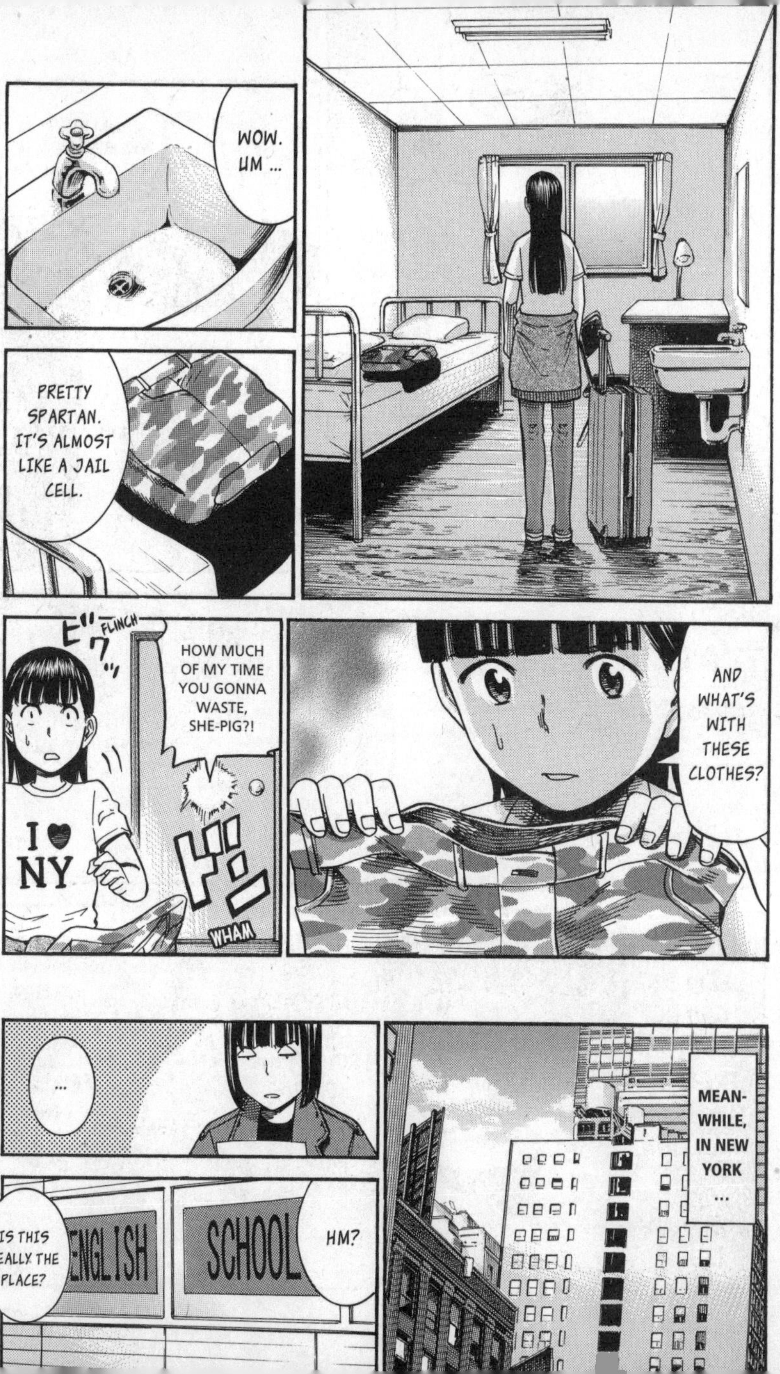
WOW. UM ...
PRETTY SPARTAN. IT'S ALMOST LIKE A JAIL CELL.
AND WHAT'S WITH THESE CLOTHES?
FLINCH
HOW MUCH OF MY TIME YOU GONNA WASTE, SHE-PIG?!
WHAM
I ♥ NY
MEAN-WHILE, IN NEW YORK ...
...
HM?
ENGLISH SCHOOL
IS THIS REALLY THE PLACE?

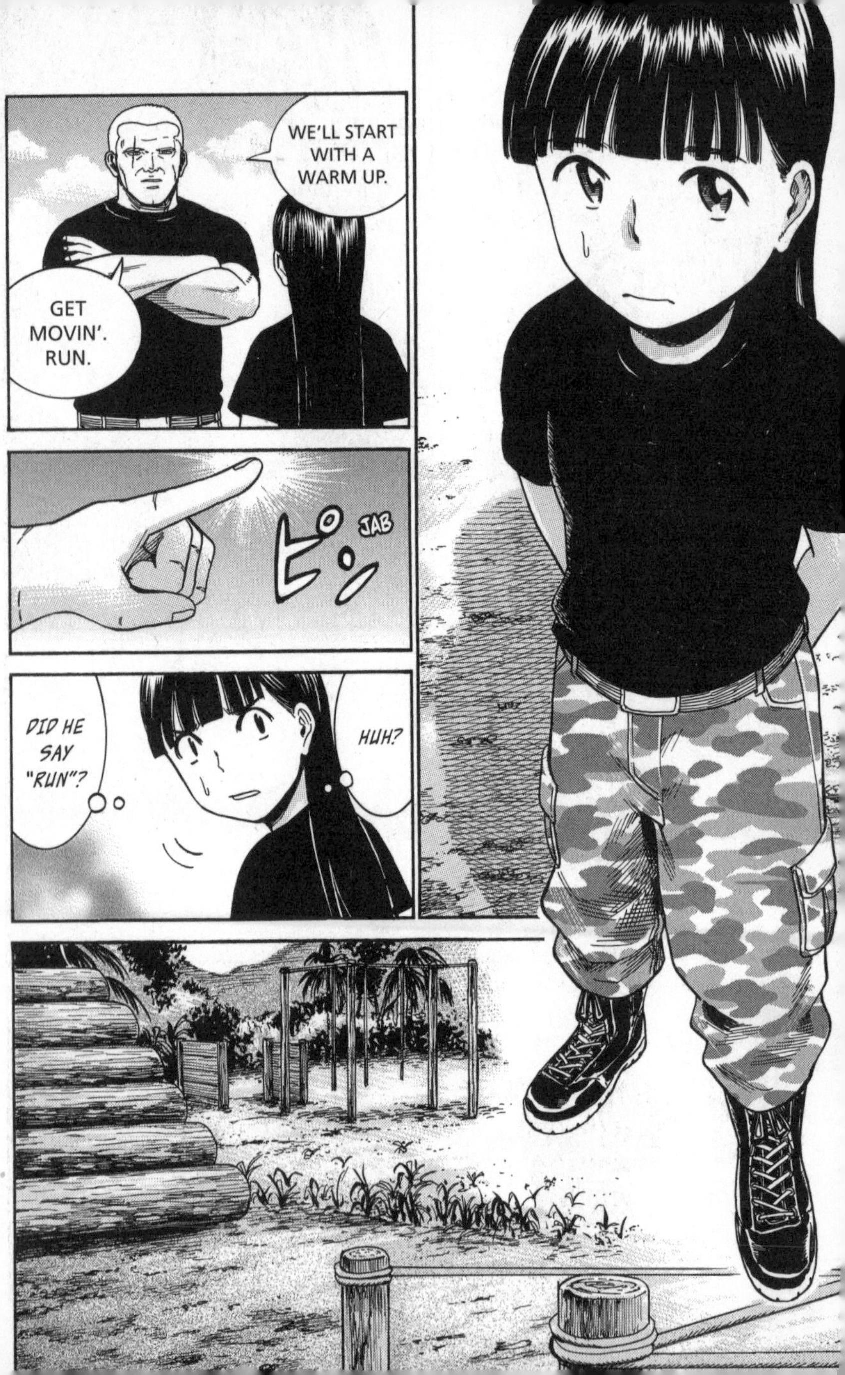
WE'LL START WITH A WARM UP.
GET MOVIN'. RUN.
ピン
JAB
HUH?
DID HE SAY "RUN"?

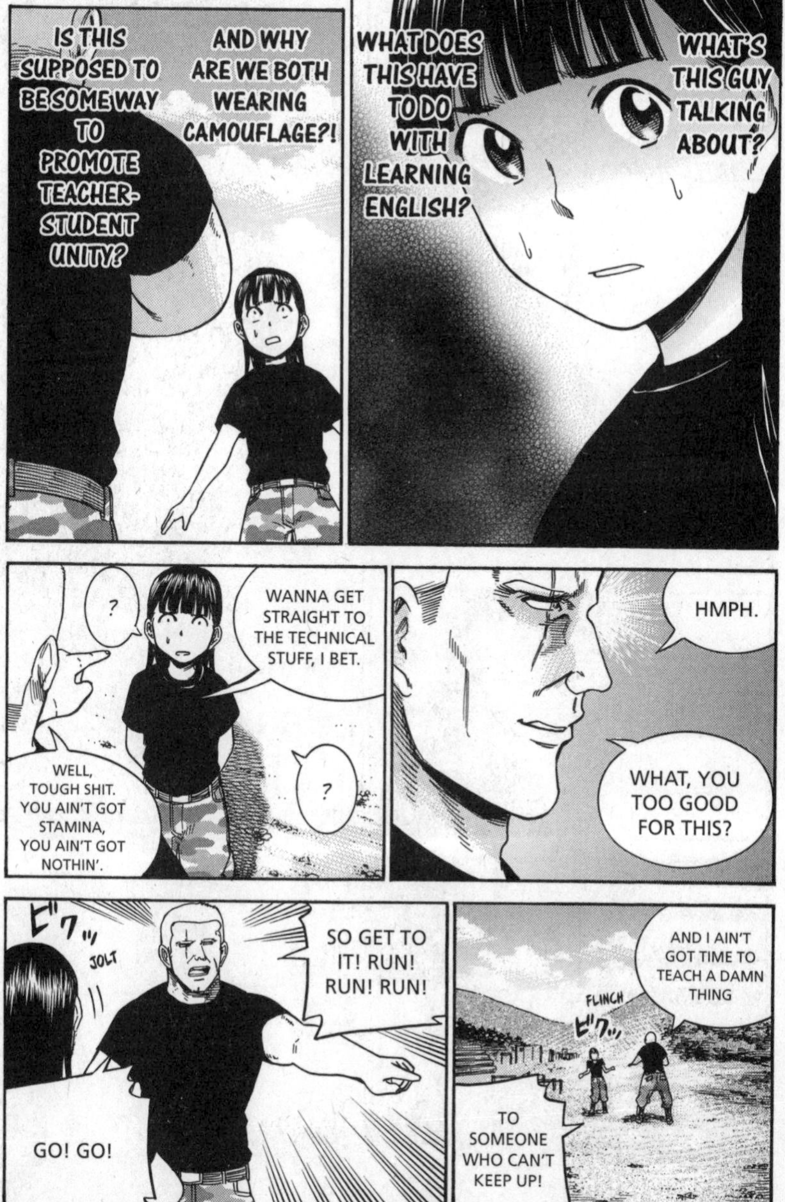
WHAT'S THIS GUY TALKING ABOUT?
WHAT DOES THIS HAVE TO DO WITH LEARNING ENGLISH?
AND WHY ARE WE BOTH WEARING CAMOUFLAGE?!
IS THIS SUPPOSED TO BE SOME WAY TO PROMOTE TEACHER-STUDENT UNITY?
HMPH.
WHAT, YOU TOO GOOD FOR THIS?
?
WANNA GET STRAIGHT TO THE TECHNICAL STUFF, I BET.
?
WELL, TOUGH SHIT. YOU AIN'T GOT STAMINA, YOU AIN'T GOT NOTHIN'.
AND I AIN'T GOT TIME TO TEACH A DAMN THING
ビクッ
FLINCH
TO SOMEONE WHO CAN'T KEEP UP!
SO GET TO IT! RUN! RUN! RUN!
ビクッ
JOLT
GO! GO!

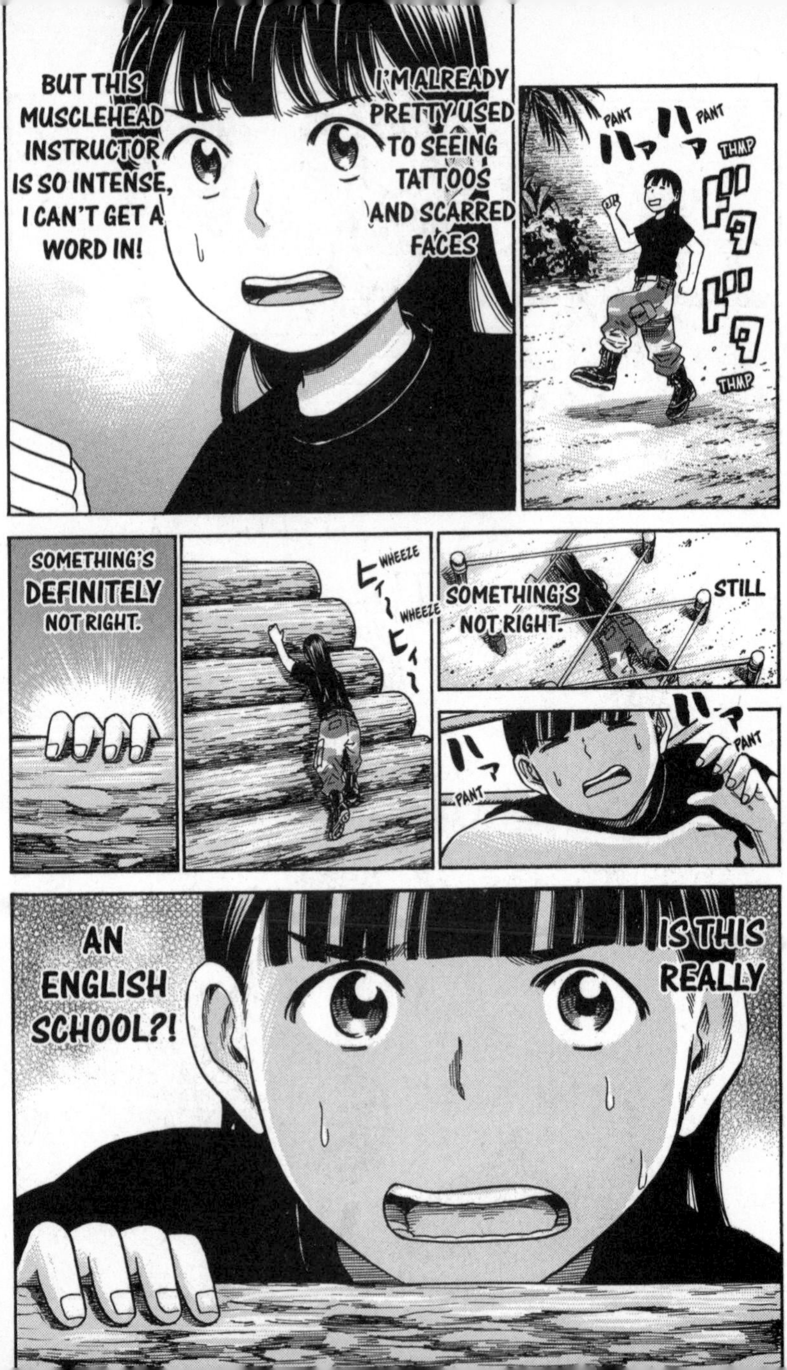
PANT ハァ PANT ハァ
THMP ドタ ドタ THMP
I'M ALREADY PRETTY USED TO SEEING TATTOOS AND SCARRED FACES
BUT THIS MUSCLEHEAD INSTRUCTOR IS SO INTENSE, I CAN'T GET A WORD IN!
STILL
SOMETHING'S NOT RIGHT.
ハァ PANT
ハァ PANT
WHEEZE ヒィ~ WHEEZE ヒィ~
SOMETHING'S DEFINITELY NOT RIGHT.
IS THIS REALLY
AN ENGLISH SCHOOL?!

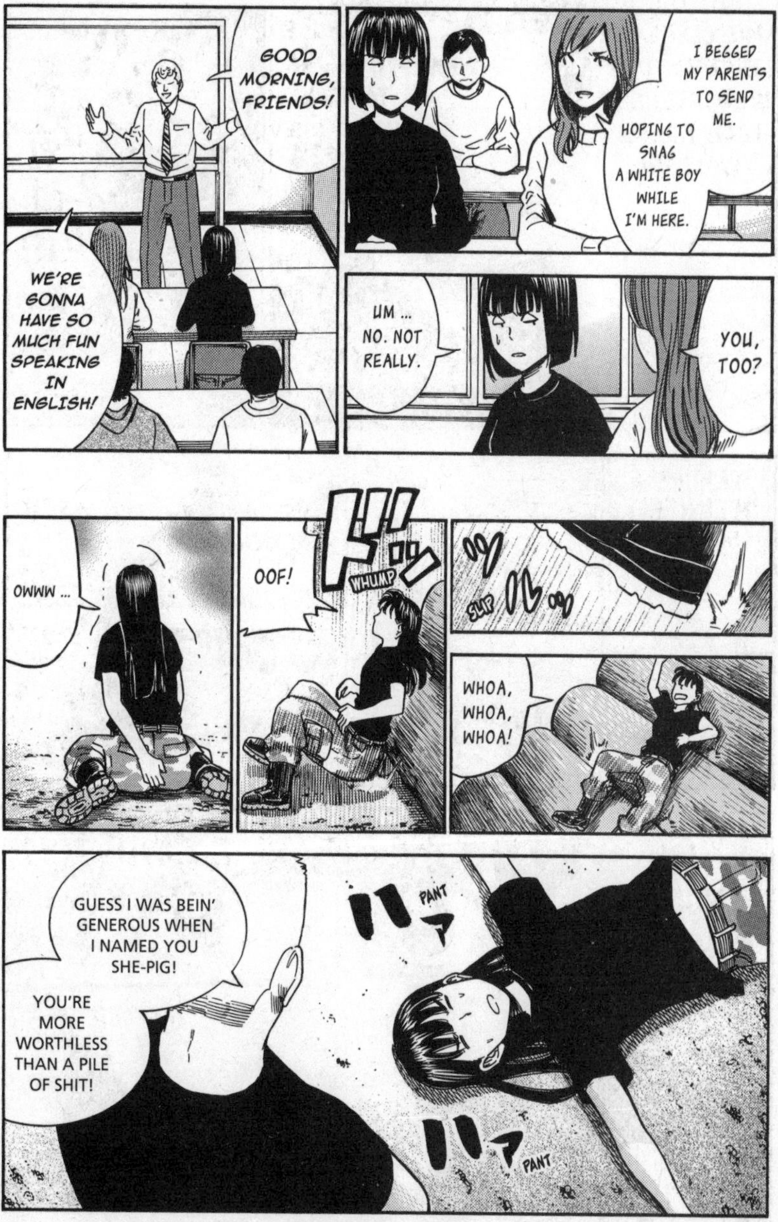
I BEGGED MY PARENTS TO SEND ME.
HOPING TO SNAG A WHITE BOY WHILE I'M HERE.
YOU, TOO?
UM ... NO. NOT REALLY.
GOOD MORNING, FRIENDS!
WE'RE GONNA HAVE SO MUCH FUN SPEAKING IN ENGLISH!
SLIP
WHOA, WHOA, WHOA!
WHUMP
OOF!
OWWW ...
PANT
GUESS I WAS BEIN' GENEROUS WHEN I NAMED YOU SHE-PIG!
YOU'RE MORE WORTHLESS THAN A PILE OF SHIT!
PANT

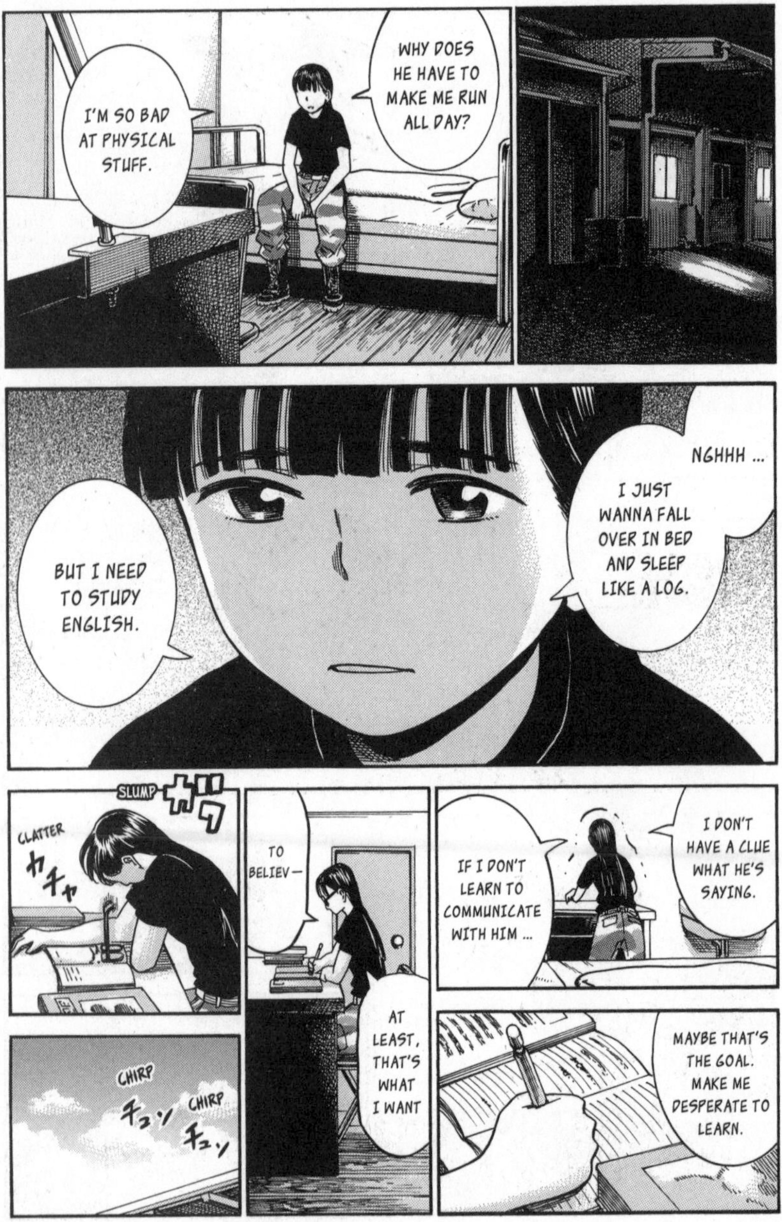
WHY DOES HE HAVE TO MAKE ME RUN ALL DAY?
I'M SO BAD AT PHYSICAL STUFF.
NGHHH ...
I JUST WANNA FALL OVER IN BED AND SLEEP LIKE A LOG.
BUT I NEED TO STUDY ENGLISH.
I DON'T HAVE A CLUE WHAT HE'S SAYING.
IF I DON'T LEARN TO COMMUNICATE WITH HIM ...
MAYBE THAT'S THE GOAL. MAKE ME DESPERATE TO LEARN.
AT LEAST, THAT'S WHAT I WANT
TO BELIEV—
SLUMP
CLATTER
CHIRP
CHIRP

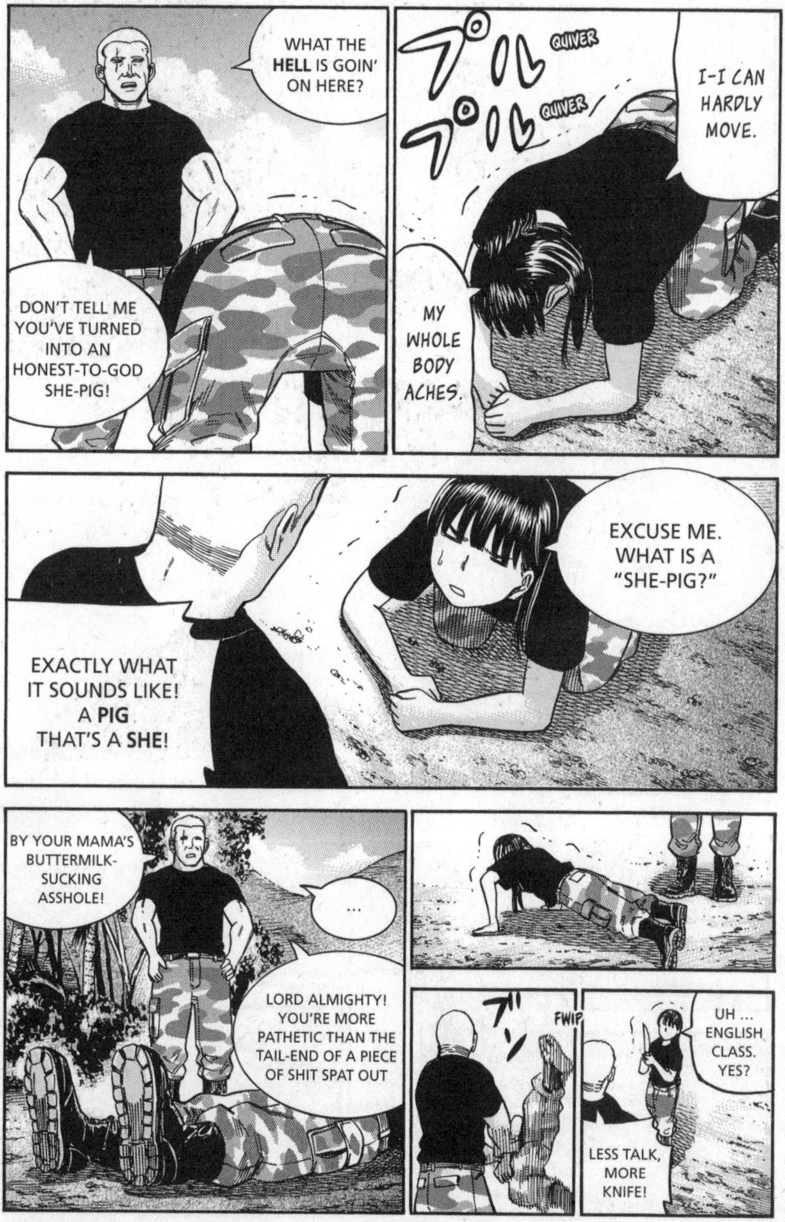
プル QUIVER
プル QUIVER
I-I CAN HARDLY MOVE.
MY WHOLE BODY ACHES.
WHAT THE **HELL** IS GOIN' ON HERE?
DON'T TELL ME YOU'VE TURNED INTO AN HONEST-TO-GOD SHE-PIG!
EXCUSE ME. WHAT IS A "SHE-PIG?"
EXACTLY WHAT IT SOUNDS LIKE! A **PIG** THAT'S A **SHE**!
UH ... ENGLISH CLASS. YES?
LESS TALK, MORE KNIFE!
FWIP
...
LORD ALMIGHTY! YOU'RE MORE PATHETIC THAN THE TAIL-END OF A PIECE OF SHIT SPAT OUT
BY YOUR MAMA'S BUTTERMILK-SUCKING ASSHOLE!

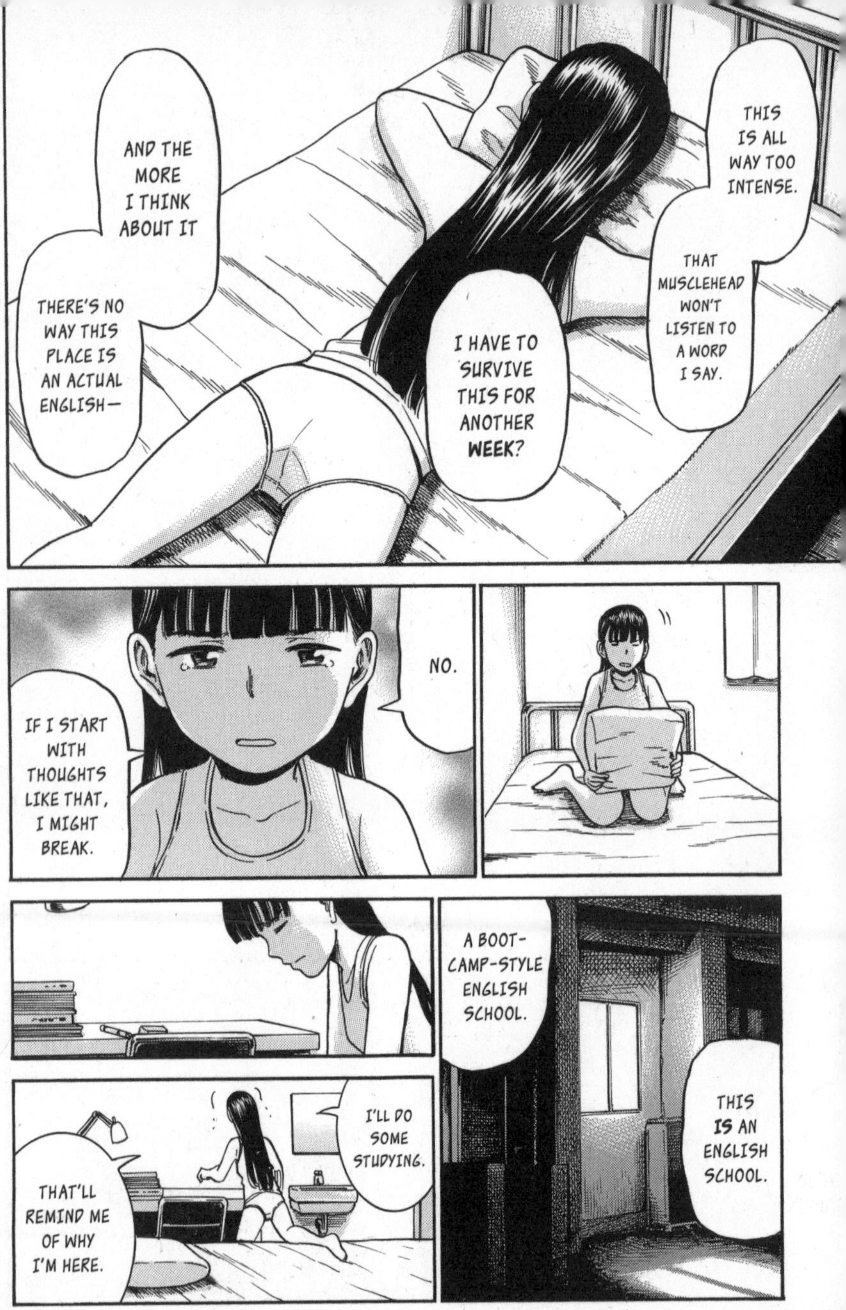
THIS IS ALL WAY TOO INTENSE.
THAT MUSCLEHEAD WON'T LISTEN TO A WORD I SAY.
I HAVE TO SURVIVE THIS FOR ANOTHER WEEK?
AND THE MORE I THINK ABOUT IT
THERE'S NO WAY THIS PLACE IS AN ACTUAL ENGLISH—
NO.
IF I START WITH THOUGHTS LIKE THAT, I MIGHT BREAK.
A BOOT-CAMP-STYLE ENGLISH SCHOOL.
THIS IS AN ENGLISH SCHOOL.
I'LL DO SOME STUDYING.
THAT'LL REMIND ME OF WHY I'M HERE.

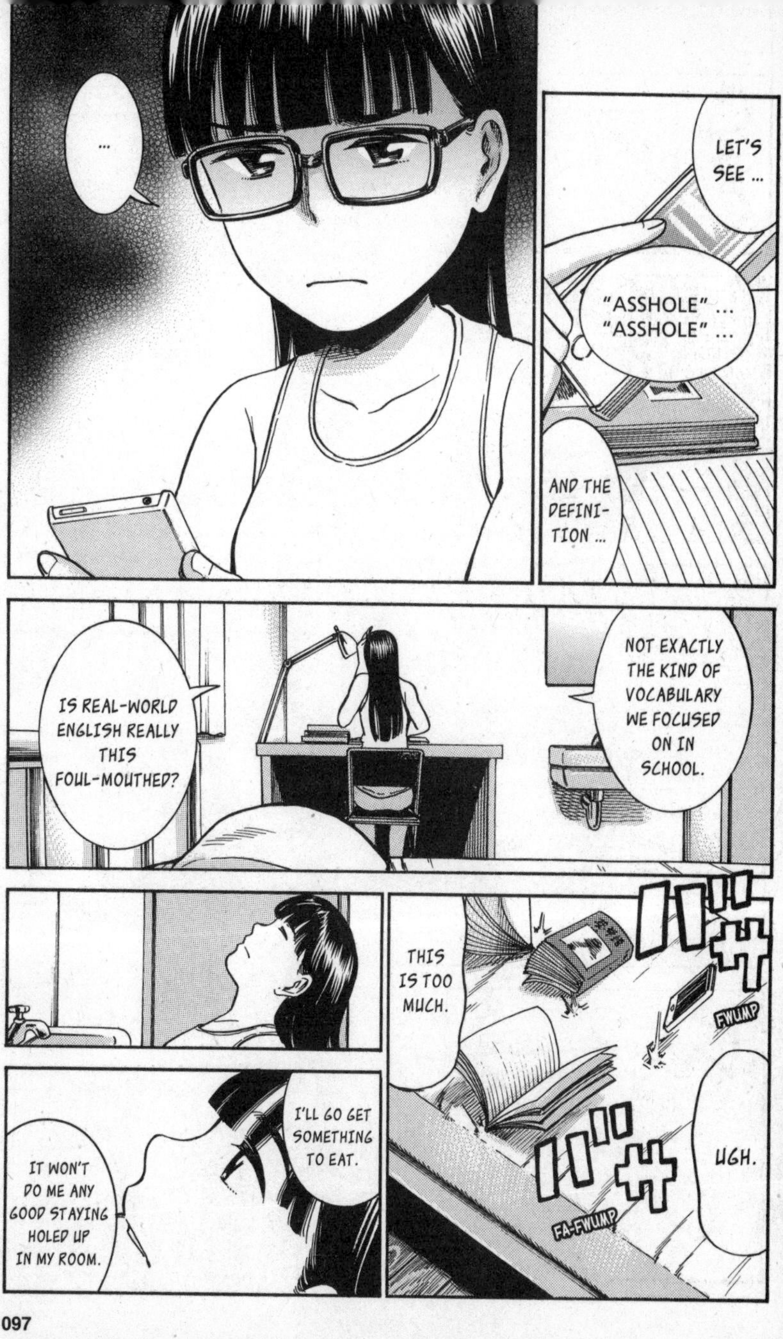
LET'S SEE ...
"ASSHOLE" ... "ASSHOLE" ...
AND THE DEFINITION ...
...
NOT EXACTLY THE KIND OF VOCABULARY WE FOCUSED ON IN SCHOOL.
IS REAL-WORLD ENGLISH REALLY THIS FOUL-MOUTHED?
FWUMP
THIS IS TOO MUCH.
UGH.
FA-FWUMP
I'LL GO GET SOMETHING TO EAT.
IT WON'T DO ME ANY GOOD STAYING HOLED UP IN MY ROOM.

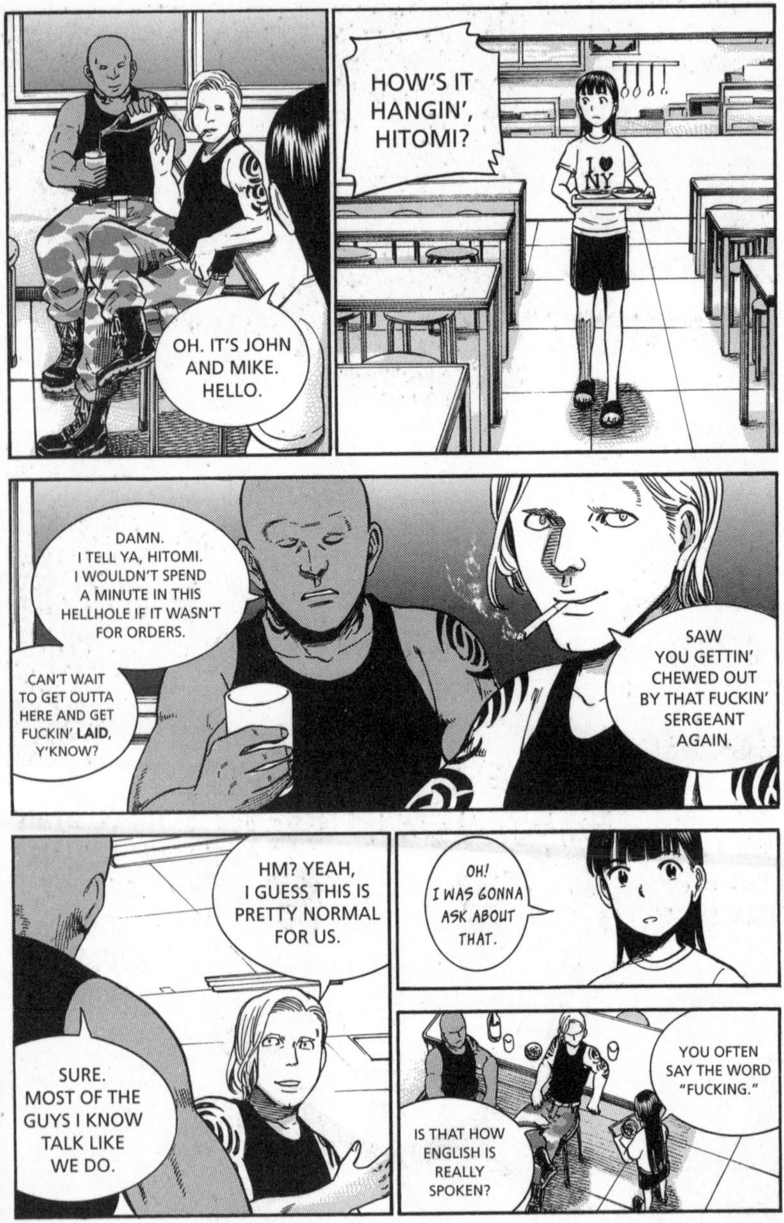
HOW'S IT HANGIN', HITOMI?
OH. IT'S JOHN AND MIKE. HELLO.
DAMN. I TELL YA, HITOMI. I WOULDN'T SPEND A MINUTE IN THIS HELLHOLE IF IT WASN'T FOR ORDERS.
CAN'T WAIT TO GET OUTTA HERE AND GET FUCKIN' **LAID**, Y'KNOW?
SAW YOU GETTIN' CHEWED OUT BY THAT FUCKIN' SERGEANT AGAIN.
OH! I WAS GONNA ASK ABOUT THAT.
YOU OFTEN SAY THE WORD "FUCKING."
IS THAT HOW ENGLISH IS REALLY SPOKEN?
HM? YEAH, I GUESS THIS IS PRETTY NORMAL FOR US.
SURE. MOST OF THE GUYS I KNOW TALK LIKE WE DO.

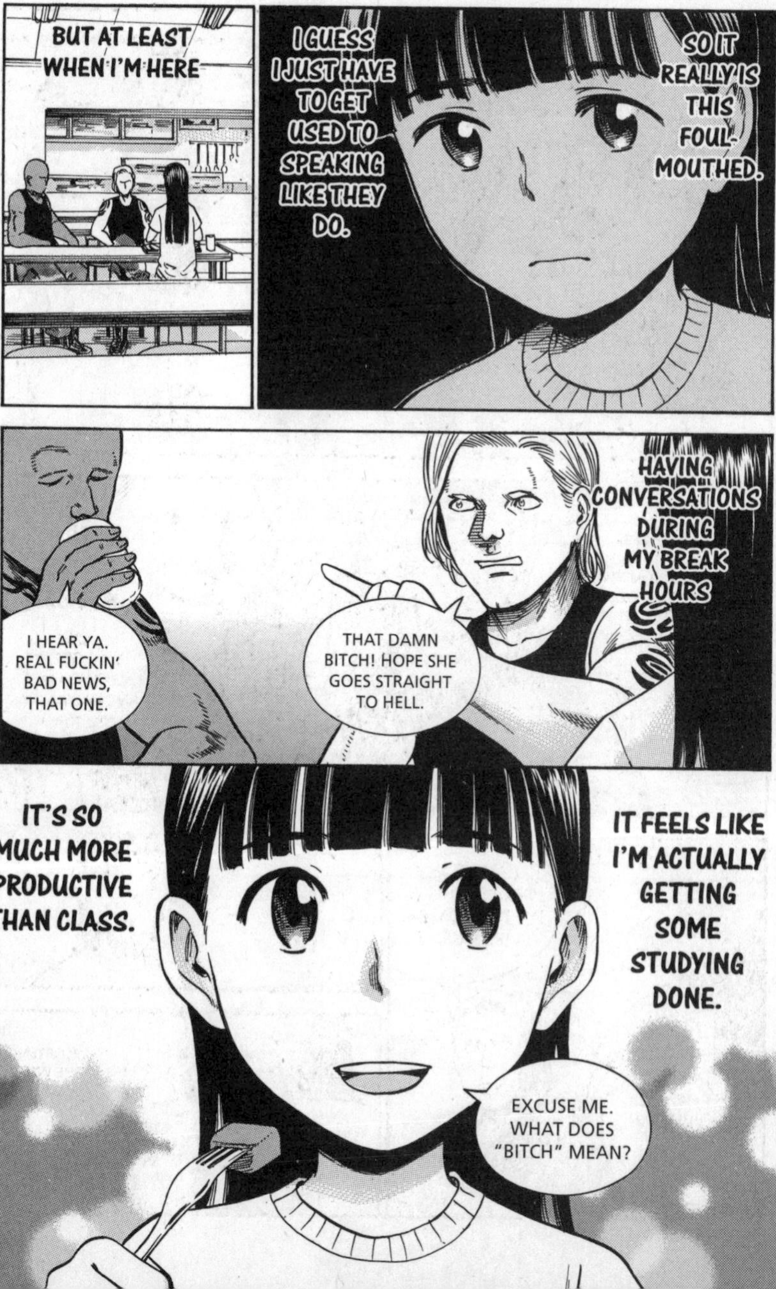
SO IT REALLY IS THIS FOUL-MOUTHED.
I GUESS I JUST HAVE TO GET USED TO SPEAKING LIKE THEY DO.
BUT AT LEAST WHEN I'M HERE
HAVING CONVERSATIONS DURING MY BREAK HOURS
THAT DAMN BITCH! HOPE SHE GOES STRAIGHT TO HELL.
I HEAR YA. REAL FUCKIN' BAD NEWS, THAT ONE.
IT FEELS LIKE I'M ACTUALLY GETTING SOME STUDYING DONE.
IT'S SO MUCH MORE PRODUCTIVE THAN CLASS.
EXCUSE ME. WHAT DOES "BITCH" MEAN?

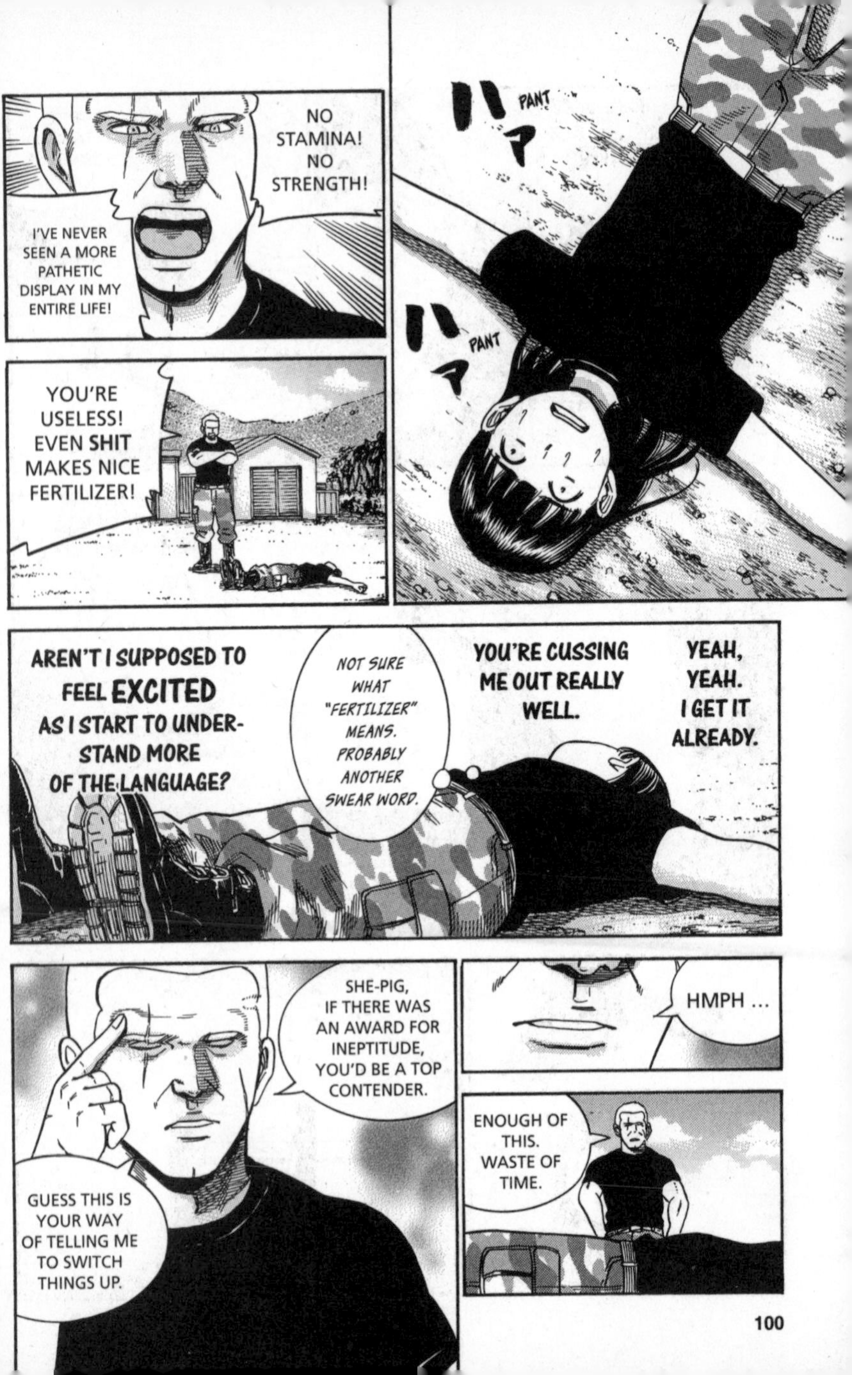

ハァ
PANT
ハァ
PANT
NO STAMINA! NO STRENGTH!
I'VE NEVER SEEN A MORE PATHETIC DISPLAY IN MY ENTIRE LIFE!
YOU'RE USELESS! EVEN SHIT MAKES NICE FERTILIZER!
YEAH, YEAH. I GET IT ALREADY.
YOU'RE CUSSING ME OUT REALLY WELL.
NOT SURE WHAT "FERTILIZER" MEANS. PROBABLY ANOTHER SWEAR WORD.
AREN'T I SUPPOSED TO FEEL EXCITED AS I START TO UNDER-STAND MORE OF THE LANGUAGE?
HMPH ...
ENOUGH OF THIS. WASTE OF TIME.
SHE-PIG, IF THERE WAS AN AWARD FOR INEPTITUDE, YOU'D BE A TOP CONTENDER.
GUESS THIS IS YOUR WAY OF TELLING ME TO SWITCH THINGS UP.

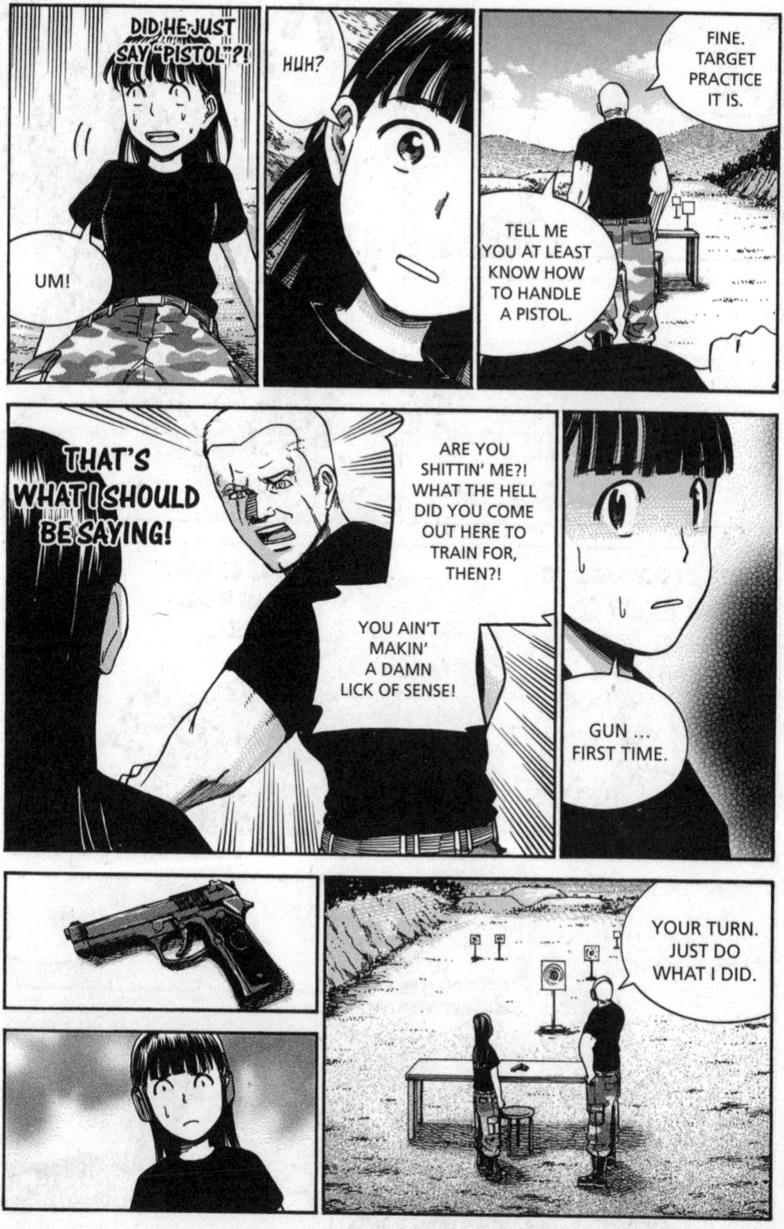
FINE. TARGET PRACTICE IT IS.
TELL ME YOU AT LEAST KNOW HOW TO HANDLE A PISTOL.
HUH?
DID HE JUST SAY "PISTOL"?!
UM!
GUN ... FIRST TIME.
ARE YOU SHITTIN' ME?! WHAT THE HELL DID YOU COME OUT HERE TO TRAIN FOR, THEN?!
YOU AIN'T MAKIN' A DAMN LICK OF SENSE!
THAT'S WHAT I SHOULD BE SAYING!
YOUR TURN. JUST DO WHAT I DID.

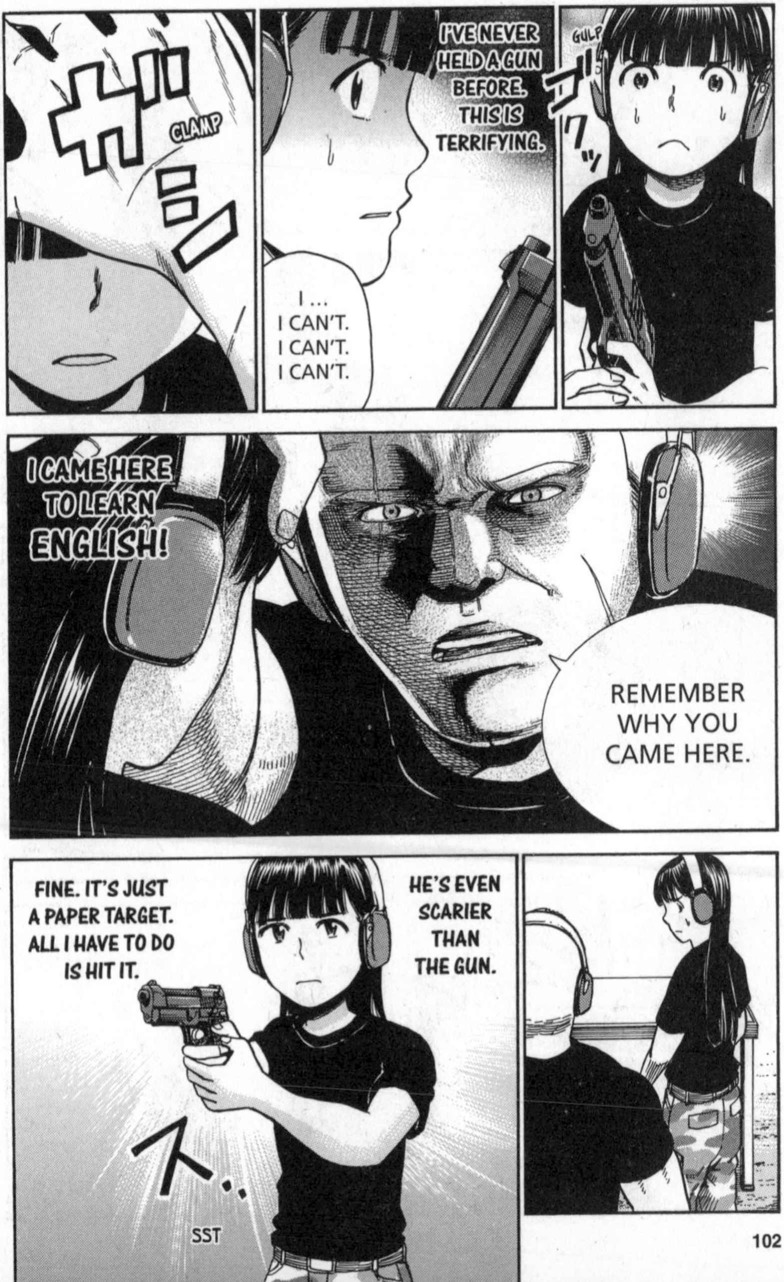
GULP
ゴクッ
I'VE NEVER HELD A GUN BEFORE. THIS IS TERRIFYING.
I ... I CAN'T. I CAN'T. I CAN'T.
CLAMP
REMEMBER WHY YOU CAME HERE.
I CAME HERE TO LEARN ENGLISH!
HE'S EVEN SCARIER THAN THE GUN.
FINE. IT'S JUST A PAPER TARGET. ALL I HAVE TO DO IS HIT IT.
SST

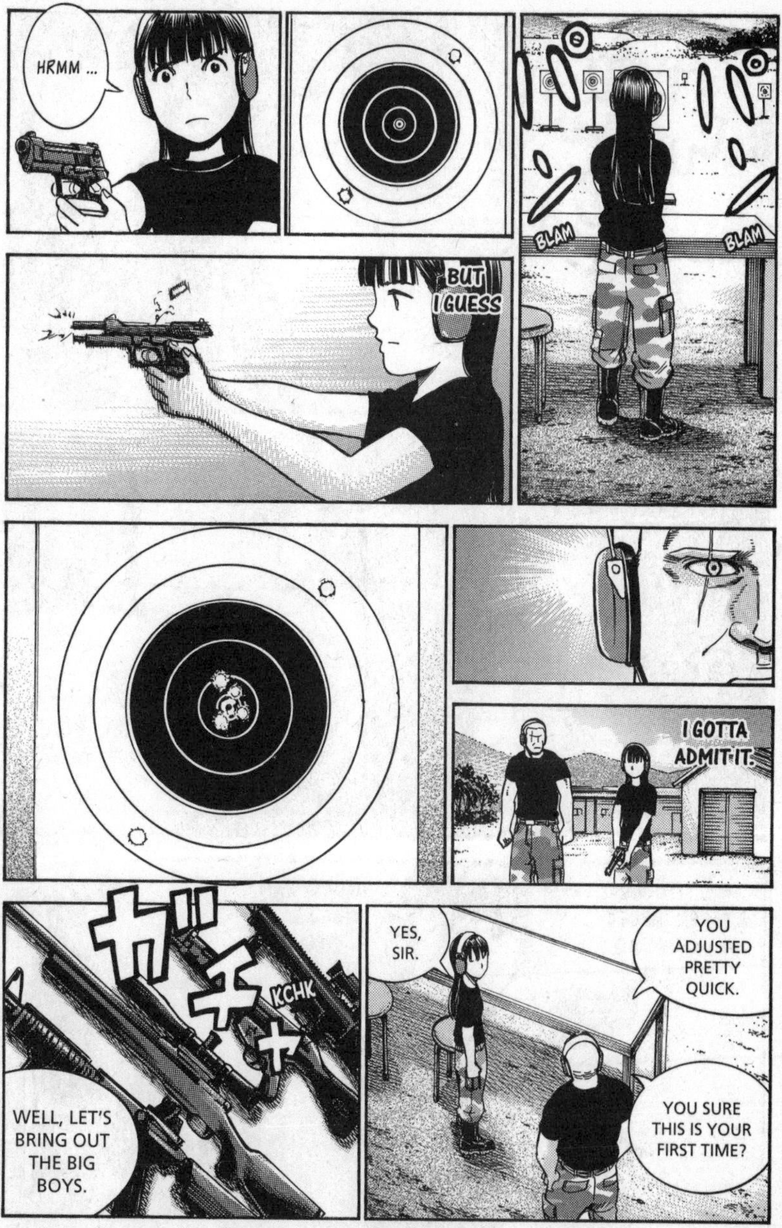
BLAM
BLAM
HRMM ...
BUT I GUESS
I GOTTA ADMIT IT.
YOU ADJUSTED PRETTY QUICK.
YOU SURE THIS IS YOUR FIRST TIME?
YES, SIR.
ガチャ
KCHK
WELL, LET'S BRING OUT THE BIG BOYS.

THERE'S NO WAY ON EARTH THIS PLACE IS REALLY A ...

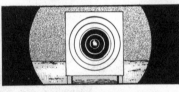

WELL, I'LL BE DAMNED.

A ONE-KLICK BULLSEYE ON YOUR FIRST RODEO.

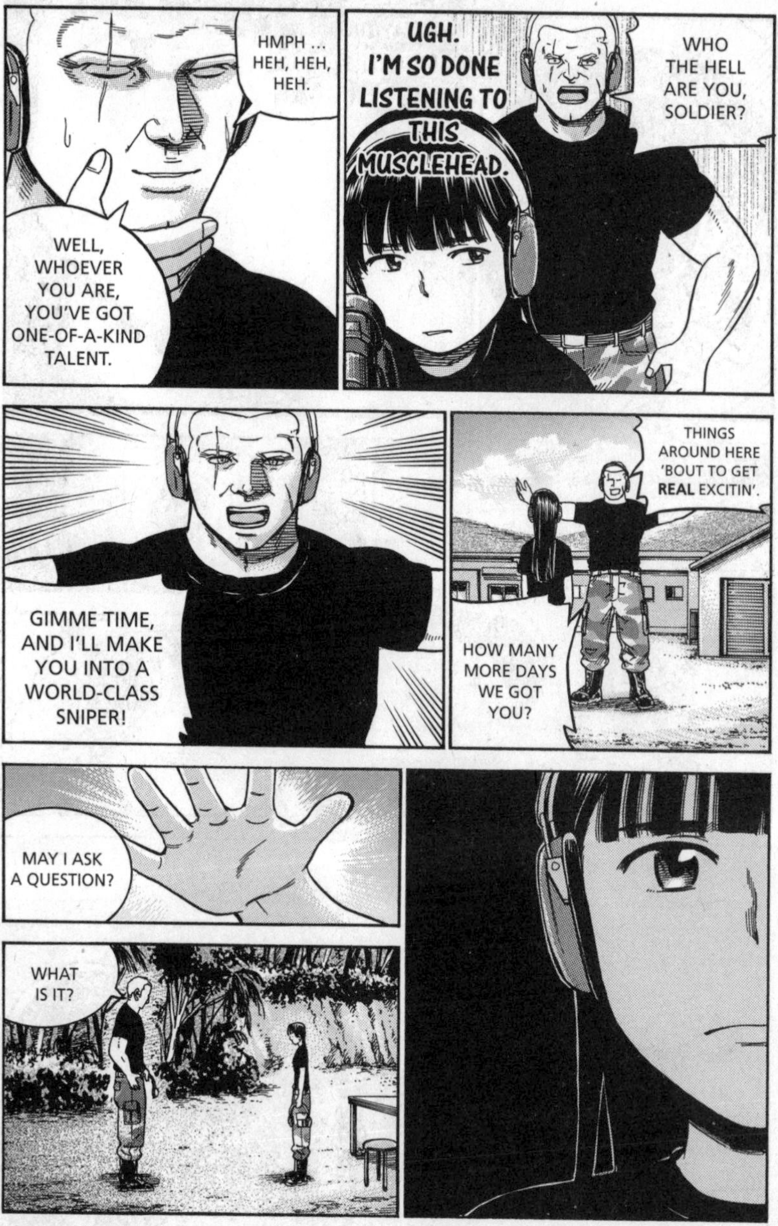
WHO THE HELL ARE YOU, SOLDIER?
UGH. I'M SO DONE LISTENING TO THIS MUSCLEHEAD.
HMPH ... HEH, HEH, HEH.
WELL, WHOEVER YOU ARE, YOU'VE GOT ONE-OF-A-KIND TALENT.
THINGS AROUND HERE 'BOUT TO GET **REAL** EXCITIN'.
HOW MANY MORE DAYS WE GOT YOU?
GIMME TIME, AND I'LL MAKE YOU INTO A WORLD-CLASS SNIPER!
MAY I ASK A QUESTION?
WHAT IS IT?

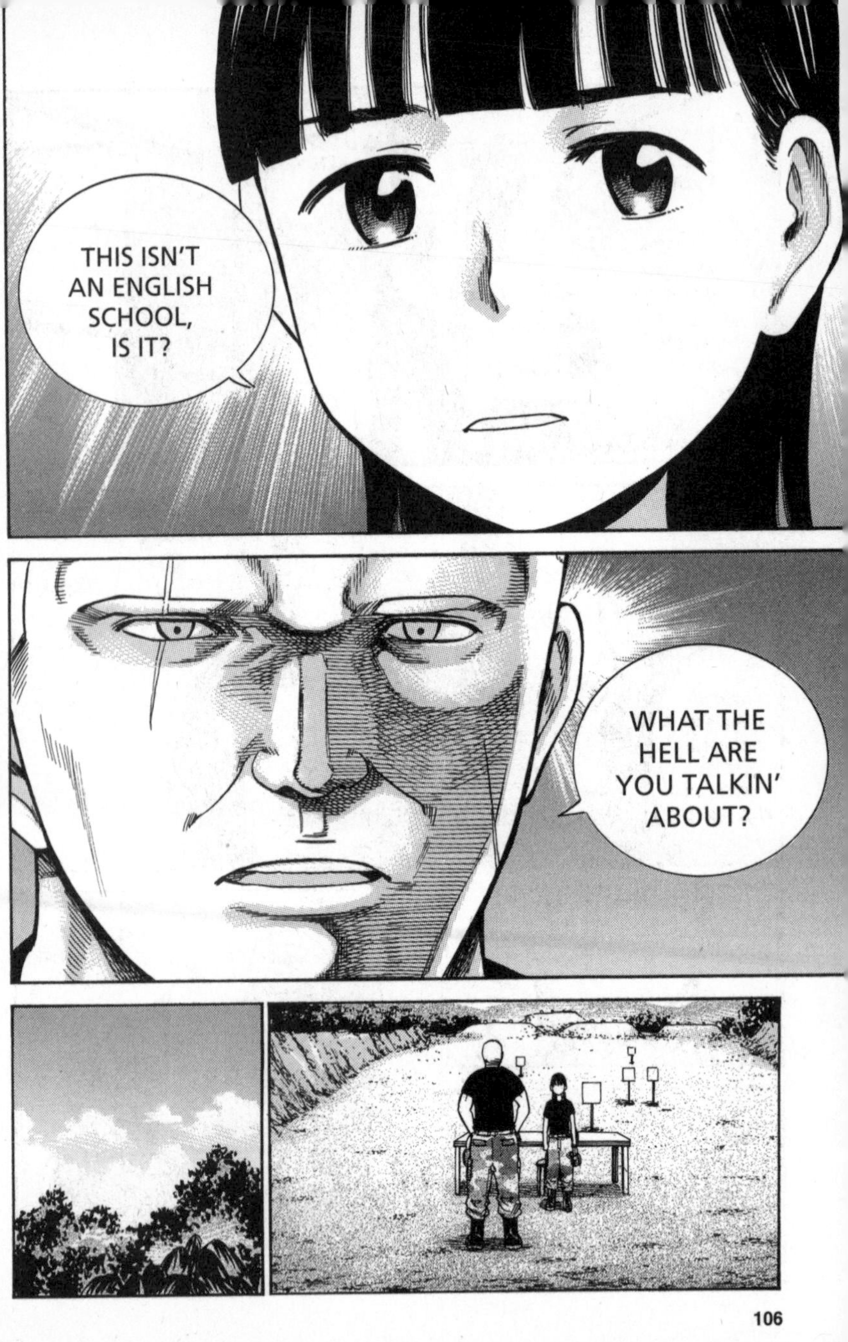
THIS ISN'T AN ENGLISH SCHOOL, IS IT?
WHAT THE HELL ARE YOU TALKIN' ABOUT?

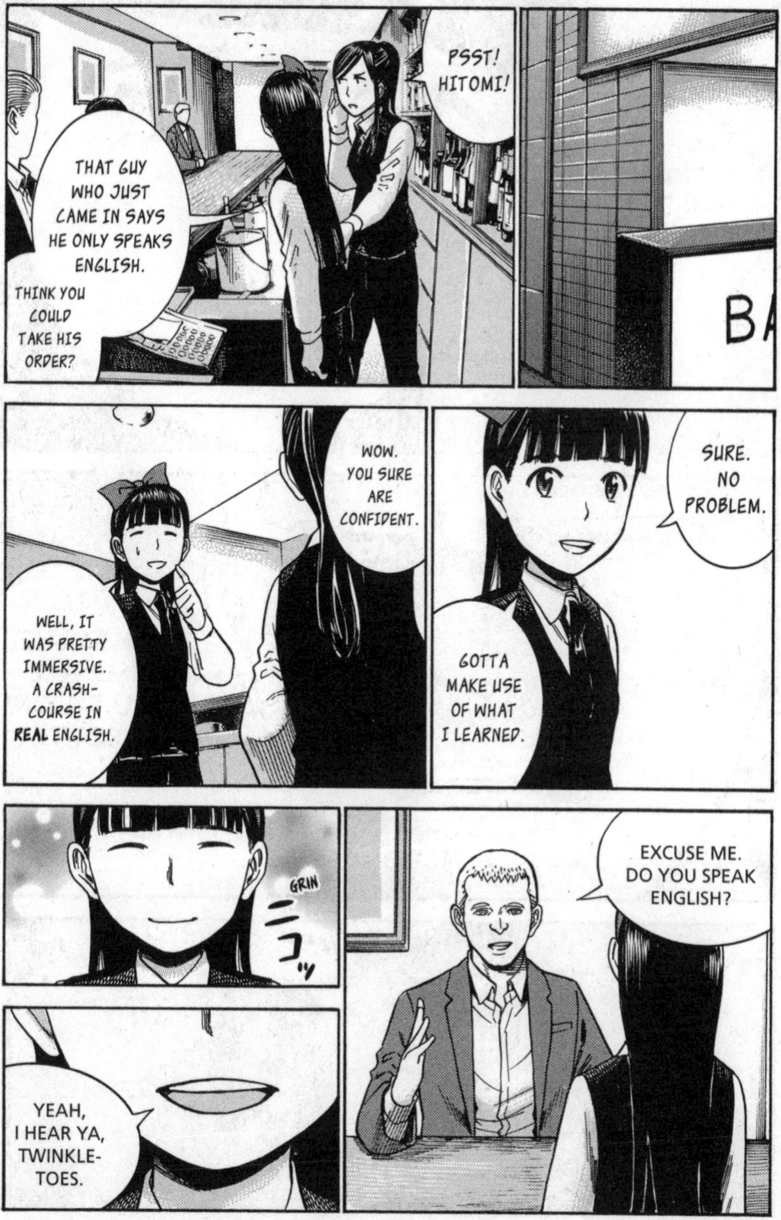
BA
PSST! HITOMI!
THAT GUY WHO JUST CAME IN SAYS HE ONLY SPEAKS ENGLISH.
THINK YOU COULD TAKE HIS ORDER?
SURE. NO PROBLEM.
GOTTA MAKE USE OF WHAT I LEARNED.
WOW. YOU SURE ARE CONFIDENT.
WELL, IT WAS PRETTY IMMERSIVE. A CRASH-COURSE IN **REAL** ENGLISH.
EXCUSE ME. DO YOU SPEAK ENGLISH?
GRIN
ニコッ
YEAH, I HEAR YA, TWINKLE-TOES.

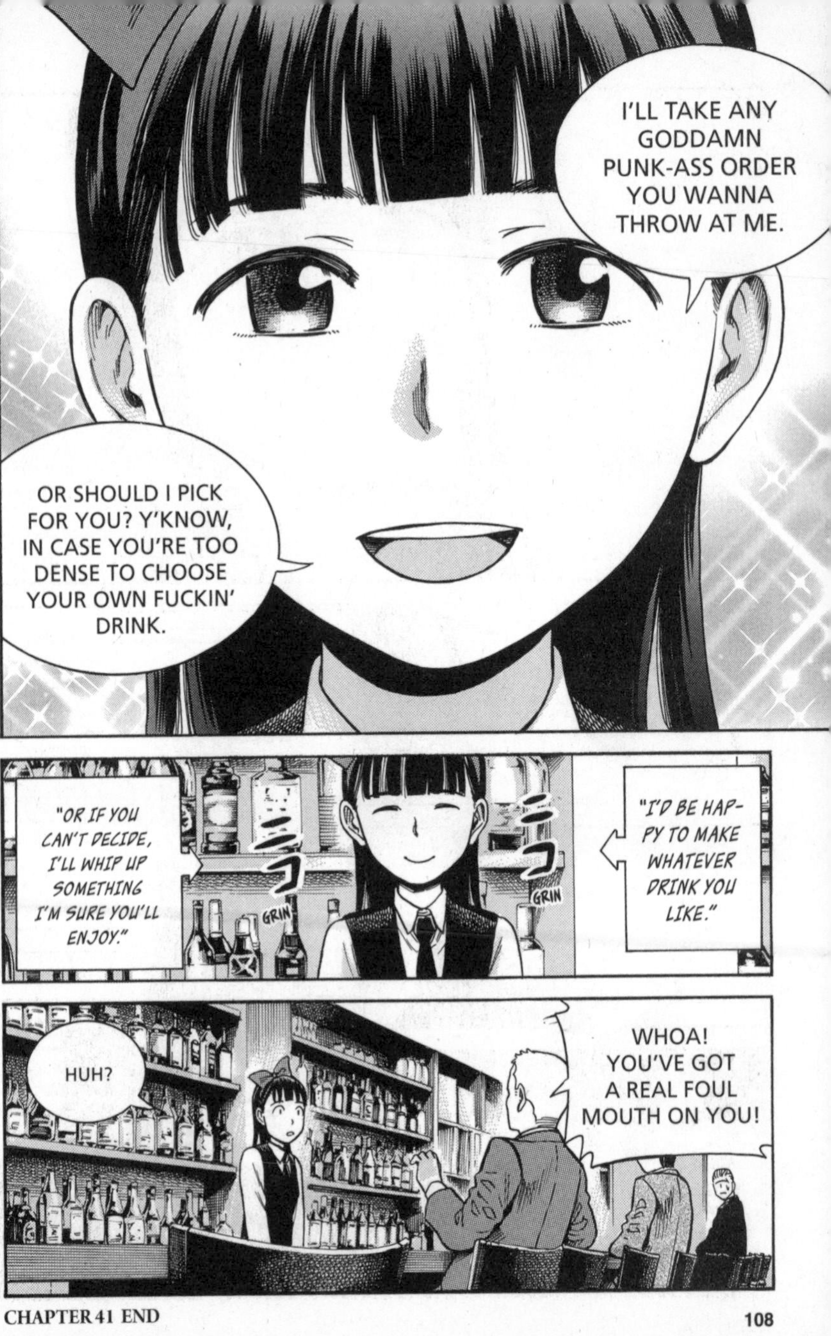
I'LL TAKE ANY GODDAMN PUNK-ASS ORDER YOU WANNA THROW AT ME.
OR SHOULD I PICK FOR YOU? Y'KNOW, IN CASE YOU'RE TOO DENSE TO CHOOSE YOUR OWN FUCKIN' DRINK.
"I'D BE HAP-PY TO MAKE WHATEVER DRINK YOU LIKE."
GRIN
GRIN
"OR IF YOU CAN'T DECIDE, I'LL WHIP UP SOMETHING I'M SURE YOU'LL ENJOY."
WHOA! YOU'VE GOT A REAL FOUL MOUTH ON YOU!
HUH?

CHAPTER 41 END

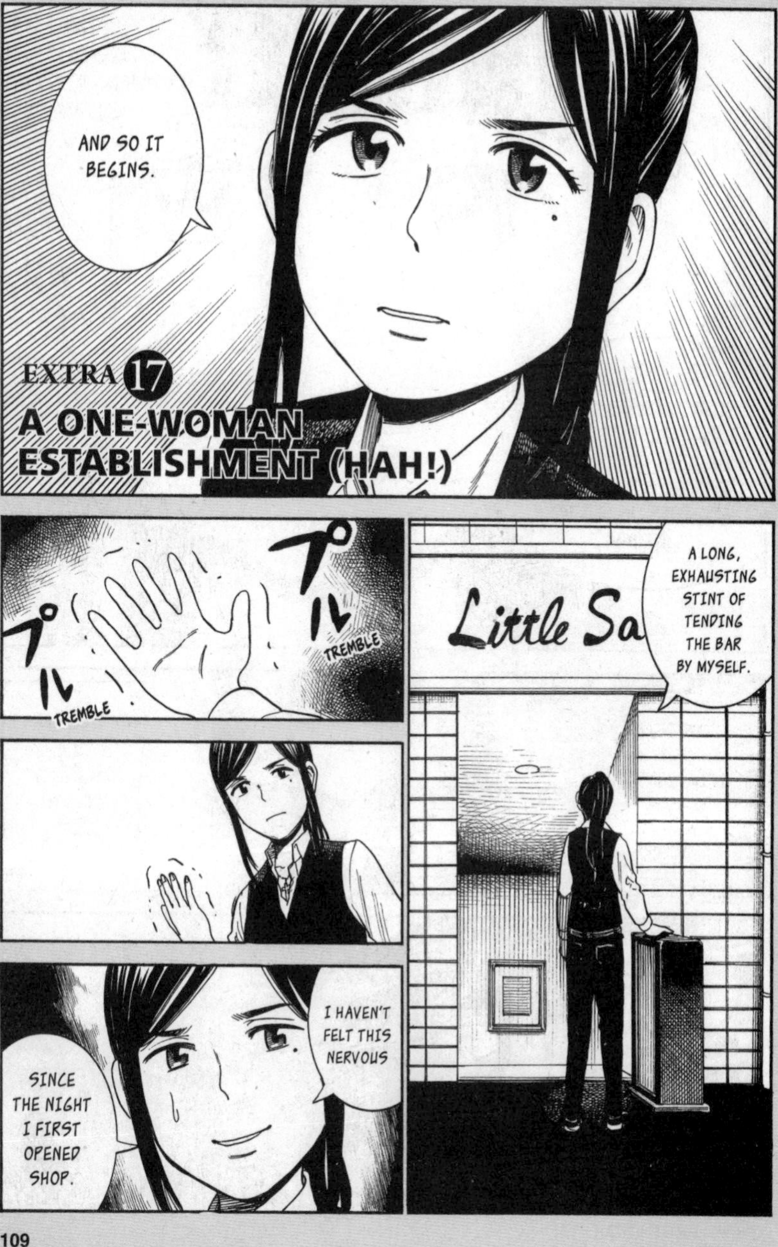
AND SO IT BEGINS.
EXTRA 17
A ONE-WOMAN ESTABLISHMENT (HAH!)
Little Sa
A LONG, EXHAUSTING STINT OF TENDING THE BAR BY MYSELF.
プル
TREMBLE
プル
TREMBLE
I HAVEN'T FELT THIS NERVOUS
SINCE THE NIGHT I FIRST OPENED SHOP.

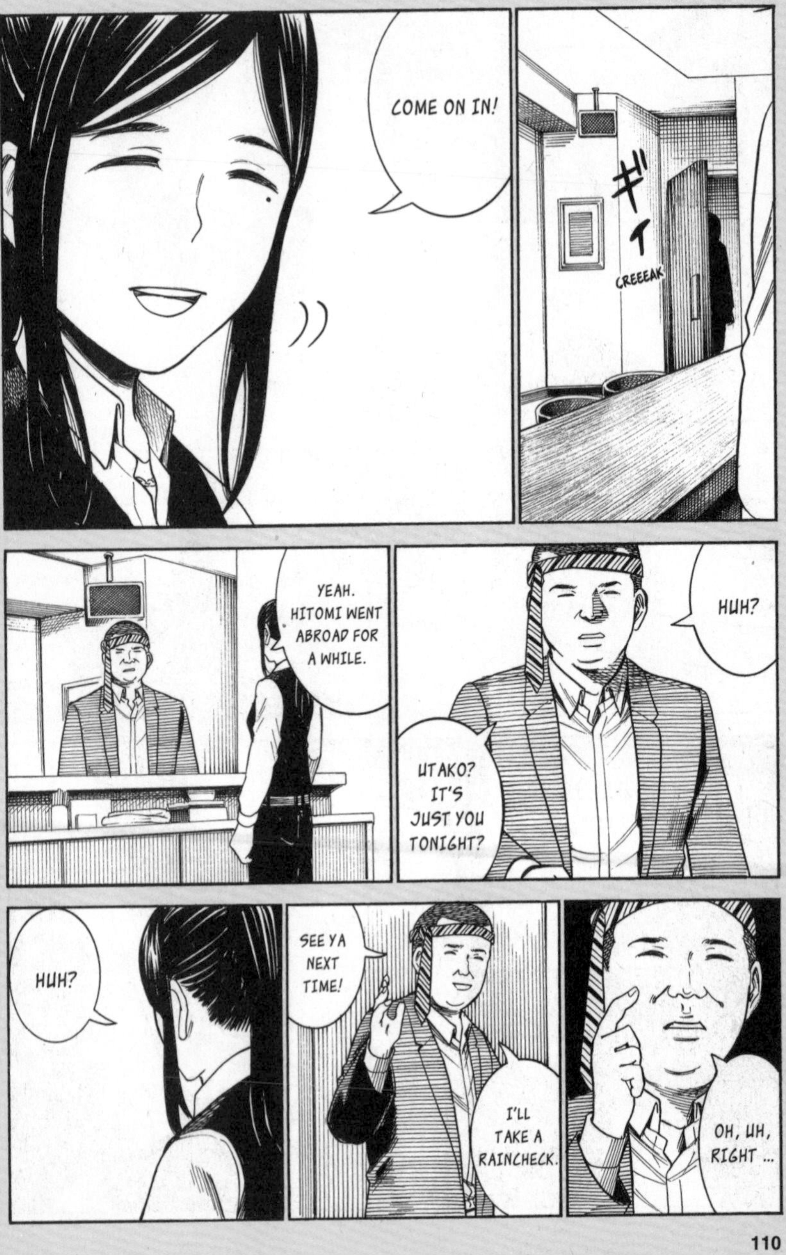
ギイ
CREEEAK
COME ON IN!
HUH?
UTAKO? IT'S JUST YOU TONIGHT?
YEAH. HITOMI WENT ABROAD FOR A WHILE.
OH, UH, RIGHT ...
SEE YA NEXT TIME!
I'LL TAKE A RAINCHECK.
HUH?

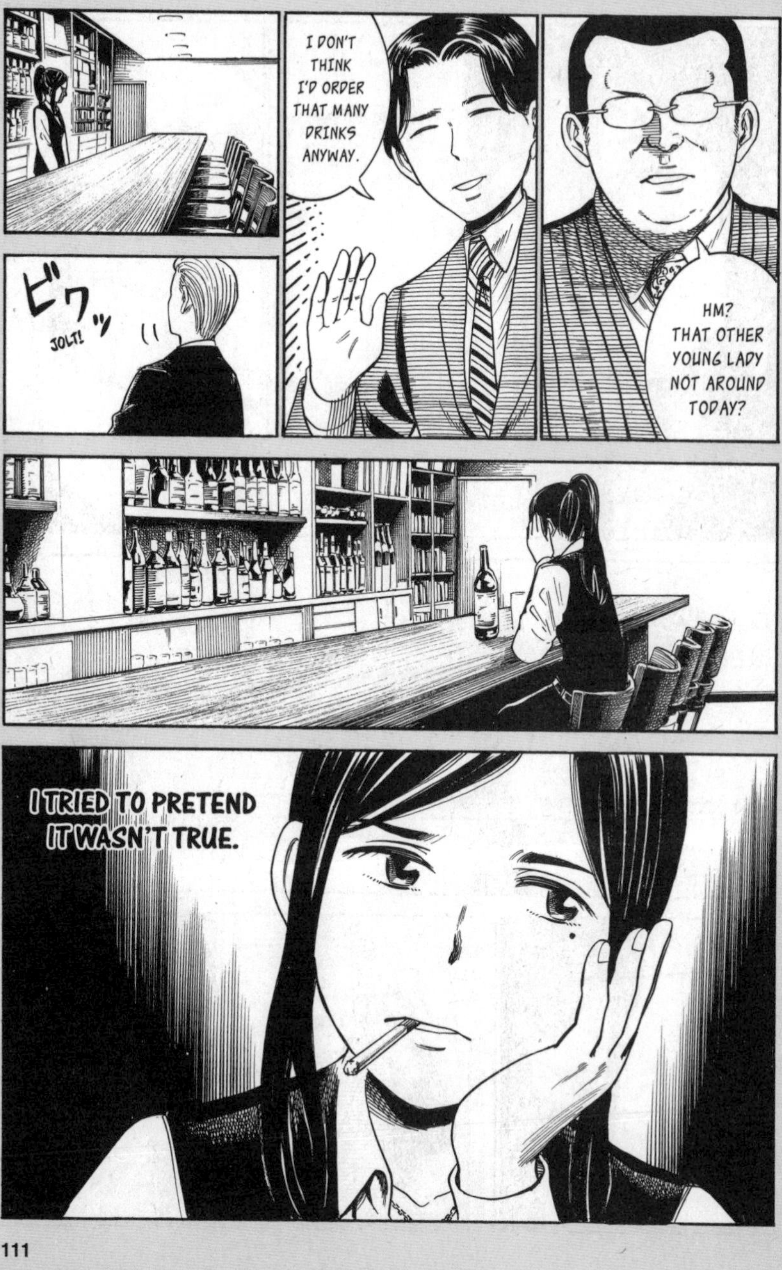
HM? THAT OTHER YOUNG LADY NOT AROUND TODAY?
I DON'T THINK I'D ORDER THAT MANY DRINKS ANYWAY.
ビクッ
JOLT!
I TRIED TO PRETEND IT WASN'T TRUE.

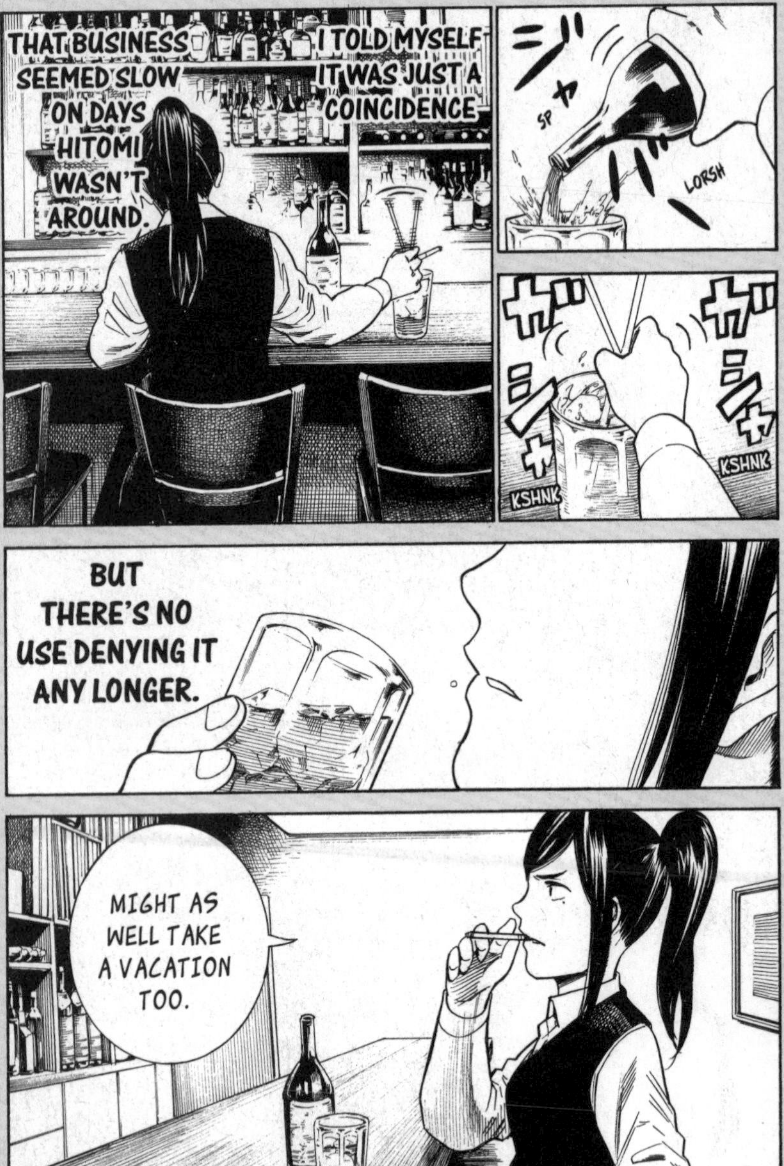
ジャ
SP
LORSH
ガシャ
KSHNK
ガシャ
KSHNK
I TOLD MYSELF IT WAS JUST A COINCIDENCE
THAT BUSINESS SEEMED SLOW ON DAYS HITOMI WASN'T AROUND.
BUT THERE'S NO USE DENYING IT ANY LONGER.
MIGHT AS WELL TAKE A VACATION TOO.

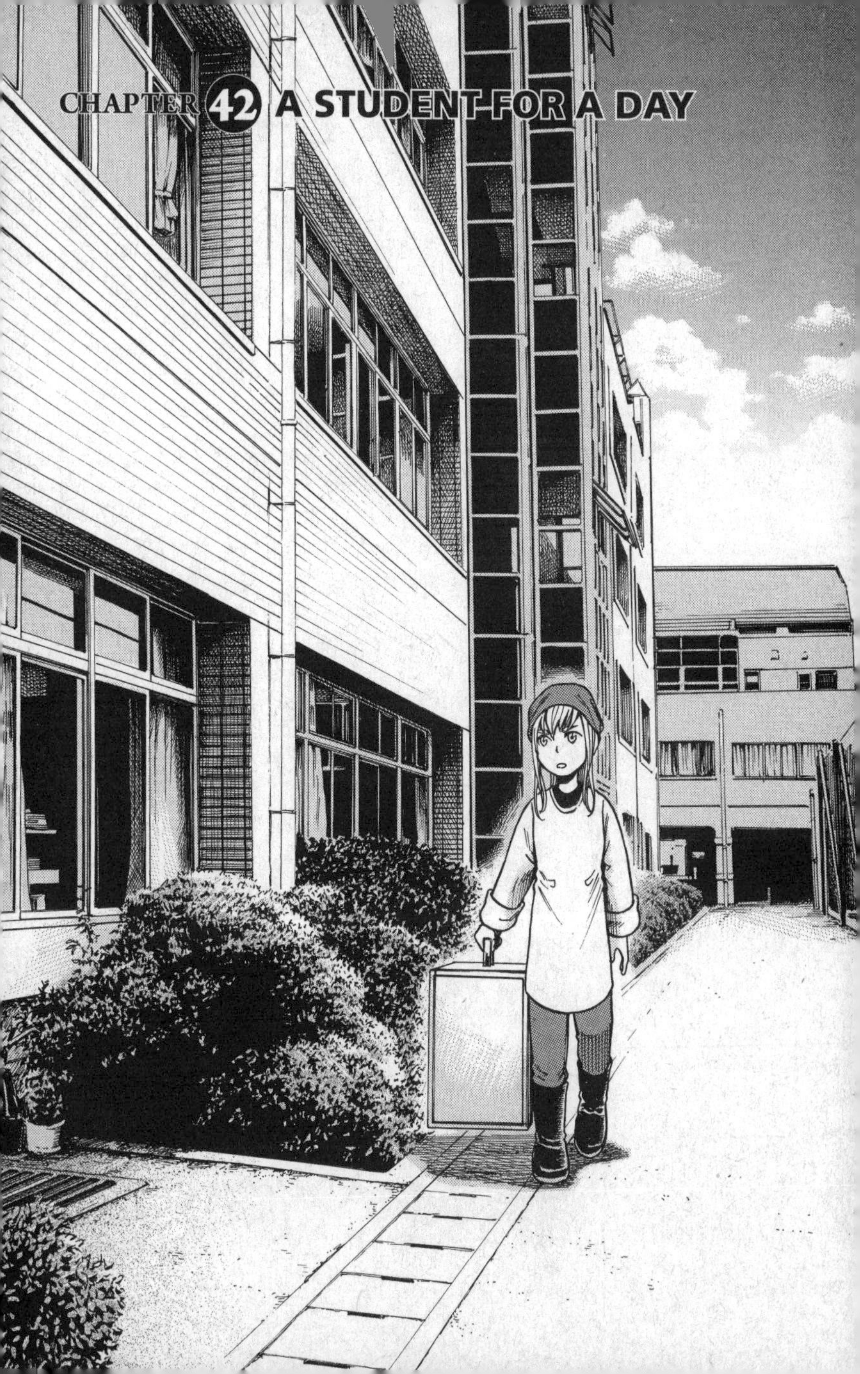
CHAPTER 42 A STUDENT FOR A DAY

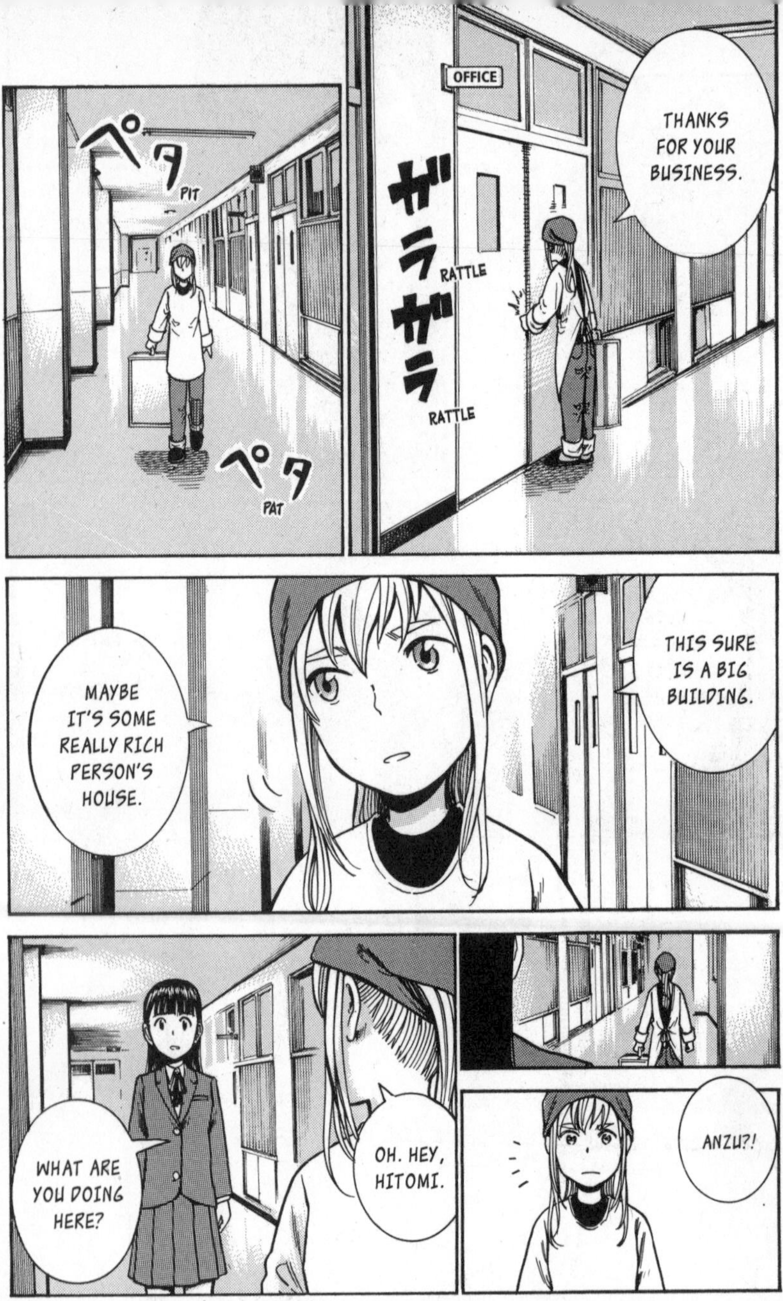
OFFICE
ガラ
RATTLE
ガラ
RATTLE
THANKS FOR YOUR BUSINESS.
ペタ
PIT
ペタ
PAT
THIS SURE IS A BIG BUILDING.
MAYBE IT'S SOME REALLY RICH PERSON'S HOUSE.
ANZU?!
OH. HEY, HITOMI.
WHAT ARE YOU DOING HERE?

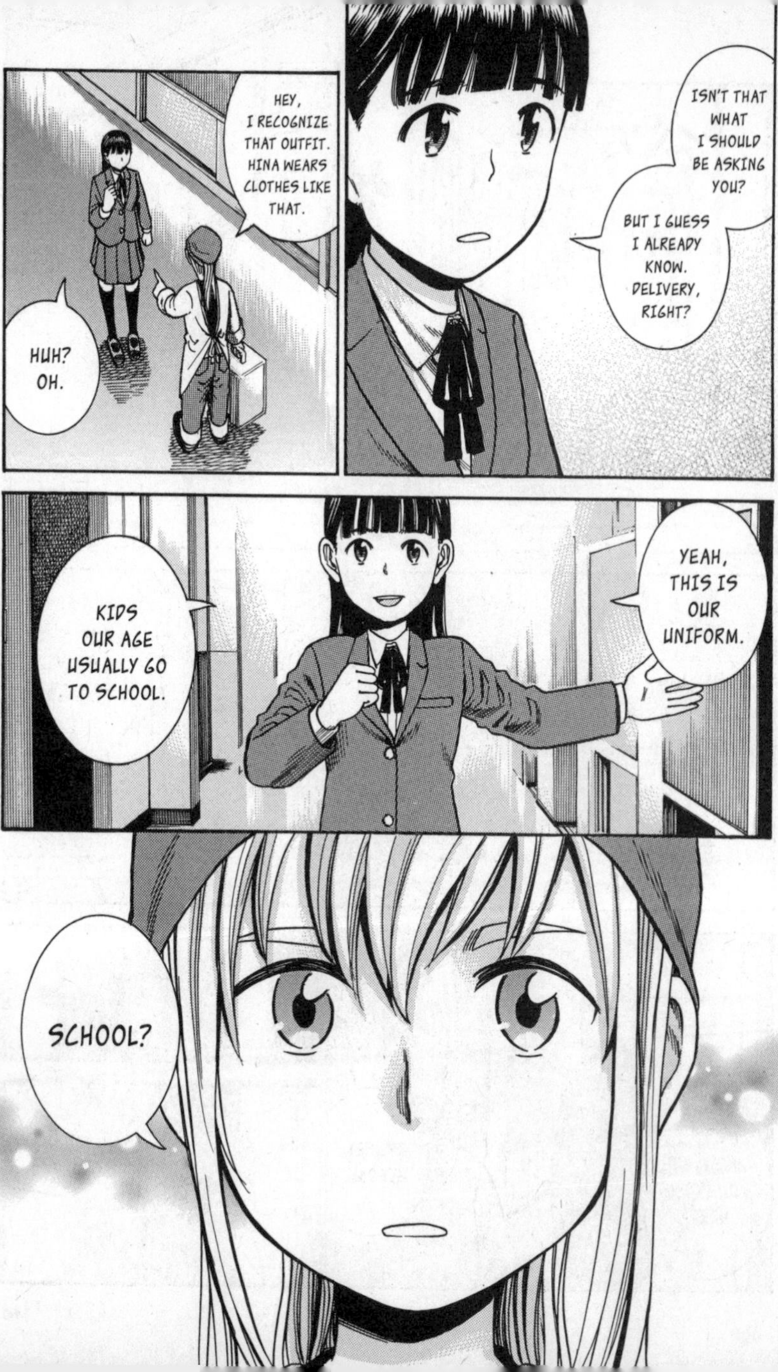
ISN'T THAT WHAT I SHOULD BE ASKING YOU?
BUT I GUESS I ALREADY KNOW. DELIVERY, RIGHT?
HEY, I RECOGNIZE THAT OUTFIT. HINA WEARS CLOTHES LIKE THAT.
HUH? OH.
YEAH, THIS IS OUR UNIFORM.
KIDS OUR AGE USUALLY GO TO SCHOOL.
SCHOOL?

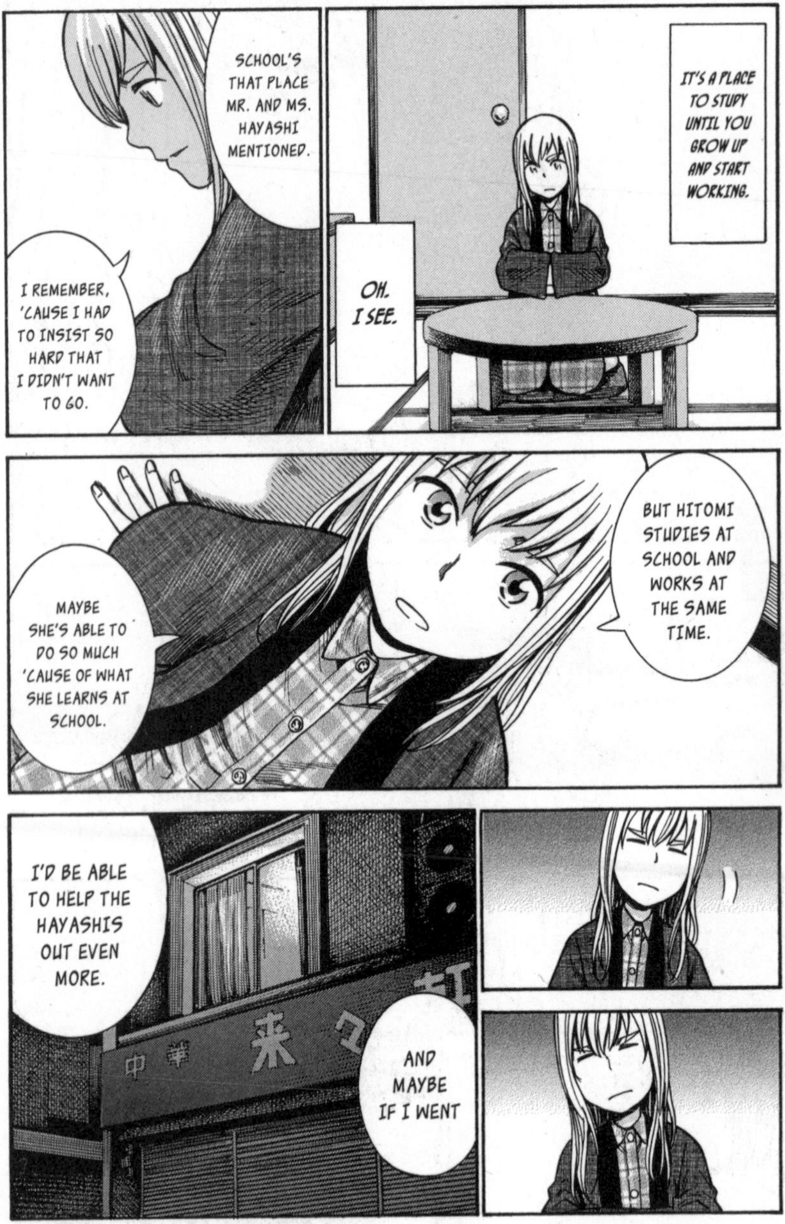
IT'S A PLACE TO STUDY UNTIL YOU GROW UP AND START WORKING.
OH. I SEE.
SCHOOL'S THAT PLACE MR. AND MS. HAYASHI MENTIONED.
I REMEMBER, 'CAUSE I HAD TO INSIST SO HARD THAT I DIDN'T WANT TO GO.
BUT HITOMI STUDIES AT SCHOOL AND WORKS AT THE SAME TIME.
MAYBE SHE'S ABLE TO DO SO MUCH 'CAUSE OF WHAT SHE LEARNS AT SCHOOL.
I'D BE ABLE TO HELP THE HAYASHIS OUT EVEN MORE.
AND MAYBE IF I WENT

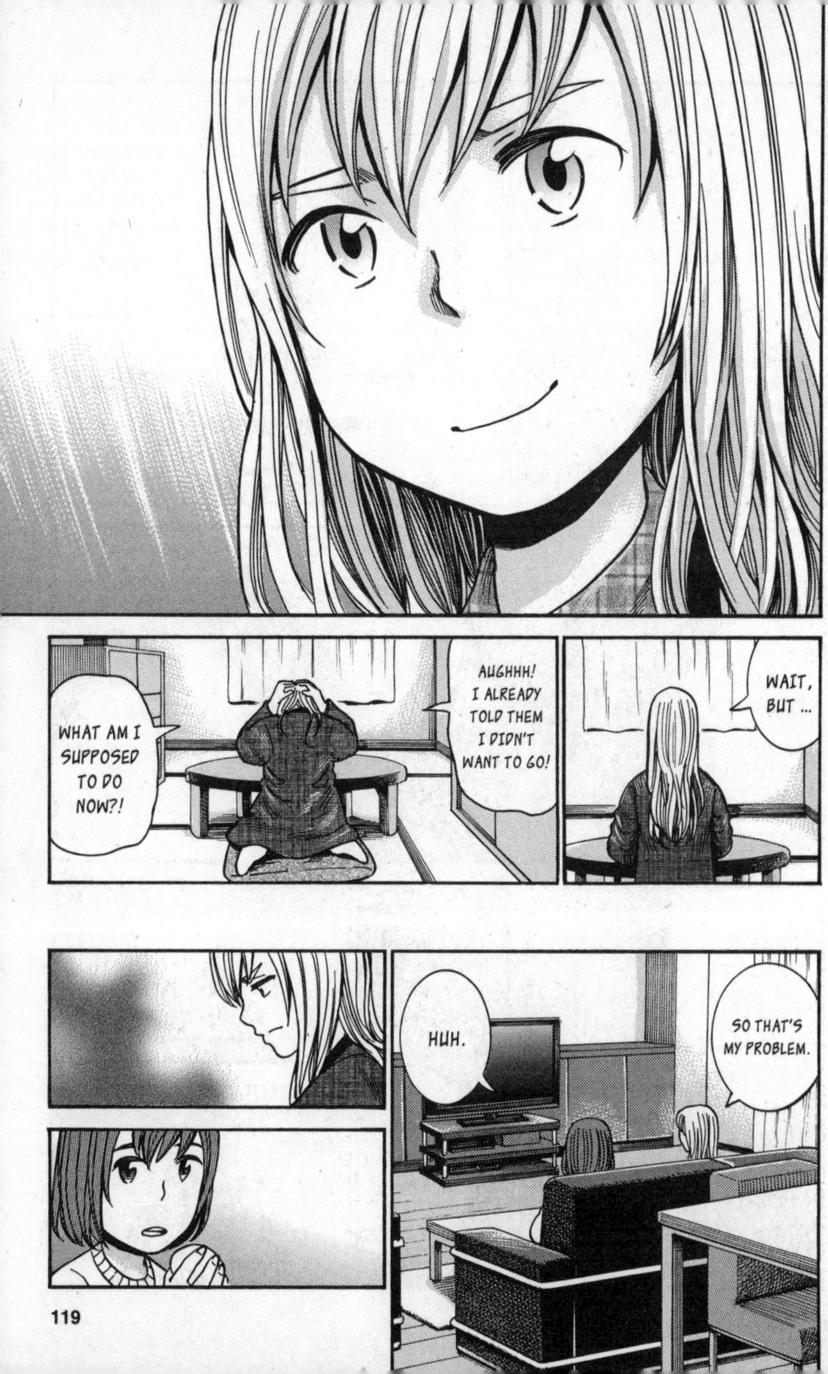
WAIT, BUT ...
AUGHHH! I ALREADY TOLD THEM I DIDN'T WANT TO GO!
WHAT AM I SUPPOSED TO DO NOW?!
SO THAT'S MY PROBLEM.
HUH.

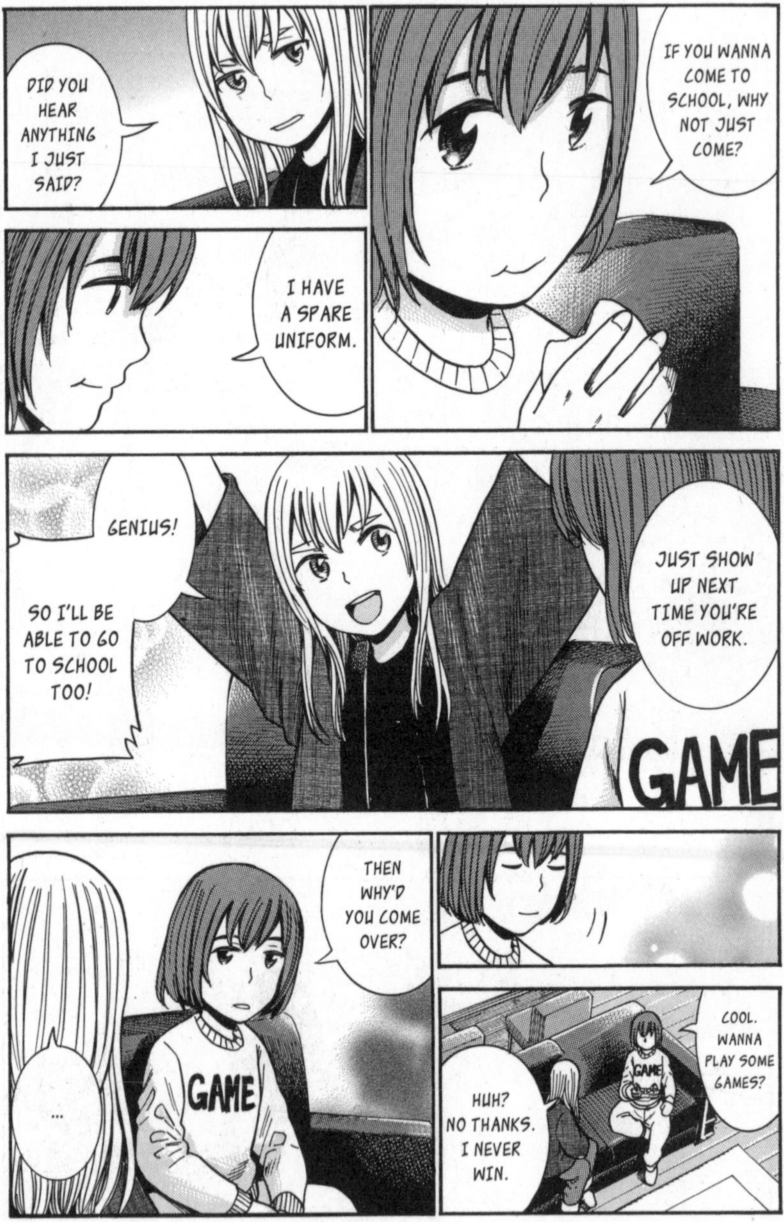
IF YOU WANNA COME TO SCHOOL, WHY NOT JUST COME?
DID YOU HEAR ANYTHING I JUST SAID?
I HAVE A SPARE UNIFORM.
JUST SHOW UP NEXT TIME YOU'RE OFF WORK.
GAME
GENIUS!
SO I'LL BE ABLE TO GO TO SCHOOL TOO!
COOL. WANNA PLAY SOME GAMES?
GAME
HUH? NO THANKS. I NEVER WIN.
THEN WHY'D YOU COME OVER?
GAME
...

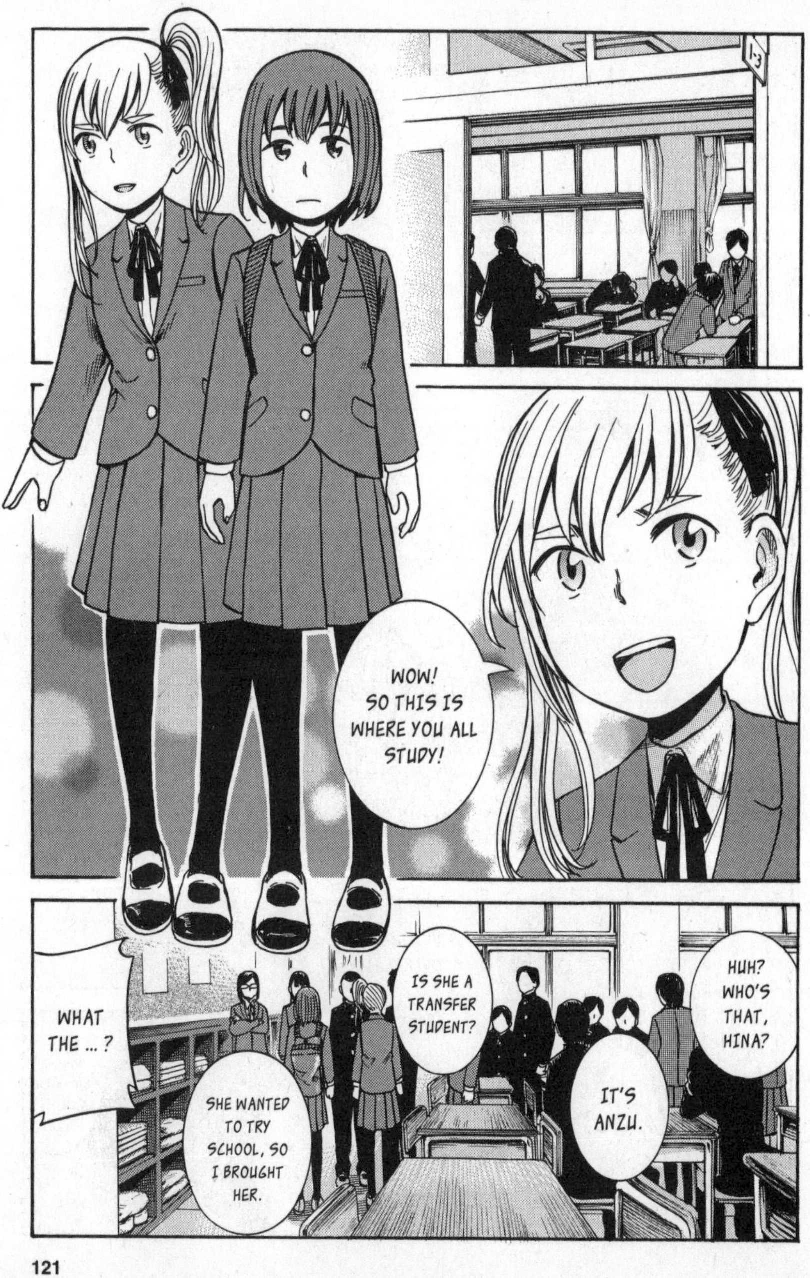
1-3
WOW! SO THIS IS WHERE YOU ALL STUDY!
HUH? WHO'S THAT, HINA?
IT'S ANZU.
IS SHE A TRANSFER STUDENT?
SHE WANTED TO TRY SCHOOL, SO I BROUGHT HER.
WHAT THE ...?

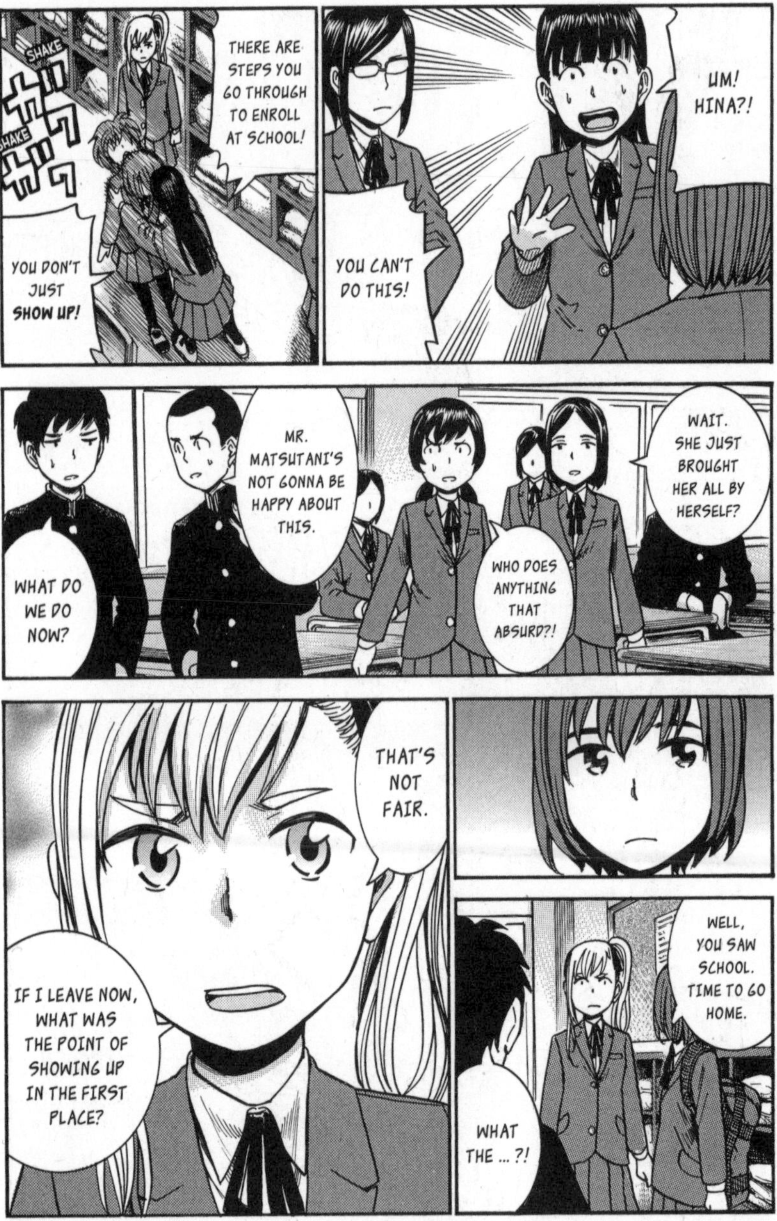
UM! HINA?!
YOU CAN'T DO THIS!
THERE ARE STEPS YOU GO THROUGH TO ENROLL AT SCHOOL!
SHAKE
SHAKE
YOU DON'T JUST SHOW UP!
WAIT. SHE JUST BROUGHT HER ALL BY HERSELF?
WHO DOES ANYTHING THAT ABSURD?!
MR. MATSUTANI'S NOT GONNA BE HAPPY ABOUT THIS.
WHAT DO WE DO NOW?
WELL, YOU SAW SCHOOL. TIME TO GO HOME.
WHAT THE ... ?!
THAT'S NOT FAIR.
IF I LEAVE NOW, WHAT WAS THE POINT OF SHOWING UP IN THE FIRST PLACE?

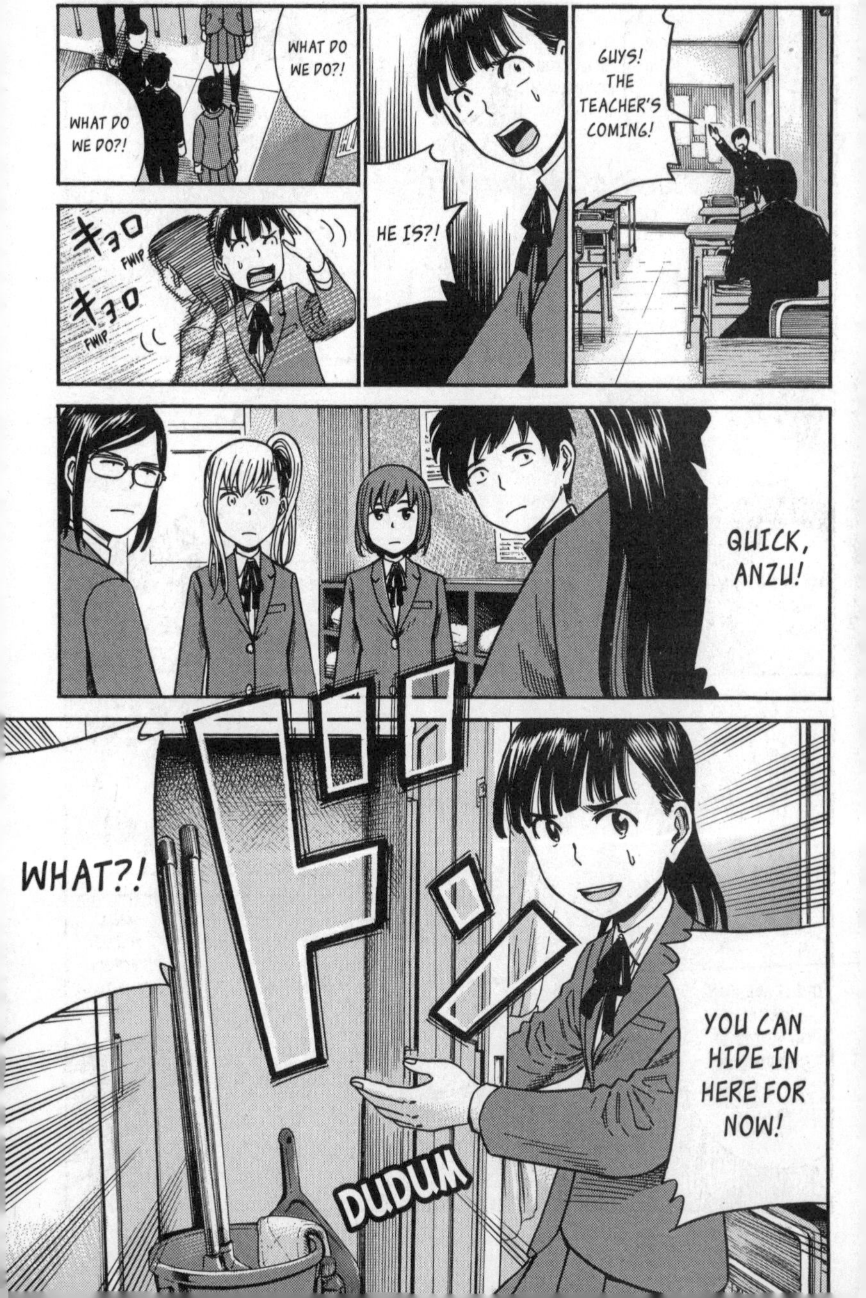
GUYS! THE TEACHER'S COMING!
HE IS?!
WHAT DO WE DO?!
WHAT DO WE DO?!
キョロ
FWIP
キョロ
FWIP
QUICK, ANZU!
YOU CAN HIDE IN HERE FOR NOW!
DUDUM
WHAT?!

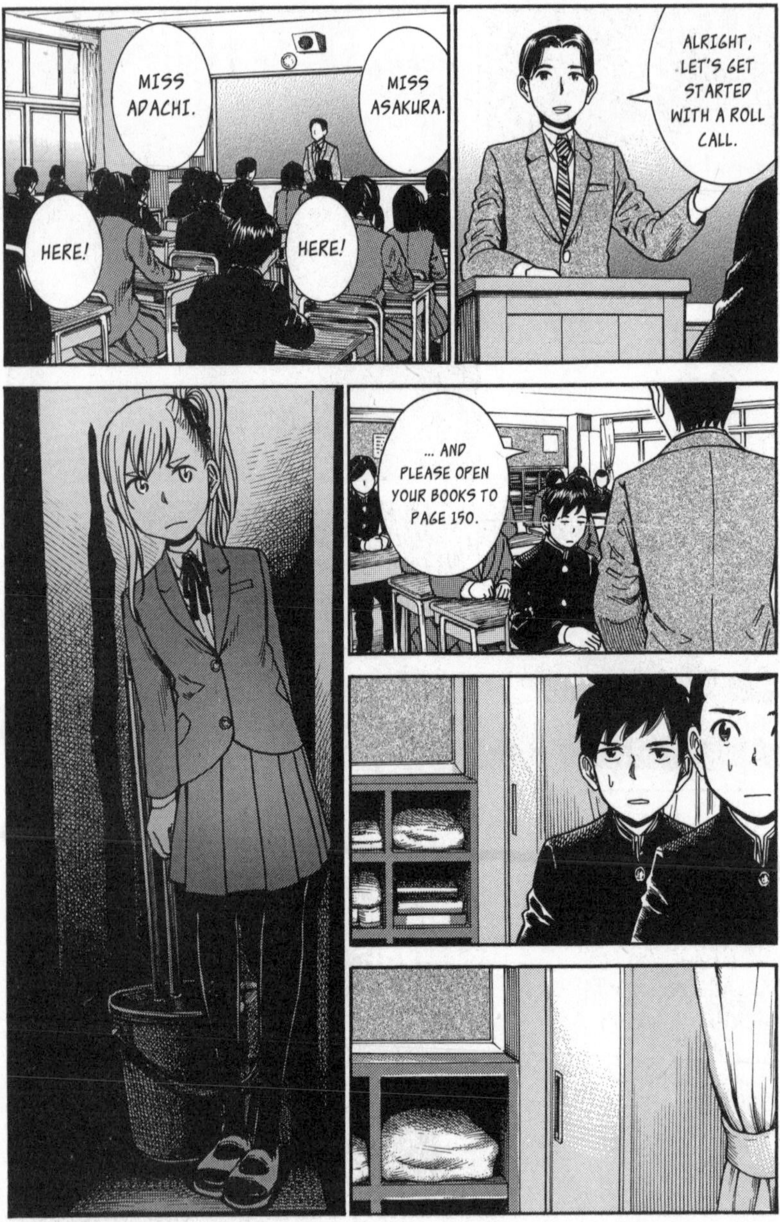
ALRIGHT, LET'S GET STARTED WITH A ROLL CALL.
MISS ASAKURA.
HERE!
MISS ADACHI.
HERE!
... AND PLEASE OPEN YOUR BOOKS TO PAGE 150.

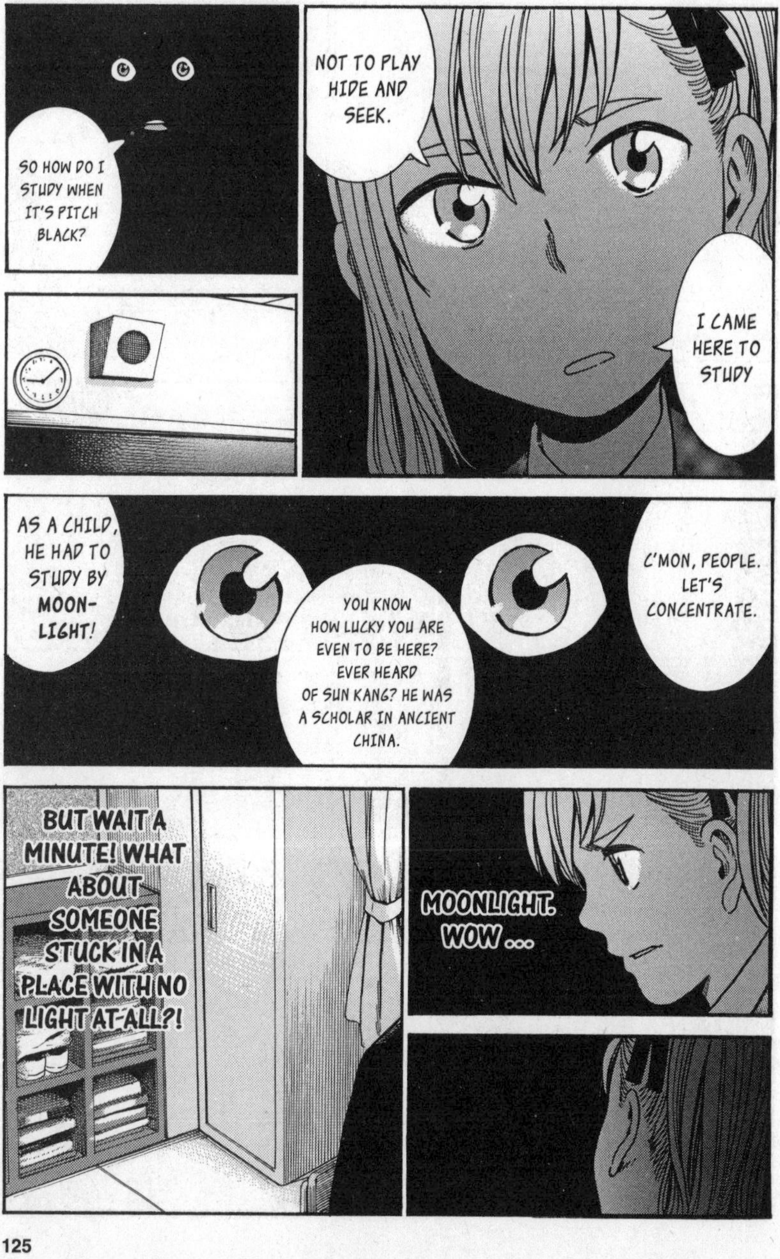
I CAME HERE TO STUDY
NOT TO PLAY HIDE AND SEEK.
SO HOW DO I STUDY WHEN IT'S PITCH BLACK?
C'MON, PEOPLE. LET'S CONCENTRATE.
YOU KNOW HOW LUCKY YOU ARE EVEN TO BE HERE? EVER HEARD OF SUN KANG? HE WAS A SCHOLAR IN ANCIENT CHINA.
AS A CHILD, HE HAD TO STUDY BY MOON-LIGHT!
MOONLIGHT. WOW ...
BUT WAIT A MINUTE! WHAT ABOUT SOMEONE STUCK IN A PLACE WITH NO LIGHT AT ALL?!

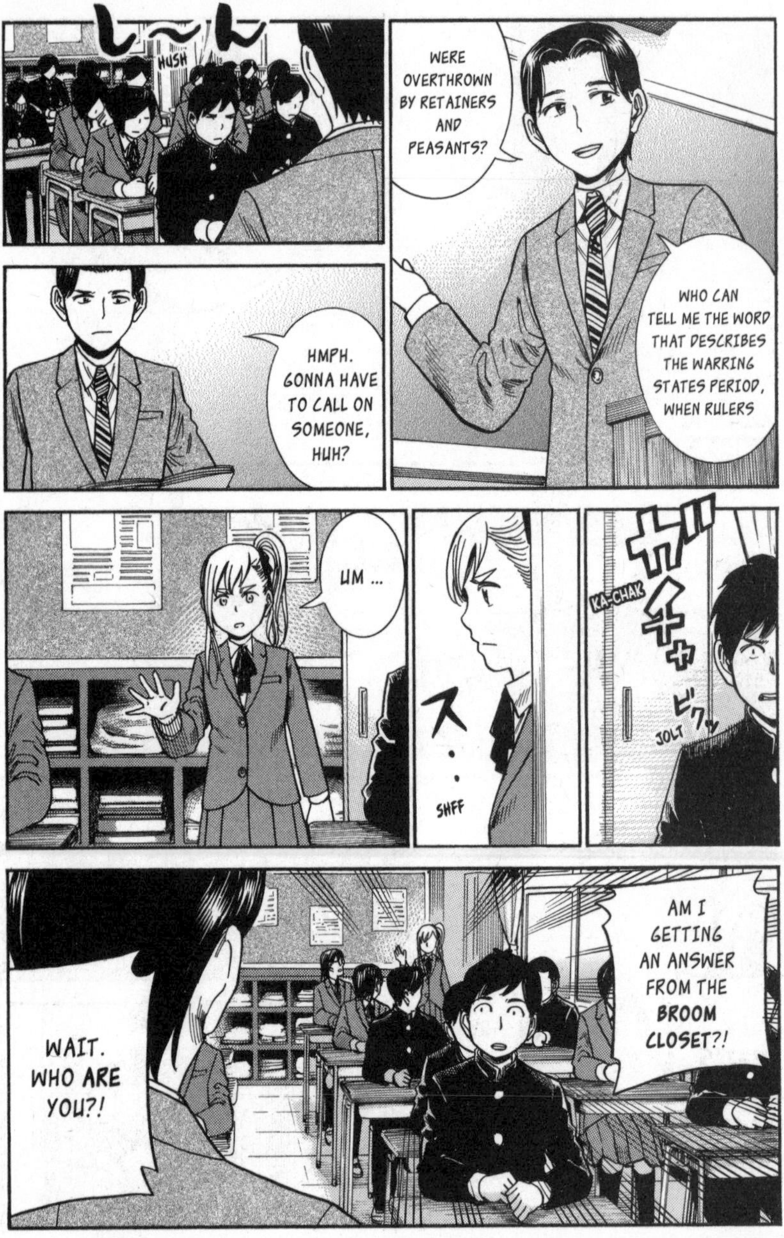
WHO CAN TELL ME THE WORD THAT DESCRIBES THE WARRING STATES PERIOD, WHEN RULERS
WERE OVERTHROWN BY RETAINERS AND PEASANTS?
しーん
HUSH
HMPH. GONNA HAVE TO CALL ON SOMEONE, HUH?
ガチャ
KA-CHAK
ビクッ
JOLT
ス…
SHFF
UM ...
AM I GETTING AN ANSWER FROM THE BROOM CLOSET?!
WAIT. WHO ARE YOU?!

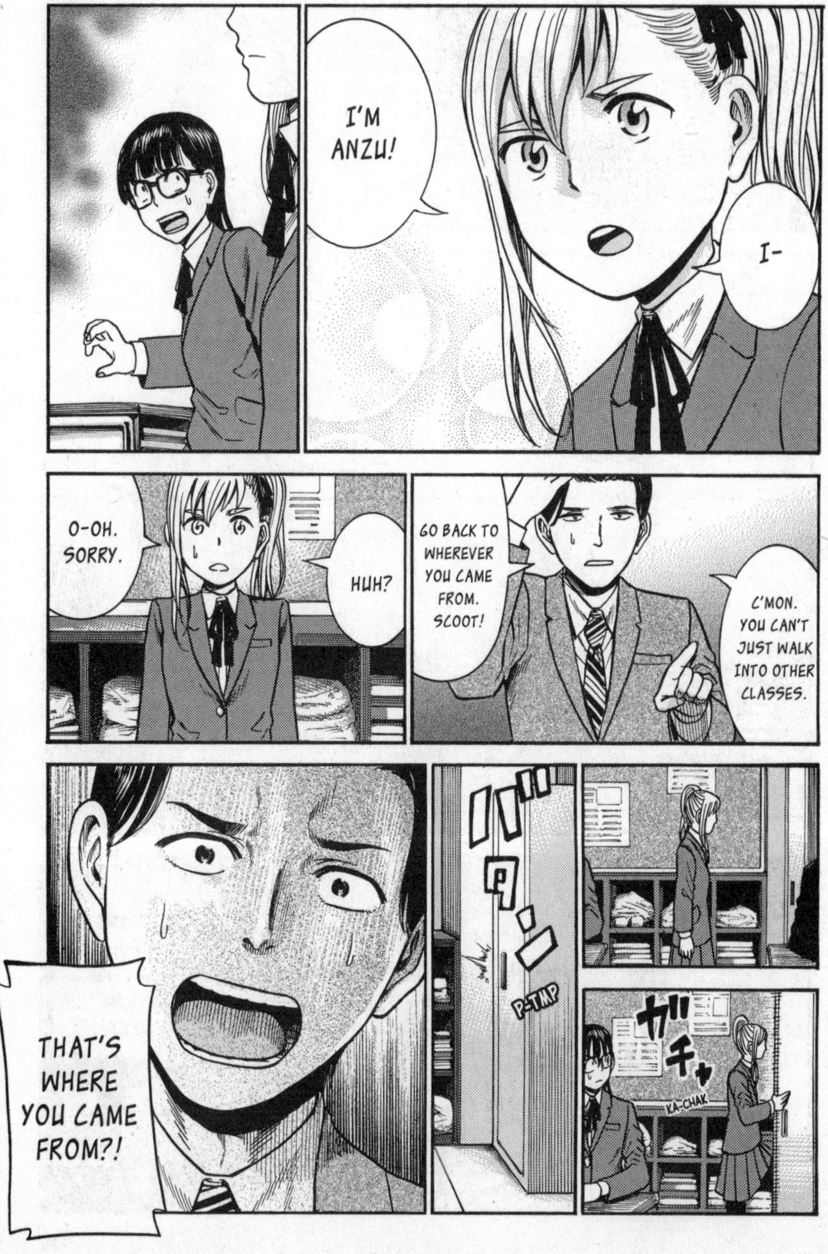
I-
I'M ANZU!
C'MON. YOU CAN'T JUST WALK INTO OTHER CLASSES.
GO BACK TO WHEREVER YOU CAME FROM. SCOOT!
HUH?
O-OH. SORRY.
ガチャ
KA-CHAK
バタン
P-TMP
THAT'S WHERE YOU CAME FROM?!

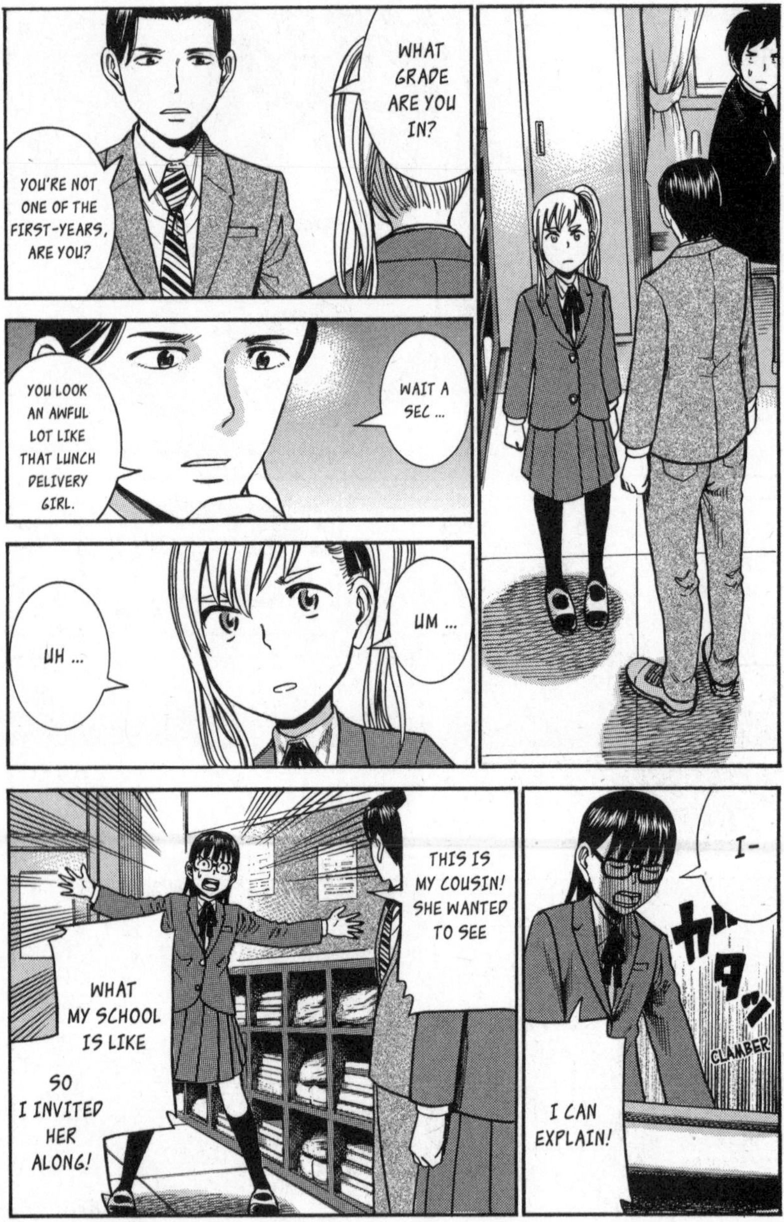
WHAT GRADE ARE YOU IN?
YOU'RE NOT ONE OF THE FIRST-YEARS, ARE YOU?
WAIT A SEC ...
YOU LOOK AN AWFUL LOT LIKE THAT LUNCH DELIVERY GIRL.
UM ...
UH ...
I-
カタッ
CLAMBER
I CAN EXPLAIN!
THIS IS MY COUSIN! SHE WANTED TO SEE
WHAT MY SCHOOL IS LIKE
SO I INVITED HER ALONG!

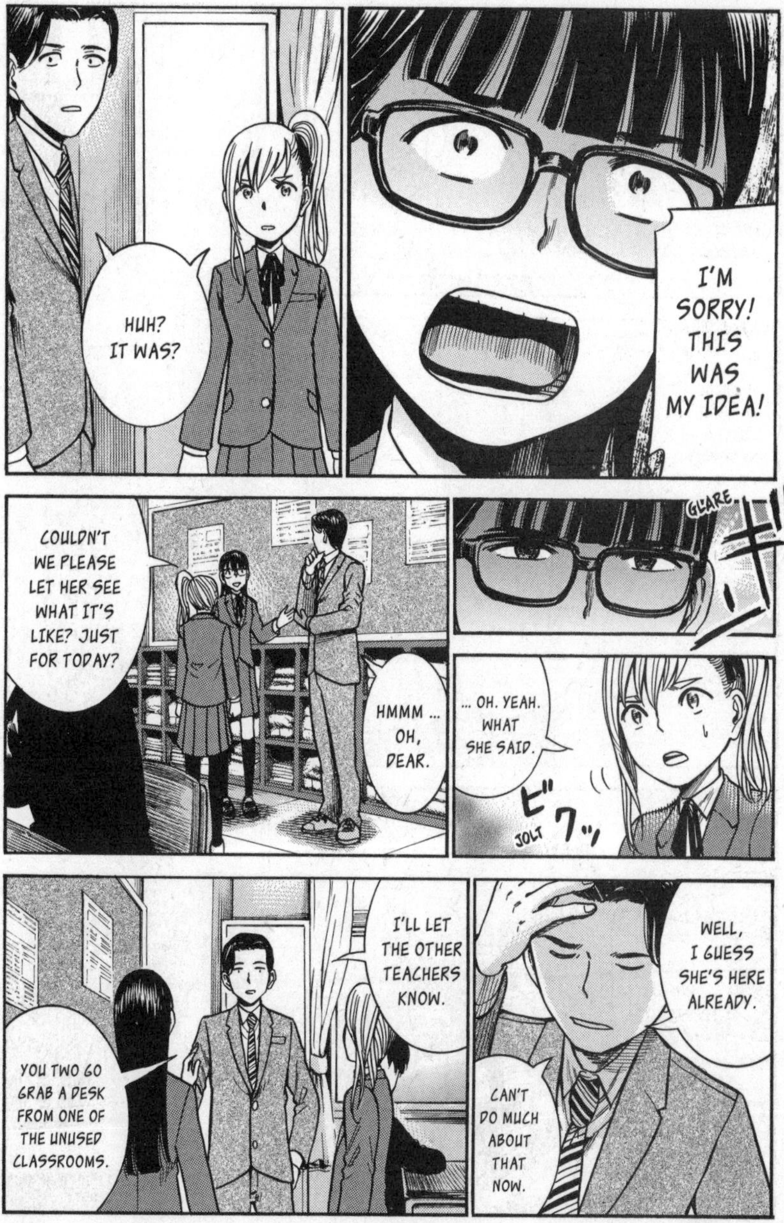
I'M SORRY! THIS WAS MY IDEA!
HUH? IT WAS?
GLARE
... OH. YEAH. WHAT SHE SAID.
JOLT
COULDN'T WE PLEASE LET HER SEE WHAT IT'S LIKE? JUST FOR TODAY?
HMMM ... OH, DEAR.
WELL, I GUESS SHE'S HERE ALREADY.
CAN'T DO MUCH ABOUT THAT NOW.
I'LL LET THE OTHER TEACHERS KNOW.
YOU TWO GO GRAB A DESK FROM ONE OF THE UNUSED CLASSROOMS.

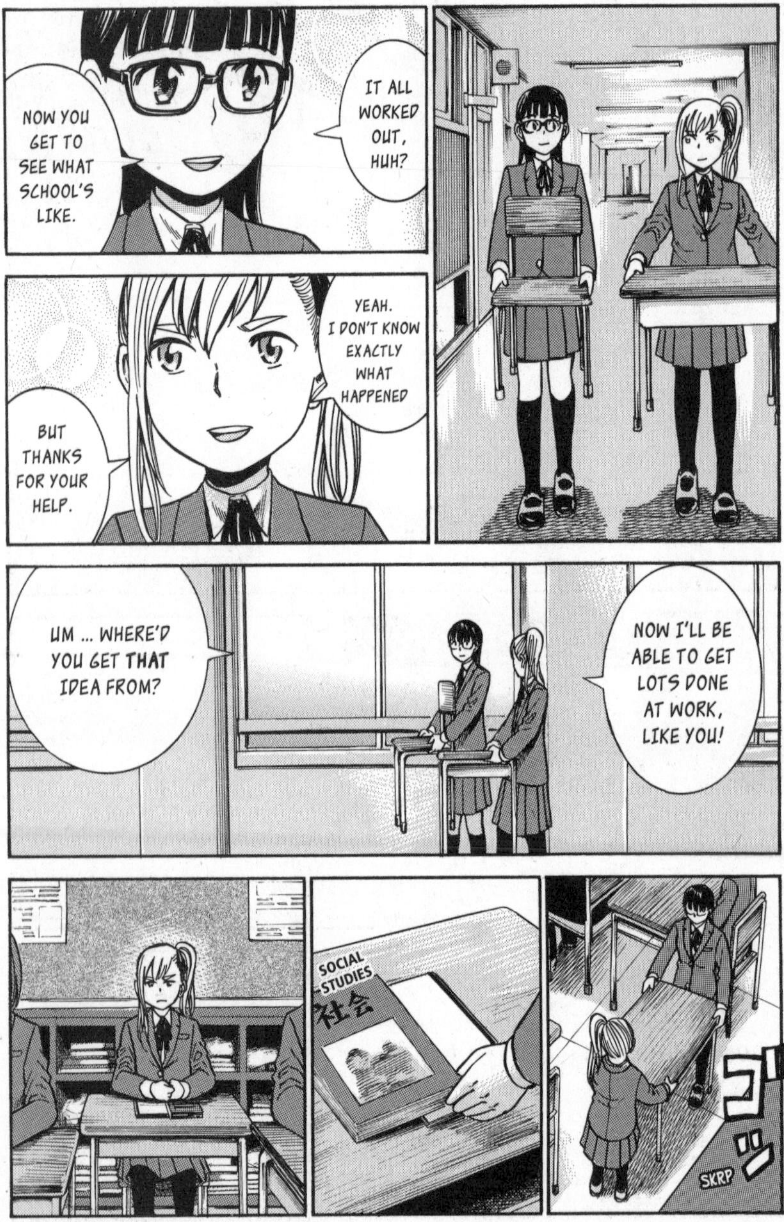
IT ALL WORKED OUT, HUH?
NOW YOU GET TO SEE WHAT SCHOOL'S LIKE.
YEAH. I DON'T KNOW EXACTLY WHAT HAPPENED
BUT THANKS FOR YOUR HELP.
NOW I'LL BE ABLE TO GET LOTS DONE AT WORK, LIKE YOU!
UM ... WHERE'D YOU GET THAT IDEA FROM?
ゴッ
SKRP
SOCIAL STUDIES
社会

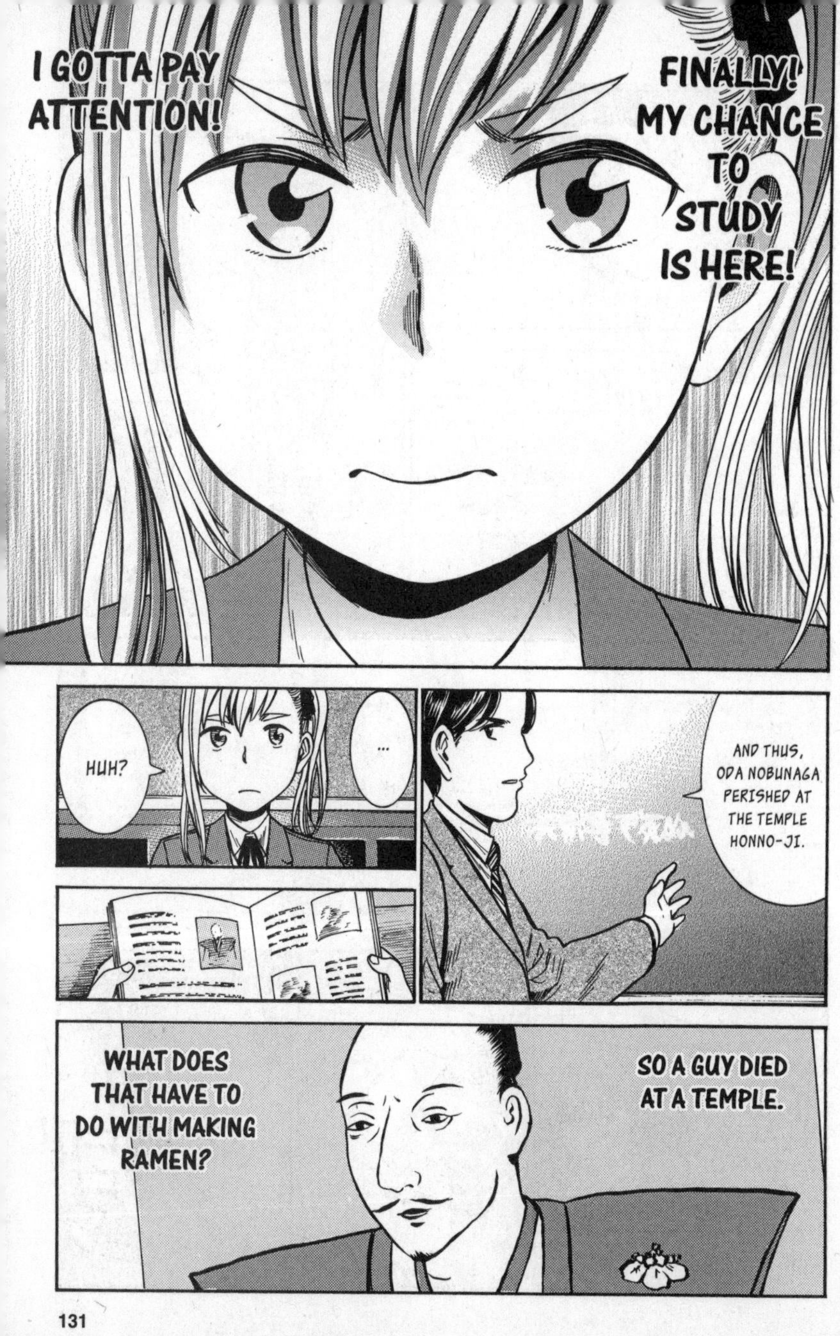
FINALLY! MY CHANCE TO STUDY IS HERE!
I GOTTA PAY ATTENTION!
AND THUS, ODA NOBUNAGA PERISHED AT THE TEMPLE HONNO-JI.
...
HUH?
SO A GUY DIED AT A TEMPLE.
WHAT DOES THAT HAVE TO DO WITH MAKING RAMEN?

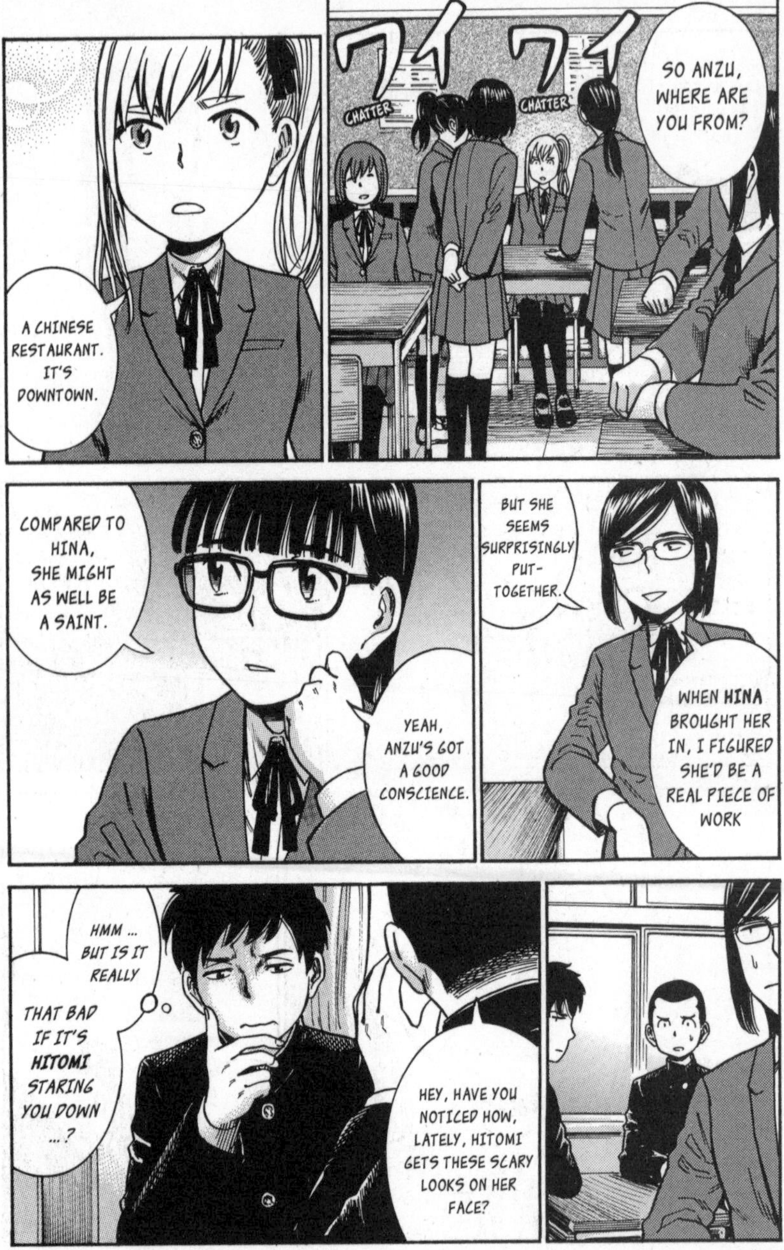

ワイ ワイ
CHATTER
CHATTER
SO ANZU, WHERE ARE YOU FROM?
A CHINESE RESTAURANT. IT'S DOWNTOWN.
WHEN HINA BROUGHT HER IN, I FIGURED SHE'D BE A REAL PIECE OF WORK
BUT SHE SEEMS SURPRISINGLY PUT-TOGETHER.
YEAH, ANZU'S GOT A GOOD CONSCIENCE.
COMPARED TO HINA, SHE MIGHT AS WELL BE A SAINT.
HEY, HAVE YOU NOTICED HOW, LATELY, HITOMI GETS THESE SCARY LOOKS ON HER FACE?
HMM ... BUT IS IT REALLY
THAT BAD IF IT'S HITOMI STARING YOU DOWN ...?

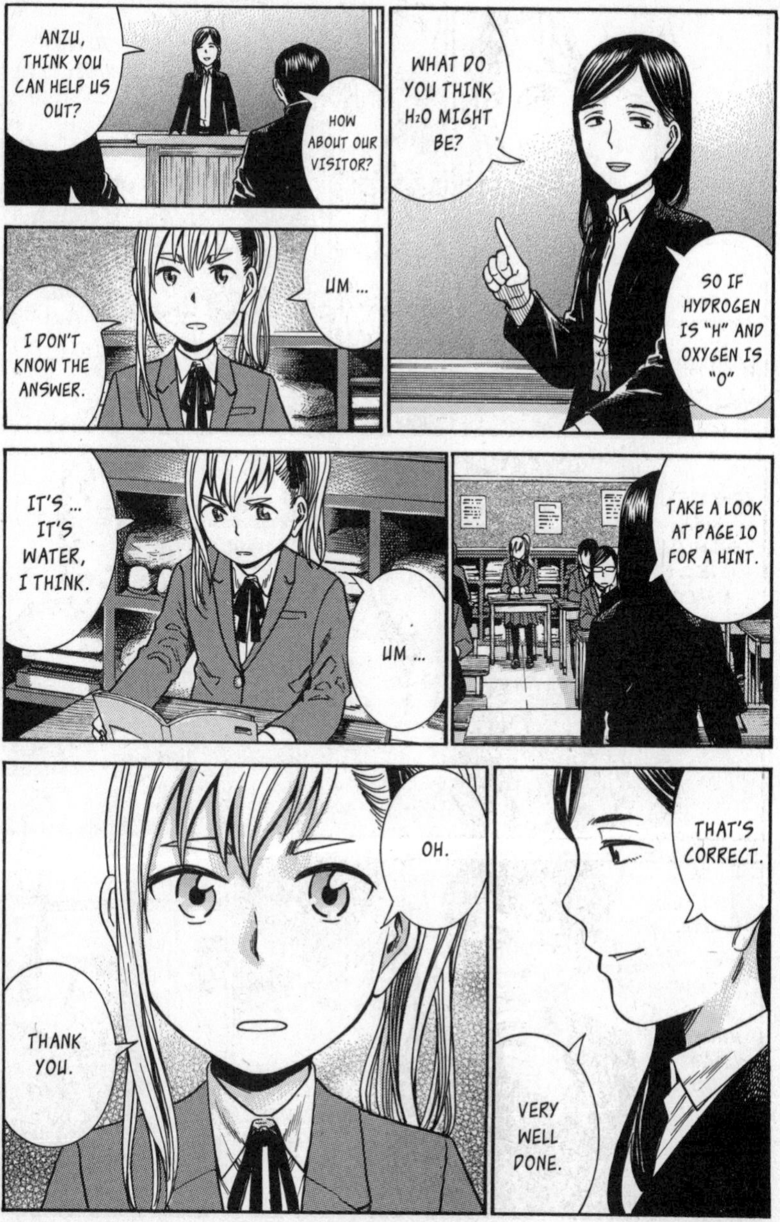
SO IF HYDROGEN IS "H" AND OXYGEN IS "O"
WHAT DO YOU THINK H_2O MIGHT BE?
HOW ABOUT OUR VISITOR?
ANZU, THINK YOU CAN HELP US OUT?
UM ...
I DON'T KNOW THE ANSWER.
TAKE A LOOK AT PAGE 10 FOR A HINT.
UM ...
IT'S ... IT'S WATER, I THINK.
THAT'S CORRECT.
VERY WELL DONE.
OH.
THANK YOU.

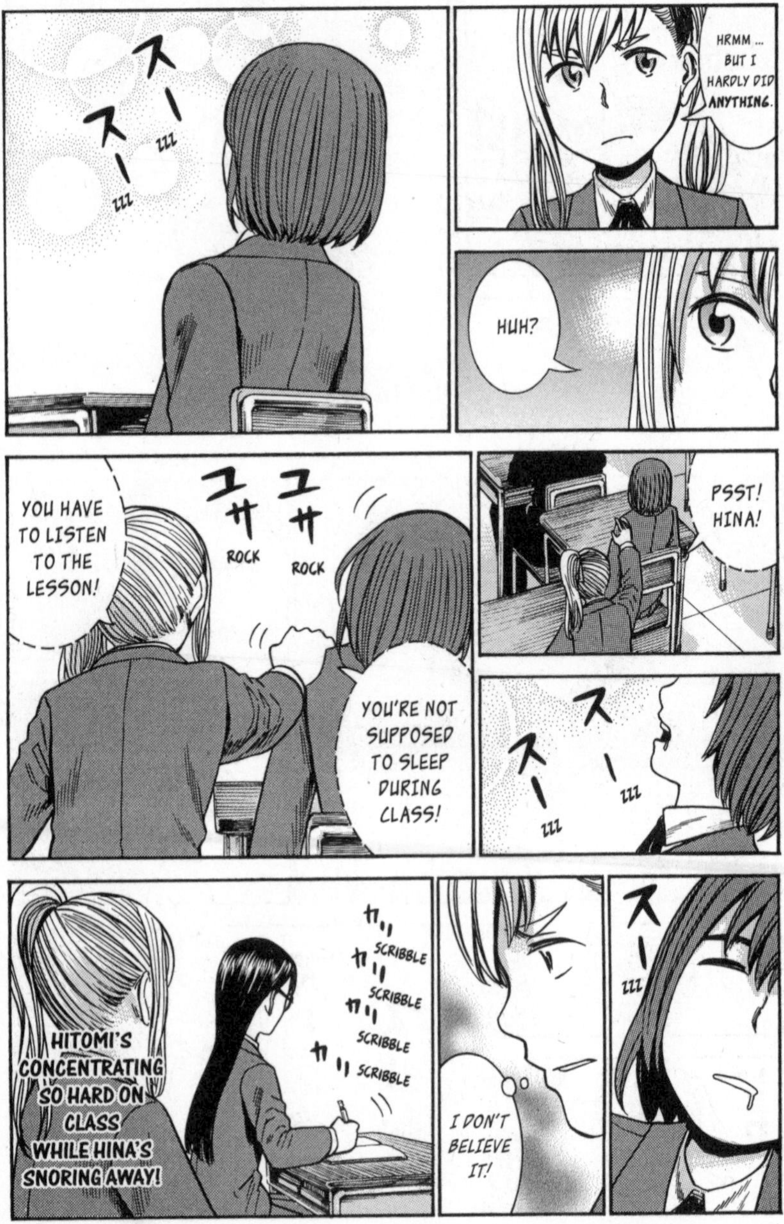
HRMM ... BUT I HARDLY DID ANYTHING.
HUH?
スー
ZZZ
スー
ZZZ
PSST! HINA!
スー
ZZZ
スー
ZZZ
ユサ
ROCK
ユサ
ROCK
YOU HAVE TO LISTEN TO THE LESSON!
YOU'RE NOT SUPPOSED TO SLEEP DURING CLASS!
スー
ZZZ
I DON'T BELIEVE IT!
カリ
SCRIBBLE
カリ
SCRIBBLE
カリ
SCRIBBLE
カリ
SCRIBBLE
HITOMI'S CONCENTRATING SO HARD ON CLASS WHILE HINA'S SNORING AWAY!

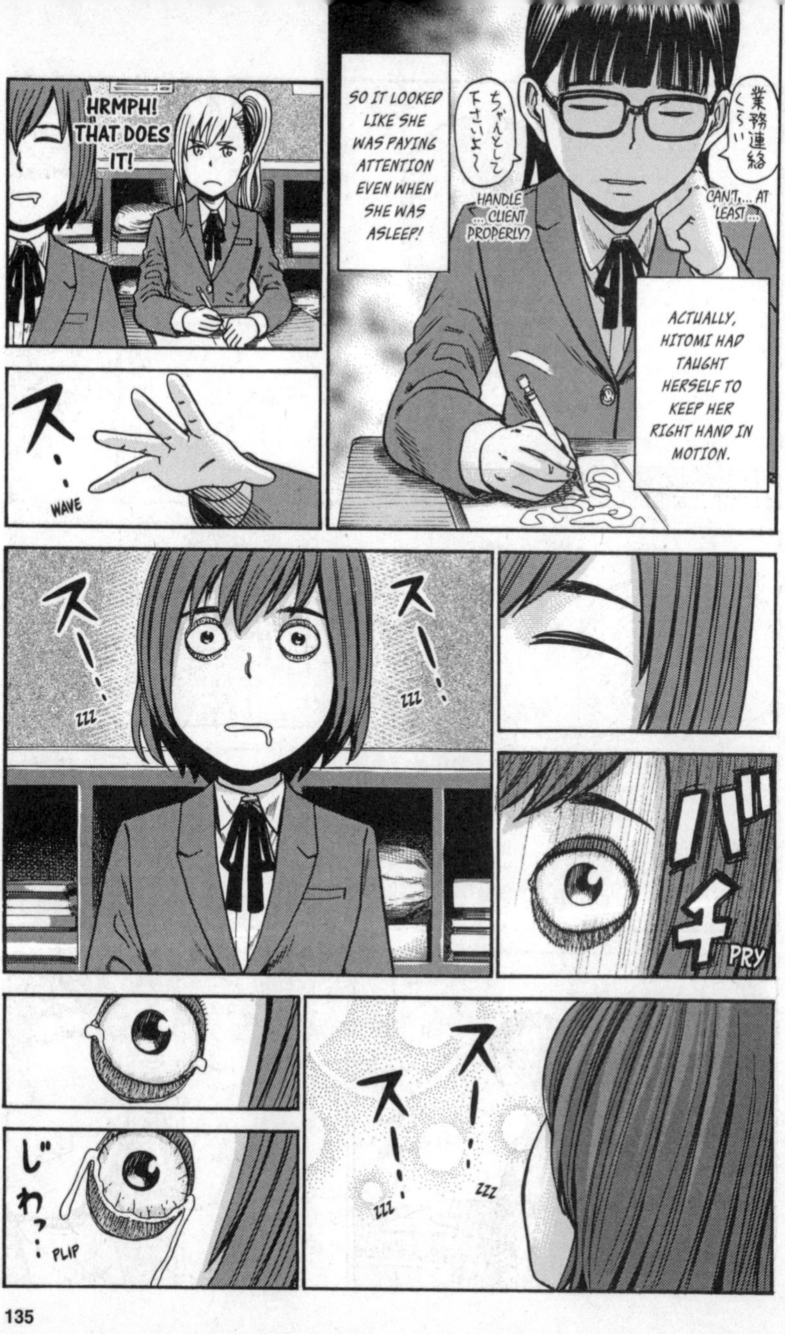
業務連絡くらい
CAN'T... AT LEAST...
ちゃんとして下さいよ〜
HANDLE ... CLIENT PROPERLY?
ACTUALLY, HITOMI HAD TAUGHT HERSELF TO KEEP HER RIGHT HAND IN MOTION.
SO IT LOOKED LIKE SHE WAS PAYING ATTENTION EVEN WHEN SHE WAS ASLEEP!
HRMPH! THAT DOES IT!
ス・・
WAVE
バチ
PRY
スー・・・
ZZZ
ス・・・
ZZZ
スー・・・
ZZZ
スー・・・
ZZZ
じわっ・・
PLIP

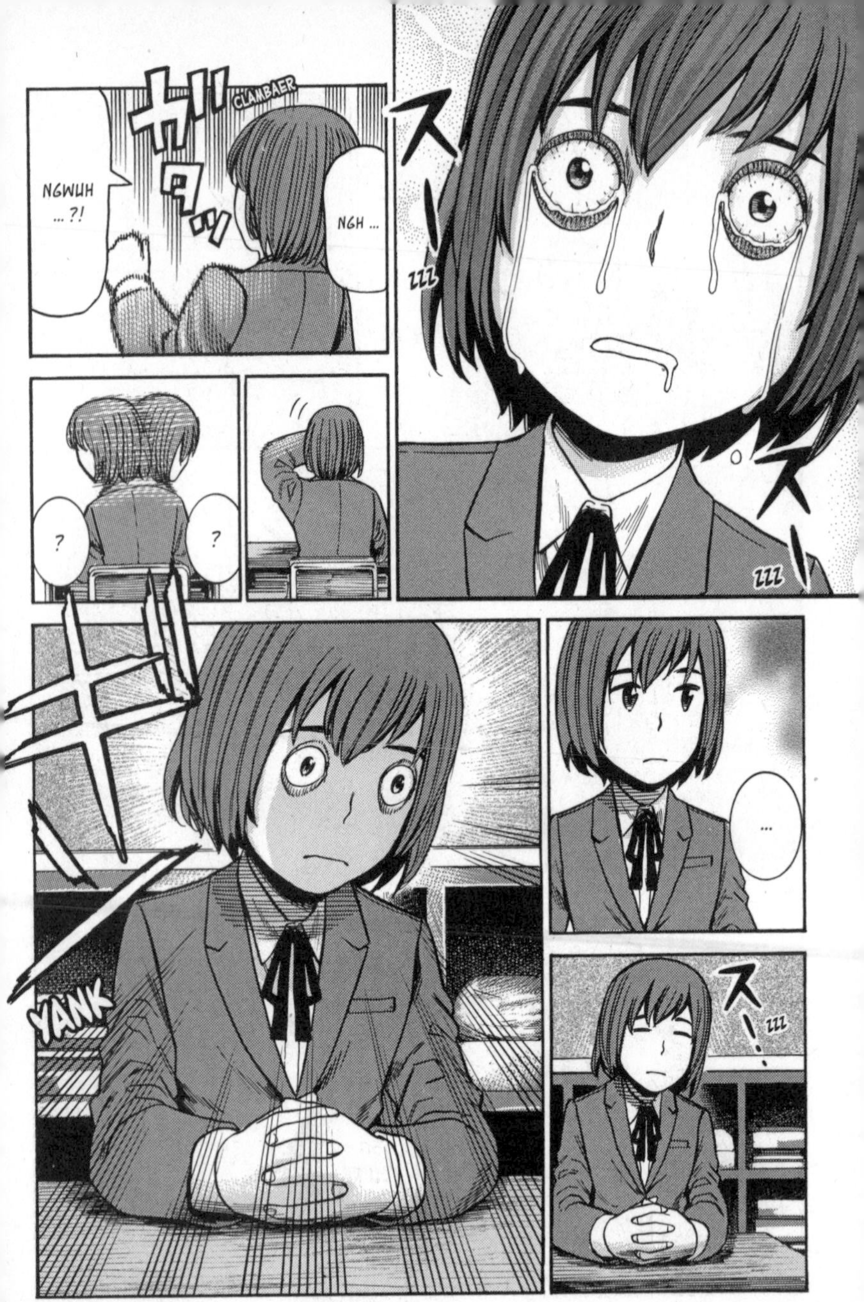
ス
ZZZ
ZZZ
ガタッ
CLAMBAER
NGH ...
NGWUH ...?!
?
?
...
ス
ZZZ
YANK

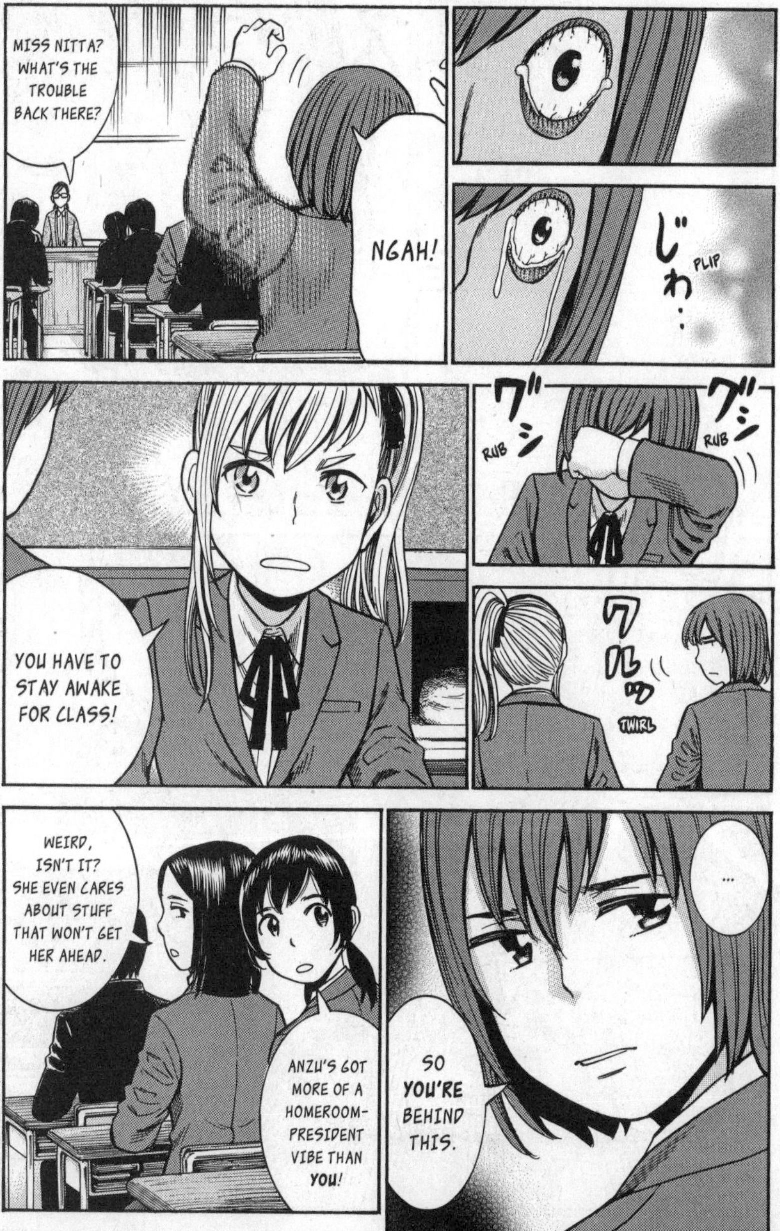
じわ…
PLIP
NGAH!
MISS NITTA? WHAT'S THE TROUBLE BACK THERE?
ゴシ
RUB
ゴシ
RUB
クルッ
TWIRL
YOU HAVE TO STAY AWAKE FOR CLASS!
...
SO **YOU'RE** BEHIND THIS.
WEIRD, ISN'T IT? SHE EVEN CARES ABOUT STUFF THAT WON'T GET HER AHEAD.
ANZU'S GOT MORE OF A HOMEROOM-PRESIDENT VIBE THAN **YOU**!

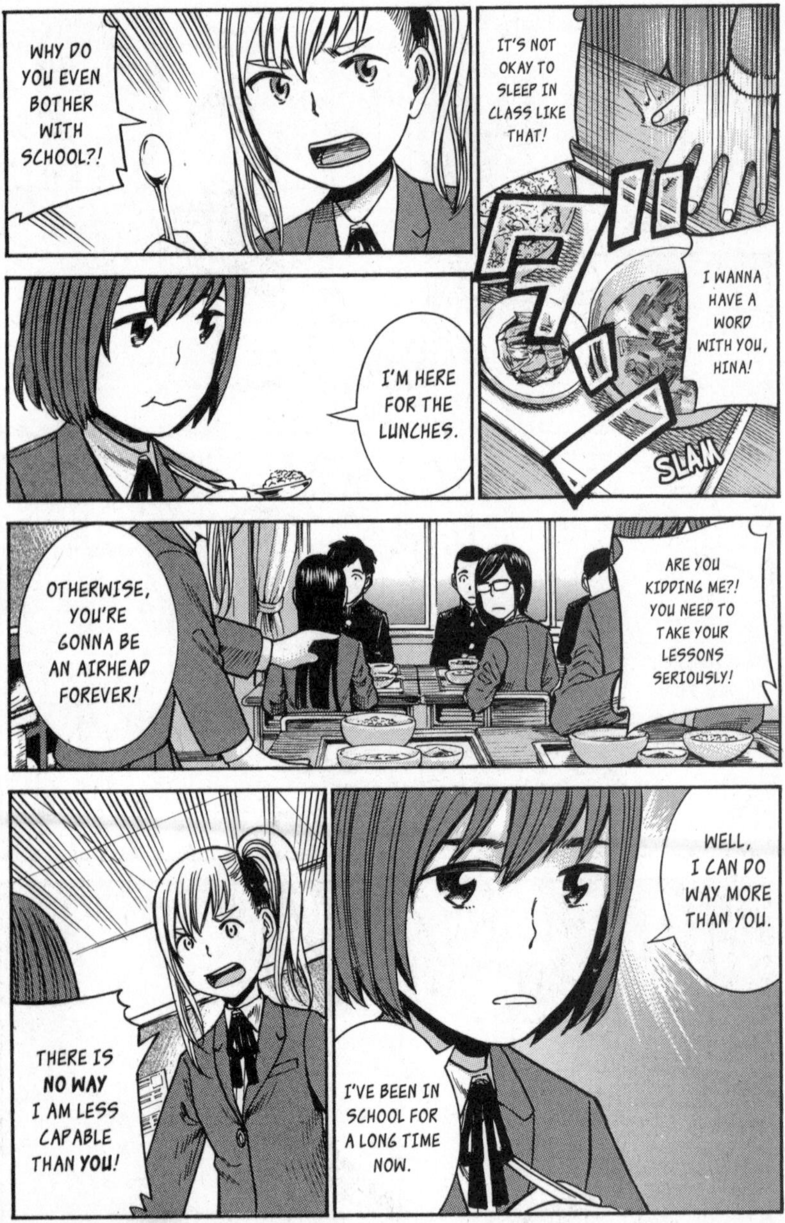
IT'S NOT OKAY TO SLEEP IN CLASS LIKE THAT!
I WANNA HAVE A WORD WITH YOU, HINA!
SLAM
WHY DO YOU EVEN BOTHER WITH SCHOOL?!
I'M HERE FOR THE LUNCHES.
ARE YOU KIDDING ME?! YOU NEED TO TAKE YOUR LESSONS SERIOUSLY!
OTHERWISE, YOU'RE GONNA BE AN AIRHEAD FOREVER!
WELL, I CAN DO WAY MORE THAN YOU.
I'VE BEEN IN SCHOOL FOR A LONG TIME NOW.
THERE IS **NO WAY** I AM LESS CAPABLE THAN **YOU**!

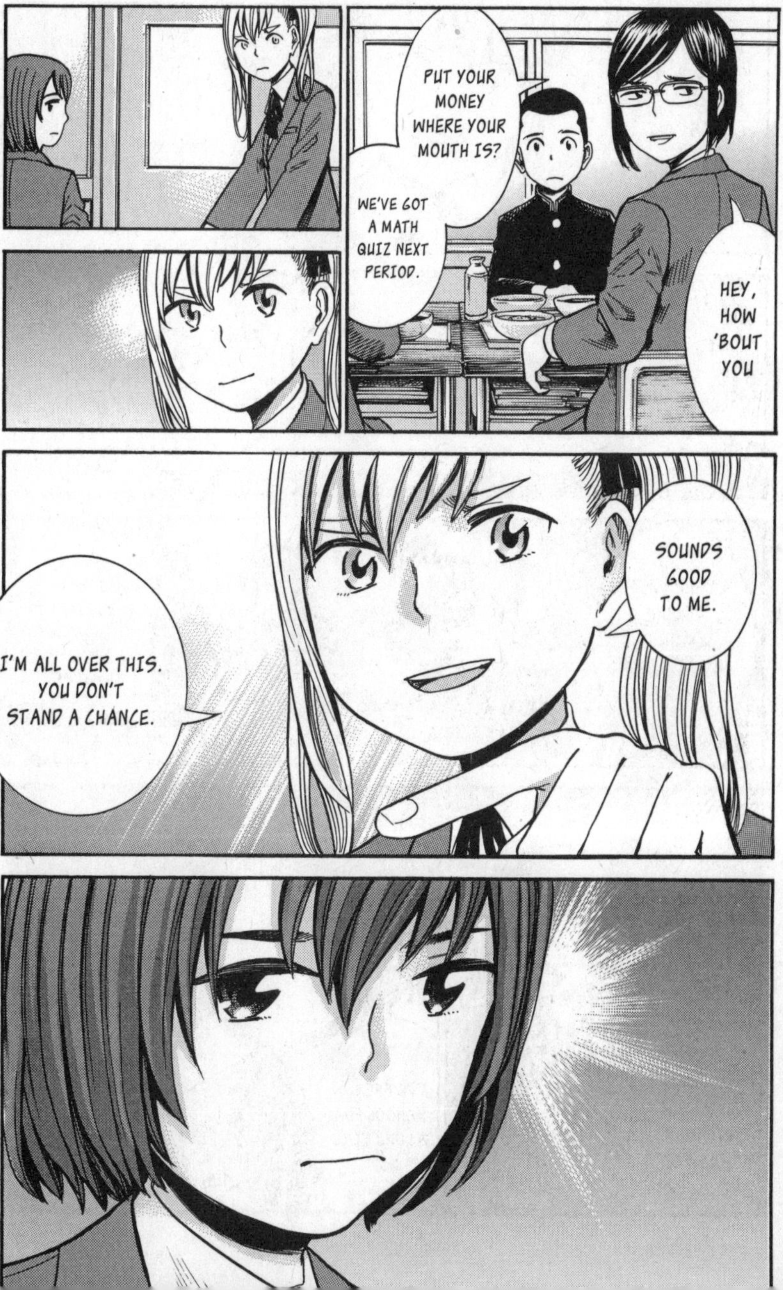
HEY, HOW 'BOUT YOU
WE'VE GOT A MATH QUIZ NEXT PERIOD.
PUT YOUR MONEY WHERE YOUR MOUTH IS?
SOUNDS GOOD TO ME.
I'M ALL OVER THIS. YOU DON'T STAND A CHANCE.

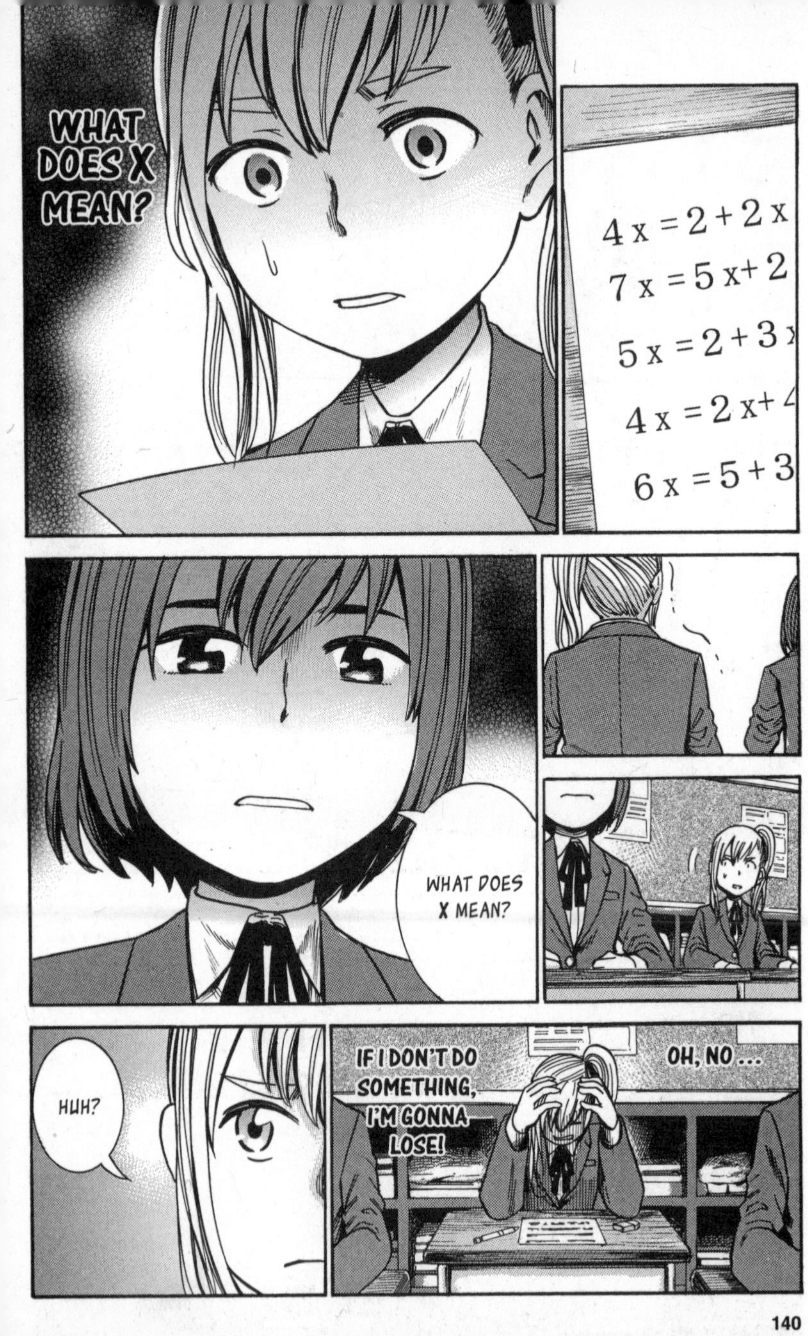
4 x = 2 + 2 x
7 x = 5 x+ 2
5 x = 2 + 3
4 x = 2 x+
6 x = 5 + 3
WHAT DOES X MEAN?
WHAT DOES X MEAN?
OH, NO ...
IF I DON'T DO SOMETHING, I'M GONNA LOSE!
HUH?

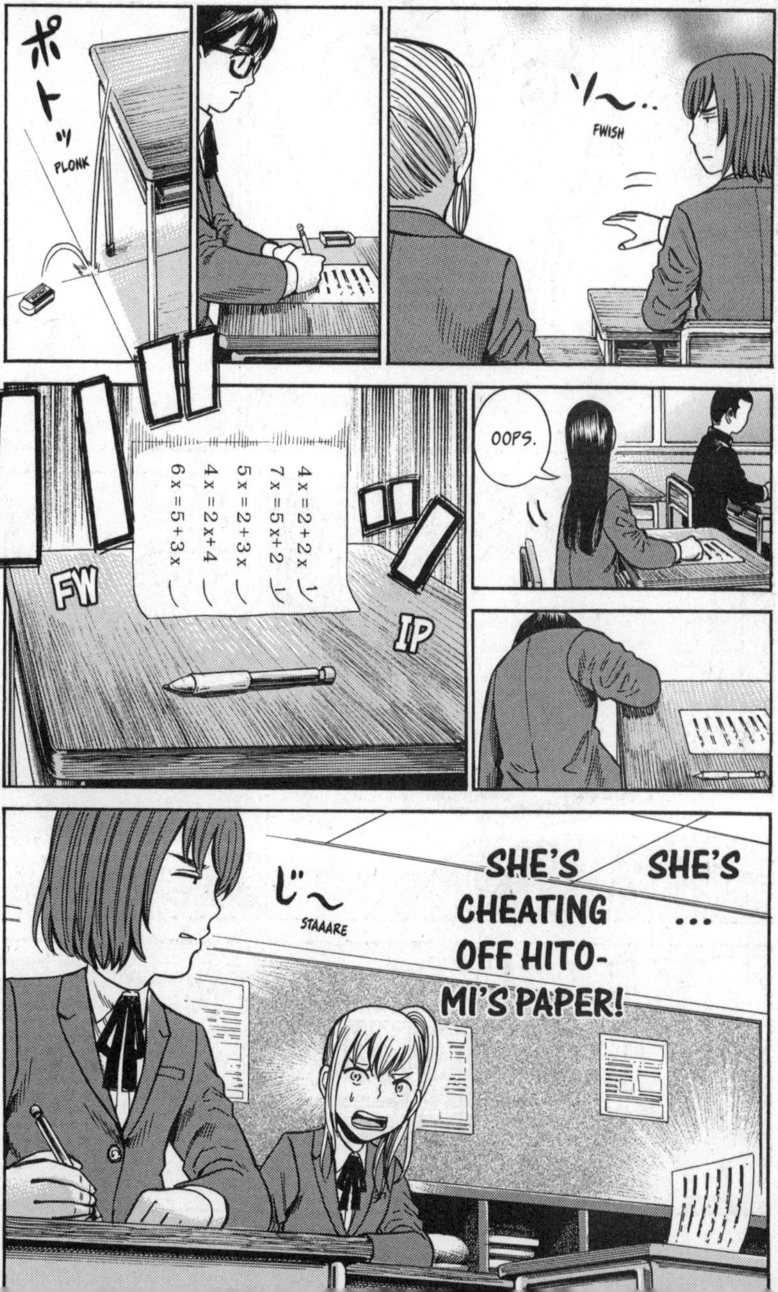
ソ〜..
FWISH
ポトッ
PLONK
OOPS.
FW
IP
4x = 2+2x ( )
7x = 5x+2 ( )
5x = 2+3x ( )
4x = 2x+4 ( )
6x = 5+3x ( )
じ〜
STAAARE
SHE'S ...
SHE'S CHEATING OFF HITOMI'S PAPER!

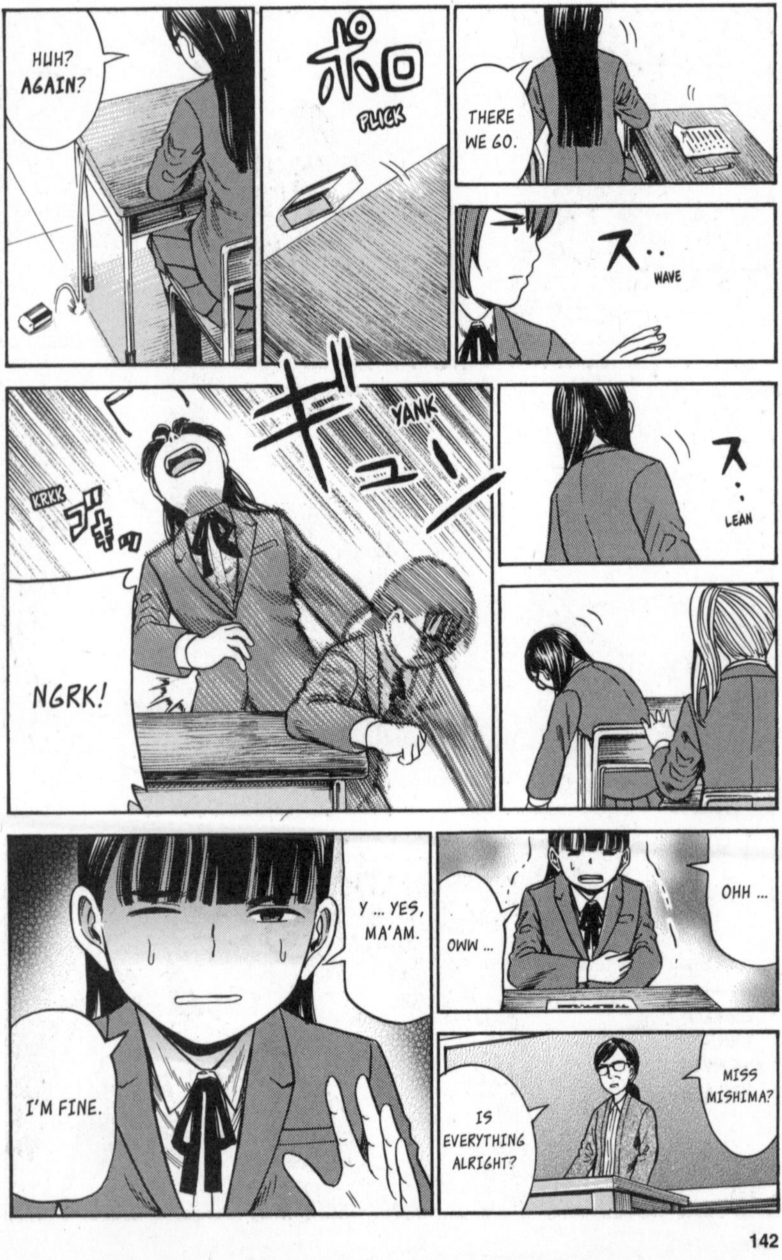
THERE WE GO.
ス..
WAVE
ポロ
PLICK
HUH? AGAIN?
ス..
LEAN
ギュー
YANK
KRKK
ゴキッ
NGRK!
OHH ...
OWW ...
MISS MISHIMA?
IS EVERYTHING ALRIGHT?
Y ... YES, MA'AM.
I'M FINE.

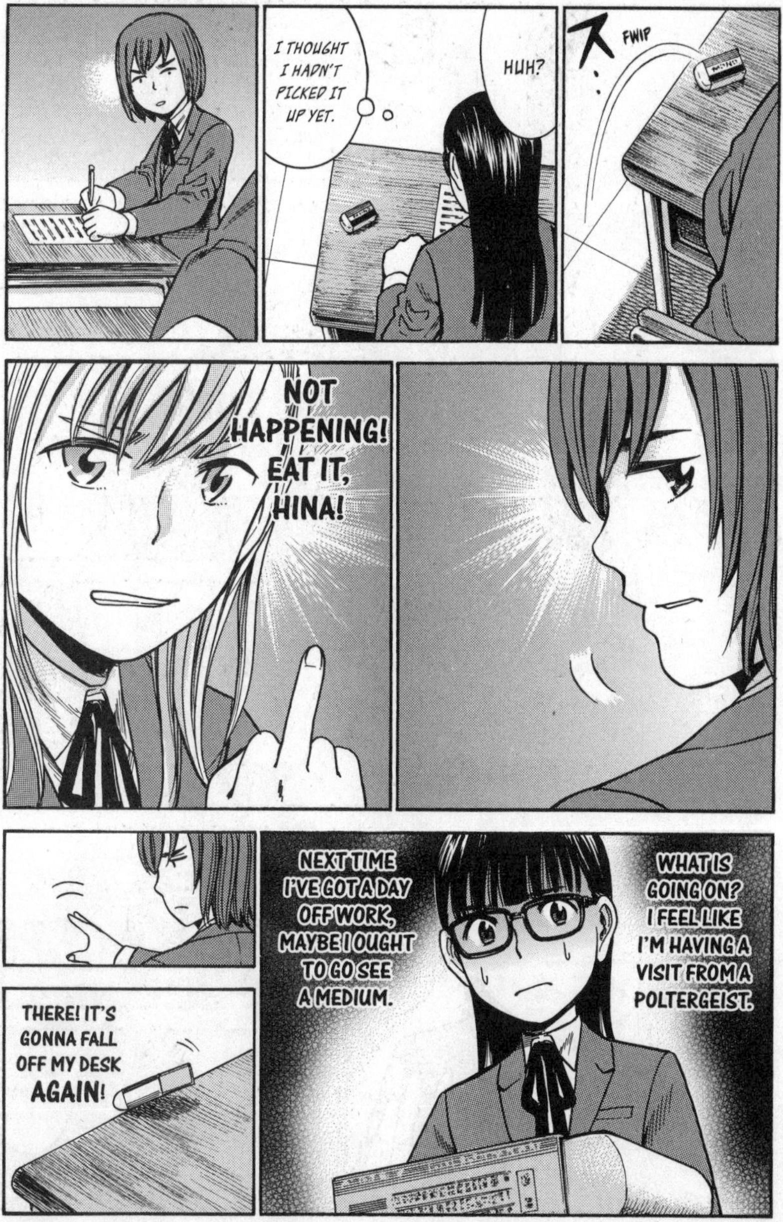
ス
FWIP
HUH?
I THOUGHT I HADN'T PICKED IT UP YET.
NOT HAPPENING! EAT IT, HINA!
WHAT IS GOING ON? I FEEL LIKE I'M HAVING A VISIT FROM A POLTERGEIST.
NEXT TIME I'VE GOT A DAY OFF WORK, MAYBE I OUGHT TO GO SEE A MEDIUM.
THERE! IT'S GONNA FALL OFF MY DESK AGAIN!

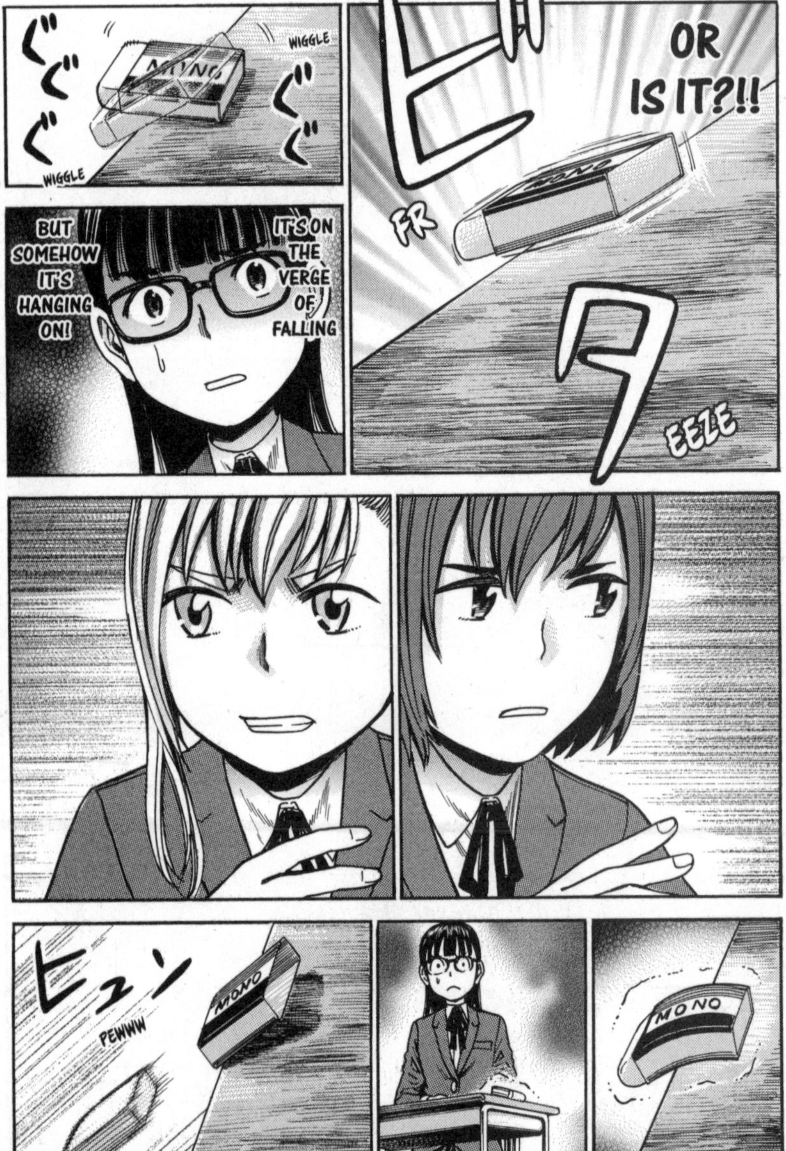

ピ
OR IS IT?!!
FR
タ
EEZE
ぐぐぐ
WIGGLE
ぐぐぐ
WIGGLE
IT'S ON THE VERGE OF FALLING
BUT SOMEHOW IT'S HANGING ON!
ヒュン
PEWWW

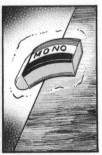

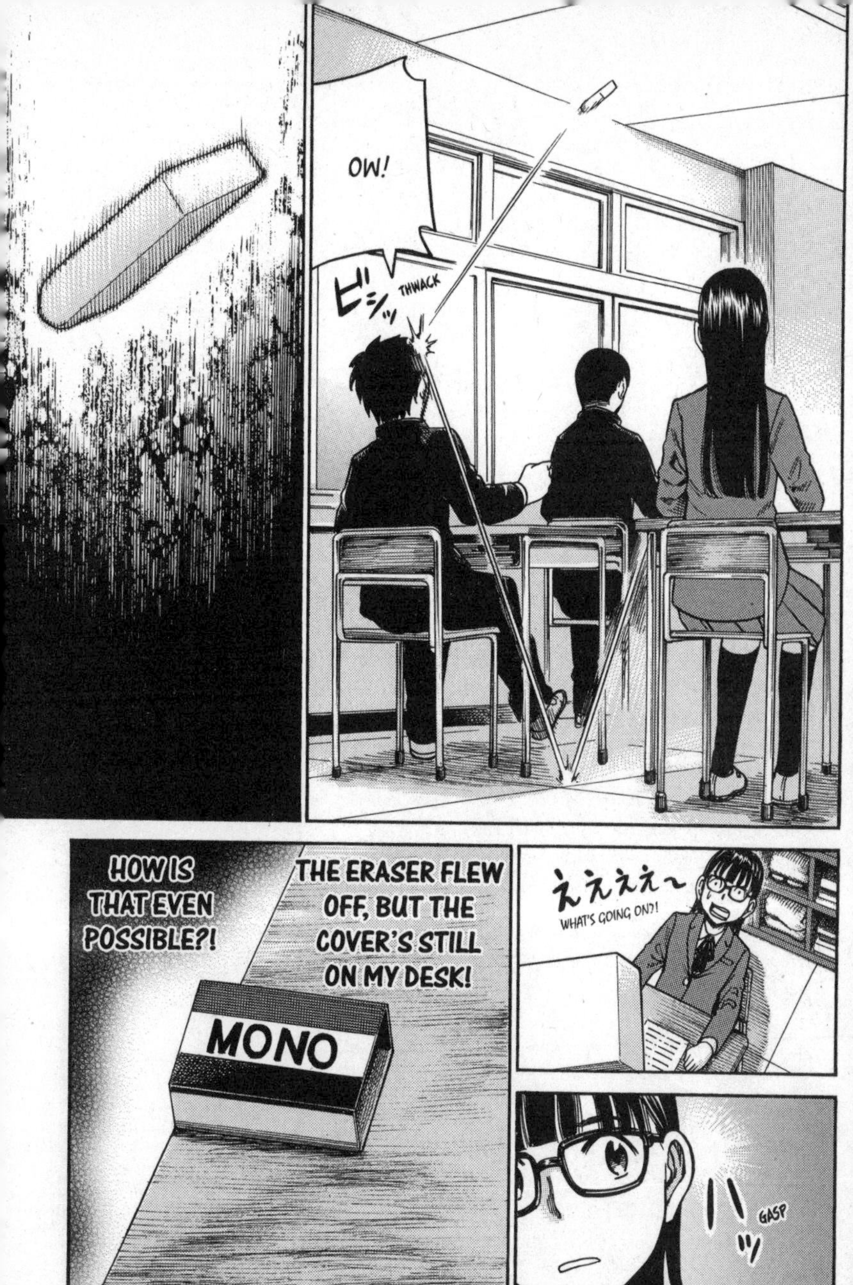
OW!
ビシッ
THWACK
ええええ~
WHAT'S GOING ON?!
GASP
THE ERASER FLEW OFF, BUT THE COVER'S STILL ON MY DESK!
HOW IS THAT EVEN POSSIBLE?!
MONO

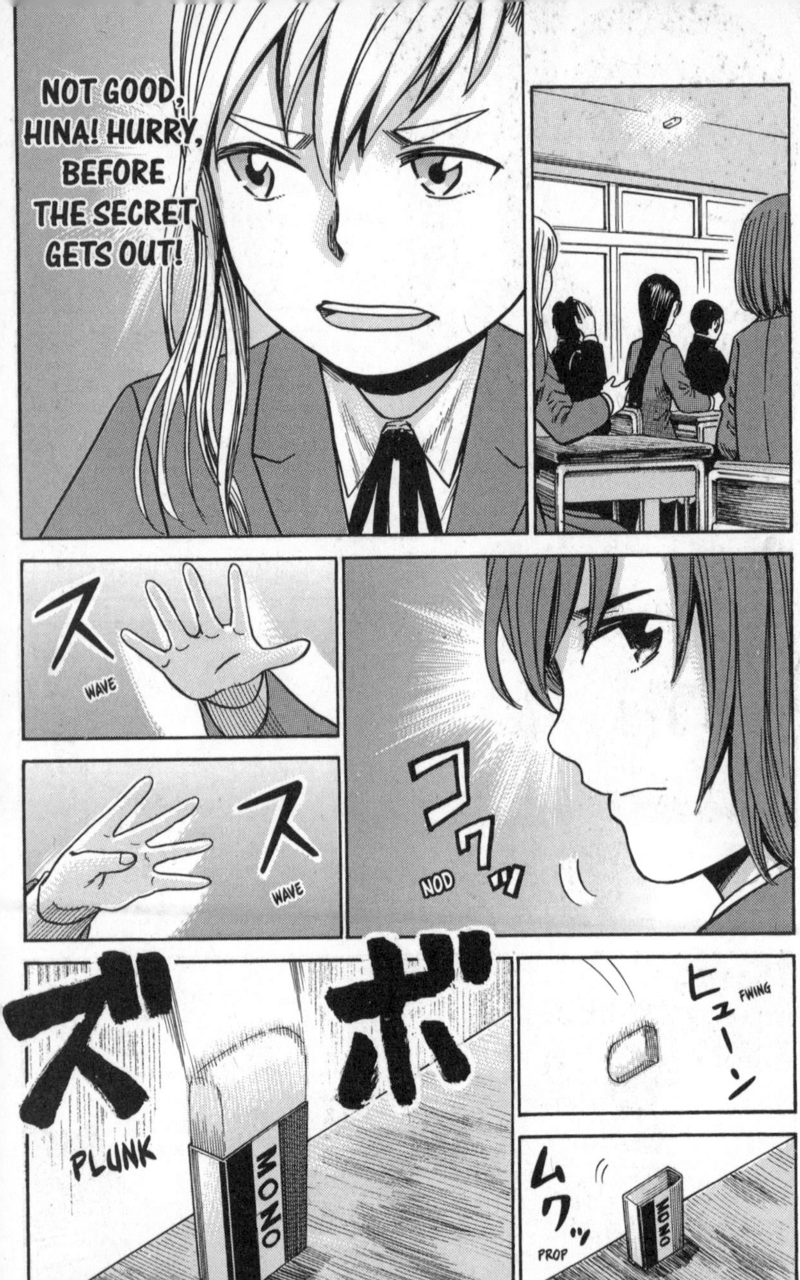
NOT GOOD, HINA! HURRY, BEFORE THE SECRET GETS OUT!
コクッ
NOD
ス
WAVE
ス
WAVE
ヒューン
FWING
ムクッ
PROP
ズボ
PLUNK
MONO
MONO

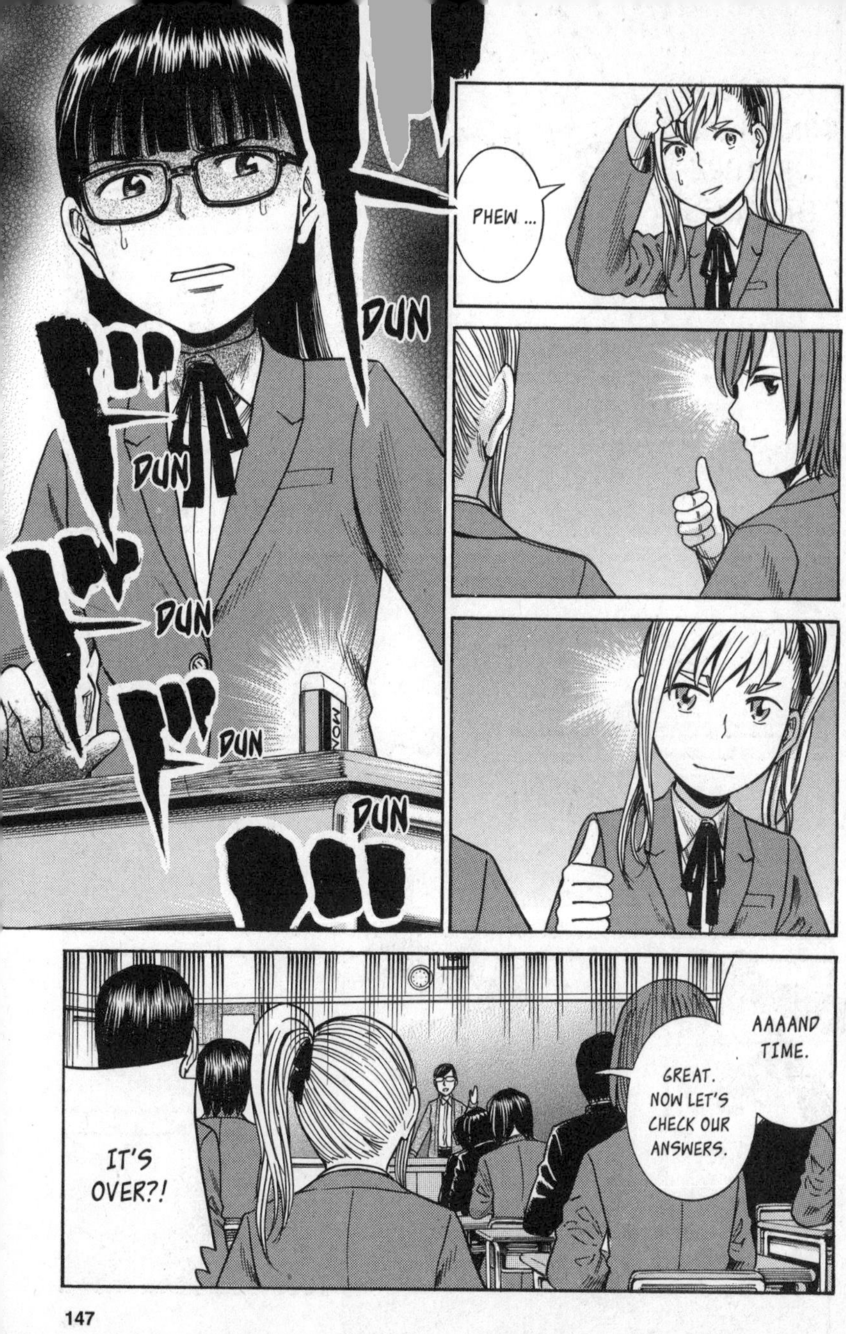
PHEW ...
DUN
DUN
DUN
DUN
DUN
AAAAND TIME.
GREAT. NOW LET'S CHECK OUR ANSWERS.
IT'S OVER?!

ONE POINT FOR ME. ZERO FOR YOU. MY WIN.

$$+ 2x \quad \checkmark$$
$$+ 2 \quad \checkmark$$
$$3x \quad \checkmark$$
$$4 \quad \checkmark$$
$$x \quad \checkmark$$

$$4x = 2 + 2x \quad ①$$
$$7x = 5x + 2 \quad \checkmark$$
$$5x = 2 + 3x \quad \checkmark$$
$$4x = 2x + 4 \quad \checkmark$$
$$6x = 5 + 3x \quad \checkmark$$

WOW. UNBELIEVABLY PATHETIC.

I THINK WE BETTER CALL THIS ONE A TIE.

YOU ONLY GOT ONE 'CAUSE YOU COPIED OFF HITOMI'S QUIZ!

NEXT PERIOD IS ETHICS.

THAT'S OUR LAST CLASS TODAY.

ALRIGHT, THEN LET'S HAVE A REMATCH. NEXT CLASS.

WE CAN'T FIGHT DURING ETHICS?

THAT'S EXACTLY WHAT WE LEARN **NOT** TO DO DURING THAT CLASS!

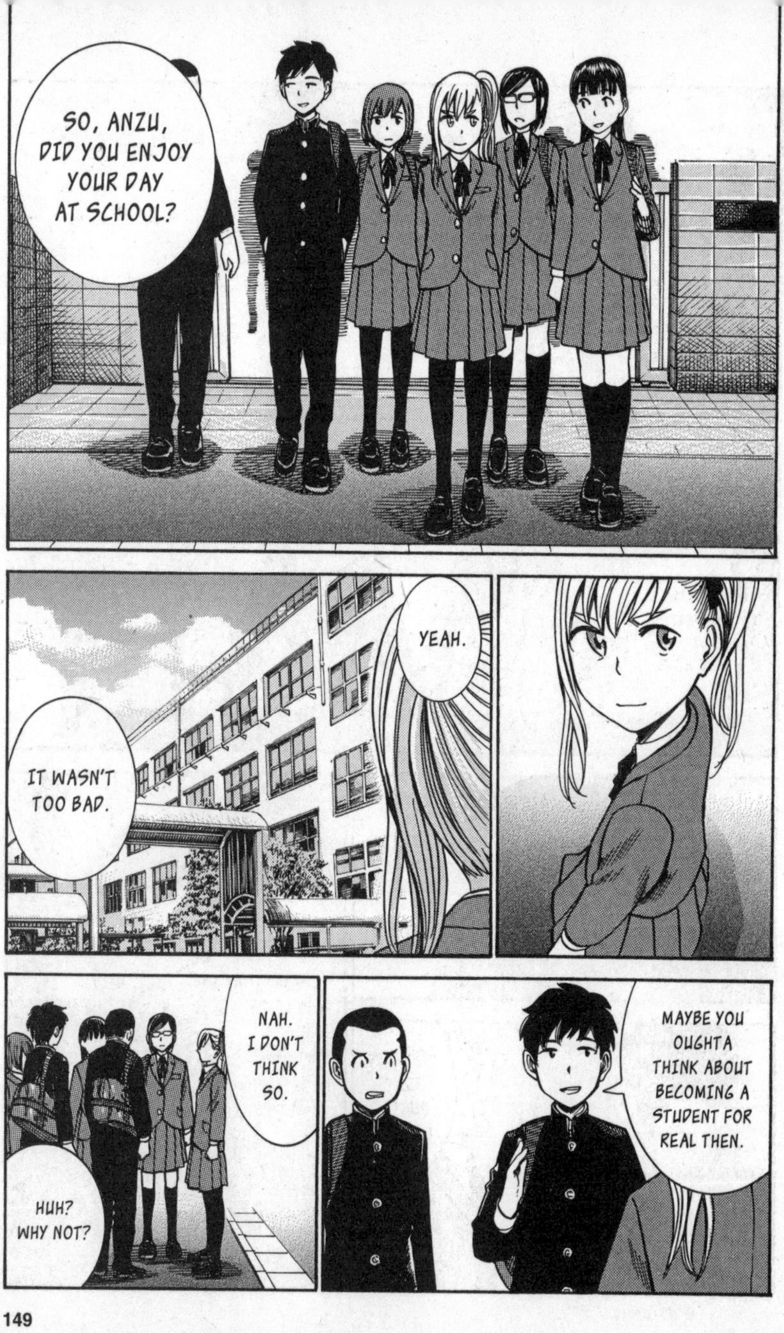
SO, ANZU, DID YOU ENJOY YOUR DAY AT SCHOOL?
YEAH.
IT WASN'T TOO BAD.
MAYBE YOU OUGHTA THINK ABOUT BECOMING A STUDENT FOR REAL THEN.
NAH. I DON'T THINK SO.
HUH? WHY NOT?

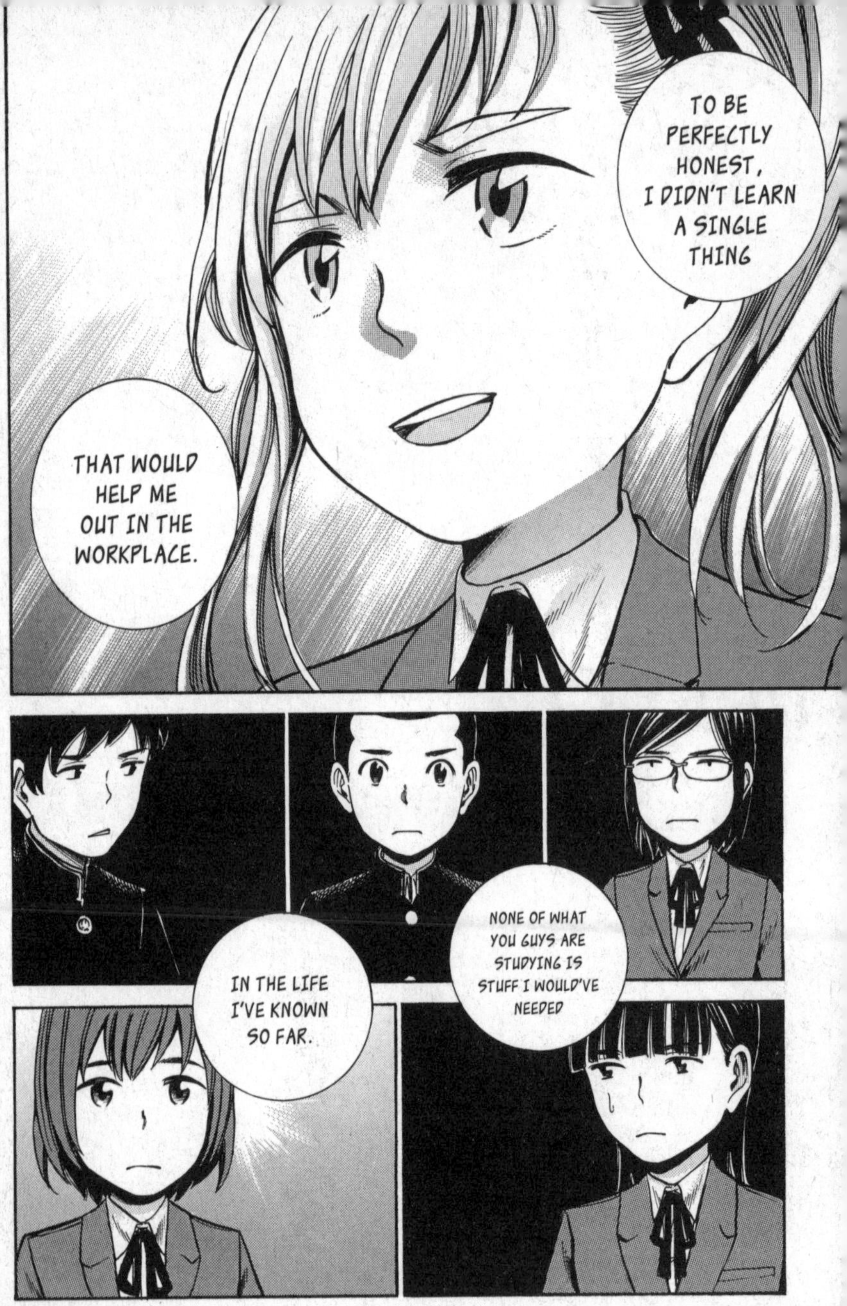
TO BE PERFECTLY HONEST, I DIDN'T LEARN A SINGLE THING
THAT WOULD HELP ME OUT IN THE WORKPLACE.
NONE OF WHAT YOU GUYS ARE STUDYING IS STUFF I WOULD'VE NEEDED
IN THE LIFE I'VE KNOWN SO FAR.

CHAPTER 42 END

ぐぐぐ
WAGGLE
MONO

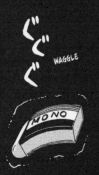

CHAPTER 43 THE VASE INSPECTORS

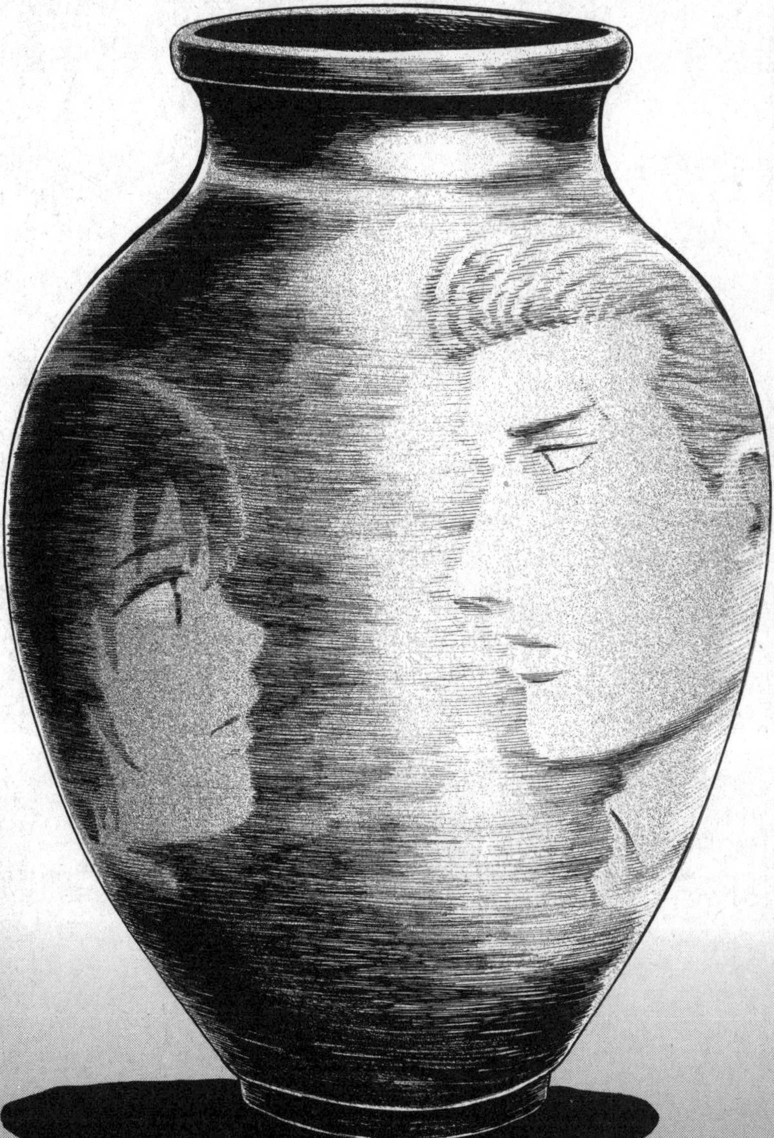

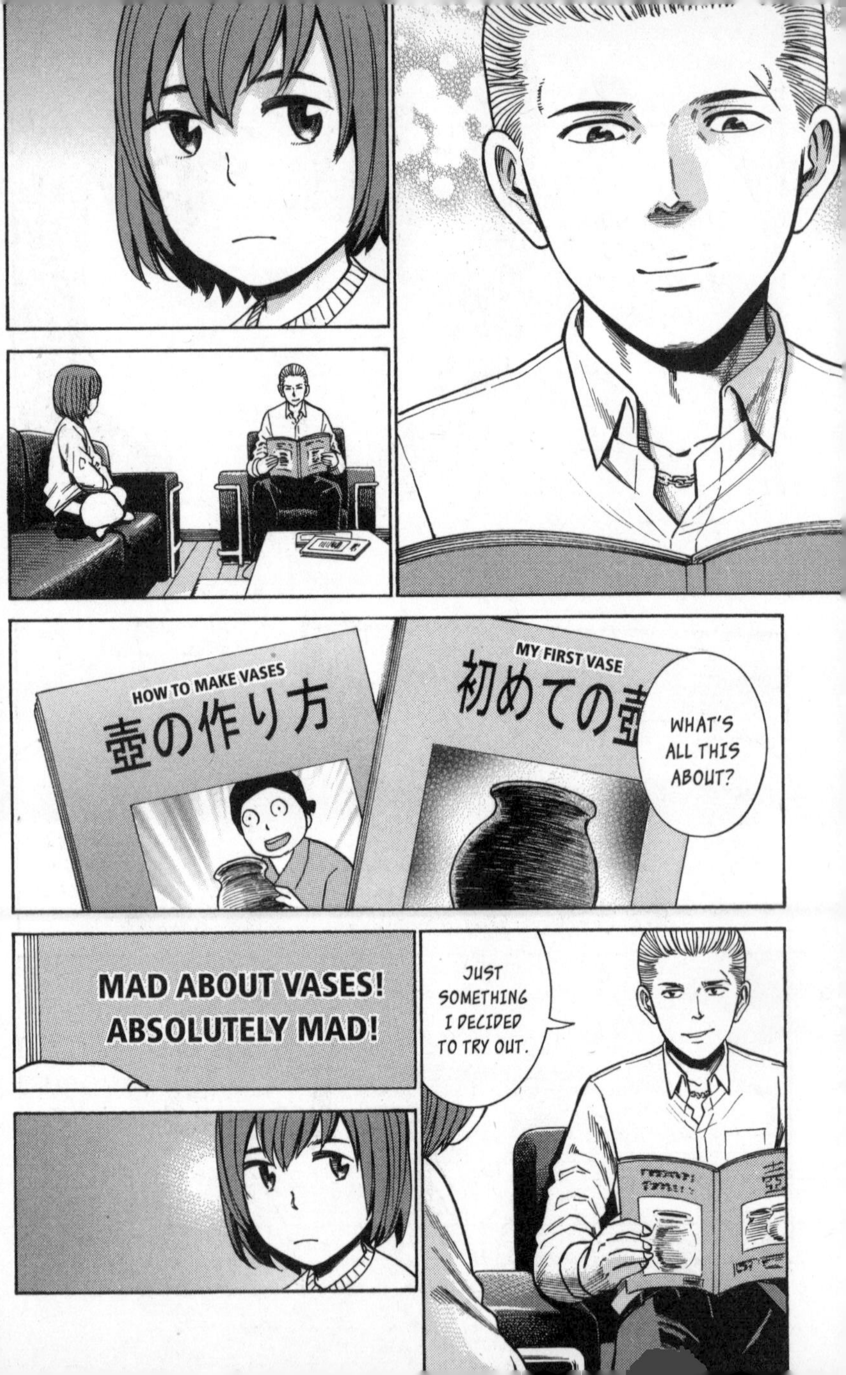
WHAT'S ALL THIS ABOUT?
MY FIRST VASE
初めての壺
HOW TO MAKE VASES
壺の作り方
JUST SOMETHING I DECIDED TO TRY OUT.
MAD ABOUT VASES! ABSOLUTELY MAD!

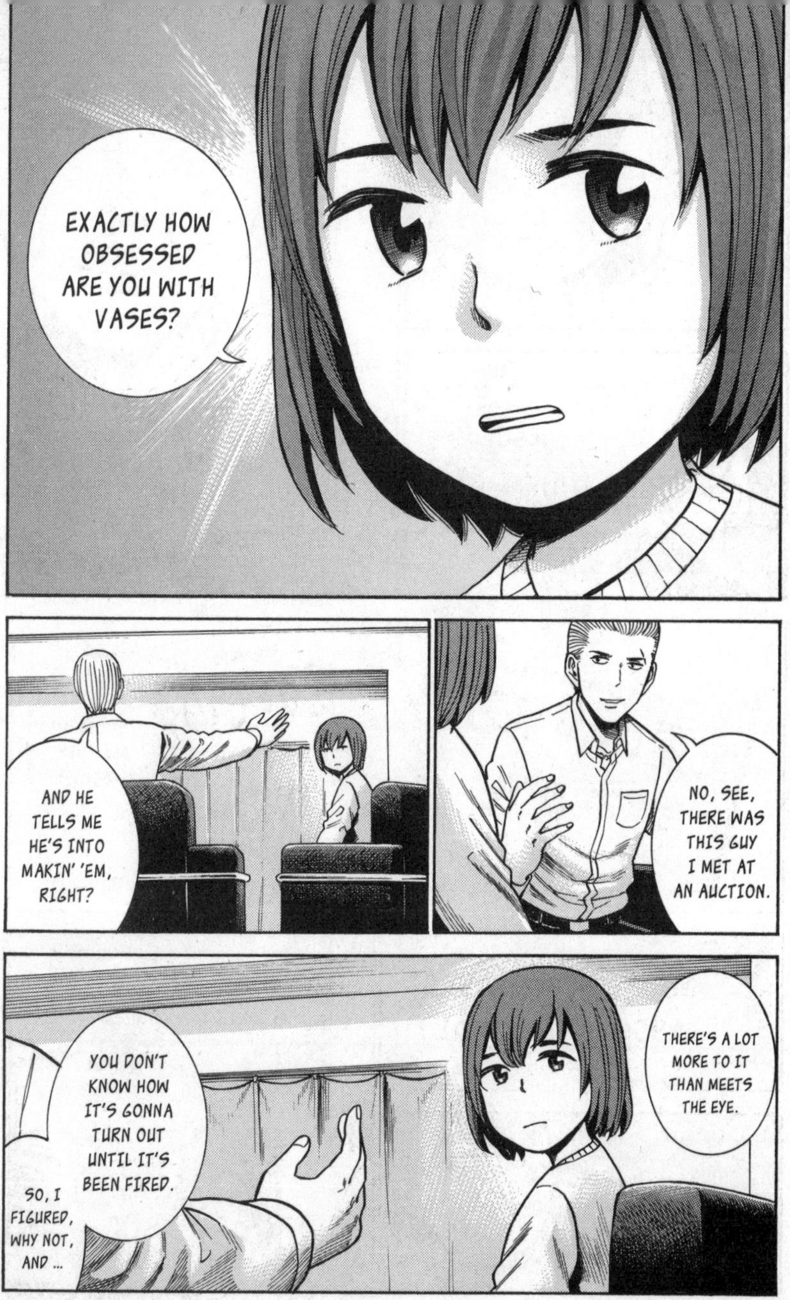
EXACTLY HOW OBSESSED ARE YOU WITH VASES?
NO, SEE, THERE WAS THIS GUY I MET AT AN AUCTION.
AND HE TELLS ME HE'S INTO MAKIN' 'EM, RIGHT?
THERE'S A LOT MORE TO IT THAN MEETS THE EYE.
YOU DON'T KNOW HOW IT'S GONNA TURN OUT UNTIL IT'S BEEN FIRED.
SO, I FIGURED, WHY NOT, AND ...

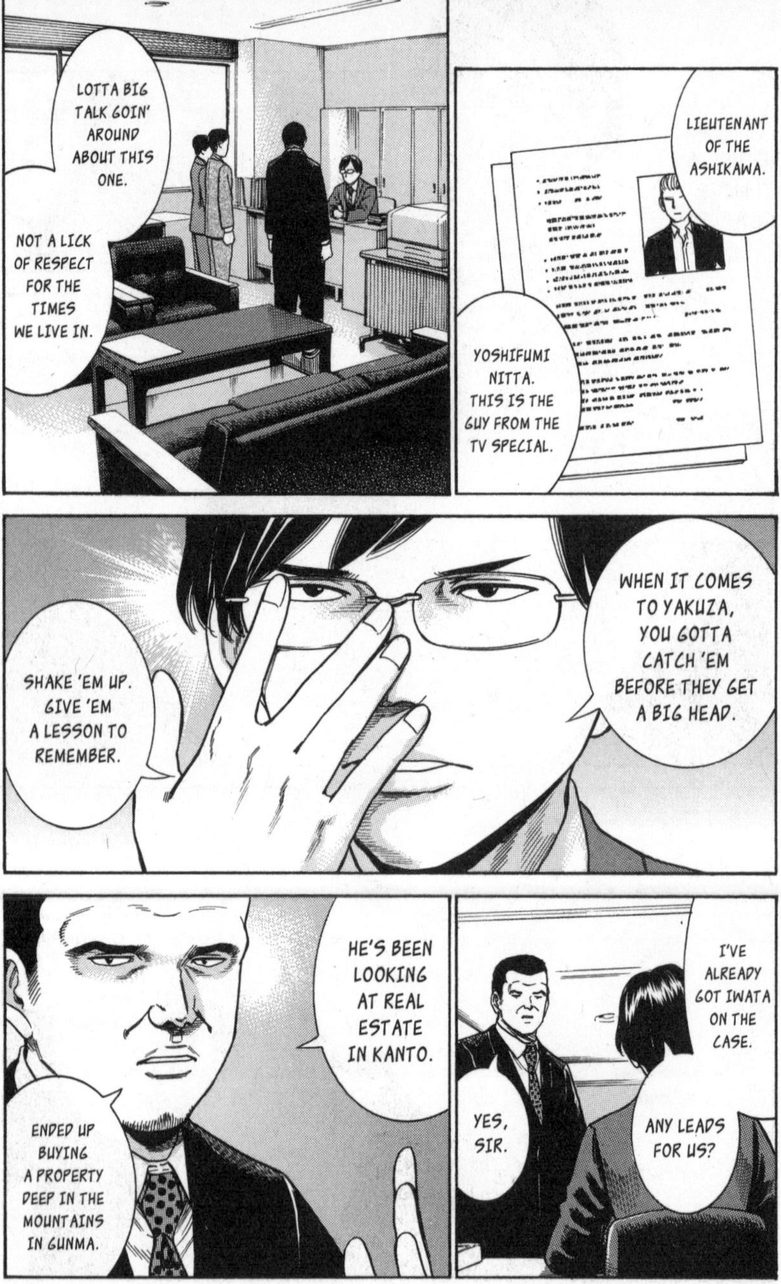
LIEUTENANT OF THE ASHIKAWA.
YOSHIFUMI NITTA. THIS IS THE GUY FROM THE TV SPECIAL.
LOTTA BIG TALK GOIN' AROUND ABOUT THIS ONE.
NOT A LICK OF RESPECT FOR THE TIMES WE LIVE IN.
WHEN IT COMES TO YAKUZA, YOU GOTTA CATCH 'EM BEFORE THEY GET A BIG HEAD.
SHAKE 'EM UP. GIVE 'EM A LESSON TO REMEMBER.
I'VE ALREADY GOT IWATA ON THE CASE.
ANY LEADS FOR US?
YES, SIR.
HE'S BEEN LOOKING AT REAL ESTATE IN KANTO.
ENDED UP BUYING A PROPERTY DEEP IN THE MOUNTAINS IN GUNMA.

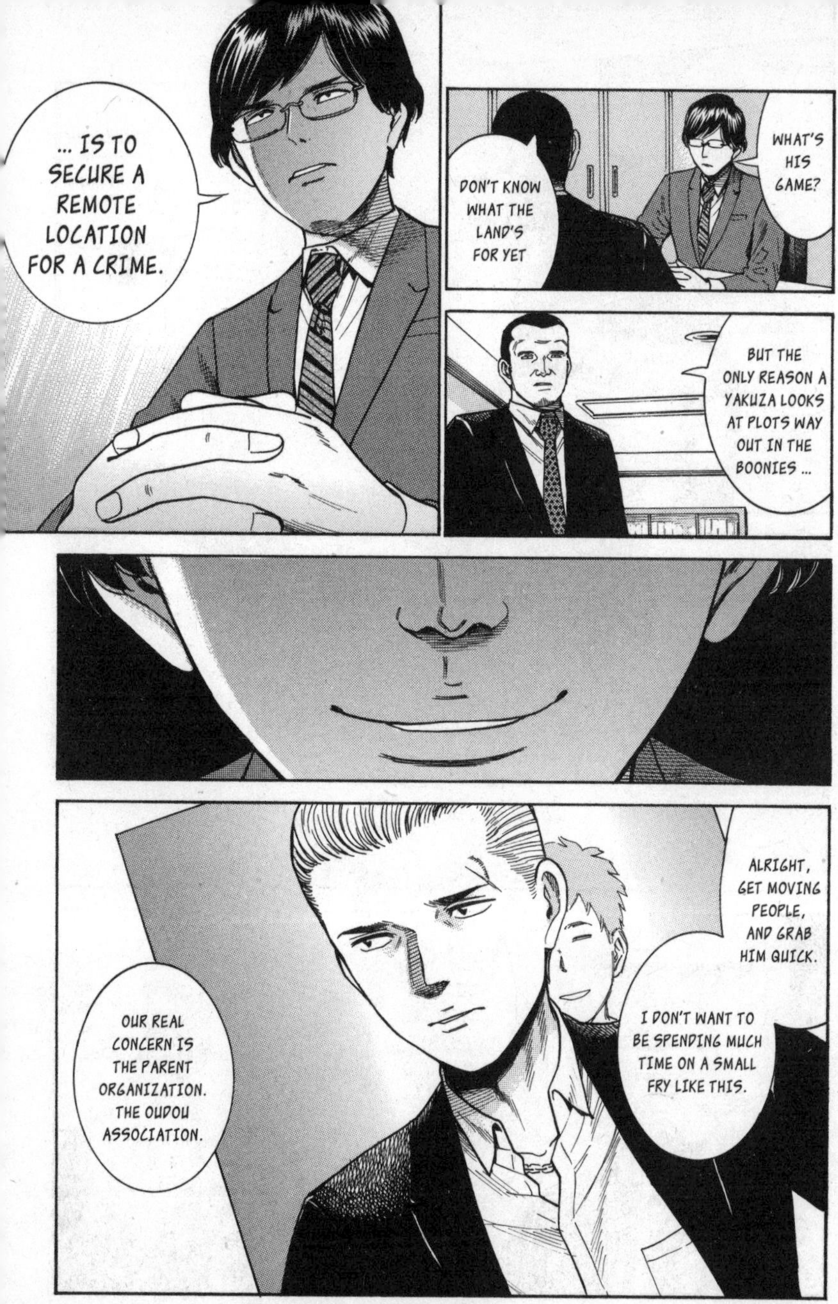
WHAT'S HIS GAME?
DON'T KNOW WHAT THE LAND'S FOR YET
BUT THE ONLY REASON A YAKUZA LOOKS AT PLOTS WAY OUT IN THE BOONIES ...
... IS TO SECURE A REMOTE LOCATION FOR A CRIME.
ALRIGHT, GET MOVING PEOPLE, AND GRAB HIM QUICK.
I DON'T WANT TO BE SPENDING MUCH TIME ON A SMALL FRY LIKE THIS.
OUR REAL CONCERN IS THE PARENT ORGANIZATION. THE OUDOU ASSOCIATION.

DEEP IN THE MOUNTAINS OF GUNMA

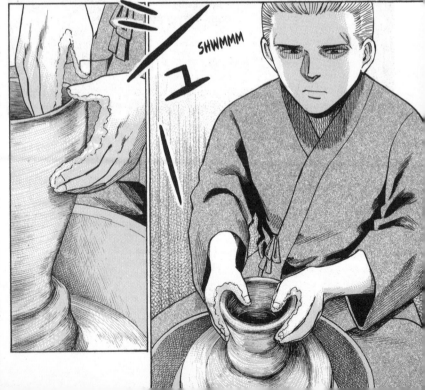

SHWMMM

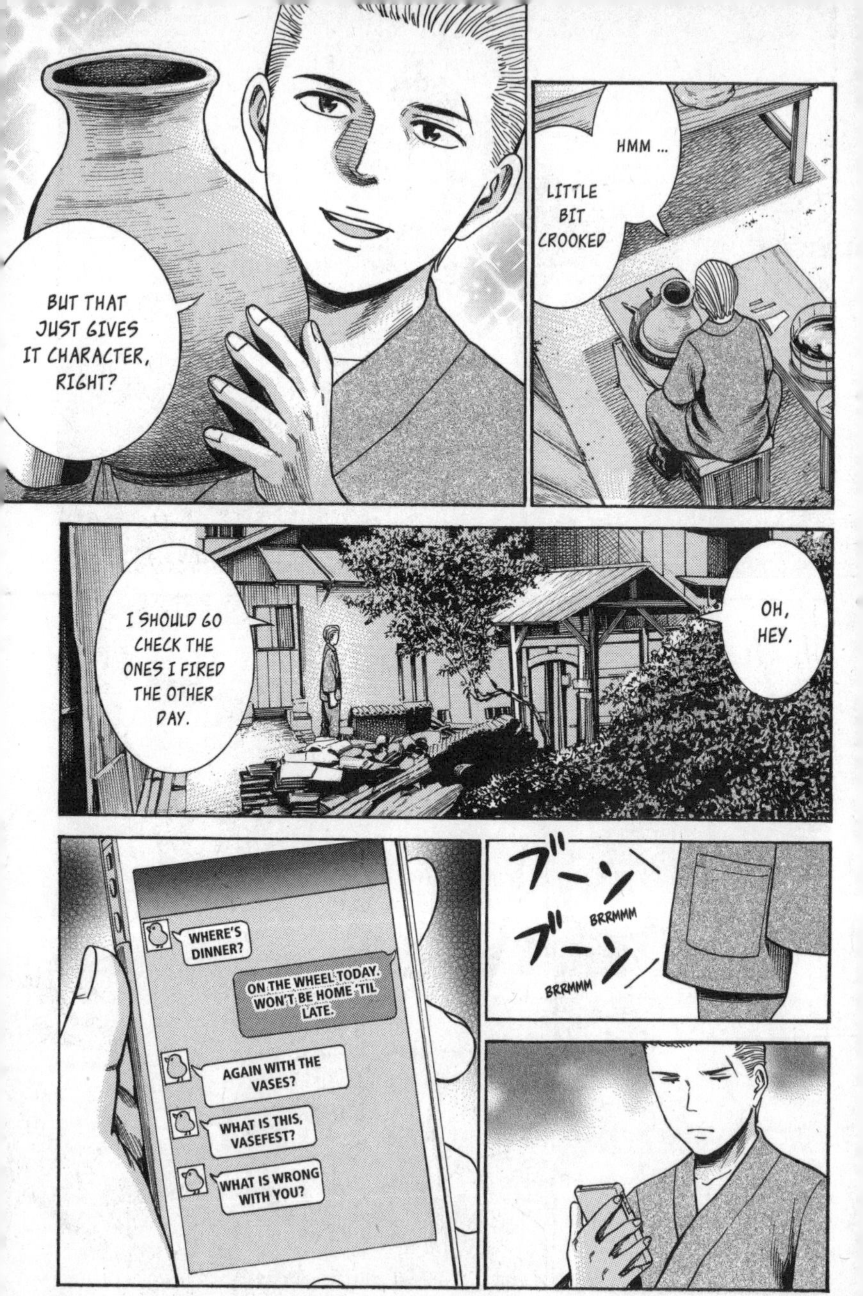
HMM ...
LITTLE BIT CROOKED
BUT THAT JUST GIVES IT CHARACTER, RIGHT?
OH, HEY.
I SHOULD GO CHECK THE ONES I FIRED THE OTHER DAY.
ブーン
BRRMMM
ブーン
BRRMMM
WHERE'S DINNER?
ON THE WHEEL TODAY. WON'T BE HOME 'TIL LATE.
AGAIN WITH THE VASES?
WHAT IS THIS, VASEFEST?
WHAT IS WRONG WITH YOU?

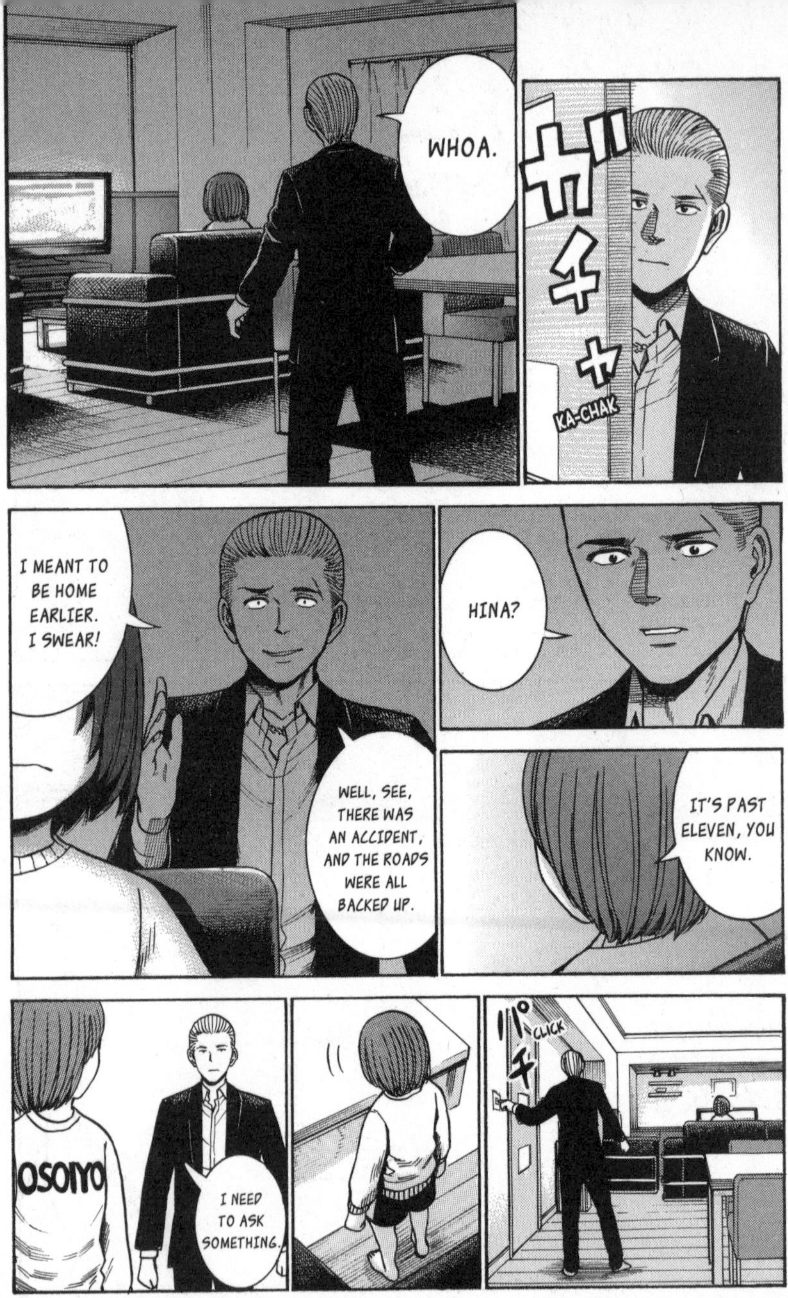
ガチャ
KA-CHAK
WHOA.
HINA?
IT'S PAST ELEVEN, YOU KNOW.
I MEANT TO BE HOME EARLIER. I SWEAR!
WELL, SEE, THERE WAS AN ACCIDENT, AND THE ROADS WERE ALL BACKED UP.
パチ
CLICK
OSOIYO
I NEED TO ASK SOMETHING.

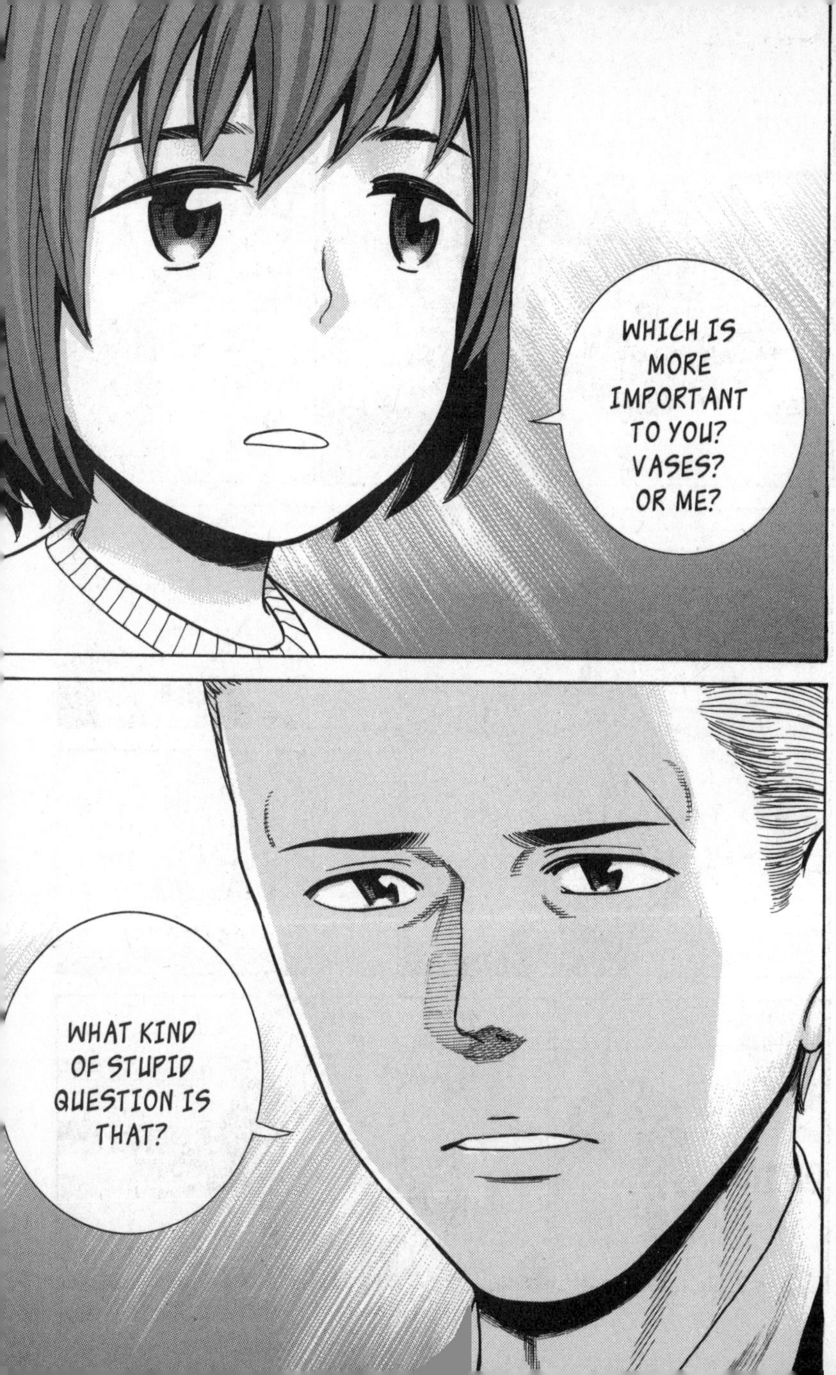
WHICH IS MORE IMPORTANT TO YOU? VASES? OR ME?
WHAT KIND OF STUPID QUESTION IS THAT?

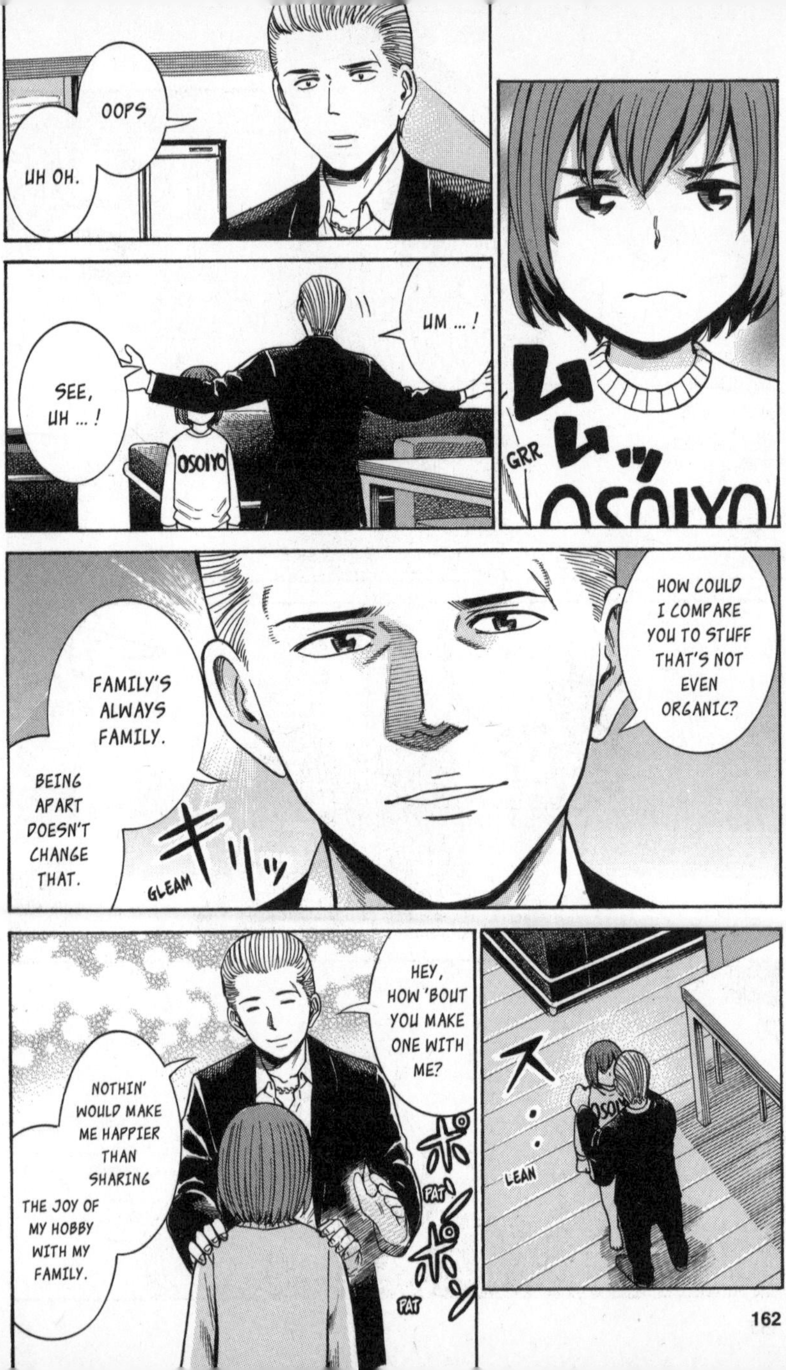
GRR
OSOIYO
OOPS
UH OH.
UM ... !
SEE, UH ... !
OSOIYO
HOW COULD I COMPARE YOU TO STUFF THAT'S NOT EVEN ORGANIC?
FAMILY'S ALWAYS FAMILY.
BEING APART DOESN'T CHANGE THAT.
GLEAM
OSOIYO
LEAN
HEY, HOW 'BOUT YOU MAKE ONE WITH ME?
NOTHIN' WOULD MAKE ME HAPPIER THAN SHARING THE JOY OF MY HOBBY WITH MY FAMILY.
PAT
PAT

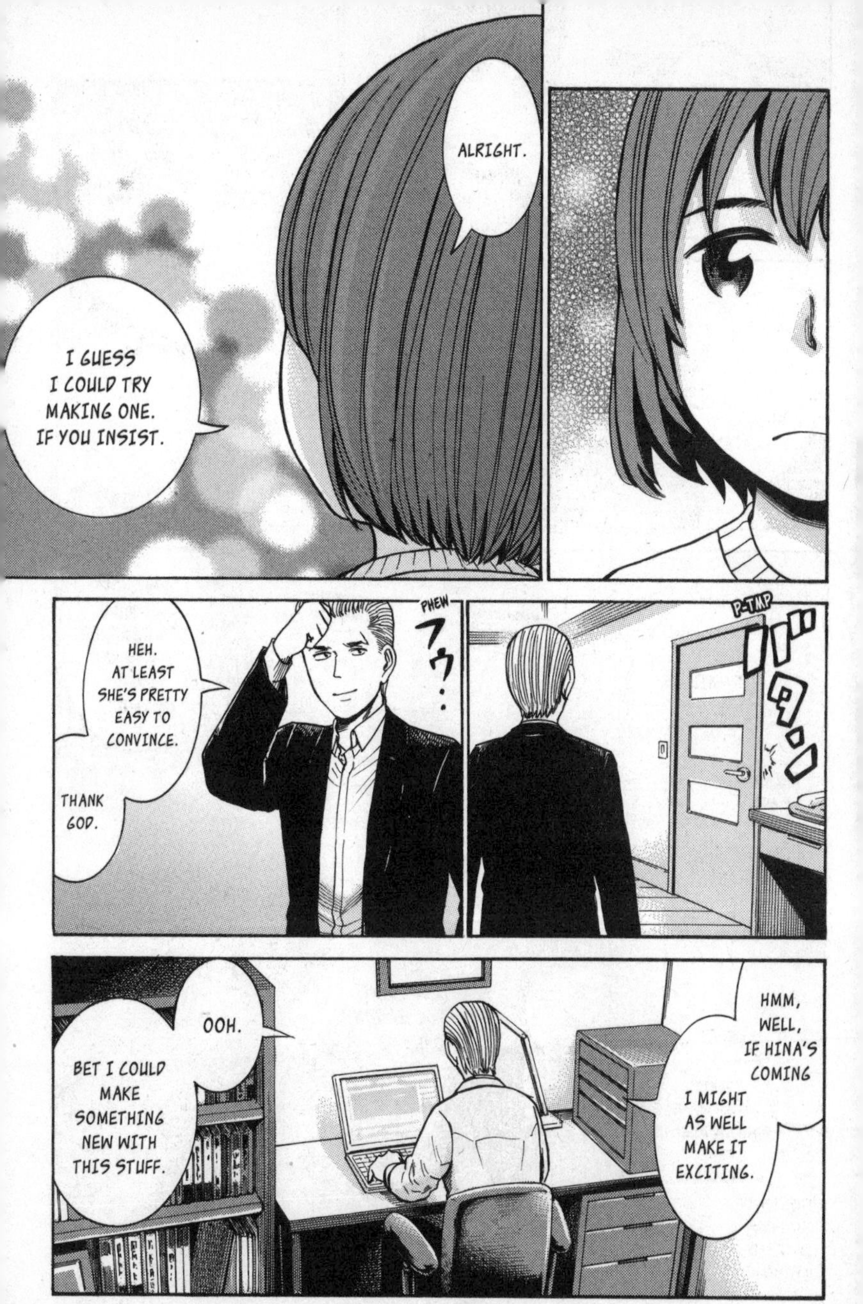
ALRIGHT.
I GUESS I COULD TRY MAKING ONE. IF YOU INSIST.
P-TMP
PHEW
HEH. AT LEAST SHE'S PRETTY EASY TO CONVINCE.
THANK GOD.
HMM, WELL, IF HINA'S COMING
I MIGHT AS WELL MAKE IT EXCITING.
OOH.
BET I COULD MAKE SOMETHING NEW WITH THIS STUFF.

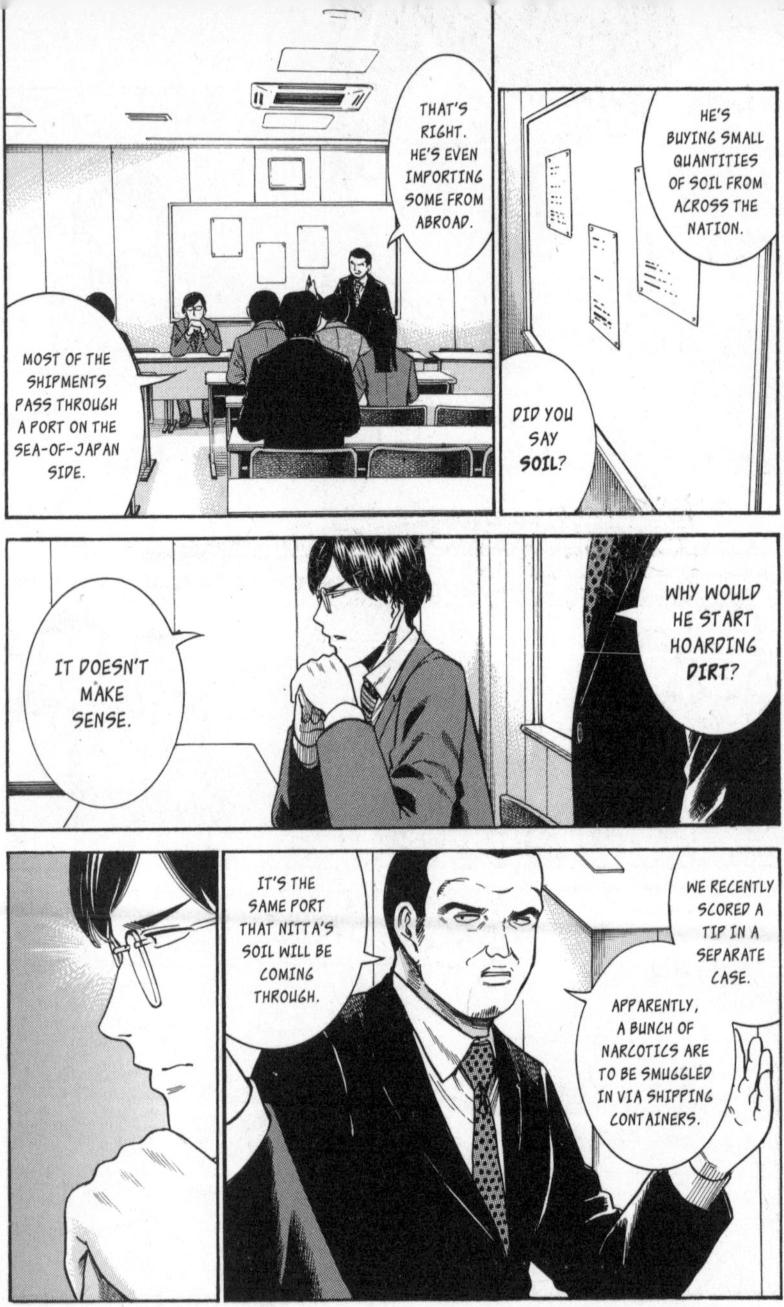
HE'S BUYING SMALL QUANTITIES OF SOIL FROM ACROSS THE NATION.
DID YOU SAY SOIL?
THAT'S RIGHT. HE'S EVEN IMPORTING SOME FROM ABROAD.
MOST OF THE SHIPMENTS PASS THROUGH A PORT ON THE SEA-OF-JAPAN SIDE.
WHY WOULD HE START HOARDING DIRT?
IT DOESN'T MAKE SENSE.
WE RECENTLY SCORED A TIP IN A SEPARATE CASE.
APPARENTLY, A BUNCH OF NARCOTICS ARE TO BE SMUGGLED IN VIA SHIPPING CONTAINERS.
IT'S THE SAME PORT THAT NITTA'S SOIL WILL BE COMING THROUGH.

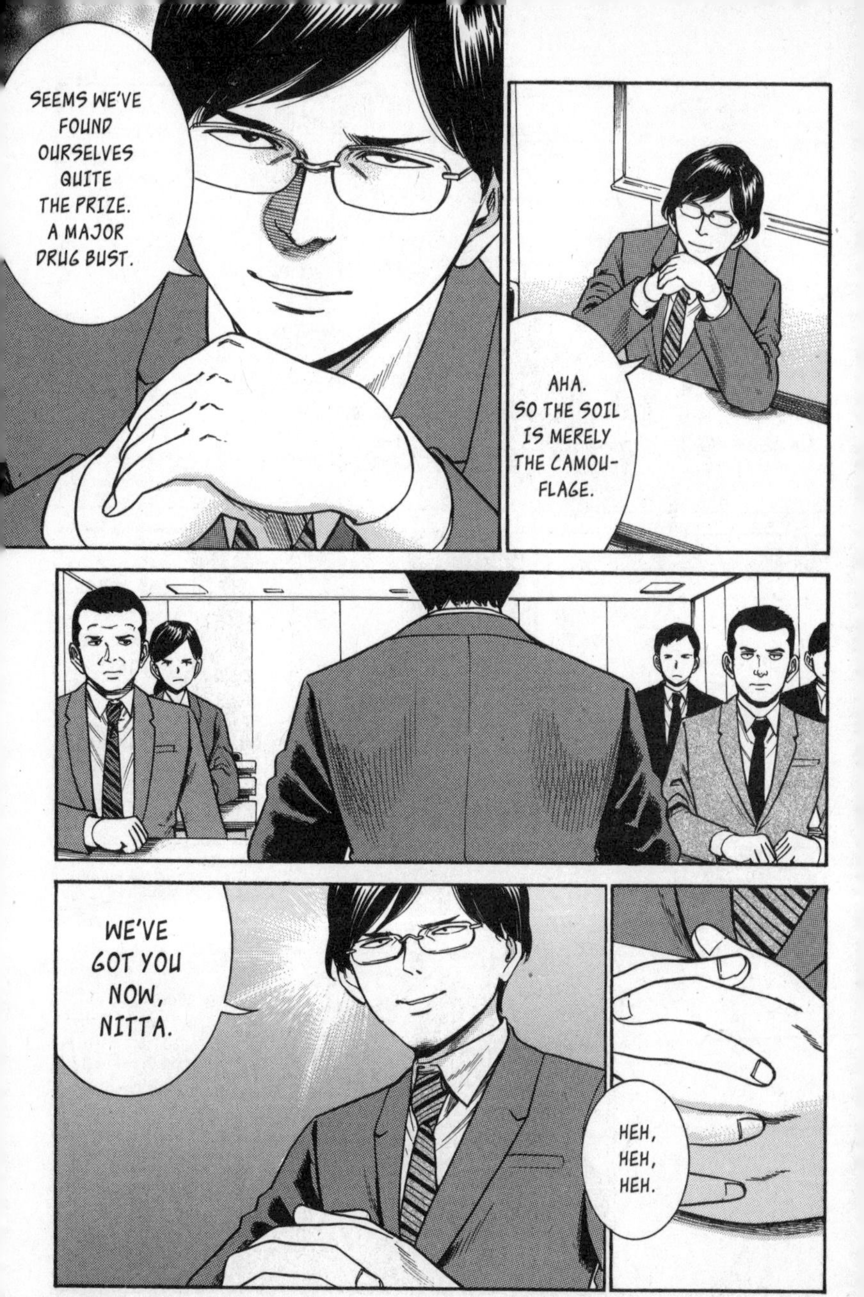
AHA. SO THE SOIL IS MERELY THE CAMOUFLAGE.
SEEMS WE'VE FOUND OURSELVES QUITE THE PRIZE. A MAJOR DRUG BUST.
HEH, HEH, HEH.
WE'VE GOT YOU NOW, NITTA.

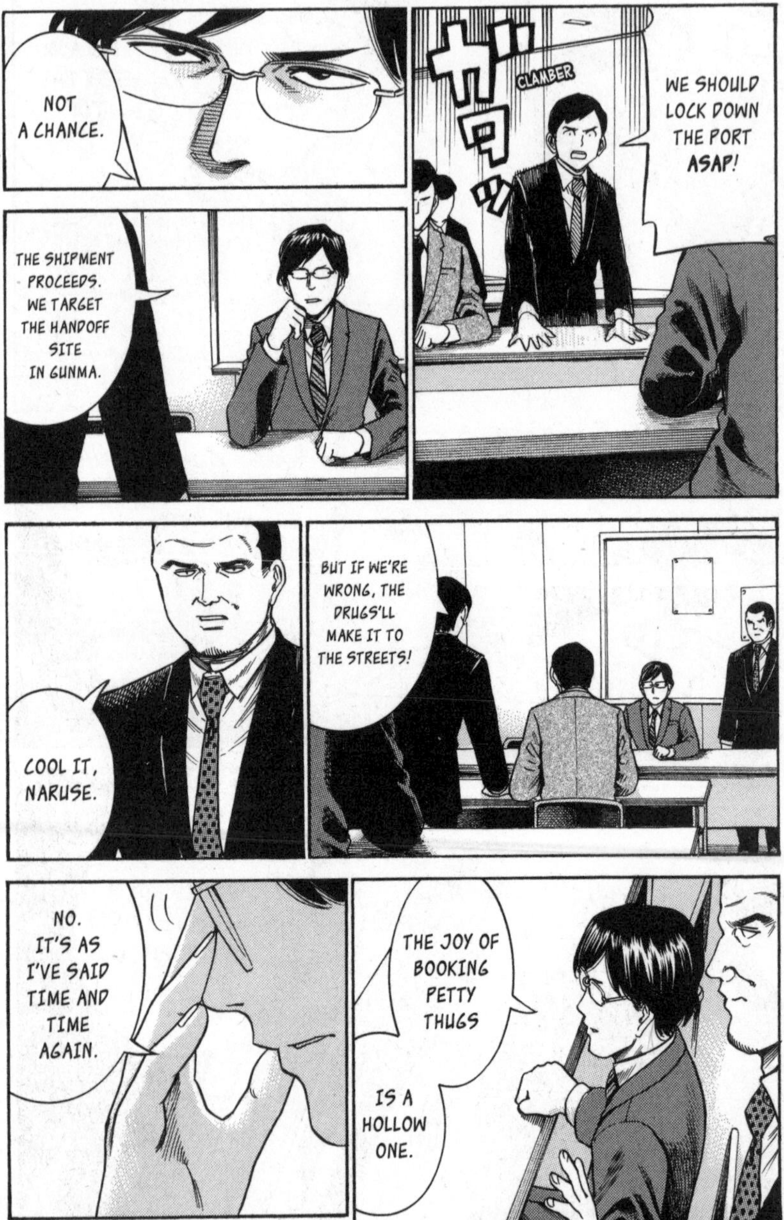
ガタッ
CLAMBER
WE SHOULD LOCK DOWN THE PORT ASAP!
NOT A CHANCE.
THE SHIPMENT PROCEEDS. WE TARGET THE HANDOFF SITE IN GUNMA.
BUT IF WE'RE WRONG, THE DRUGS'LL MAKE IT TO THE STREETS!
COOL IT, NARUSE.
THE JOY OF BOOKING PETTY THUGS
IS A HOLLOW ONE.
NO. IT'S AS I'VE SAID TIME AND TIME AGAIN.

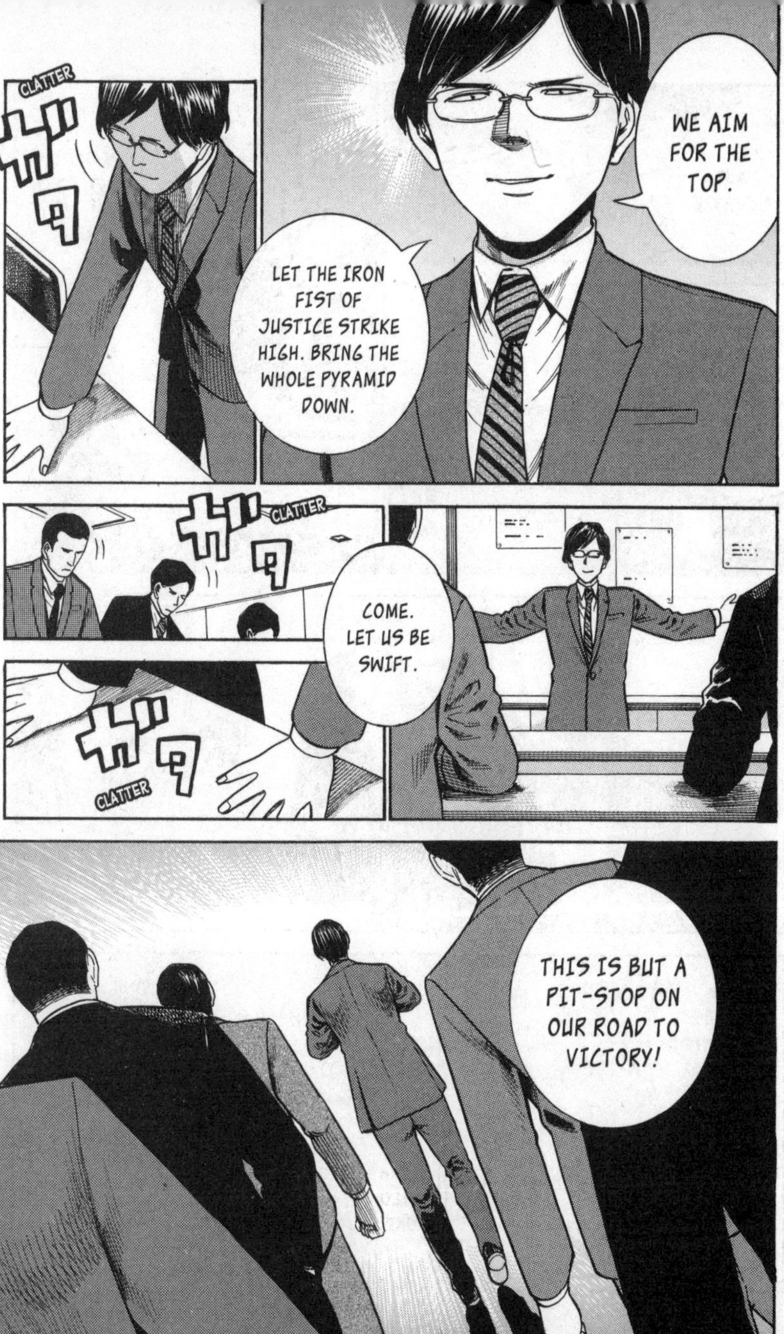
WE AIM FOR THE TOP.
LET THE IRON FIST OF JUSTICE STRIKE HIGH. BRING THE WHOLE PYRAMID DOWN.
ガタ
CLATTER
COME. LET US BE SWIFT.
ガタ
CLATTER
ガタ
CLATTER
THIS IS BUT A PIT-STOP ON OUR ROAD TO VICTORY!

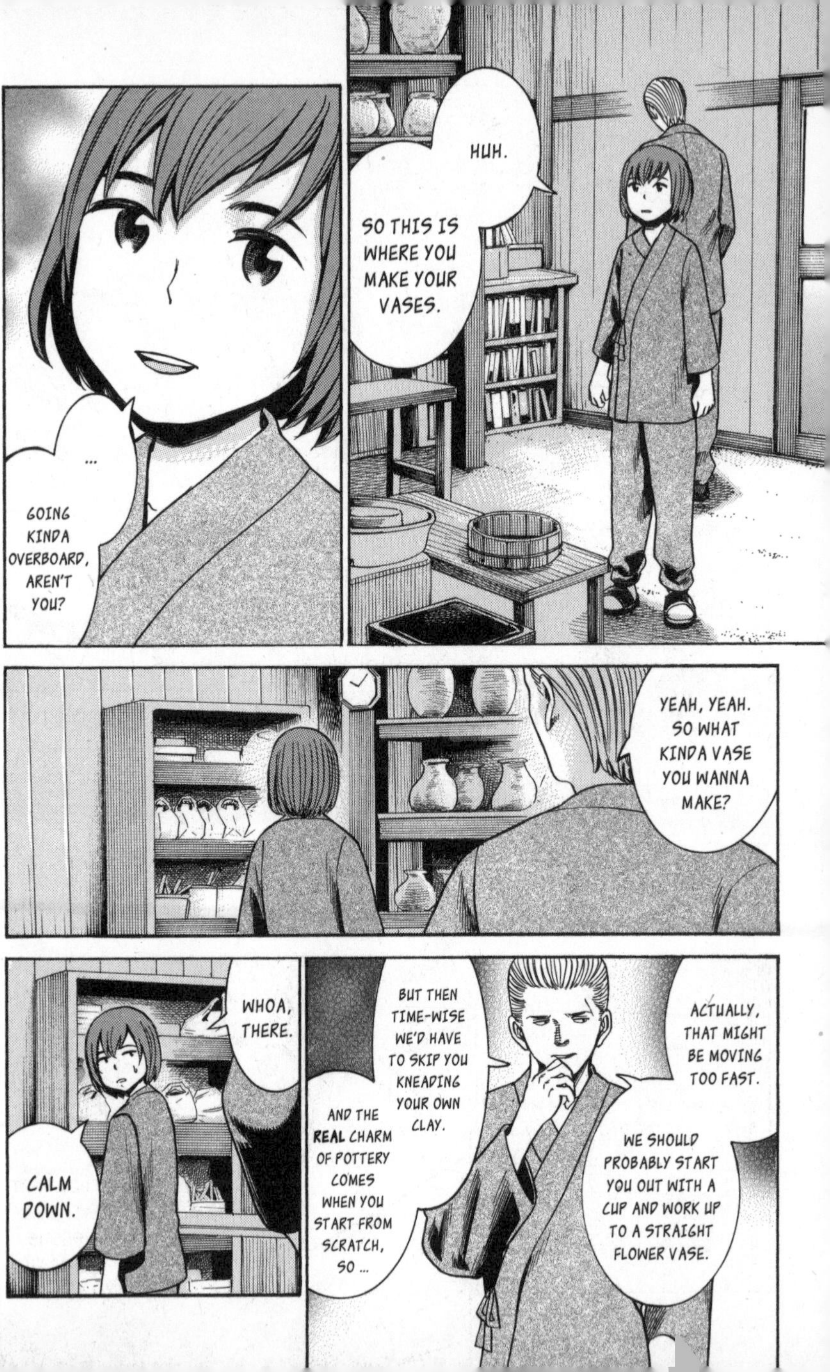
HUH.
SO THIS IS WHERE YOU MAKE YOUR VASES.
...
GOING KINDA OVERBOARD, AREN'T YOU?
YEAH, YEAH. SO WHAT KINDA VASE YOU WANNA MAKE?
ACTUALLY, THAT MIGHT BE MOVING TOO FAST.
WE SHOULD PROBABLY START YOU OUT WITH A CUP AND WORK UP TO A STRAIGHT FLOWER VASE.
BUT THEN TIME-WISE WE'D HAVE TO SKIP YOU KNEADING YOUR OWN CLAY.
AND THE **REAL** CHARM OF POTTERY COMES WHEN YOU START FROM SCRATCH, SO ...
WHOA, THERE.
CALM DOWN.

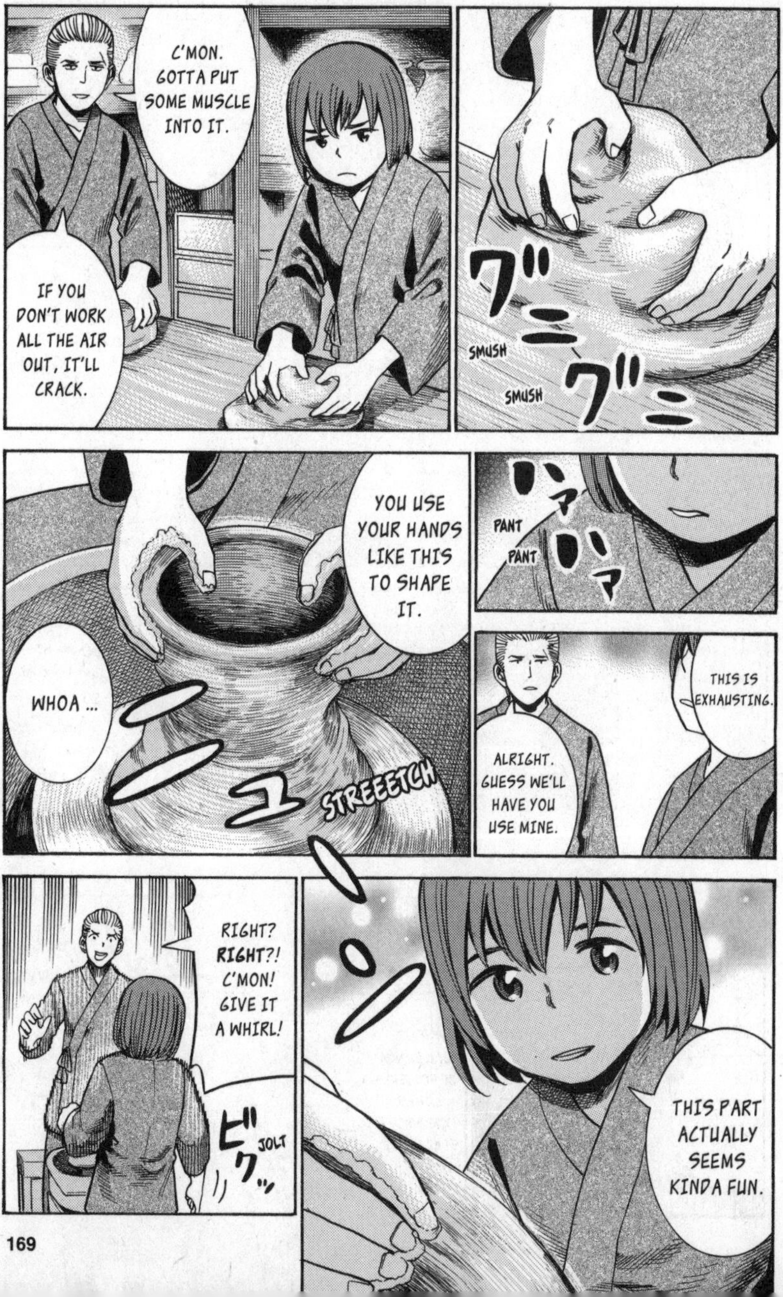
グニ グニ
SMUSH
SMUSH
C'MON. GOTTA PUT SOME MUSCLE INTO IT.
IF YOU DON'T WORK ALL THE AIR OUT, IT'LL CRACK.
ハァ ハァ
PANT
PANT
THIS IS EXHAUSTING.
ALRIGHT. GUESS WE'LL HAVE YOU USE MINE.
YOU USE YOUR HANDS LIKE THIS TO SHAPE IT.
WHOA ...
STREEEETCH
THIS PART ACTUALLY SEEMS KINDA FUN.
RIGHT? **RIGHT?!** C'MON! GIVE IT A WHIRL!
ビクッ
JOLT

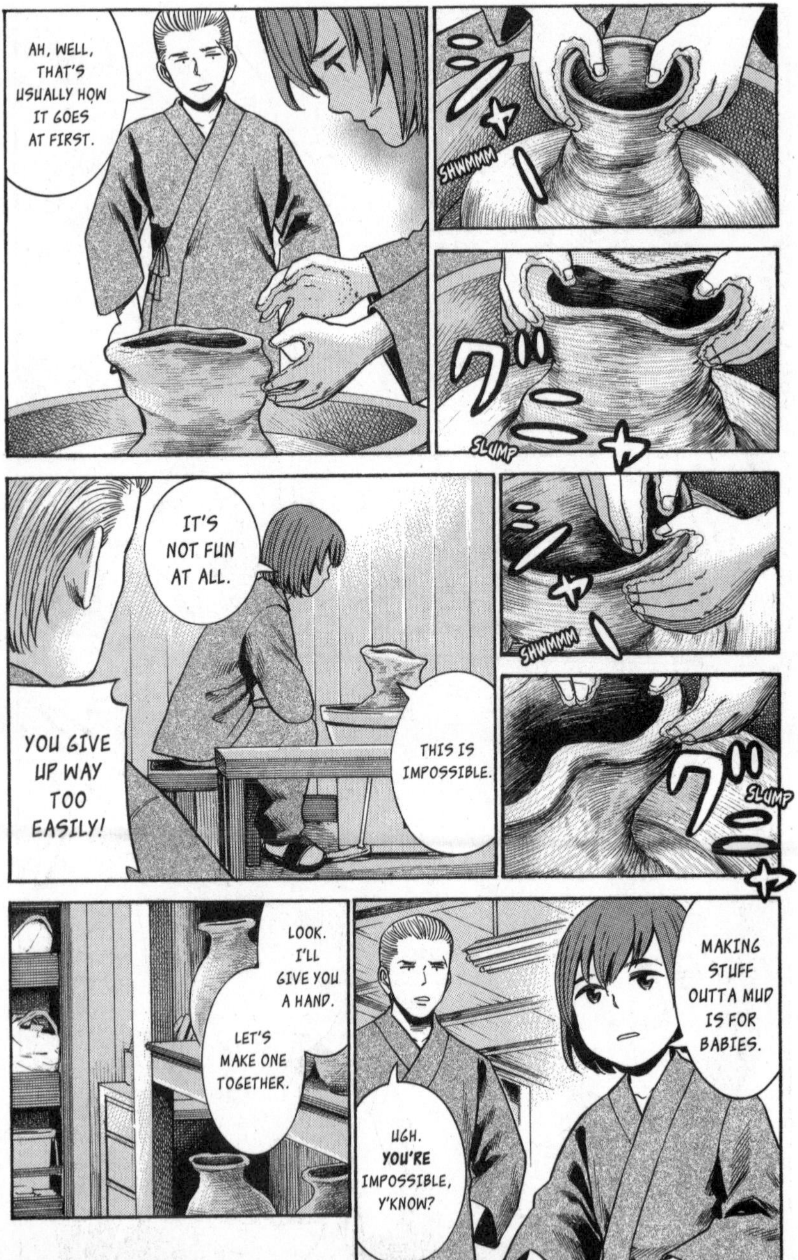
SHWMMM
SLUMP
AH, WELL, THAT'S USUALLY HOW IT GOES AT FIRST.
SHWMMM
SLUMP
IT'S NOT FUN AT ALL.
THIS IS IMPOSSIBLE.
YOU GIVE UP WAY TOO EASILY!
MAKING STUFF OUTTA MUD IS FOR BABIES.
UGH. **YOU'RE** IMPOSSIBLE, Y'KNOW?
LOOK. I'LL GIVE YOU A HAND.
LET'S MAKE ONE TOGETHER.

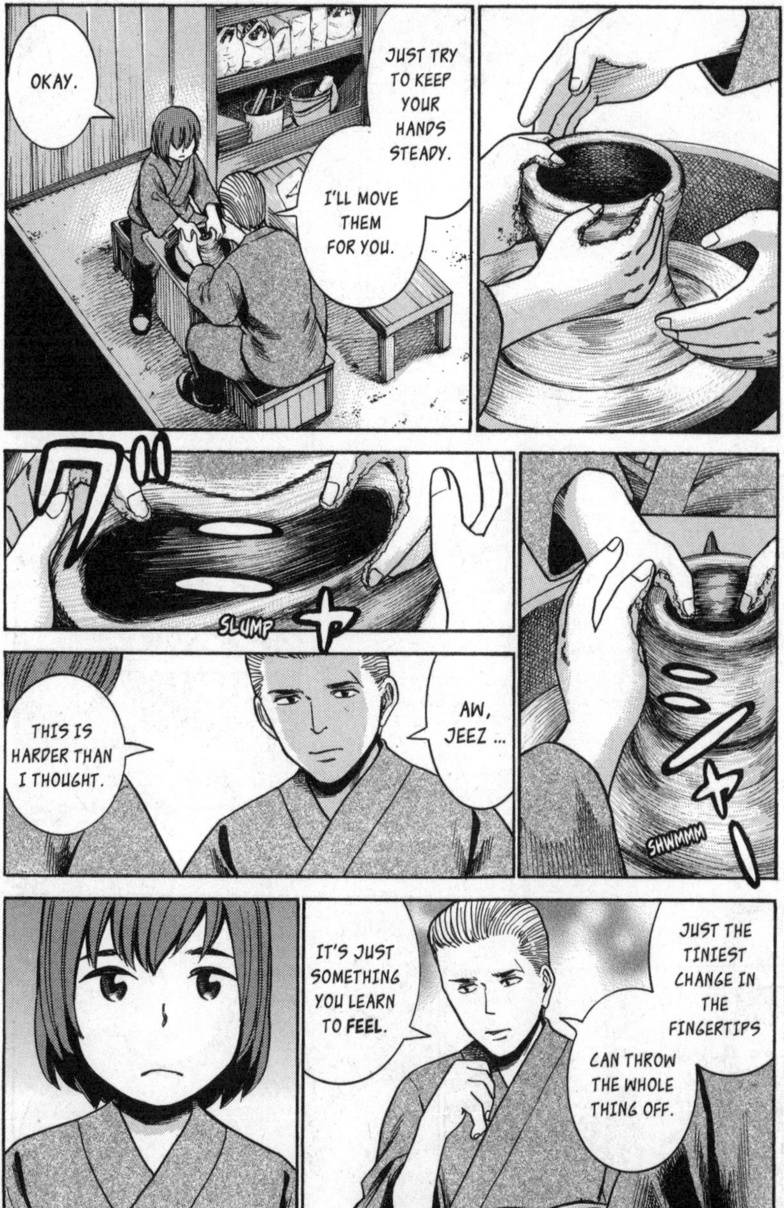
JUST TRY TO KEEP YOUR HANDS STEADY.
I'LL MOVE THEM FOR YOU.
OKAY.
SHWMMM
SLUMP
AW, JEEZ ...
THIS IS HARDER THAN I THOUGHT.
JUST THE TINIEST CHANGE IN THE FINGERTIPS
CAN THROW THE WHOLE THING OFF.
IT'S JUST SOMETHING YOU LEARN TO FEEL.

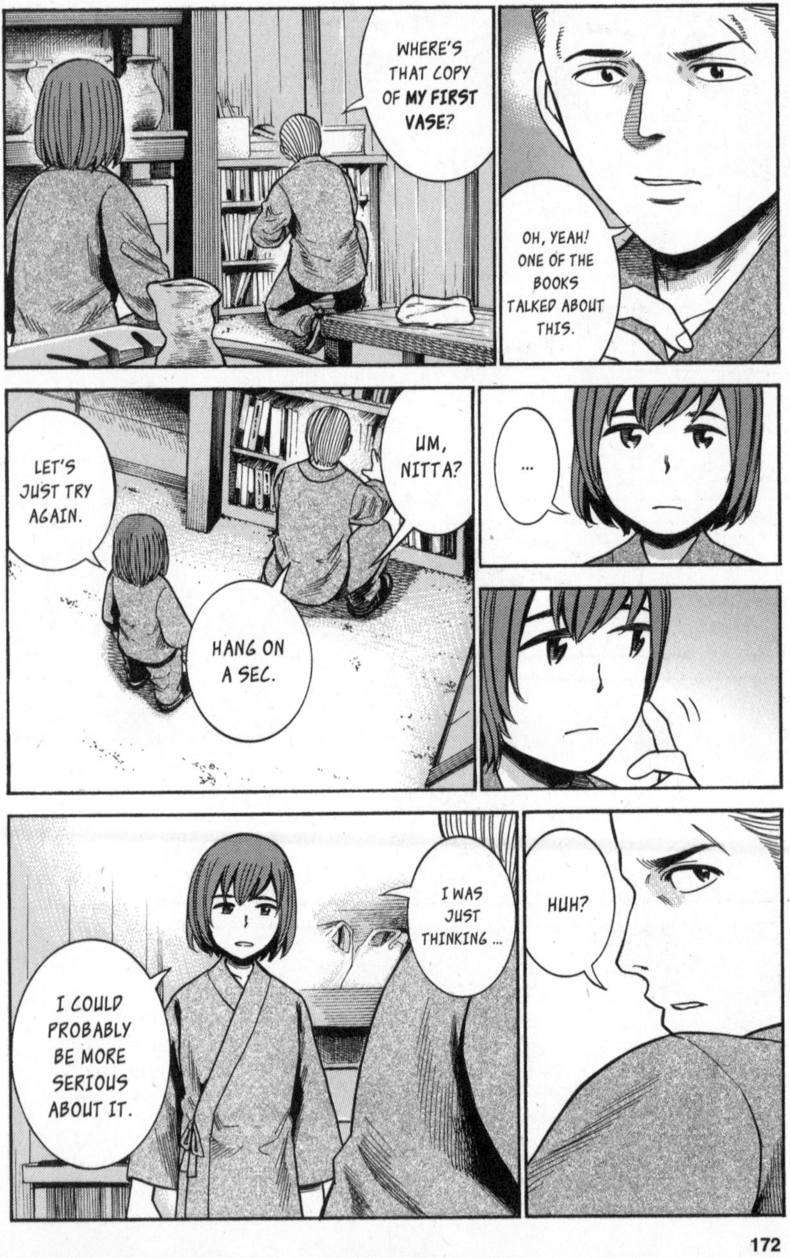
OH, YEAH! ONE OF THE BOOKS TALKED ABOUT THIS.
WHERE'S THAT COPY OF **MY FIRST VASE**?
...
UM, NITTA?
LET'S JUST TRY AGAIN.
HANG ON A SEC.
HUH?
I WAS JUST THINKING ...
I COULD PROBABLY BE MORE SERIOUS ABOUT IT.

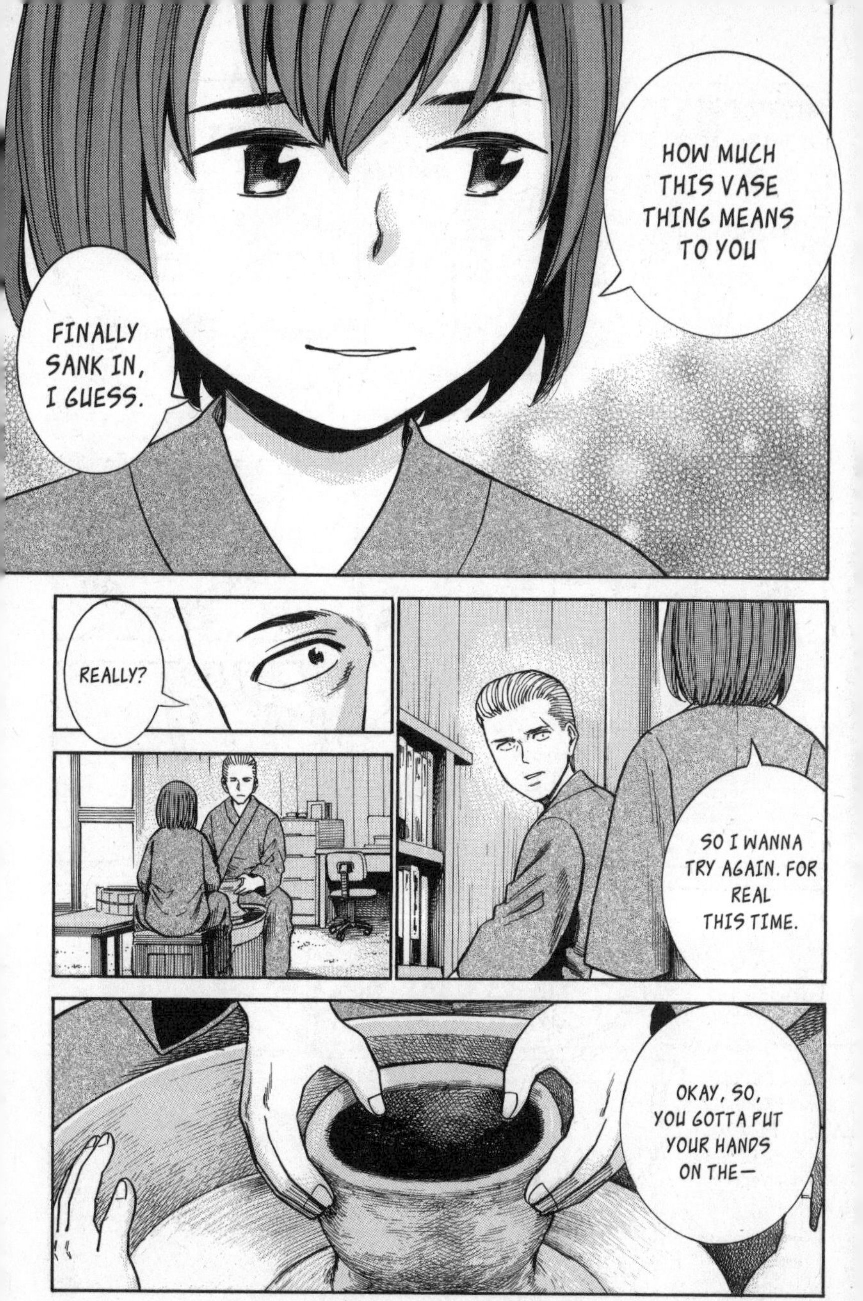
HOW MUCH THIS VASE THING MEANS TO YOU
FINALLY SANK IN, I GUESS.
SO I WANNA TRY AGAIN. FOR REAL THIS TIME.
REALLY?
OKAY, SO, YOU GOTTA PUT YOUR HANDS ON THE—

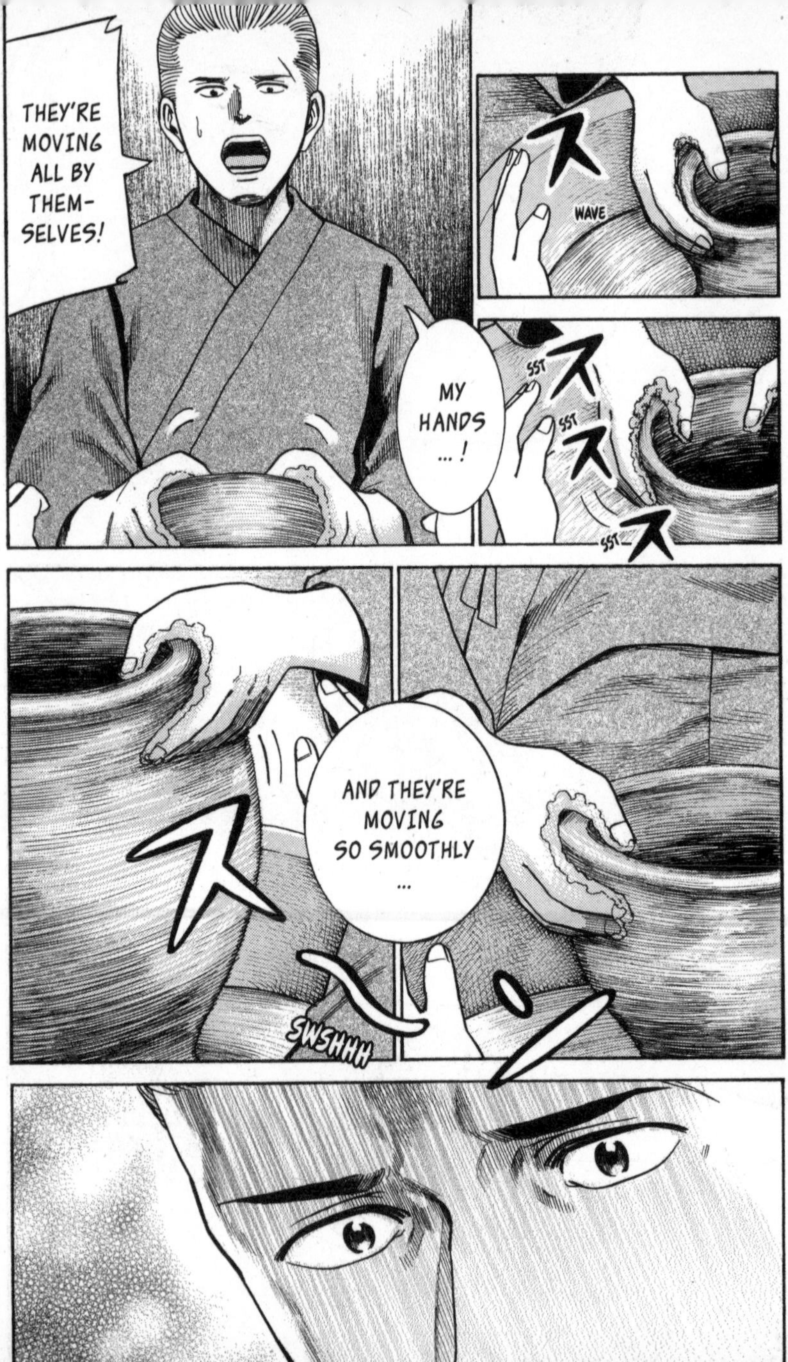
WAVE
SST
SST
SST
MY HANDS ...!
THEY'RE MOVING ALL BY THEM-SELVES!
AND THEY'RE MOVING SO SMOOTHLY ...
SWSHHH

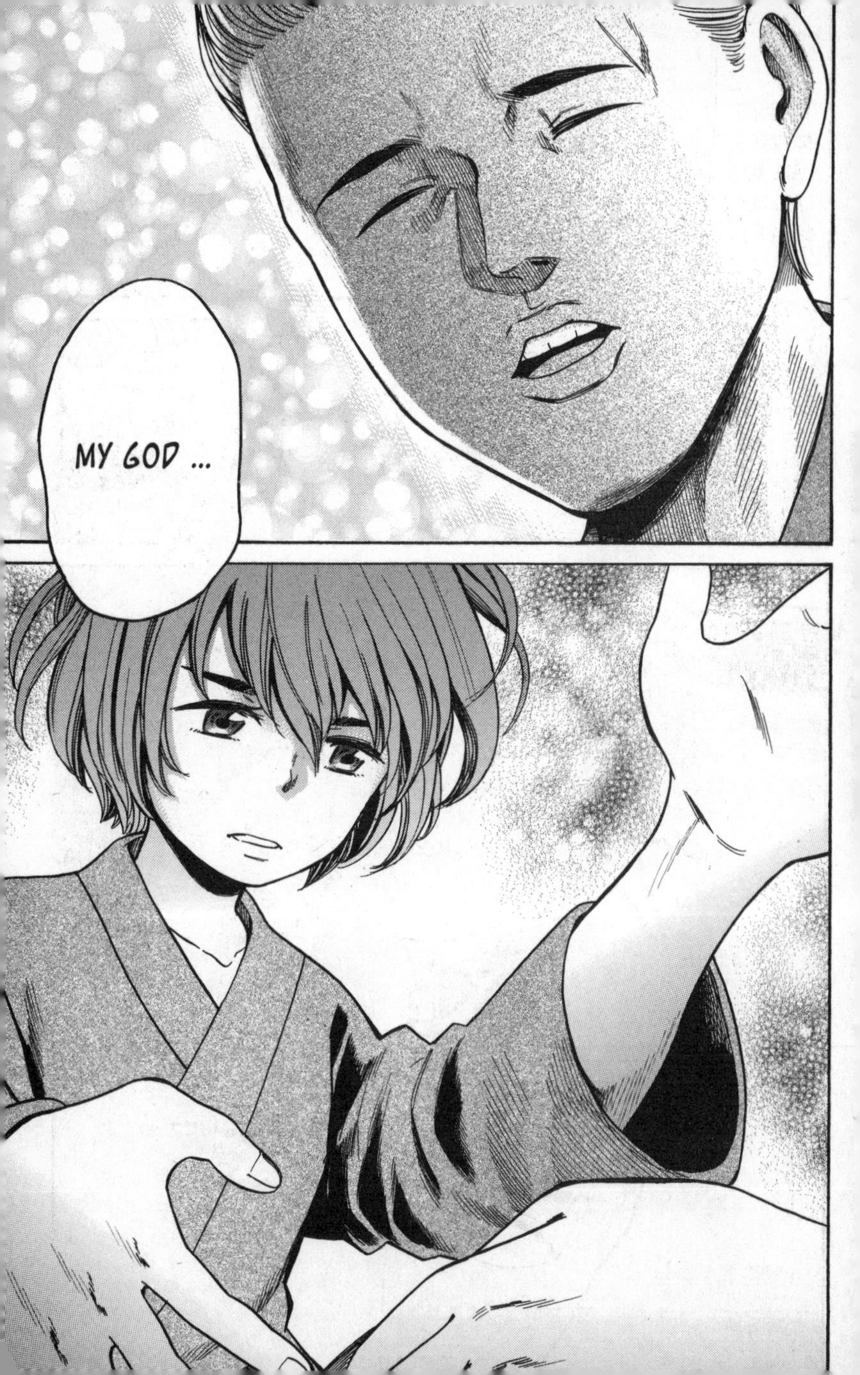
MY GOD ...

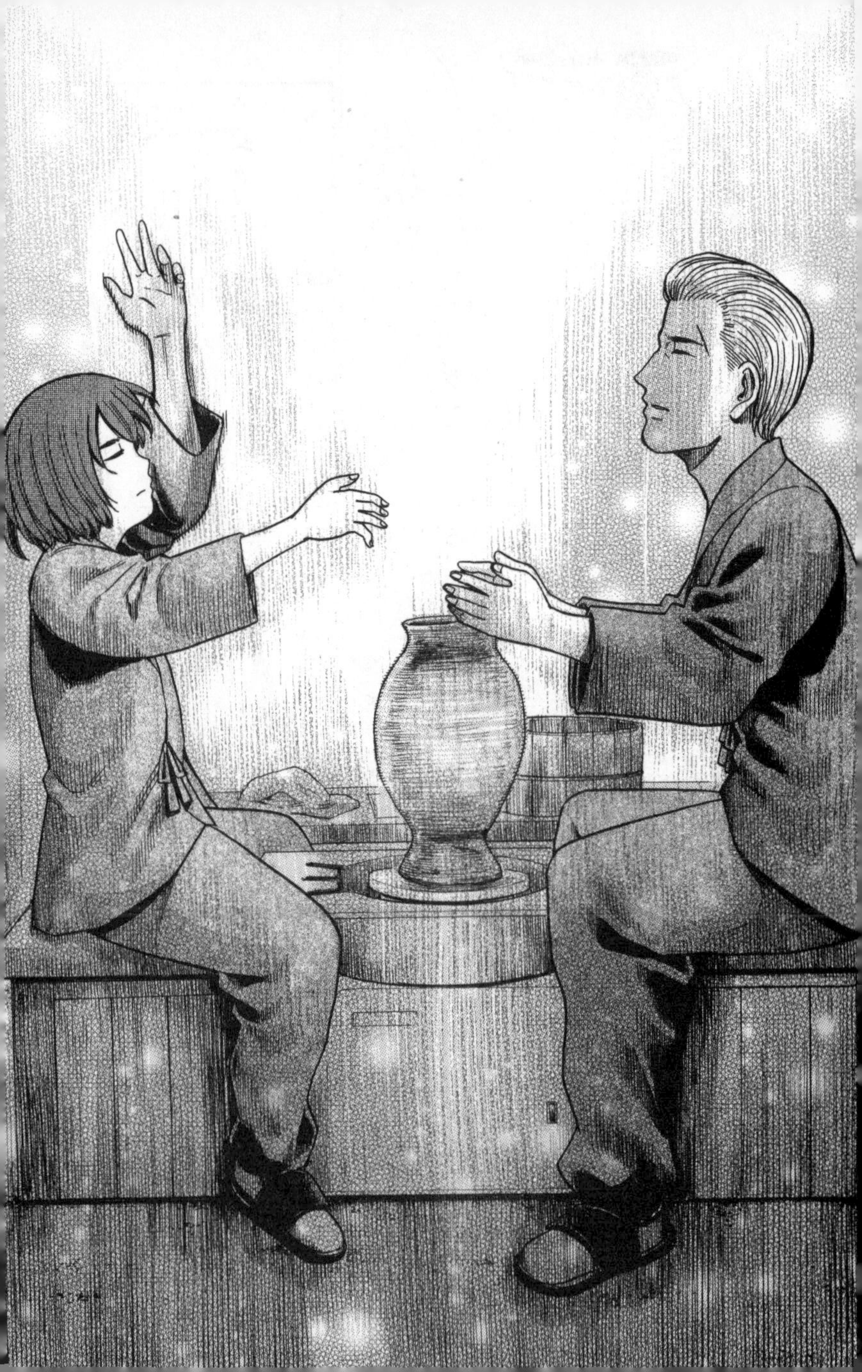

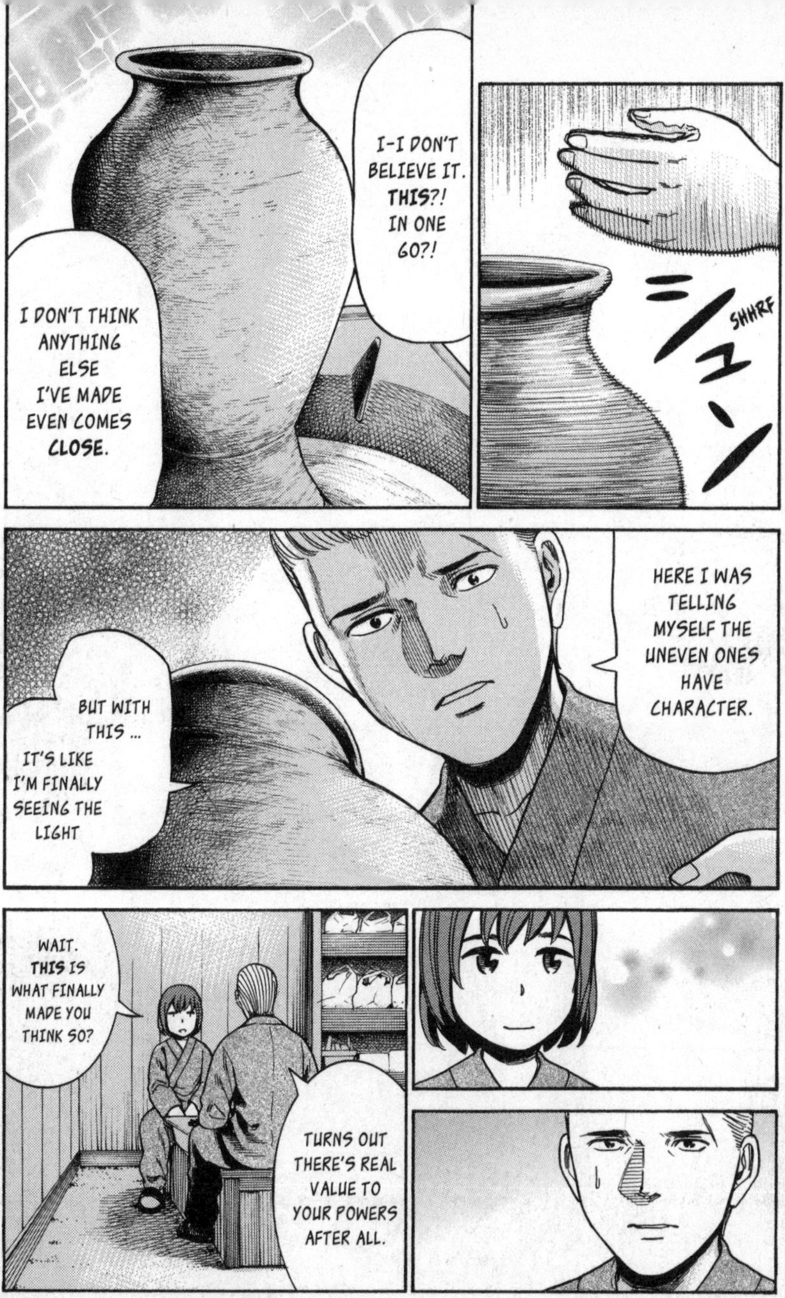
SHHRF
I-I DON'T BELIEVE IT. THIS?! IN ONE GO?!
I DON'T THINK ANYTHING ELSE I'VE MADE EVEN COMES CLOSE.
HERE I WAS TELLING MYSELF THE UNEVEN ONES HAVE CHARACTER.
BUT WITH THIS ... IT'S LIKE I'M FINALLY SEEING THE LIGHT
WAIT. THIS IS WHAT FINALLY MADE YOU THINK SO?
TURNS OUT THERE'S REAL VALUE TO YOUR POWERS AFTER ALL.

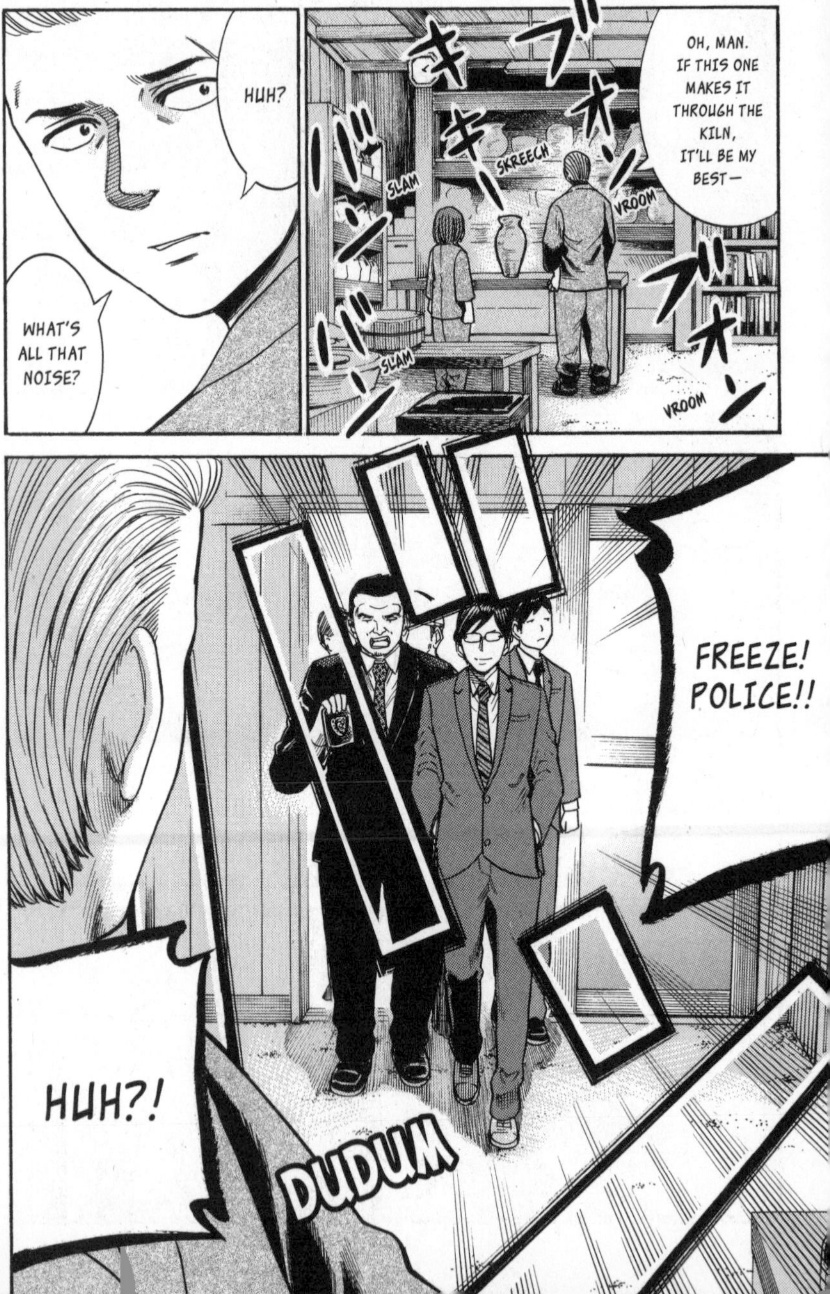
OH, MAN. IF THIS ONE MAKES IT THROUGH THE KILN, IT'LL BE MY BEST—
VROOM
SKREECH
VROOM
SLAM
SLAM
HUH?
WHAT'S ALL THAT NOISE?
FREEZE! POLICE!!
DUDUM
HUH?!

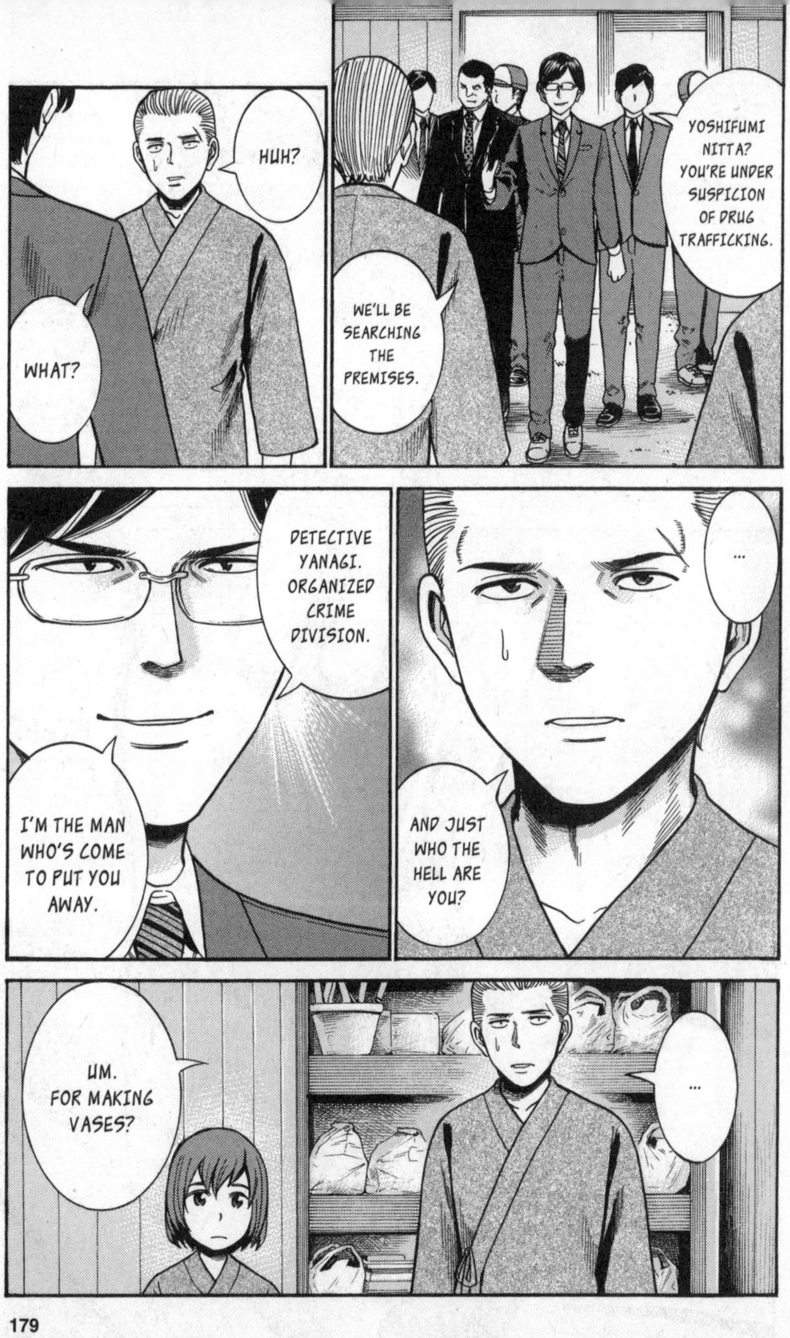
YOSHIFUMI NITTA? YOU'RE UNDER SUSPICION OF DRUG TRAFFICKING.
WE'LL BE SEARCHING THE PREMISES.
HUH?
WHAT?
...
AND JUST WHO THE HELL ARE YOU?
DETECTIVE YANAGI. ORGANIZED CRIME DIVISION.
I'M THE MAN WHO'S COME TO PUT YOU AWAY.
...
UM. FOR MAKING VASES?

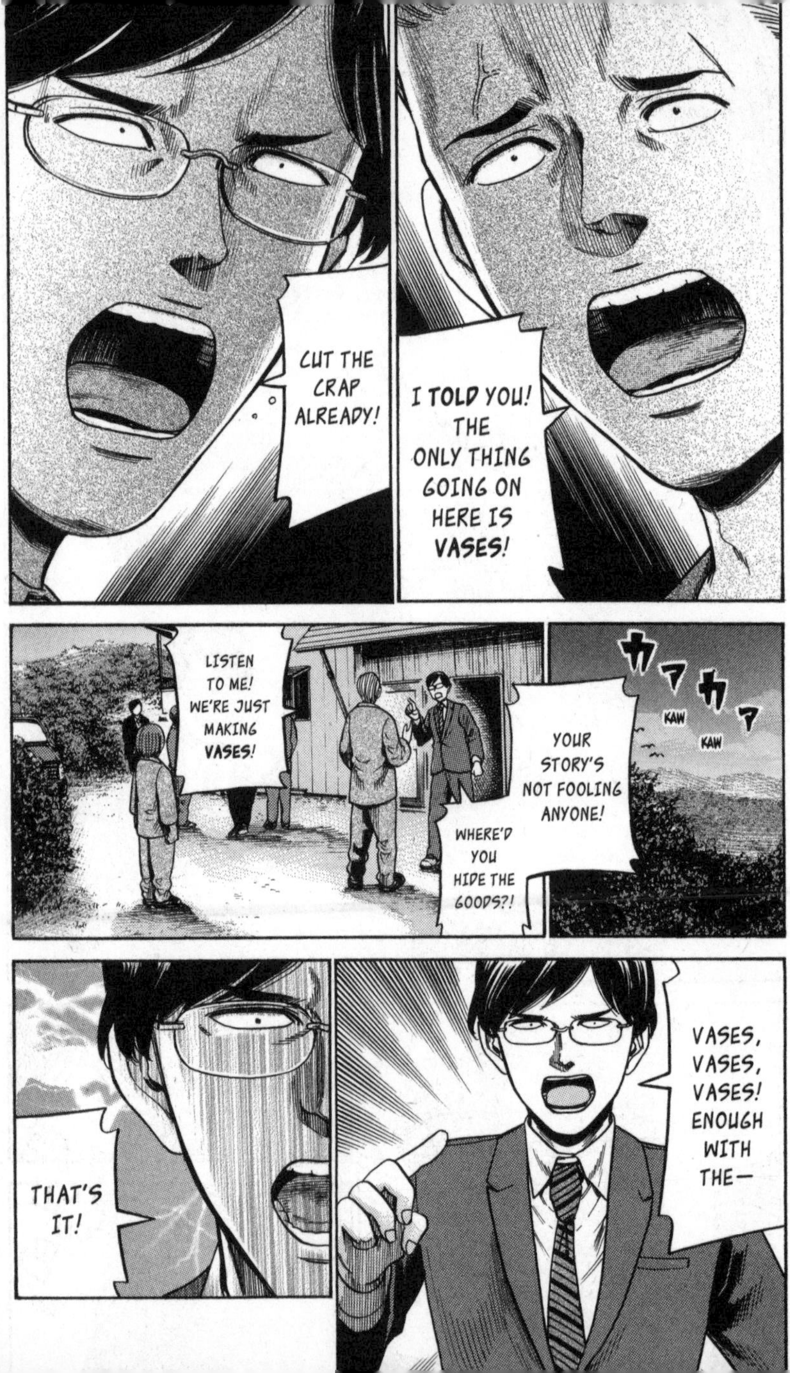
I TOLD YOU! THE ONLY THING GOING ON HERE IS VASES!
CUT THE CRAP ALREADY!
カァカァ
KAW KAW
YOUR STORY'S NOT FOOLING ANYONE!
WHERE'D YOU HIDE THE GOODS?!
LISTEN TO ME! WE'RE JUST MAKING VASES!
VASES, VASES, VASES! ENOUGH WITH THE—
THAT'S IT!

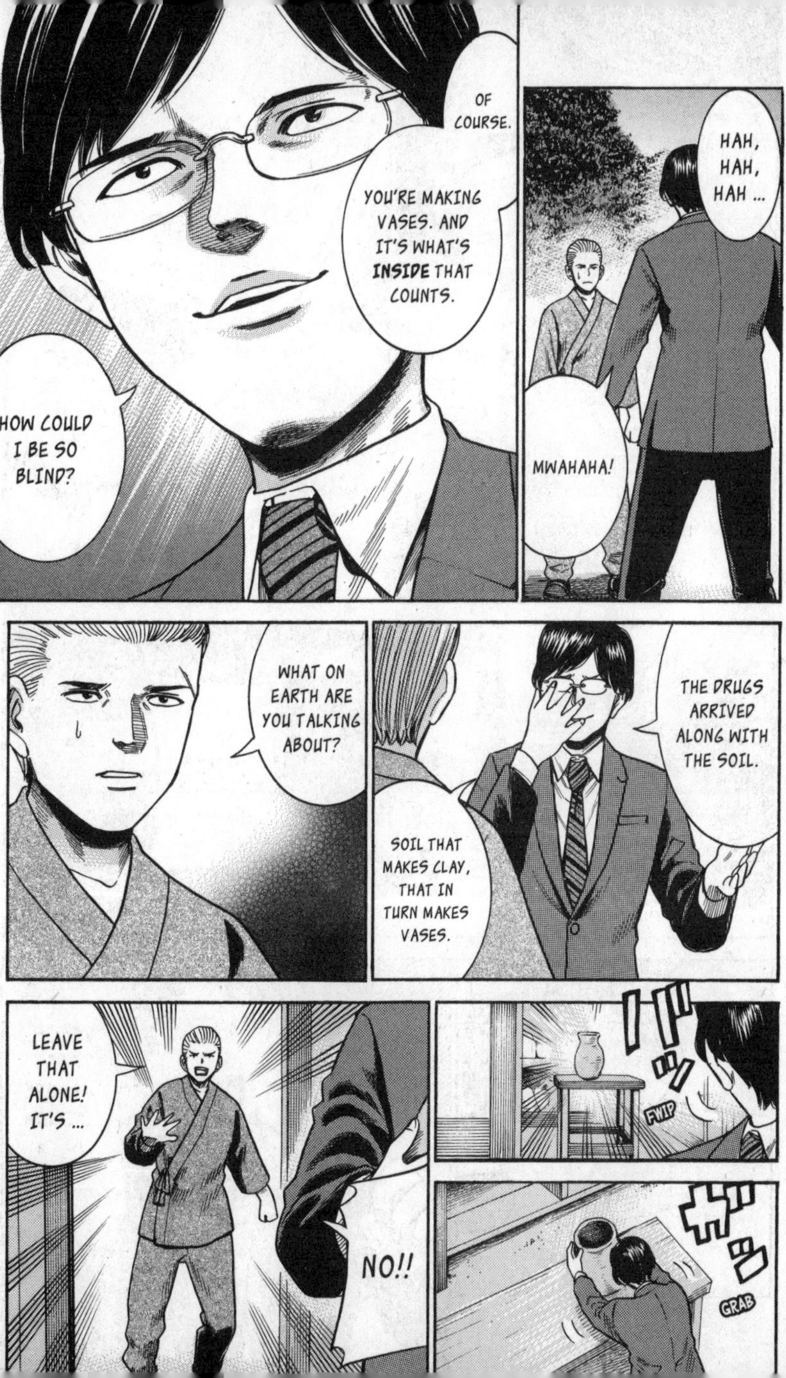
HAH, HAH, HAH ...
MWAHAHA!
OF COURSE.
YOU'RE MAKING VASES. AND IT'S WHAT'S **INSIDE** THAT COUNTS.
HOW COULD I BE SO BLIND?
THE DRUGS ARRIVED ALONG WITH THE SOIL.
SOIL THAT MAKES CLAY, THAT IN TURN MAKES VASES.
WHAT ON EARTH ARE YOU TALKING ABOUT?
FWIP
GRAB
LEAVE THAT ALONE! IT'S ...
NO!!

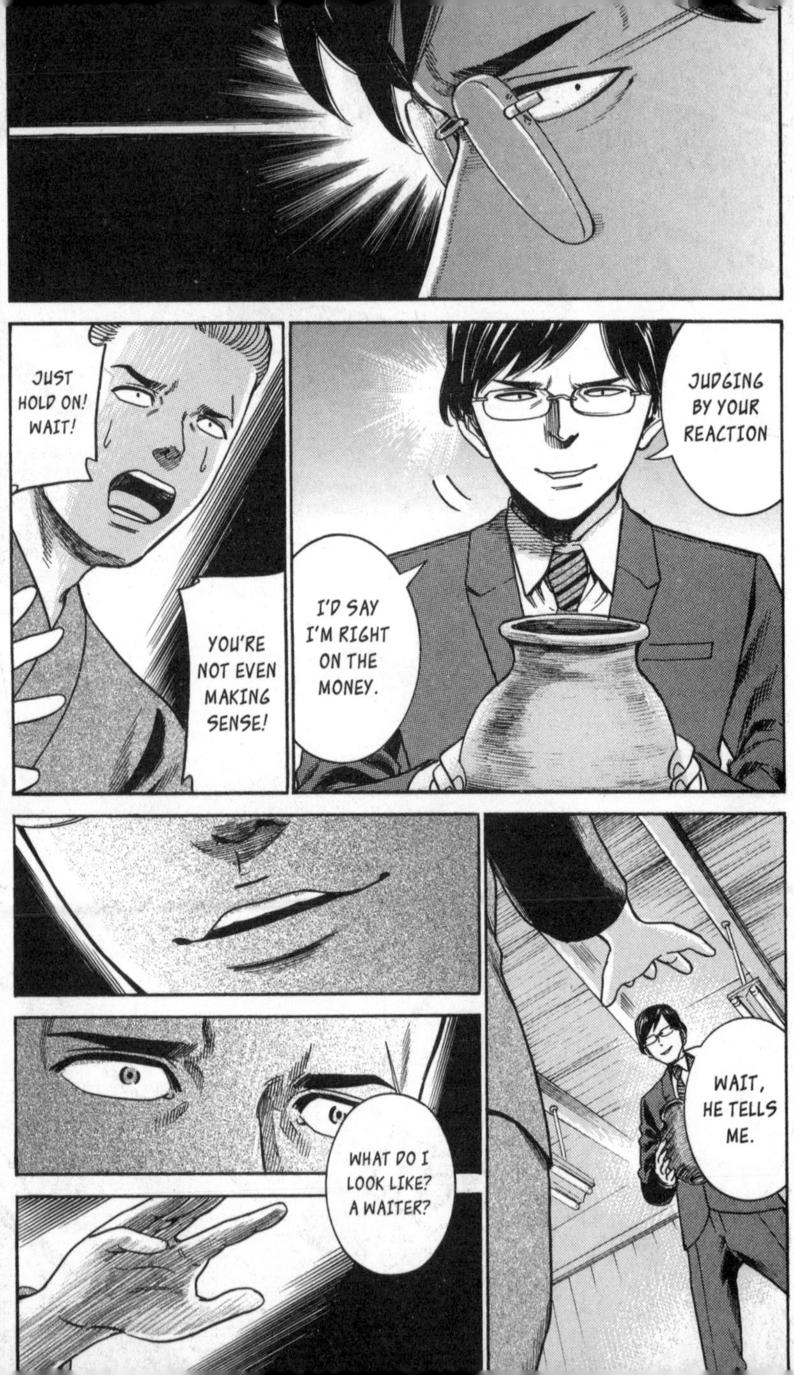
JUDGING BY YOUR REACTION
I'D SAY I'M RIGHT ON THE MONEY.
JUST HOLD ON! WAIT!
YOU'RE NOT EVEN MAKING SENSE!
WAIT, HE TELLS ME.
WHAT DO I LOOK LIKE? A WAITER?

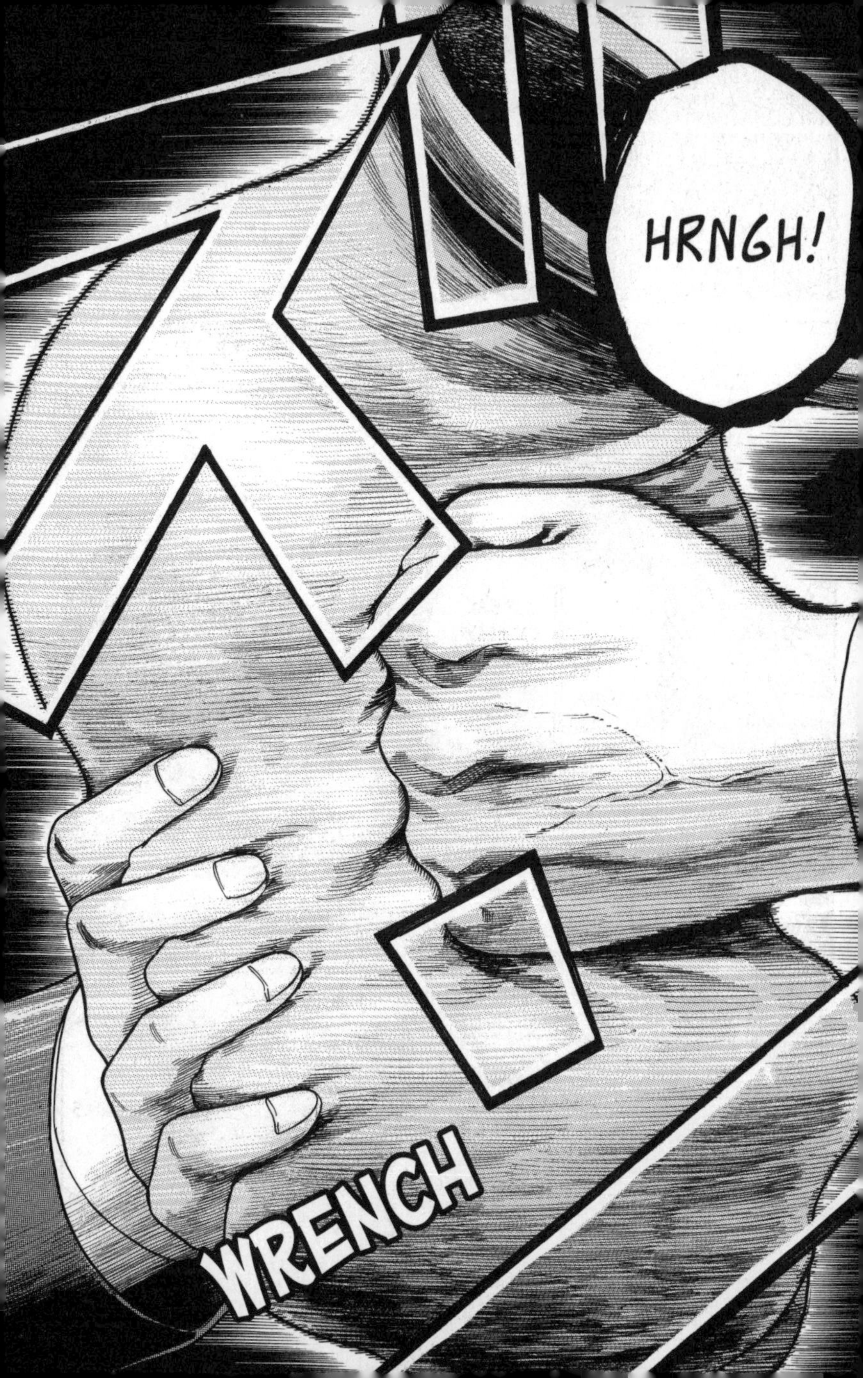
HRNGH!
WRENCH

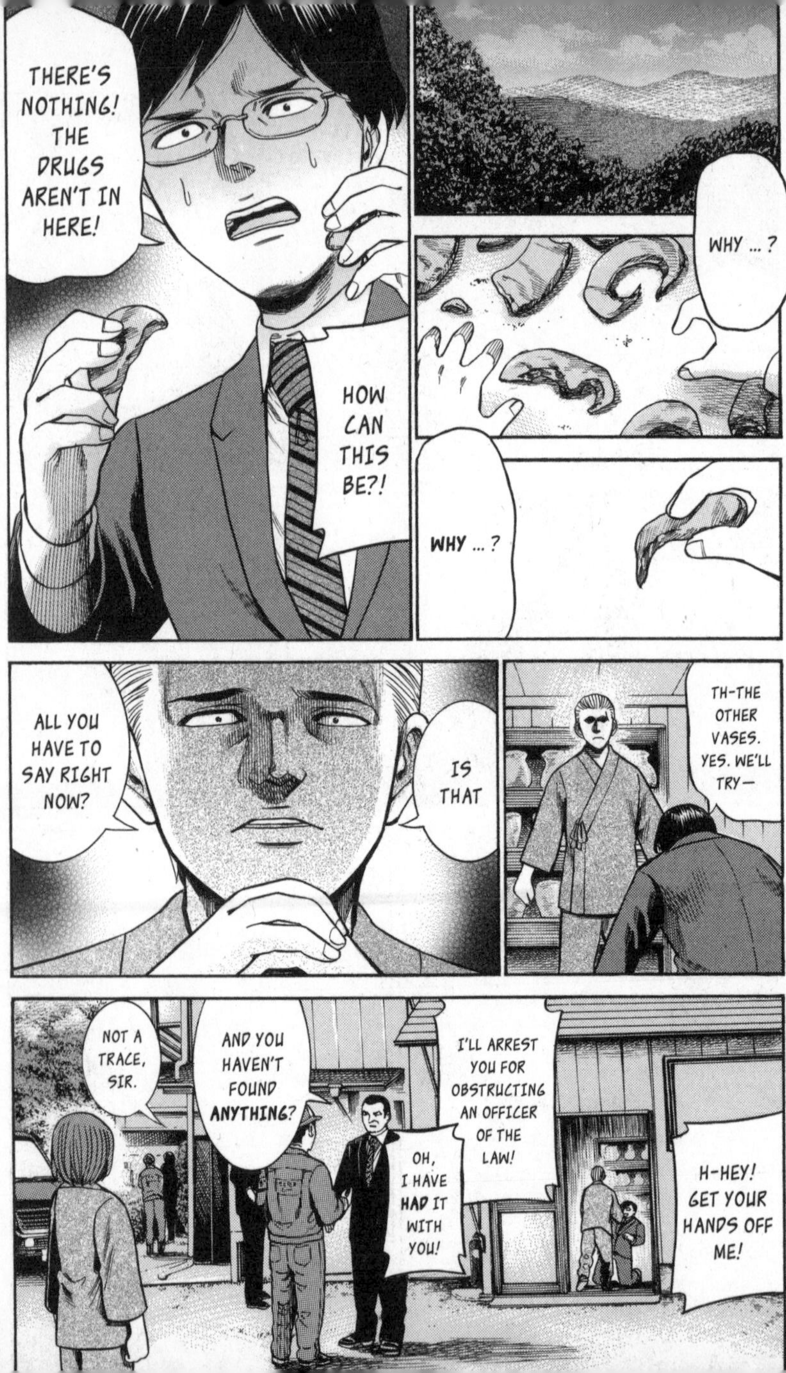
WHY ...?
WHY ...?
THERE'S NOTHING! THE DRUGS AREN'T IN HERE!
HOW CAN THIS BE?!
TH-THE OTHER VASES. YES. WE'LL TRY—
IS THAT
ALL YOU HAVE TO SAY RIGHT NOW?
H-HEY! GET YOUR HANDS OFF ME!
I'LL ARREST YOU FOR OBSTRUCTING AN OFFICER OF THE LAW!
OH, I HAVE **HAD** IT WITH YOU!
AND YOU HAVEN'T FOUND **ANYTHING**?
NOT A TRACE, SIR.

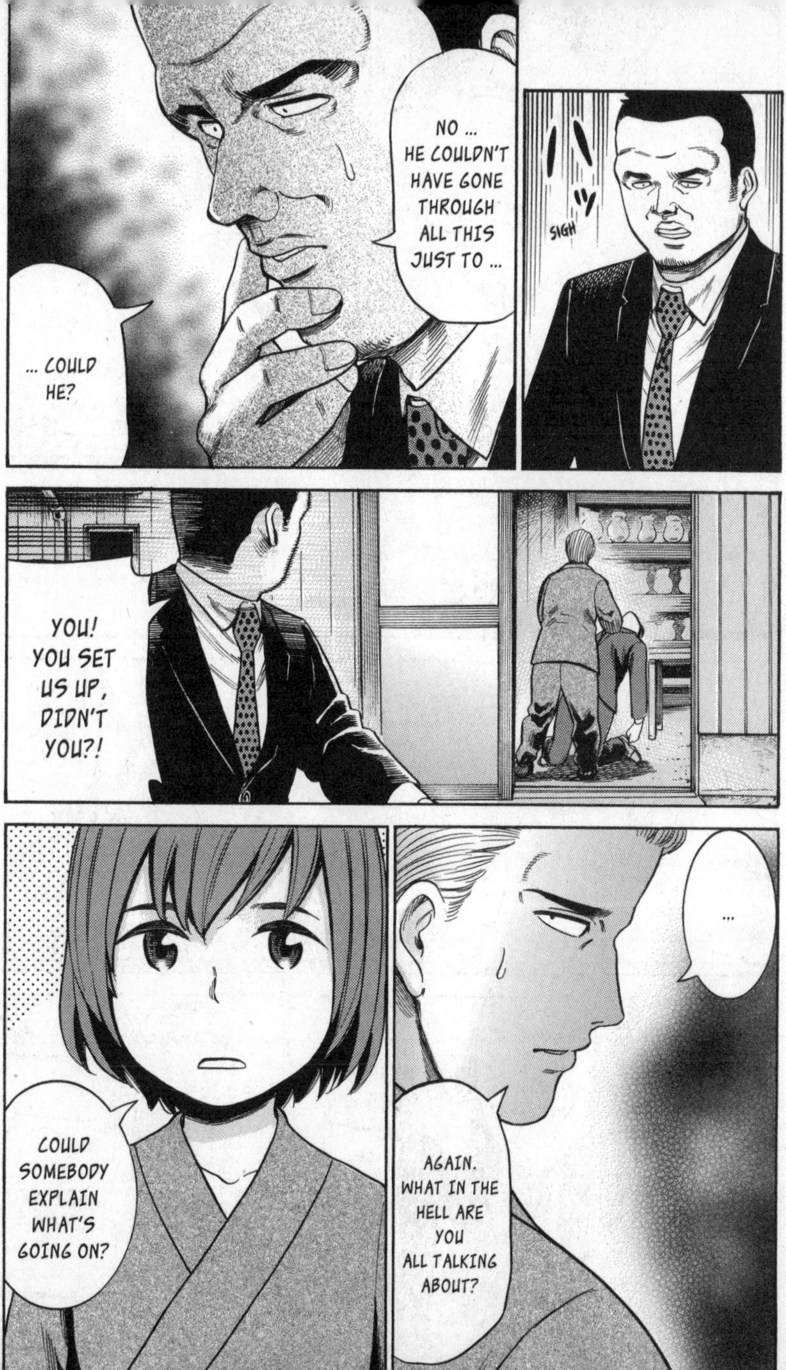
SIGH
NO ... HE COULDN'T HAVE GONE THROUGH ALL THIS JUST TO ...
... COULD HE?
YOU! YOU SET US UP, DIDN'T YOU?!
...
AGAIN. WHAT IN THE HELL ARE YOU ALL TALKING ABOUT?
COULD SOMEBODY EXPLAIN WHAT'S GOING ON?

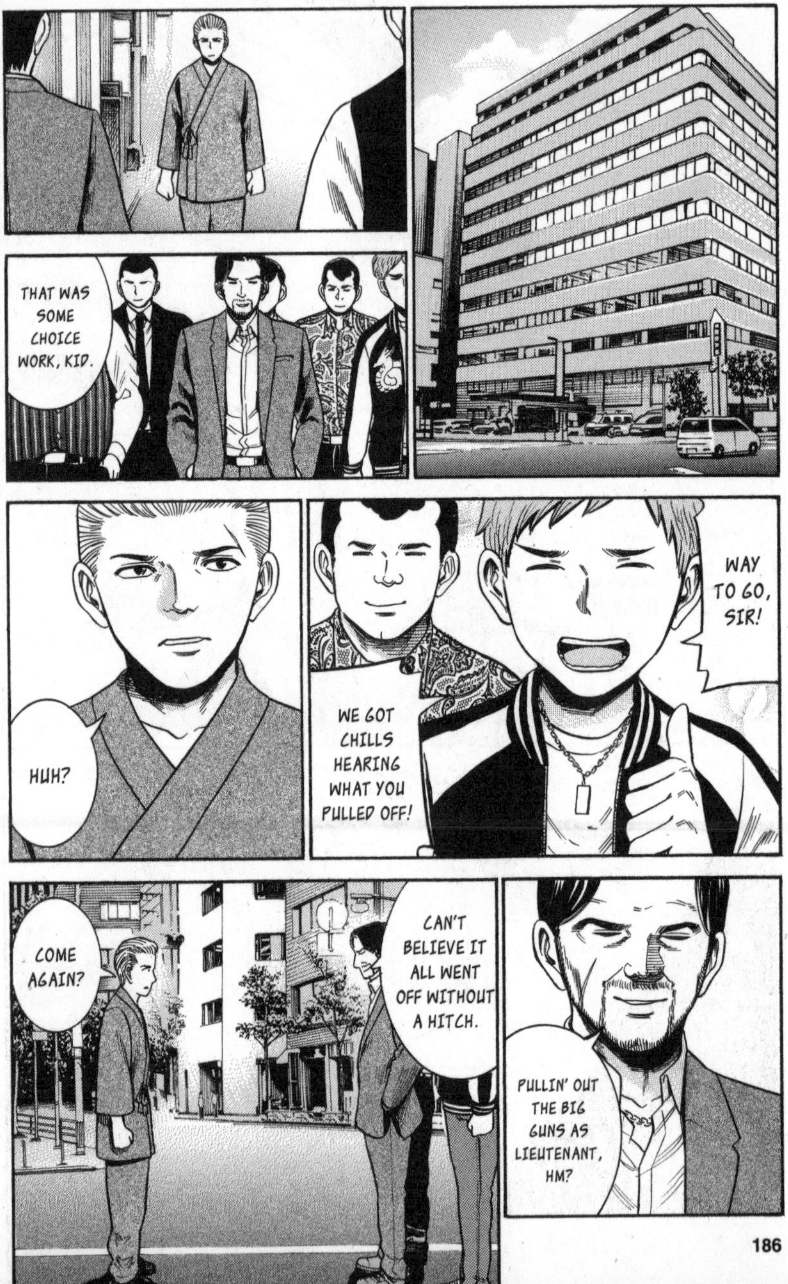
THAT WAS SOME CHOICE WORK, KID.
WAY TO GO, SIR!
WE GOT CHILLS HEARING WHAT YOU PULLED OFF!
HUH?
PULLIN' OUT THE BIG GUNS AS LIEUTENANT, HM?
CAN'T BELIEVE IT ALL WENT OFF WITHOUT A HITCH.
COME AGAIN?

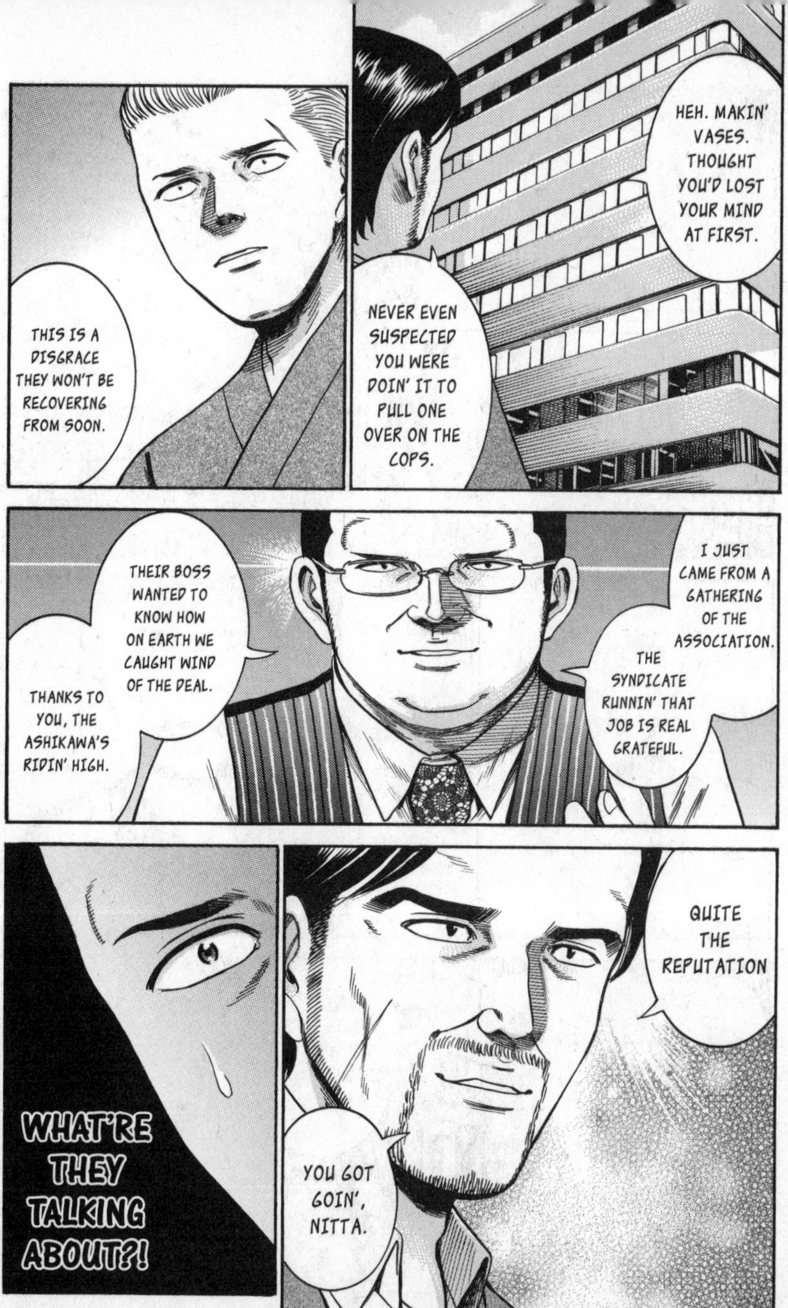
HEH. MAKIN' VASES. THOUGHT YOU'D LOST YOUR MIND AT FIRST.
NEVER EVEN SUSPECTED YOU WERE DOIN' IT TO PULL ONE OVER ON THE COPS.
THIS IS A DISGRACE THEY WON'T BE RECOVERING FROM SOON.
I JUST CAME FROM A GATHERING OF THE ASSOCIATION.
THE SYNDICATE RUNNIN' THAT JOB IS REAL GRATEFUL.
THEIR BOSS WANTED TO KNOW HOW ON EARTH WE CAUGHT WIND OF THE DEAL.
THANKS TO YOU, THE ASHIKAWA'S RIDIN' HIGH.
QUITE THE REPUTATION
YOU GOT GOIN', NITTA.
WHAT'RE THEY TALKING ABOUT?!

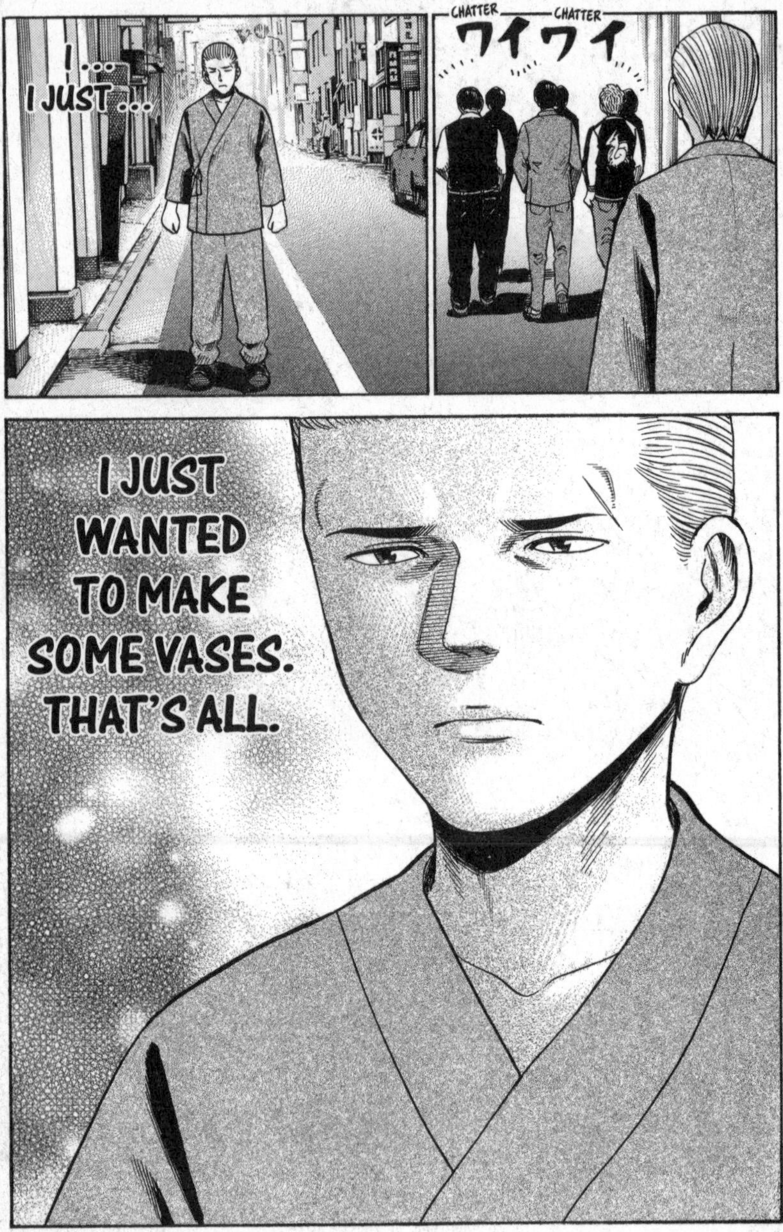
CHATTER CHATTER
ワイワイ
I ... I JUST ...
I JUST WANTED TO MAKE SOME VASES. THAT'S ALL.

CHAPTER 43 END

HOW TO MAKE VASES

壺の作り方

HINAMATSURI.
TO BE CONTINUED
IN VOLUME 9.

HINAMATSURI Volume 8
© Masao Ohtake 2015
First published in Japan in 2015 by KADOKAWA CORPORATION, Tokyo
English translation rights arranged with KADOKAWA CORPORATION, Tokyo

ISBN: 978-1-64273-057-9

Translated by Stephen Kohler
English Edition Published by One Peace Books 2020

Printed in Canada
1 2 3 4 5 6 7 8 9 10

One Peace Books
43-32 22nd Street STE 204 Long Island City New York 11101
www.onepeacebooks.com